STORM FRONT

www.rbooks.co.uk

STORM FRONT

Rowland White

BANTAM PRESS

LONDON • TORONTO • SYDNEY • AUCKLAND • JOHANNESBURG

TRANSWORLD PUBLISHERS
61–63 Uxbridge Road, London W5 5SA
A Random House Group Company
www.rbooks.co.uk

First published in Great Britain
in 2011 by Bantam Press
an imprint of Transworld Publishers

A CIP catalogue record for this book
is available from the British Library.

ISBNs 9780593064344 (cased)
9780593064351 (tpb)

Addresses for Random House Group Ltd companies outside the UK
can be found at: www.randomhouse.co.uk
The Random House Group Ltd Reg. No. 954009

The Random House Group Ltd supports the Forest Stewardship
Council (FSC®), the leading international forest-certification organization. All our
titles that are printed on Greenpeace-approved FSC®-certified paper carry the FSC® logo.
Our paper procurement policy can be found at
www.rbooks.co.uk/environment

Typeset in 11.5/14pt Sabon by
Falcon Oast Graphic Art Ltd.

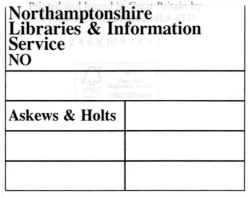

For Rory, Jemima and Lexi

Contents

Author's Note

As with my first two books, *Vulcan 607* and *Phoenix Squadron*, *Storm Front* represents, to the best of my knowledge, a true and accurate account of events that took place in Oman in the first years of the 1970s. There have been a handful of personal accounts of the war in Oman – and one notable academic study in John Peterson's *Oman's Insurgencies* – but such was the secrecy surrounding the war that it remains little known or understood beyond a relatively small circle. That is beginning to change. And I hope that this book accelerates the process. They were extraordinary events and, whatever happens to Oman and Sultan Qaboos as a result of the democratic change sweeping across the Middle East, his success in the Dhofar war, supported by the British, was unarguably a good thing for the country. The veterans of the campaign remain justifiably proud of what they achieved and it was a pleasure to listen to them talk about it.

Inevitably, over forty years, memories fade though, and in interviewing so many people for the book I have, as before, been presented with sometimes contradictory accounts. On the occasions when this has happened, I've done my best to establish a consensus – and check against contemporary documents. I've drawn on a wide variety of sources and this is reflected in the dialogue in the book. Where it appears in quotation marks it's either what I've been told was said, or what has been reported in previous accounts or records, published and unpublished. Where speech is in italics – often the call and response checks that accompany any military flying – it represents genuine dialogue that has been taken from another source to add richness to a scene. I hope it can be argued, with a degree of certainty, that it's what would have been said. Finally, where internal thoughts are included in italics, they are an accurate record of what participants told either me or others that they were thinking at the time.

R.W.
Nant-y-Feinen
March 2011

Acknowledgements

As ever, there are large numbers of people without whom the book simply couldn't have been attempted, let alone finished. From the outset there have been a handful of key supporters who have helped make introductions and open doors. Any attempt to write about the SAS means inevitable disappointment along the way, so I'm hugely grateful to those who have helped me tell the story. Chief amongst them must be Sekonaia Takavesi, whom I've been privileged to meet and spend time with. Of all those who fought at Mirbat, only Tak is still able to provide a first-hand account of the fight from the forward gunpit position. Talaiasi Labalaba was killed during the battle; Tommy Tobin died of his injuries; and the Troop Commander, Mike Kealy, was to die of exposure during training in the Brecon Beacons in 1979. Without Tak's generous support of this project it would have hardly been possible to pursue. Special mention, too, of Tak's wife Jacqui for her help, encouragement and hospitality.

Similarly willing to help was Major General Tony Jeapes, author of the excellent *SAS: Secret War* and ex-CO of 22 SAS Regiment. Tony was kind enough to contact a number of his contemporaries on my behalf, including John Russell, who shared his memories of Johnny Watts and Operation JAGUAR with me.

Still with the SAS, particular thanks must go to Shaun

Brogan, who recalled his time in Oman in vivid detail. His enthusiasm for his subject was infectious and the book hugely richer for his contribution.

There are a handful of other Regiment veterans who spoke to me who have asked to remain anonymous. They know who they are and I'm grateful to them.

One whom I did not meet, nor talk to, was Alistair Morrison, ex-2ic of 22 SAS. While feeling that current MoD rules prevented him from helping more directly, he did kindly provide me with permission to listen to an interview he gave to Charles Allen in 1990, now archived at the Imperial War Museum.

Charles, too, helped the cause by generously sharing the transcript of his long and fascinating interview with the ex-CO of 22 SAS and Director SAS, Johnny Watts. Again, it was invaluable.

The war in Dhofar was not, however, fought and won by the SAS alone. Far from it. While in Oman they were attached to the Sultan's Armed Forces (SAF) and under the Operational Command of the Sultan's military commander. Throughout the period I focus on in *Storm Front*, that man was John Graham, whom, again, I felt privileged to speak to. His time, hospitality and willingness to share his memories of some extraordinary times in Oman have helped underpin the book.

Other important SAF veterans have been similarly supportive. The ex-Desert Regiment CO, Nigel Knocker, still a lynchpin of the very active SAF Association, provided a fascinating insight into Operation SIMBA. So too did Graeme Smyth-Piggott of the Northern Frontier Regiment, along with his recollections of Mirbat, when he had responsibility for the SAF standby force. Bryan Ray and Ewen Southby-Tailyour, too, were helpful. In mentioning the SAF Association, I should also just nod to the membership secretary, Neil Fawcett, and Richard Owens of the Anglo-Omani Association, both of whom helped put me in touch with people I was trying to track down. One other SAF Association stalwart – and historian – I should thank is Colin Richardson, who has been patient and helpful in answering my questions.

Following *Vulcan 607* and *Phoenix Squadron*, my route to *Storm Front* began with aviation, and the largely British-manned Sultan of Oman's Air Force. With around half its aircrew seconded from the RAF (and many of the rest under contract to SOAF after leaving the RAF, Fleet Air Arm, Army Air Corps or 3 Commando Brigade Air Squadron Royal Marines), it was, in the early seventies, the only place that RAF fast-jet pilots were flying on operations. SOAF veterans were unfailingly enthusiastic about sharing their memories of flying for the Sultan's little Air Force, from RAF Salalah in Dhofar. The first of these was the ex-Commander of SOAF, Curly Hirst. After Curly had provided a fascinating introduction to the air war, he then put me in touch with Neville Baker, who raised SOAF's first helicopter squadron. Neville's career is an extraordinary one that provided all the surprises and variety which draw me to stories like this. From Neville's squadron, I was lucky to meet Nick Holbrook, gunner turned pilot, whose vivid memories of Oman were as entertaining as they were useful, and Charlie Gilchrist, accordion-player and Neville's co-pilot at Mirbat.

On the jet front, Nigel Charles was kind enough to put me in touch with Bob Ruskell, who introduced me to the core of pilots at the heart of this story: David Milne-Smith, Sean Creak and Denis 'Nobby' Grey. All three flew at Mirbat and helped bring it to life for me in way that I hope it's been my privilege to try to bring to a wider audience. For all that the Battle of Mirbat holds a kind of mythical status in military circles, the crucial contribution of the pilots has never before been given adequate recognition. Another ex-Strikemaster pilot who flew into Mirbat that day was Barrie Williams. Although by then no longer flying jets, he too had a fascinating story to tell, which he did with warmth and generosity. There's one more Strikemaster pilot who was central to the battle and whom I'd have liked to talk to, but sadly, after he passed away in May 2010 following a long illness, I never had the opportunity to: Bill Stoker. I'm extremely grateful to his sons, James and Bill, for their support of my efforts.

I must also thank two SOAF veterans who, although not in Oman at the time I've written about, were able to make a huge difference to my ability to tell the story. First of all, Baron Stirrup – formerly Air Chief Marshal Sir Jock Stirrup – ex-Chief of the Defence Staff, was kind enough to take time to talk to me and provide an introduction to Air Chief Marshal Sir Erik Bennett, the last British Commander of SOAF. Sir Erik's support paved the way for a hugely useful research trip to Oman in late 2010. While I was there, the current Commander of the Royal Air Force of Oman (as SOAF has been since 1990) could not have been more generous. I can only thank Air Vice Marshal Yahya Al Juma for somehow making time to meet me. Again, it was a privilege. While I was in Oman, I was extremely well looked after by Squadron Leader Khalid Al Kharusi, himself an author and book-lover. I enjoyed Khalid's enthusiasm and deep knowledge of Oman greatly. Finally, in advance of my flying out, Group Captain Musallam Al Zeidi performed miracles in assembling a fantastic, full itinerary at very short notice.

He and Khalid were also kind enough to help me make contact with two Omani SOAF/RAFO veterans, Brigadier Malallah and Group Captain Hamed Nasser. Although the Omanization of the Sultan's forces was in its infancy, both men were serving with the Air Force in 1971/72 – and in Malallah's case, since 1959 – and both went on to enjoy long, distinguished careers, both of which intersect with the story I've told. It was a great pleasure to meet the two of them.

RAFO's support allowed me, during a brief week in Oman, to visit all the locations I've written about in *Storm Front* and provided me with an absolutely invaluable sense of place. I hope that the book is a welcome addition to the RAFO archive Khalid is assembling.

As well as those serving with the SAS and seconded to SAF, there were a handful of other British servicemen in Oman. The skill of the FST – Field Surgical Team – at Salalah was a crucial part of SAF's ability to fight the war. I was extremely lucky that Bill de Bass of the RAMC, whose website, 55fst-ramc.org, has become a wonderfully rich resource on the Dhofar war, was in Salalah during the period I was writing about.

Other than the SAS, the only other formed unit in Oman was the RAF Regiment, in whose capable hands the defence of RAF Salalah rested. I thoroughly enjoyed meeting and talking to ex-2 Squadron 2ic Paul Ryan, and only wish I'd found a way of weaving in more of what he shared. Also from the RAF Regiment, Rick Hardy – Paul's CO – Marcus Witherow and Harry Foxley were kind enough to answer my questions. Thanks to Martin Hooker for putting me in touch with them. Overall responsibility for Salalah's safety lay with the Station Commander. In 1971/72 that was Gerry Honey. Again, it was a great pleasure hearing Gerry share his vivid recollections of his time in Oman.

Staying with the RAF, I had the privilege to talk to Air Chief Marshal Sir Richard Johns about his time flying Hunters out of Aden in the sixties. The connection Sir Richard highlighted helped open up another part of the story which subsequently led me to Chris Granville-White, Tim Webb and the Radfan. It was a fascinating and unexpected direction and I'm grateful to them all.

Unsurprisingly enough perhaps, civilians play very little part in this account of a secret war in Oman. But there were a few. First of all, Andy Dunsire, ex-Airwork radio engineer, photography guru for SOAF and Oman enthusiast, was hugely generous with his time, energy and support for my efforts. I'm thankful to him for knocking on so many doors on my behalf. Another, who was able to provide me with a fascinating perspective on Oman, was diplomat and ex-British Ambassador to both Oman and Syria, Ivor Lucas. I should also thank ex-BAC engineer Paul Lewis for his enthusiasm and willingness to help.

Once again, it's been Lalla Hitchings who, through thick and thin, has managed to transcribe all of the conversations detailed above. Her efforts this time round have been, I know, little short of heroic. Thank you.

My agent Mark Lucas and editor Bill Scott-Kerr continue to

demonstrate that there's simply no better combination for a book like this than the two of them. Together and alone they offer experience, judgement, perspective, enthusiasm, irreverence and tact. Thanks again. Alongside Bill at Transworld, there's a hugely talented team who continue to demonstrate that no one does it better. Thanks once more to publicist Polly Osborn, designer Steve Mulcahey, production editor Vivien Garrett, and the whole of the Ealing marketing and sales team. Still nobody does it better. Copy editor Mark Handsley once again sorted things out – thank goodness.

Friends Tom Petch and James Holland have both offered great encouragement throughout when even pretending to be interested would have been enough.

And while he's not, sadly, going to see the book hit the shelves this time, there could not have been a greater supporter of mine than my friend Jonny. Everything's a little bit tougher and a little less fun without him. No doubt he'd have seen it differently. Damned if I can find a positive spin on it though.

I must also, once again, thank my wife Lucy. Only Lucy's love, generosity, good sense, patience and, let's face it, endurance allow me the freedom to write. I'm always aware that it's me who gets the easier half of the deal – not that I imagine that's much consolation.

I don't really know how to thank you. Although I appreciate that jewellery and a long, indulgent weekend in a country house hotel might be a good start . . .

Dramatis Personae

Sultan's Armed Forces
Brigadier John Graham
Seconded from the British Army as Commander of the Sultan's Armed Forces between 1970 and 1972. A Second World War veteran and ex-Commanding Officer of 1 PARA. Alongside the Sultan and the Oman Defence Secretary, Colonel Hugh Oldman, Graham was responsible for the prosecution of the Dhofar war.

Lieutenant Colonel Nigel Knocker
Seconded from the British Army as Commanding Officer of SAF's Desert Regiment. Knocker was the architect of Operation SIMBA.

Captain Graeme 'Smash' Smyth-Piggott
British contract officer serving with SAF's Northern Frontier Regiment.

22 SAS Regiment
Lieutenant Colonel Johnny Watts
Commanding Officer of 22 SAS Regiment between 1970 and the end of 1971. Architect of the SAS campaign in Oman, codenamed Operation STORM. Previously Royal Ulster Rifles.

Lieutenant Colonel Peter de la Billière
Second-in-Command of 22 SAS Regiment under Johnny Watts in 1970–71 before replacing him as CO in January 1972. Previously Durham Light Infantry.

Major Alistair Morrison
Commanding Officer of G Squadron, 22 SAS. Previously Scots Guards.

Major Richard 'Duke' Pirie
Commanding Officer of B Squadron, 22 SAS. Previously Parachute Regiment.

Captain Shaun Brogan
Troop Commander with A Squadron, 22 SAS. Previously Royal Anglians.

Captain Mike Kealy
Troop Commander of Eight Troop, B Squadron, 22 SAS. Previously Queen's Royal Regiment.

Trooper Sekonaia 'Tak' Takavesi
Fijian serving with Eight Troop, B Squadron, 22 SAS. Trained medic and Arabist, with responsibility for running the Firqa al Umri and the 25 pounder gun. Veteran of SAS operations in Aden and Borneo. Previously King's Own Border Regiment.

Corporal Talaiasi 'Laba' Labalaba
Fijian NCO with Eight Troop, B Squadron, 22 SAS. Trained Arabist with responsibility for Mirbat's 25 pounder gun. Previously Royal Irish Rangers (ex-Royal Ulster Rifles).

Corporal Peter 'Snapper' Winner
NCO with Eight Troop, B Squadron, 22 SAS. Signals specialist with responsibility for the Mirbat .50 calibre Browning heavy machine gun. Previously Royal Engineers.

Trooper Austen 'Fuzz' Hussey
Lancastrian Mortar specialist with Eight Troop, B Squadron, 22 SAS.

Sergeant Bob Bennett
Second-in-Command of Eight Troop, B Squadron. Trained Forward Air Controller and mortar plotter.

Corporal Roger Cole
Bristolian NCO with responsibility for the Mirbat GPMG SF. Trained Medic and Forward Air Controller.

Trooper Tommy Tobin
Newest member of Eight Troop. Trained Medic. Previously Army Catering Corps.

Corporal Jeff Taylor
Member of the G Squadron advance party. Previously Irish Guards.

Trooper Jim Vakatali
Third Fijian member of B Squadron, 22 SAS. Joined the British Army in the early sixties alongside Takavesi and Labalaba. Served with them both in Aden in an undercover anti-terrorist role.

Sergeant Lofty Wiseman
Quartermaster at SAS HQ in Um al Gwarif camp outside Salalah, Oman.

Sultan of Oman's Air Force
Wing Commander 'Curly' Hirst
Seconded from the Royal Air Force, fast-jet pilot Hirst had been Station Commander of RAF Salalah in 1960 before returning to Oman as Commander of the Sultan of Oman's Air Force in 1970.

Flight Lieutenant David Milne-Smith

Seconded from the RAF to 1 Squadron SOAF(Tac) to fly Strikemaster attack jets. A Qualified Flying Instructor with experience of flying Hawker Hunters in the Middle East.

Squadron Leader Neville Baker

A contract pilot serving as Commanding Officer of SOAF's helicopter squadron at Salalah. An experienced search and rescue pilot, Baker joined the RAF during the Second World War and flew DC3 Dakotas before converting to helicopters.

Squadron Leader Bill Stoker

Seconded from the Royal Air Force, Stoker was Commanding Officer of 1 Squadron SOAF(Tac), the Sultan's only jet squadron. An experienced fighter-bomber pilot with long experience flying in the Middle East.

Flight Lieutenant Sean Creak

Originally seconded from the RAF, after leaving he rejoined SOAF as a contract pilot with 1 Squadron SOAF(Tac) to fly Strikemasters and DeHavilland Beavers. Responsible for much of the conversion course for pilots new to Oman.

Flight Lieutenant Denis 'Nobby' Grey

Seconded from the RAF to fly Strikemasters with 1 Squadron SOAF(Tac). A nuclear bomber pilot and flying instructor before volunteering for service in Oman.

Flight Lieutenant Barrie Williams

A contract pilot and veteran Fleet Air Arm fast-jet pilot. Saw combat at Suez in 1956. Joined SOAF to fly Strikemasters but converted to Skyvans after injuring his back after ejecting from his jet.

Wing Commander Peter Hulme

Ex-RAF pilot under contract to SOAF as Commander of all

SOAF's assets in the Dhofar Operational Area, based at RAF Salalah.

Captain Nick Holbrook
An Ex-Army Air Corps contract pilot flying helicopters with 3 Squadron SOAF at Salalah.

Flight Lieutenant Charlie Gilchrist
Seconded from the RAF to fly helicopters with 3 Squadron SOAF at Salalah.

Aircrewman Hamed Nasser
Helicopter Aircrewman for 3 Squadron SOAF. One of the first Omanis recruited into SOAF as aircrew.

Sergeant Malallah
The longest-serving member of SOAF and its first Omani recruit. Later SOAF's first Omani officer.

Aircrewman Leader Stan Standford
Under contract to 3 Squadron SOAF. Ex-Fleet Air Arm Aircrewman and Search and Rescue Diver.

Civilians
Sultan Qaboos bin Said
Ruler of Oman since deposing his father in 1970. Sandhurst-educated and Anglophile, Sultan Qaboos instigated much-needed reforms in Oman as soon as he assumed power, aged twenty-nine.

Sultan Said bin Taimur
Ruler of Oman between 1932 and 23 July 1970, until deposed in a coup by his son Qaboos. Under him, Oman remained almost biblically underdeveloped.

Hugh Oldman
Defence Secretary to both Said bin Taimur and, subsequently,

Qaboos. A former Commander of the Sultan's Armed Forces, the ex-British Army Colonel was, during the early years of Qaboos's reign, perhaps his key advisor.

Donald Hawley
After a diplomatic career that had taken him from Sudan to the Trucial States (now UAE) and Baghdad, Hawley became the first British Ambassador to Oman in May 1970.

Andy Dunsire
An ex-RAF radio engineer, Dunsire was one of a handful of civilian aircraft engineers employed by Airwork to maintain SOAF's aircraft. He also pioneered SAF's photo-reconnaissance capabilities.

British Military
Wing Commander Gerry Honey
Station Commander at RAF Salalah. A fast-jet pilot with no previous Middle East experience, Honey was promised a place on the RAF's Harrier programme in exchange for accepting the posting to Oman.

Flight Lieutenant Paul Ryan
Second-in-Command of 2 Squadron RAF Regiment, the force's only parachute trained field squadron and, in summer 1972, responsible for RAF Salalah's ground defence.

Captain Bill de Bass
Royal Army Medical Corps anaesthetist with 55 Field Surgical Team. Alongside surgeons Joe Johnston and Nick Cetti, de Bass was at the Salalah field hospital when the injured from Mirbat were flown in.

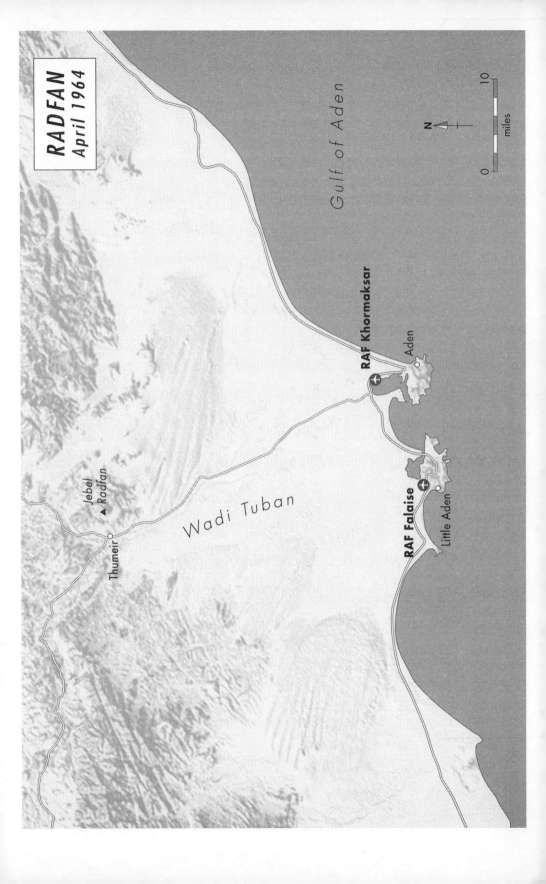

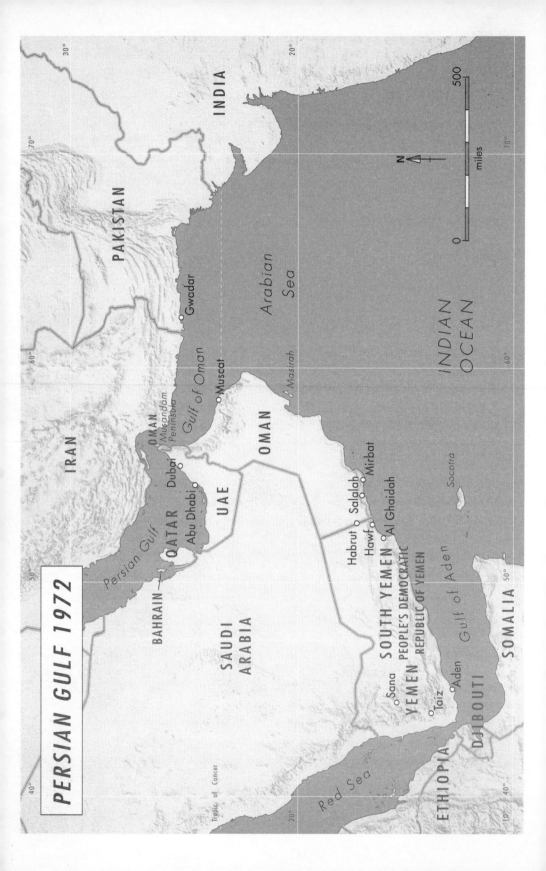

PERSIAN GULF 1972

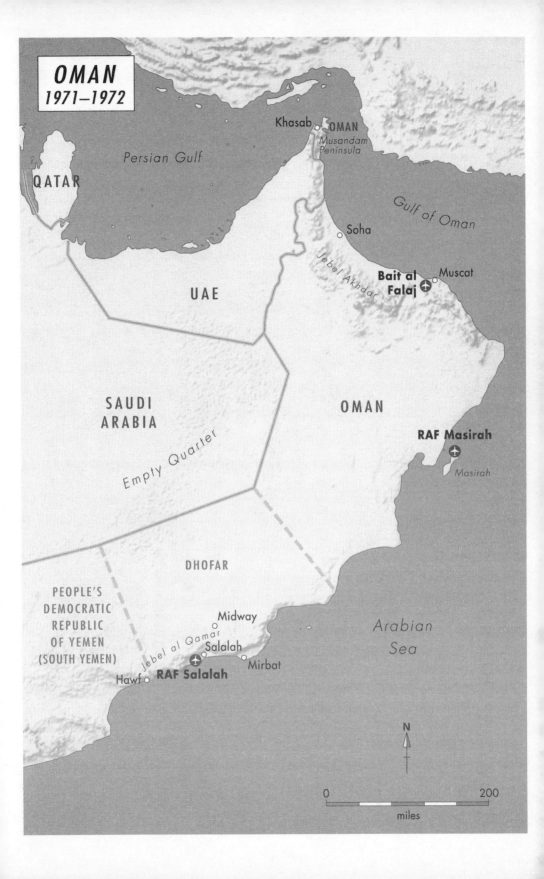

OMAN
1971–1972

QATAR

Persian Gulf

Khasab **OMAN**
*Musandam
Peninsula*

Gulf of Oman

UAE

Soha

Jebel Akhdar

**Bait al
Falaj** Muscat

SAUDI
ARABIA

OMAN

RAF Masirah

Empty Quarter

Masirah

DHOFAR

Arabian
Sea

PEOPLE'S
DEMOCRATIC
REPUBLIC
OF YEMEN
(SOUTH YEMEN)

Midway

Jebel al Qamar Salalah
RAF Salalah Mirbat

Hawf

N

0   200

miles

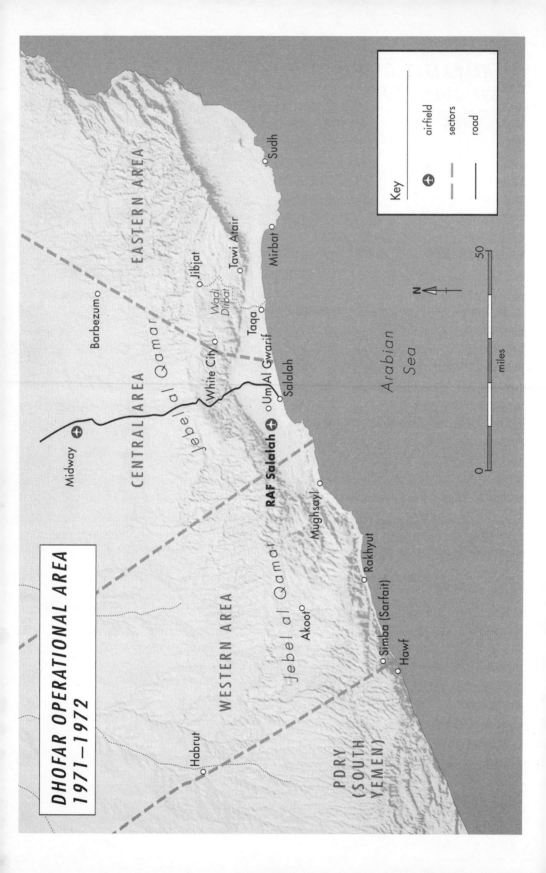

DHOFAR OPERATIONAL AREA 1971–1972

Key
- airfield
- sectors
- road

Midway

Barbezum

EASTERN AREA

Jibjat

Tawi Atair

Sudh

Wadi Dirbat

Mirbat

CENTRAL AREA

Jebel al Qamar

White City

Taqa

Um Al Gwarif

Salalah

RAF Salalah

Arabian Sea

Mughsayl

WESTERN AREA

Akoot

Jebel al Qamar

Rakhyut

Habrut

Simba (Sarfait)

Hawf

PDRY (SOUTH YEMEN)

N

miles

0   50

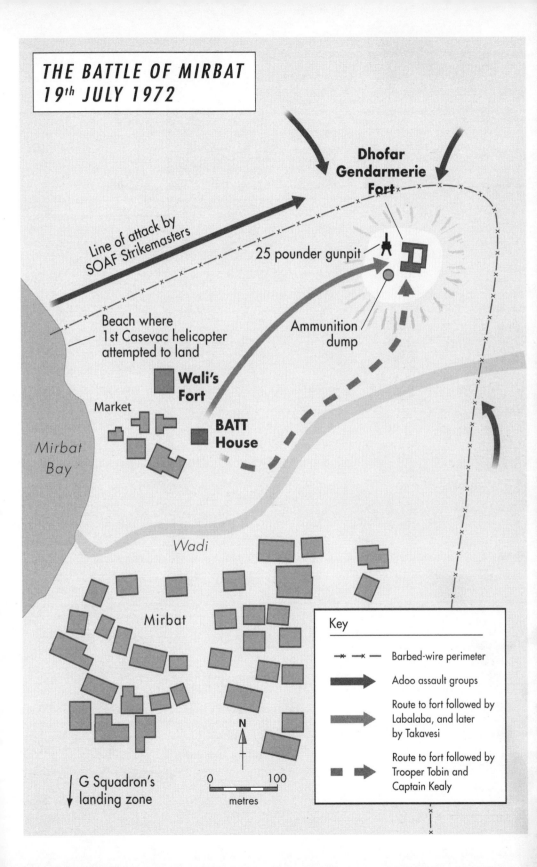

THE BATTLE OF MIRBAT
19th JULY 1972

Dhofar
Gendarmerie
Fort

Line of attack by
SOAF Strikemasters

25 pounder gunpit

Beach where
1st Casevac helicopter
attempted to land

Ammunition
dump

Wali's
Fort

Market

BATT
House

Mirbat
Bay

Wadi

Mirbat

N

Key

—✕——✕—— Barbed-wire perimeter

Adoo assault groups

Route to fort followed by
Labalaba, and later
by Takavesi

Route to fort followed by
Trooper Tobin and
Captain Kealy

0   100
metres

G Squadron's
landing zone

Prologue

April 1964, Aden

The two Royal Air Force Hawker Hunter FGA9s were armed, the magazines of each jet's four 30mm cannons filled with big high-explosive shells. There was always the possibility of a quicksilver glint in the sky that might signal a MiG probing south into British-controlled airspace. But as Flight Lieutenant Bill Stoker and his wingman, Martin Herring, cruised up and down the border with Yemen to the north, the possibility of a little excitement seemed remote. And that's how it stayed this time. Again. For 43 Squadron, flying out of RAF Khormaksar in Aden, the action usually took place a little closer to the ground.

Flying in support of ground troops was where 43 and 208, the other Hunter unit based at Aden, really earned their crust. The two fighter squadrons practised relentlessly. And while doing so, leading a section firing 60lb rocket projectiles, Martin Herring crashed and died. Pulling out of a dive, the front pin connecting the drop tank to his jet sheered and then swung round, swiping at the wing and fuselage behind, making the aircraft completely uncontrollable. So close to the ground, Herring didn't have a chance.

So just eleven days after they were together on the Beihan patrol, Bill Stoker was airborne again, providing top cover for the 26 Squadron Belvedere HC1 helicopter that salvaged the wreckage of his wingman's Hunter from the crash site.

Everyone lost friends in Aden.

The deteriorating security situation in the South Arabian colony was fomented from outside the Federation. And in 1964 Britain was forced to take action against rebel tribesmen from the Radfan whose attacks had closed the road between Aden and Yemen. The rebels were known as the Red Wolves. Their formidable mountain stronghold, twenty miles long and fifteen miles wide, rose to a height of 7,000 feet above sea level. It was an area no European was known to have entered since a visiting missionary before the First World War. And he had never been seen again.

But while the preacher's unhappy demise was predictable enough, the SAS, well armed, well trained and with long experience fighting successful counter-insurgency wars around the globe, flew into the colony expecting much better odds of survival.

In March, just four days after the order was received in Hereford, the Regiment headed out into the wild ridges and wadis of the Radfan. The new Commanding Officer of A Squadron, 22 SAS, Major Peter de la Billière – known as DLB – had deployed to Aden and moved quickly to tented accommodation at Thumeir, the British forward operating base sixty miles north of the city.

He and his men patrolled at night, protected by darkness and from daytime temperatures that rose to 120°F. But de la Billière quickly realized that leading the patrols himself made him a less effective Squadron Commander. He needed to be able to see the big picture and direct events. With some reluctance, he decided that one of the A Squadron troop commanders, his close friend Captain Robin Edwards, should lead the next one. Even within the SAS, the big Cornishman with the ready smile was regarded as a remarkable character. It was hard to believe that someone who had contracted polio as a child could find the strength and will to push himself through Selection. All the same, DLB still wished he were leading the patrol in himself.

Edwards's men were to secure a dropzone for the Parachute

Regiment over ten miles behind enemy lines. Man-packing all their equipment, hard decisions had to be made about what had to be discarded. Water and ammunition for the SLR rifles and Bren light machine guns invariably took priority. Each of the men carried a blood chit, promising a £1,000 reward to anyone who returned them safely to the British High Commissioner in Aden.

The first of the Three Troop soldiers climbed aboard a Westland Scout AH1 of 653 Squadron Army Air Corps. It would take three runs to lift in the whole patrol. Flying into hostile territory 5,000 yards from Thumeir, the little helicopter had been stripped of all doors and safety straps to save weight and reduce offloading time to a bare minimum. The soldiers sat, facing out, their feet resting on the skids. If they encountered enemy opposition during the insertion, they'd been instructed to return fire through the open doors.

At 1820 as the light was fading, the pilot, Sergeant Scott, increased the power and pulled the heavily loaded machine into the air. Even with a light fuel load she was still reluctant to get airborne carrying the SAS men and their equipment.

Like flying in porridge, Scott thought as he pitched down the nose of the Scout to gain airspeed. He accelerated to 80 knots, flying low under covering fire from armoured cars and a 105mm artillery gun. Twenty minutes later, Edwards and his eight-man patrol were on their own.

Inside a sweltering tent at Thumeir, Hunter pilot Flight Lieutenant Tim Webb knew quickly that things had gone wrong. Grounded by a broken arm, Webb was the RAF's Brigade Air Support Officer – BASO – responsible for providing the link between the RAF and the troops on the ground. At dawn on 30 April, de la Billière put Webb on notice that Edwards and his men had failed to reach their objective, an Observation Point overlooking the dropzone. After setting off, Signaller Nick Warburton had been hit by sickness and stomach cramps, which slowed their progress overnight. They had no choice but to stop short of the OP, hide themselves as best they could under camouflaged nets, and lie up for the day before pushing on after nightfall. But they were in the lee of high ground, out of reach of artillery support from Thumeir camp. If there was trouble, de la Billière told Webb over the phone, his men would need the jets. Webb didn't have to wait long.

As the morning sun began to grow fierce, Three Troop's position was approached by a lone goatherd. From inside the hide, Edwards knew he had three options when compromise was beyond doubt: let the tribesman go; overwhelm and restrain him; or shoot him. The report of the single shot echoed around the jagged mountain walls, but it was in the silence that followed when Edwards understood they were in serious trouble. He and his men couldn't see that they were being surrounded, but in the intense heat and oppressive stillness of midday, they could almost feel the advance of the Radfan tribesmen as they closed in on them.

Just after 1100 hours, the A Squadron Boss asked Webb to put the Hunters on standby to go. Then de la Billière's arrival inside the BASO tent quickly rammed home the gravity of the Regiment patrol's position. DLB brought with him all the SAS's own radio equipment.

With Edwards pinned down, overlooked by high ground and vulnerable to unseen approaches from surrounding dead ground, DLB knew that his men's only hope of survival was air support from the Hunters. He couldn't allow any possibility of communications between the Regiment and the RAF breaking down.

The first pair of Hunters sped down the Khormaksar runway and tucked up their undercarriage at 1145 hours. Each was armed with eight 60lb rockets and 30mm ADEN cannons. Webb's own 208 was the duty squadron, but Edwards's patrol needed seamless air cover for the rest of the day. So, alongside 208, 43 Squadron, Bill Stoker's unit, was drafted into the plan.

Ten minutes later, the first pair streaked over the SAS position. For the next three quarters of an hour the 43

Squadron pair dived in, firing on positions passed back from Edwards to de la Billière and on to the pilots from Webb. Eight hundred cannon shells and thirteen rockets later, they passed the baton to mission number 204, another 43 Squadron pair.

208 was next, led by one of the squadron's flight commanders, Flight Lieutenant Anthony Mumford. He and his wingman nearly emptied their magazines and rocket racks. But it was Mumford's next sortie that would prove to be remarkable.

There were carefully established techniques and procedures for guiding jets in against targets on the ground. But none of the besieged SAS patrol had been trained in them. Instead, without any formal Forward Air Control – FAC – from Three Troop the RAF Hunter pilots had to make do with the best that the common sense and experience of the SAS men could provide. But in barren, rocky terrain in which one ridge or wadi could easily be mistaken for another, great care was needed to make sure that attacks were effective.

In the BASO tent there was little or no talk, save for the messages coming in and out; a continuous stream of inform-ation exchanged between the Special Forces team and the pilots via Webb at Thumeir. An unwieldy system, but holding up. Throughout the day, as he passed directions to the jets, Webb overheard intense discussions amongst the soldiers about the possibility of relieving or evacuating the patrol. There was certainly no shortage of volunteers. But nothing seemed to offer anything except the prospect of even greater loss of life. And so Three Troop's survival remained squarely on the shoulders of the two RAF fighter squadrons.

Only one thing was certain: at sundown, darkness would put an end to the air support from the Hunters. In the mean-time, the SAS position was coming under increasing pressure, under attack from rifle fire and at least three different machine-gun positions. From inside, the soldiers returned fire where and when clear targets presented themselves, conserving their ammunition. Making it count. It was enemy they couldn't see, though, that were the greater threat. And there were still two hours of daylight left. That was when Anthony Mumford returned to the fight.

At 1600 hours, the landscape beneath him looked quite different. The late-afternoon sun had begun to throw dark shadows across the precipitous, serrated landscape. Webb crackled across the RT from Thumeir. Edwards had reported enemy approaching up the hill below them. The SAS men couldn't see anyone, but were sure they were there.

Mumford rolled in and swept across the SAS position, hoping that he was going to be able to pick out the approaching threat. No mean task a few hundred feet up, travelling at three or four hundred knots. He pressed the transmit button.

'I've got him,' he told Webb. 'He's twenty-five yards from them.'

There was a pause as it was relayed from BASO HQ.

'OK. Go for it,' Edwards confirmed.

The 30mm ADEN cannon was not a subtle weapon. Each milk-bottle-sized nine-ounce round, leaving the barrel with a muzzle velocity of 1,320 feet per second, could take out a Land Rover. The Hunter carried four of the guns under the nose. Fire them all at once and they tended to pop circuit breakers in the jet's cockpit. On the ground the effect was even more dramatic. They had the power, one SAS officer reflected, to wobble the horizon. With 600 rounds loaded in the magazines, a strafing attack from a Hunter could be utterly devastating. But this time round, Mumford didn't have that option.

With the enemy just twenty-five yards away from the SAS position there was too much danger of hitting Edwards and his men. Instead, Mumford would have to try to use the ADEN cannon like a sniper's rifle. He had to try to take his man down with a direct hit. Mumford carved round and set himself up for the attack. He uncaged the sight and settled into a shallow dive, placing the aiming pipper over the target. He put everything else out of his mind. With a shallow 10 degree grazing angle and the impossible closeness of the target to the good guys, there was simply no margin for error. Certain of his aim, he gently squeezed off three rounds, careful not to let his trigger finger affect the stability of the diving Hawker.

At BASO HQ in Thumeir, Peter de la Billière and Tim Webb waited for news of Mumford's attack.

Then Edwards's voice crackled over the A41 radio. 'Bloody good shooting . . .'

The roar of the Rolls-Royce Avon turbojet as Mumford pulled into a climb, away from the besieged position, could be heard in the background. But Mumford's efforts had only removed the immediate threat. Edwards's patrol were still in a desperate situation. And three of them were already carrying injuries; victims of the day's sniping attacks.

One last pair of Hunters replaced Mumford and his wingman. For six hours the RAF had kept the enemy at bay. In doing so they'd fired 127 60lb rockets and 7,131 high-explosive rounds. But with the light fading they too turned south for Khormaksar.

Now Edwards and his men had no choice but to break out.

At BASO HQ, de la Billière received a message from Trooper Nick Warburton telling him that the patrol was about to slip away from their position. Then nothing. At the other end of the radio, and powerless to intervene, the A Squadron Commander could only hope that his men's training, skill and courage would be enough.

Around the Three Troop position, some ninety enemy fighters launched their attack.

Days later, intelligence reached Aden that the bodies of Edwards and Warburton had been decapitated. Their heads had been carried north across the border into Yemen, where they were paraded on stakes in the city of Taiz as a grotesque trophy of the SAS's humiliation in the Radfan. The news caused outrage in the UK and huge distress to the next of kin, who had not yet been informed of their deaths.

Peter de la Billière was devastated by the losses. He took himself off alone into the desert to try to absorb what had happened. He would write letters of condolence, of course. He would also visit his friend's parents on his return to the UK.

On 11 May, the camouflaged Scout helicopters from 653 Squadron flew north into an almost impossible landing site to bring back the two SAS men's headless bodies for burial. One of the RAF Hunter pilots watched the Land Rover cortège driving them back to the Aden hospital, relieved they were home. But the grim deaths had an electrifying effect on the two Hunter squadrons. It changed the tone of the campaign that followed completely. They were going to get the bastards that had done this.

On 43 Squadron, Flt Lt Bill Stoker had always had a particular affinity for what he called the PBI – the Poor Bloody Infantry. He felt a responsibility towards them; only too aware that whatever risks were taken by fighter pilots like him, it was usually a great deal worse at ground level. As a ground attack pilot he knew that the troops were in his care and, like the rest of the aircrew on 43 and 208, he was determined to do whatever it took to stop this happening again.

PART ONE

1970
On the Ropes

Chapter 1

David Milne-Smith joined the RAF the same year Tak passed Selection. As a boy, Milne-Smith couldn't remember a time when he hadn't loved flying. Because his father worked for a company that produced demerara sugar in British Guiana, he'd endured a peripatetic upbringing constantly flicking between a prep school near Tunbridge Wells, a public school in Derbyshire, and South America. But he took advantage of holidays with his parents to realize his dream. He took flying lessons and, aged just sixteen, he'd earned his private pilot's licence. A year later, after the blond-haired seventeen-year-old walked into the RAF's Adastral House in London and told the recruiting officer he wanted to join the Air Force, it meant he was spared elementary flying training and posted straight on to the advanced course flying jets.

But by the summer of 1970, the gloss was coming off a little.

After being awarded his Wings, the driven young fighter pilot was posted to fly Hunters with 8 Squadron at RAF Muharraq in Bahrain. Life on a frontline squadron was what he'd signed up for. Just twenty-one, he felt like he'd been given the keys to the kingdom. And although his thirteen-month tour was free from significant operations, the flying was as challenging and varied as he'd hoped. He practised air combat, trained with the Navy and Army over the Gulf and the vast open spaces of the interior, and flew low-level patrols along disputed desert borders, but what really distinguished 8 Squadron and the capability upon which their recent reputation was built, was the accuracy of their air-to-ground attacks. Demand from the training school for Forward Air Controllers at Sharjah meant that live-firing the Aden cannons, 3in rocket projectiles and SNEB rocket pods against targets on the Yas Island range became bread and butter. There was every opportunity to become a very good shot indeed. But it wasn't just the flying. Milne-Smith enjoyed every aspect of squadron life and, inevitably, the Mess christened him DMS.

He loved it. Not so what followed.

The RAF told him they had a plan for him. Perhaps that was no surprise. Milne-Smith certainly had all the trappings of an Air Force high-flyer. Sharp, thoughtful and capable he also possessed a toughness that was plain to see. The powers that be sent him to Central Flying School at RAF Leeming as a flying instructor. He was *definitely* a non-volunteer.

Chuntering around the skies of Yorkshire working his way methodically through a syllabus, all the while being endlessly patient with the students coming through, wasn't his idea of fun. He wanted to get back on to the frontline. And strangely enough, the clues to his future could be found in his past.

8 Squadron had long been connected with the Middle East. Throughout the sixties, it had rotated between Aden and Bahrain along with 43 and 208. After the British withdrawal from Aden, 8 Squadron had remained in the Gulf. But the association with the region had begun earlier. During the Second World War the squadron had been based at RAF Salalah in the Dhofar region of Southern Oman flying twin-engine Vickers Wellington medium bombers on long maritime patrol missions over the Indian Ocean. It was Oman that lent one of its most recognizable national symbols, the distinctively shaped *kunjah* ceremonial dagger, to 8 Squadron's crest.

And, in 1970, it was the Dhofar region again where things were just starting to get really interesting.

March 1970

Immigration was rudimentary: a small wooden hut with a door at each end. Not much more than a corridor with a flat roof.

Inside, an old man dressed in a white dishdash sat at a simple wooden table. 'Mr Smith' handed him a British passport. The old man flicked through the pages to find the visa permitting his visitor's entry into Oman. Smith was not the new arrival's name, and yet the document wasn't counterfeit, exactly. But while it had been produced by British government officials, it was not genuine; a necessary deception in a country where the ruler, Sultan Said bin Taimur, personally checked and approved every single visa application. And the name of the new guest to his country would have been well known to him.

Lieutenant Colonel Johnny Watts had been to Oman before. Eleven years earlier he'd been awarded the Military Cross for his part in an audacious SAS operation to crush a rebellion against Sultan bin Taimur in the mountains of the Jebel Akhdar. Since then, following a botched assassination attempt in 1966, the Sultan hadn't left his summer palace in Salalah, 500 miles to the south-west. It's a good thing there was no prospect of Watts being seen by bin Taimur as, in mufti, without the safety net of a uniform, the Commanding Officer of 22 SAS cut a distinctively rumpled figure. Olive-skinned and compact, Watts cared little for his appearance. He had many strengths, but they were not sartorial. Most of his clothes were reckoned to have been bought secondhand in Okehampton market. To complete the look he kept a hand-rolled cigarette more or less permanently on the go.

Satisfied, the old man in the immigration hut stamped Mr Smith's passport. *Shukran.* Watts thanked him in Arabic and entered the Sultanate of Oman and Muscat. It hadn't changed a bit. Literally. And therein lay the problem. And the opportunity. Watts pulled on his roll-up and sucked the smoke down into his lungs. This had potential.

Watts was looking for work. The SAS hadn't been in a fight since Aden in 1967. He sensed his men were getting bored.

There wasn't anything, he thought, *to get the adrenalin really going.* Watts realized how this made the men sound: *like psychopaths.* But he knew it was nothing like that. He'd seen it happen with the Ghurkas in Hong Kong after the end of the

Indonesian Confrontation. Without operations, Watts thought, *training gets pedestrian; men lose their edge; hard-won, valuable lessons are lost and skills go rusty.* With Britain's withdrawal from its global empire substantially complete, the MoD was now focused on Northern Europe and NATO. Watts, however, continued to take a wider view.

The history of the Regiment was defined by its restless, relentless need to prove its usefulness. It had been that way from the day in July 1941 when a young Scots Guards lieutenant called David Stirling had rushed the guards at Cairo HQ to secure a chance to present his ideas to General Auchinlek, Commander of British Forces in North Africa.

The Special Air Service itself began life as a deception: a name conjured up by A-Force, a British psychological operations outfit in Second World War Cairo, to describe dummy paratroops dropped to confuse enemy informers. What was eventually to become the SAS Regiment was first labelled L Detachment of the entirely fictitious SAS Brigade for no other reason than to ensure the support of A-Force's Commanding Officer. That was the way Lieutenant David Stirling approached things. The end justified the means. The young Scots Guards officer was contemptuous of the inefficiency of the Regular Army. His vision and persistence had allowed him to create a unit that was able, to a large extent, to act independently of what he termed the 'fossilized layers of shit' of the usual bureaucratic chain of command. His men operated in small patrols, deep behind enemy lines, attacking and disrupting strategic targets that directly affected the enemy's ability to wage war: airfields, fuel dumps, stores depots. By delegating much of the on-the-ground decision-making to the 'Originals', as the founder members of the SAS became known, Stirling ensured that they were flexible and unpredictable. They operated like irregular guerrilla fighters and so were able to stay one step ahead of the regular Afrika Korps forces they faced in North Africa. It proved to be an unusually successful approach, with small SAS raids being, by some counts, responsible for the destruction of more Luftwaffe aircraft in North Africa than the RAF. Beyond North Africa, the SAS operated with great success in Italy, Northern Europe and Scandinavia working alongside SOE, SIS and local partisans. But it was in Greece, where British forces defeated an attempt by Communist guerrillas to take Athens, that an SAS observer, attached to an SBS unit, saw that the Regiment's future might lie in counter-insurgency operations. If, that is, the SAS survived long enough to make its case.

With the war's end there were many senior Army commanders who questioned the continuing value of Special Forces at all. The Americans, after all, had none. But when, during the war, Stirling had been unable to secure official support for an operation, he was quite prepared to pursue it as a private enterprise if he believed the cause to be important enough. And the officers at the heart of the SAS, faced with the unit's disbandment at the end of the Second World War, believed that the preservation of the SAS was firmly in that category. Here, too, the end justified the means.

Conventional wisdom has it that the SAS was disbanded in autumn 1945, its last action of the war being the disarming of German units in Norway in Operation APOSTLE. The truth is a little murkier than that. The Regiment, perhaps unsurprisingly, proved to be rather hard to kill off.

While much of the regimental apparatus was done away with in October 1945, a two-month stay of execution was granted by the War Office for the arrangement of a small number of 'special jobs'. This gave those at the head of the Regiment a little breathing space. With it they secured approval for the creation of an SAS War Crimes Investigation Team whose members, while listed under their parent regiments, continued to wear the SAS beret and winged dagger to preserve *esprit de corps*. And SAS men were despatched to Greece where, ultimately, they formed an independent SAS International Squadron. Unacknowledged but supported in secret by the British government they fought a counter-insurgency campaign during the Greek Civil War in the late 1940s.

At the heart of all this activity was the SAS Regimental Association, which soon after the war had accumulated over 1,000 members. With Winston Churchill as its patron the Association had clout. The ex-Prime Minister also helped with the creation of a phantom SAS HQ inside the Hyde Park Hotel in Knightsbridge. From here, the semi-official operations set up in the dying days of the Regiment's wartime incarnation were run by the last CO of 2 SAS, Lieutenant Colonel Brian Franks. This regimental rump – relentlessly vocal in its lobbying on behalf of the SAS cause – was enough to ensure the Regiment's survival until, in 1947, with the creation of the Territorial Army, a Royal Warrant was signed to officially reconstitute the SAS on 8 July as 21 SAS (Artists Rifles) (TA).

David Stirling had formed the SAS as a unit designed to have a strategic effect. And a brief glance at a map was more than enough to confirm that Oman was a country that was of great strategic importance. Looking out south-east across the Indian Ocean, the southern face of the Arabian peninsula runs for over 1,000 miles from the Red Sea to the Persian Gulf; a bridge connecting Africa to Asia. Oman and Yemen inhabit a 300-mile-deep strip across the entire coastline that cuts off their larger northern neighbour, Saudi Arabia, from the open ocean. And this was key. Oman's Musandam peninsula, the northern extremity of her territory, extended north like an upright thumb into the Strait of Hormuz. Iran stood guard fifty miles across the water, controlling the south gate of the Strait of Hormuz. Saudi Arabia, Kuwait, Qatar and the other oil-producing Gulf States relied on passage through the strait to deliver their goods to market. In the early seventies 51 per cent of all Britain's oil was transported by tanker through the narrow channel of water. If the SAS were able to play a role in Oman, it was abundantly clear that it was the kind of thing that would have its founder's approval.

The idea that Watts should visit Oman to assess what the SAS might contribute to the Sultanate's security and stability had first been mooted in January. Three months later Watts flew in. He spent a week considering the situation on the ground, taking advice from trusted sources, not least SAS veteran Johnny Cooper, now back in Oman serving with the Sultan's Armed Forces after his protracted involvement in the civil war in Yemen. Watts's report on what he saw was unequivocal. The Regiment could make a crucial difference. Even allowing for what they acknowledged was Watts's 'boundless enthusiasm' for the possibilities of an SAS deployment, both the Foreign Office and the MoD were convinced. They knew something had to be done.

Britain's interest in Oman was longstanding. The treaty granting a trading monopoly to the English East India Company was first signed in 1646, but it was in 1798 that the first meaningful agreement between Britain and Oman was signed, prompted by the prospect that Napoleon might get in there first. The friendship between the two countries, it established, 'would endure till the end of time or the sun and moon cease in their revolving careers'. It was not a treaty imposed on Oman by a conquering power, although it could, on occasions, seem a little one-sided. In signing, the Sultan was committed to take the British side in international affairs and deny help to the French or Dutch. When the Sultan gifted the Omani Kuria Muria Islands to Queen Victoria in perpetuity, her wrong-footed Foreign Secretary responded with the gift of a snuff box. But the real value to the Sultan of the treaty with Britain, though, was in the security his powerful ally provided. On at least three occasions during the last years of the nineteenth century Royal Navy warships helped to suppress rebellions. And in 1915 British Indian troops defeated an attack on Muscat. Each time the British had been helping quell an internal dispute within what, as even its name – Muscat and Oman – reflected, was a divided country.

That too is how the rebellion in Dhofar had started.

The catalyst for its leader's discontent was supposedly his being thrown into jail for riding a bicycle. In 1963 Mussalim bin Nufl and his brother launched their first act of armed rebellion with a bomb attack on an oil company lorry. In 1964, following a trip to Saudi Arabia and now leader of the Dhofar Liberation Front, or DLF, bin Nufl returned to Oman across the desert from the north in a column of seven Dodge trucks armed with 3in mortars, old .303 rifles and 3.5in rocket launchers. Over the year that followed irregular attacks continued until, in August 1965, just like his predecessors, Sultan bin Taimur requested British help.

Two RAF Hunter FR10 reconnaissance jets from 1417 Flight deployed to Oman from Aden to mount long-range recces out into the desert in search of rebel columns. It was like looking for a needle in a haystack. The detachment was given the title Operation THESIGER after the British explorer whose book *Arabian Sands* recorded his voyages across the Empty Quarter with the Bedouins between 1945 and 1950. It turned out to be more appropriate than had been imagined. In the absence of anything more up to date or accurate, the two Hunter pilots carried copies of sketch maps drawn by Thesiger folded into the pockets of their flightsuits. But it was stopwatch and compass stuff. The two jets had little choice but to get airborne, pick a heading and start the clocks as they crossed over the airfield at 360 knots. And they found nothing.

Whatever it was that had first fuelled his own personal rebellion, bin Nufl's action had been timely, harnessing genuine and serious grievances amongst Dhofaris, who, in a poor, undeveloped country, were the most neglected of all. But what began as an understandable reaction to the highly conservative rule of the Sultan, containable by the old ruler's own relatively unsophisticated military, had by early 1970 become something much more dangerous.

When Britain withdrew from Aden in 1967, the Communists filled the vacuum. The Federation of South Arabia became the People's Republic of Yemen, supported by the Soviet Union, China, East Germany, Cuba and North Korea. And it provided a secure, sympathetic base for the guerrillas fighting across the border to operate from. But worse than that, as well as having a haven, the DLF now also enjoyed substantial military support from China: AK47s, mortars, RCLs, mines and military training strengthened their threat to the Sultanate. Dhofar had become part of the Cold War frontline; and SAF, the Sultan's Armed Forces, one of the combatants in the long campaign.

They're on a hiding to nothing, Watts thought as he realized how precarious SAF's position in Dhofar had become. But, as much as the situation had been allowed to deteriorate, Johnny Watts didn't believe that it was irretrievable. In fact the charismatic Boss of 22 SAS saw that Oman might be the place where everything the Regiment had learnt since its restoration to regular Army Corps status in 1950 might be brought together; a blank canvas to which the SAS could apply its expertise in counter-insurgency. Watts drew up a document which he called his Five Fronts plan:

1. A national aim. In fighting the rebels, there had to be an objective beyond killing people.
2. An intelligence front. A proper, coherent intelligence picture needed to be built.
3. Psy-Ops (Psychological Operations). There needed to be a propaganda cell working to discredit the enemy, promote the virtues of the government and encourage defections.
4. 'Hearts and minds'. Watts wanted to set up CATs – Civil Action Teams – to provide medical, dental, veterinary and administrative support in a country that provided virtually none of the above.
5. Counter-revolution. Watts wanted to arm and train irregular units made up of Dhofaris to fight the Communist insurgency.

Sultan bin Taimur knew all about the capabilities of the SAS. The 1959 Jebel Akhdar campaign had been of great mutual benefit to him and the Regiment. While bin Taimur owed his continued grip on power to its intervention, the SAS had also been gifted an opportunity to demonstrate to its political masters back home that its members were much more than outstanding jungle fighters and to further solidify its place in the British Army's order of battle.

With the successful conclusion of the Malayan campaign, A Squadron was pulled out of the jungle, where it had been conducting mopping-up operations along the Thai border, and flown to Oman. D Squadron, under the command of Johnny Watts, was already there. The exceptional toughness displayed by A and D Squadrons in climbing the 6,000ft peaks of the Jebel Akhdar overnight, in order to engage in combat with and put down rebels intent on deposing him, had left the Sultan in no doubt. Centuries earlier 10,000 Persians had been killed trying and failing to dislodge Omani tribesmen from the same imposing heights.

And now, it seemed, the SAS was in a position to ride to bin Taimur's rescue again. The connection made in 1959 might be re-established.

Except that when, behind the thick walls of his summer palace in Salalah, Watts's Five Fronts plan to recover the situation in Dhofar was put to the old Sultan, he was not in the slightest bit interested.

Watts had known his plan was risky. By arming and training Dhofari irregulars, and by encouraging surrendered enemy guerrillas to join their ranks, he was, in essence, trying to start a civil war; pitting brother against brother and family against family.

The nastiest, Watts thought, *of all wars. But the only solution.*

The Sultan, though, was having none of it.

Chapter 2

June 1970

The directions were clear enough: drive to the big tree, turn right, bounce along the uneven sand, gravel and rock, then through the customs post manned by the one-armed warden. The Sailing Club hut was beyond that. Five miles west of the capital, Muscat, in the north of Oman, Blackpool Beach was the name given to a secluded cove inside the exclusive seaside enclave run by PD(O), Petroleum Development Oman. It was where, in swimming trunks and bikinis, oil workers and their wives, PD(O) administrators and off-duty SAF officers let their hair down. There were water sports, cold beers, neatly cut sandwiches and fresh food shipped in from overseas. It was a single, small oasis of Western prosperity inside Oman.

A little distance out to sea, away from the other swimmers, two Englishmen trod water and looked back towards the people relaxing on the beach. Behind them, half a mile out, the rusted hull of a half-submerged wreck broached the sea's surface. Both men were cast from the same mould. Military men. The older of the two, sporting a neatly trimmed salt-and-pepper moustache, was rarely seen without a dark suit and tie. Today was an exception. Needs must.

Colonel Hugh Oldman had been in Oman since 1962, when he took over as CSAF, Commander of the Sultan's Armed Forces. He was now Oman's Defence Secretary. Brigadier John Graham swam alongside him, his arms out wide, gently kicking his legs in the warm water of the Persian Gulf. A mane of thick brown hair swept back from his forehead. A veteran of the Second World War invasion of Europe with the Cameron Highlanders before later taking command of 1 PARA, Graham was the new CSAF. He'd been sent to Oman with specific instructions to come down hard on any complaints about the old Sultan's rule. He'd driven to the beach today at Oldman's invitation. And it had seemed like more than a social call. Calmly, Oldman got to the point.

'What would your reaction be,' he asked, 'if Said bin Taimur was deposed?'

In the two months since he'd been in Oman, Graham had seen enough to realize that, under Sultan bin Taimur, the situation was hopeless. At the end of his first meeting with the Sultan in Salalah, bin Taimur had ended the meeting by saying, in perfect, barely accented English: 'Those people on the Jebel are very bad, Brigadier. I want you to kill them all.' With bin Taimur at the helm, he realized, *we're sunk*. The Sultan reminded him, he thought, *of a tenacious Hanoverian monarch who was singlehandedly trying to govern England from Balmoral Castle.*

Graham looked at the Defence Secretary.

'I'd give three cheers.'

Oman was unusual among the countries of the southern Arabian peninsula. Its history was one of trade; or reaching out to the rest of the world. For 500 years until AD 400 Dhofar was home to the most important trading port in Arabia, its wealth built almost entirely on frankincense. This precious, fragrant resin travelled north across overland routes to the Holy Land controlled by the kings of Shabwa. But the most famous of all these monarchs was actually female, the Queen of Sheba, a contemporary of King Solomon. For the next thousand years Oman continued to look beyond its own shores. Omani merchants had plied routes that extended as far as China. It was an Omani captain who had helped the Portuguese explorer Vasco da Gama navigate his ships around the Cape of Good Hope – for his trouble, Portugal was eventually to seize territory in Oman until being ejected in 1650. But that humiliation did drive the development of a powerful navy able to conduct joint anti-piracy operations with the Royal Navy off the Horn of Africa. By the first half of the nineteenth century, under Sultan bin Taimur's great-great-grandfather, Oman controlled a coastal empire that extended from Zanzibar and mainland East Africa to Gwadar enclave on the Indian subcontinent inside modern-day Pakistan. Such was the country's ambition that in 1840 a trade mission sailed to New York for the purpose of acquiring weapons to use against the Portuguese in Mozambique.

By 1970, though, Oman was a shadow of her former self. Zanzibar was gone. So too was Gwadar. And Sultan Said bin Taimur had retreated into an isolationism that kept his country in the dark ages. It was divided between north and south, divided between Muscat and the interior, and fractious. Bin Taimur had ruled parsimoniously. When he took over from his father he'd had to. The country was crippled by debt. But once he'd rebalanced the books he did no more. As a consequence Oman was staggeringly undeveloped, while bin Taimur's rule became increasingly characterized by his eccentricities and neglect. Sunglasses were banned. The gates of Muscat were locked at dusk. Anyone walking around the city after dark had to carry a hurricane lantern. A torch would not do. There were only three miles of blacktop road in the country, linking Muscat with what passed for an international airport at Bait al Falaj – little changed since it was opened by the RAF in 1930. There were two other graded roads. In June 1970, Oman had one hospital and three primary schools. The total school population throughout a country the same size as the UK was just 750 pupils. Faced with this, wealthy Omanis sent their children abroad for an education. Which was exactly what Sultan bin Taimur did. And his son, Qaboos, provided the Sultan's desperate country with a glimmer of hope.

Before Oldman and Graham swam ashore, the new SAF Commander quizzed the Defence Secretary further.

'I assume that Qaboos wishes to take over himself as Sultan.'

'Yes, he's indicated that he is resolved to take over to save the Sultanate, and that he has the means and the following to achieve that.' Oldman told Graham that his role would simply be to keep the peace and not get involved. The Brigadier's mind was already churning.

'And if he fails?' he asked Oldman, already anxious that the young heir would be lucky to survive, let alone succeed in seizing power.

Qaboos bin Said lived in semi-isolation, enforced by his father, in a small house in Salalah some distance from the palace. This restriction was his father's reaction to his son's return from his education overseas. On the face of it, bin Taimur had been reasonably far-sighted in realizing that he needed to prepare his only son to one day take over. Until he was eighteen Qaboos was educated by tutors in Dhofar, but in 1960, after two years' private schooling in Oxford, he entered Sandhurst Royal Military College. His two years there did not go unnoticed by the British authorities. Nor did the friendships he made. After passing out with good reports he served for six months with the Cameron Highlanders in Germany before returning to Salalah. His last real exposure to the world beyond Dhofar came in 1963, when, at the end of March, he was escorted on what his father described as a 'world tour' with Major Leslie Chauncy, the ex-British Consul-General, and his wife. In a letter to his friend Colin Maxwell, a long-serving SAF officer, the Sultan explained, in neat, clear handwriting, that Chauncy would be 'accompanying him, or rather he will be in charge of Qaboos during the tour'.

Since returning, Qaboos had been largely confined to his quarters, studying the Quran and indulging a passion for classical music, particularly Beethoven, Mozart and Haydn. There was only one British officer allowed to visit Qaboos with any regularity.

Captain Tim Landon had been Qaboos's classmate at Sandhurst. After passing out with Qaboos in 1962, Landon had joined the 10th Hussars, but just five years later the young cavalry officer left the British Army to join SAF as a contract officer. Once Landon was in theatre, Sultan bin Taimur was persuaded by the SAF Intelligence Officer, Malcolm Dennison, that Landon might provide Qaboos with a small measure of the broad-ranging conversation he'd enjoyed while outside Oman. Landon became Qaboos's friend and confidant. During his visits they would play bridge and talk. Their conversations and, when Landon could get his hands on one, the occasional recent copy of *The Times* provided Qaboos with his only window on the world. By 1970, Landon was the Dhofar Region Intelligence Officer. And he knew more than anyone about Qaboos's resolve to save Oman from his father.

Qaboos needed to know how the British government would react. In late spring, the young heir found a way to send a secret emissary to London in search of answers to two questions: if his father was deposed would he be accepted into exile in Britain; and if he, Qaboos, took over from his father would he be regarded as Oman's lawful ruler. In both cases, the answer came back, yes.

The prospect of Qaboos taking control was one Graham greeted with optimism. It was the process of Qaboos actually doing so that alarmed him.

Sultan bin Taimur had allowed Graham to meet Qaboos for tea at his house. Bach played quietly on a record player. Their conversation was frequently interrupted by servants bringing cakes and buns, but Graham was impressed by the young man's charm. Dressed in traditional Omani robes and a richly coloured turban, and wearing a thick, long black beard, Qaboos spoke in elegant, unaccented English. Graham described how the British Army regiment Qaboos had joined, the Cameronians, chosen by his father because of its involvement in the Jebel Akhdar campaign, had been raised by one of Graham's own ancestors in 1794. The Brigadier asked Qaboos if he had enjoyed his time with them. Small talk. Then Qaboos fixed Graham with doe-brown eyes and asked him quietly: 'If there was an attempt to change the ruler, what action would the Army take?' Graham wondered if the room was bugged.

He thought quickly before answering carefully: 'I'm quite confident that the Army would do whatever was best for the country.' He felt sure that Qaboos had read him correctly. But the Brigadier had heard nothing to assuage his fears that action by Qaboos might end in tragedy.

Until now, Graham had been told nothing from London regarding any transition of power. But he understood that there had been one final attempt in late May to try to persuade bin Taimur to change course. The British Political Resident in the Persian Gulf, Sir Stuart Crawford, had flown to Oman to make the case to the Sultan in person. The visit achieved nothing. And attitudes in London began to harden.

In mid-July the British Consul-General in Muscat, David Crawford, visited Graham at Flagstaff House, Graham's bungalow home in Bait al Falaj, bringing with him a message from London: if Qaboos successfully carried out a coup he was to immediately switch the allegiance of the Armed Forces. On Friday the 17th, Crawford returned with further instructions from London: if Qaboos attempts something and fails you are to use the Army to restore the situation in his favour. Graham had had enough.

'This is totally unrealistic,' he told Crawford, '*totally* unrealistic! The Army is several miles from the palace, we've no idea what's going on, the palace garrison is strong – no idea *how* strong. By the time we get there Qaboos and his followers are bound to be dead. The situation must never be allowed to reach that stage and if you and the world want Qaboos to win, there's only one solution: summon the Army. We've got to be involved from the very beginning in the planning. And the person doing that must be me . . .'

Crawford reported the Brigadier's reaction to the Foreign Office. The signal he received for Graham from London by return was succinct and unambiguous:

USE THE ARMY TO MAKE SURE HE WINS

After his first meeting with Sultan bin Taimur, John Graham

was cornered by Tim Landon and Colonel Teddy Turnill, the Commanding Officer of SAF's Desert Regiment, based in Dhofar. They had asked him his impression of the Sultan.

'Seems like a nice old boy,' he replied, not revealing his hand, 'firm ideas about how his country should be run. Optimistic about the progress of the war.' Graham noticed the despairing glance shared between Landon and Turnill.

Now, finally given the licence he needed to act, CSAF drafted a secret signal that he telegraphed south to Landon and Turnill at the Um al Gwarif army camp outside Salalah. The Brigadier reminded his officers of the necessity and urgency of bin Taimur's removal. And he set three conditions:

1. Qaboos, he insisted, had to provide him with a signed, handwritten paper explaining why he wanted to take action against his father for the sake of the country and what he wanted the Armed Forces to do.
2. Initial overt movements as the coup got underway must be seen to be done by the civilian conspirators. The Army must merely come in as back-up; not the other way round.
3. There must be no bloodshed.

Chapter 3

July 1970

Leaning back against the slope of the fuselage, John Graham made his way along the aisle to the door at the back of the DC-3 Dakota and down the steps. The veteran airliner was still a handsome machine, painted white and silver with a red cheatline running along its length. Now reaching the end of its career with the Sultan of Oman's Air Force, Dakota 501 had enjoyed an interesting history. During the Second World War it had been General Eisenhower's personal aircraft. It was subsequently loaned to the post-war German Chancellor, Konrad Adenauer. But it was the name of Adenauer's predecessor that nagged away at Graham as he was greeted off the plane by Teddy Turnill and Tim Landon. It was Monday, 20 July. The anniversary, Graham pointed out with a wry smile, of Von Stauffenberg's 1944 bomb plot against Hitler: Operation VALKYRIE.

We'll have to do better, he thought. And yet even as they steeled themselves to act it felt as if the plot was in danger of coming apart.

A palace bombing in Sharjah and rumours of a reference by the BBC claiming that 'a palace coup is imminent in Muscat' did nothing for Graham's nerves. Nor those of the conspirators. The two young sheikhs supporting Qaboos were getting cold feet, Landon reported. Buraik, the son of the local governor, or *wali*, and Hilal bin Sultan, who controlled one

28

half of bin Taimur's Palace Guard, were crucial to success. And if there was one thing guaranteed to lead to disaster it was faint hearts at this point. Bold action carried out with conviction was the conspiracy's only hope. Graham sent a sharp written message via Landon to share with Buraik and Hilal.

'You are committed,' he reminded them, 'and furthermore if there is any more backsliding by you I will personally tell the Sultan. Think of the retribution from bin Taimur on you and your families . . .'

The next day, Graham received a personal letter from Sultan bin Taimur inviting him to tea on Thursday. There was no indication at all of what was on the old man's mind.

Inside the palace, informants had told the Sultan that there existed a plot to kill him.

Flight Lieutenant Barrie Williams thought: *They've got it all wrong*, every time he picked his way down through the high saw-toothed ridges to land on the strange, kinked runway at Bait al Falaj. But, three weeks into his contract with the Sultan of Oman's Air Force, Williams was starting to get used to the airfield's quirks.

23 July had started off normally enough for him. Or what passed for normal in what had, since the Welshman had left the Fleet Air Arm, become an increasingly colourful flying career. He'd delivered aircraft to Singapore and flown Jet Provosts to Khartoum for the fledgling Sudanese Air Arm. He'd been expecting to go to South Yemen to help them establish their own, post-independence Air Force. That hit the buffers when the British government realized that supplying men and expertise to both South Yemen and Saudi Arabia, where a sophisticated new air defence system was a largely British affair, might not be such a good idea. When simmering border disputes flared into armed action, they didn't want Yemen's British pilots flying into battle against Saudi's British pilots. Then, in the company offices, he spotted paperwork on the secretary's desk mentioning Muscat and Oman.

Faced with old kit and the growing intensity of the war in

Dhofar, the Sultan's Air Force had been undergoing a recent expansion and re-equipment programme that had introduced a fleet of more modern aircraft. Now SOAF needed pilots to fly them.

That sounds good, Williams thought. And on a tax-free salary of a little over £4,000 a year he'd be able to pay off his mortgage in three years too. He just had one question: would he have to shave off his beard?

In June 1970, strawberry blond naval beard intact, he flew out to Muscat, arriving at SOAF's Bait al Falaj headquarters in 114°F heat. SOAF's newest pilot was greeted by the recently appointed head of the country's little Air Force, another Brit, Wing Commander 'Curly' Hirst. Now, three weeks later, Williams was about to be pressed into service with one of the Air Force's very earliest recruits.

In March 1959, SOAF's first seven pilots assembled at RAF Manby in Lincolnshire, under Squadron Leader Barry Atkinson, the Second World War veteran chosen to bring the Sultan's new Air Force into existence. All seconded from the RAF, they began with just five aeroplanes, three of which had to be flown out to Muscat from the UK. The journey itself was an adventure and an indication of what was to come. The little piston-engined two seaters took eighteen days to reach Aden, 5,000 miles away, via France, Spain, Algiers, Nigeria and Sudan. Forty-eight hours in the air. They finally reached Bait al Falaj in August. The camouflaged Hunting Percival Provost T52s were a throwback. Even the manufacturer admitted, when enquiries were first made, that their 'literature on armed Provosts was now somewhat depleted'. The Provost would have been shown a clean pair of heels by the RAF's last biplane, the Gloster Gladiator. It was no guntruck either, with just two of the Gladiator's four .303 machine guns in the wings. There was something incongruous about young RAF fighter pilots wearing modern bonedome helmets strapping themselves into the old taildraggers while their contemporaries back home looked beyond the sound barrier. But, for all their limitations, they were the sort of aircraft SOAF needed to be getting on with. It needed to walk before it could run. So too did the country itself.

The son of a shopkeeper, Staff Sergeant Malallah was the first Omani to join the Air Force. His mother had cried when he said he wanted to join in 1959. The recent fighting in Jebel Akhdar made her fear for the safety of her only surviving child. He was her twelfth. His eleven brothers and sisters had all died. Despite coming from a moderately affluent family, he spoke little English, had no schooling or certificates, and couldn't even be certain of his age. Because of bin Taimur's neglect, these were universal problems facing British recruiters trying to bring young Omanis into their own Armed Forces. But Barrie Atkinson saw something in Malallah and forced his application through – ignoring the complaints of a Pakistani admin officer. Malallah understood enough English to appreciate that. The doctor who did his medical guessed his age as fourteen. He became an airman clerk. Now, a decade later he was a sergeant specializing in radio and communication. And there was about to be a lot of traffic over the airwaves.

A car arrived to pick up Malallah at 2.30 in the afternoon. At the same time there was a knock on the door of Barrie Williams's room in the accommodation block. As Duty Officer he was obliged to be found there or in the Mess. Williams opened the door to a soldier.

'Good afternoon, sir,' the soldier said, 'would you come up and see Colonel Oldman?' Williams went straight over to the Defence Secretary's office. Oldman was, as ever, charming.

Real old school gentleman, thought Williams, but this time, the Colonel's manner, for all his politeness, seemed less easy.

'Could you,' he asked, 'go down to the operations room and put the HF sets on. I'll be down in about half an hour. Lock the door after you.'

Williams took a Land Rover straight to the airfield and parked outside the Ops Room. Inside, the HF radio provided the only communications link with RAF Salalah. Williams was joined by Malallah and the two of them opened the system, switching it all on and preparing it.

Oldman entered the room and announced himself. With a slightly uncomfortable half-smile he turned to Williams.

'What is about to happen,' he explained, 'hasn't happened, if you get my meaning. Would you step outside?'

The sky above Salalah was grey and overcast; the air wet with drizzle. But rain in Arabia was a blessing. John Graham took it to be a good omen. By noon, the Brigadier had the letter he'd requested from Qaboos. A long, forceful explanation from the young heir explaining what he needed to do and why, calling on the Army to support him. Time to act.

Graham ordered Turnill to deploy the Desert Regiment, but he still had his doubts about the vital role of the civilian conspirators. The Army couldn't act pre-emptively, *they* had to. But Graham had no starting gun; no way of telling them: 'Go!' Then he realized he had at his disposal something unmissable. He wrote a brief note and handed it to Turnill, for Landon to pass to Buraik and Hilal; then he climbed into his Land Rover and headed to the airfield.

First, he called on the Station Commander. Neither he nor any of RAF Salalah's facilities came under Graham's command, but CSAF knew he must be confident of their support.

'I have an exceptional request,' he explained, 'the reasons for which will become clear. I've no jurisdiction whatever over you but I'm going to ask that, for the rest of the day, you and your subordinates, if you receive any orders or are asked for any help from Turnill or me, comply.' The readiness with which the Squadron Leader agreed led Graham to believe he'd already been tipped off about what was planned by his superiors in Bahrain. Then Graham walked to the office of No. 1 Squadron SOAF to arrange his starting gun.

'At 1515 hours,' he told two fighter pilots, 'I want you to take off and fly over Salalah town, then circle the area for about half an hour reporting any large numbers of enemy or people coming off the hills.' The intelligence would be useful, but it was the sound of the two jets streaking low over the palace that Graham was really after. The handwritten note left with Turnill told Buraik and Hilal that the arrival of the jets should be their trigger.

As Graham returned to Salalah, the RAF Station Commander sent a secret FLASH signal to Commander British Forces Gulf. He warned:

STRONG POSSIBILITY THAT SULTAN SAID BIN TAIMUR DEPOSED BY SON. SULTAN'S ARMED FORCES AND SULTAN'S AIR FORCE SUPPORTING TAKEOVER. COUP TIMED FOR 1520 LOCAL.

In town, Teddy Turnill was organizing his soldiers. He passed a handwritten card to Graham as the Brigadier returned from the airfield. It was from Qaboos.

'Are you sure it will work?' he asked CSAF. 'Have you approved our plans?'

'Yes,' wrote Graham in reply, 'leave it to us. You must remain totally out of sight until this is done. Just return this to me with your signature on it so that I know you've received it safely.' Landon, again, was the go-between. With the counter-signed return of Graham's note, they were set. And Graham, having laid the foundations, could only wait by the radio for news.

With Turnill's Desert Regiment positioned around Salalah in a conspicuous show of strength, the two SOAF jets roared overhead. Buraik's men cut the power to the palace communications room. Then a small group, led by Buraik, entered the Sultan's palace, not through the locked main gate, but by a small side door, guarded, but unlocked. Buraik's men were followed by a half-platoon of Desert Regiment soldiers led by an Omani Lieutenant, Said Salem, picked by Graham and Turnill. As they advanced past the outer walls to the palace in search of bin Taimur one of the Sultan's African slaves, loyal to the last, raised his rifle and was shot and killed.

Once inside, they searched for the Sultan through the

interior of the palace. It was a surreal setting for the hunt. Loaded weapons of every description lined the walls: pistols, rifles, machine guns and tear gas. There were careful piles of state papers on every surface, in every nook and cranny. Cinema equipment, perfumes, leather-bound books, radios and expensive drapery filled the rooms. Heaps of glossy Western magazines suggested long subscriptions. There were bricks, too, of fresh foreign currencies and an extensive collection of clocks and watches. Part department store, part Batcave. The men continued the hunt, the arsenal contained within the palace a constant reminder of the danger of ambush.

They found the Sultan in the North Tower counting his money. Buraik approached him first and called on him to surrender. Bin Taimur drew a gun from the folds of his dishdash and shot the Sheikh in the gut before making a break for it, trying to escape into the maze of the interior; firing in every direction as he went. At the sound of gunfire, Said Salem's soldiers were reinforced by two British SAF officers, Dick James and Ray Kain, and a Rhodesian, Captain Spike Powell, who joined the hunt. But there was nowhere to go. The Sultan made his last stand in a bedroom at the end of a corridor, refusing to surrender to anyone but a senior British officer. James, Kain and Powell didn't cut it. Teddy Turnill was fetched from the courtyard below only for bin Taimur to pull a machine pistol on him. The Desert Regiment CO stood his ground and softened his expression.

'Sir,' he said, 'put that gun down. I've come to save you.' The game was up.

'I don't think I'll need this any more,' the old man said as he lowered the weapon. In the firefight, bin Taimur had received a gunshot wound to the foot and had, apparently, been cut by shards of broken glass, although a later RAF signal to Bahrain, requesting an aircraft with an onboard aeromedical team to evacuate the injured Sultan, recorded four bullet wounds: to the foot, upper thigh, abdomen and arm. The wound to the foot, particularly, would need close supervision to prevent infection. As the Desert Regiment medic treated him, the

Sultan turned to Turnill and asked him bitterly how he could have been so disloyal; how could he do this?

'I didn't overthrow you,' Turnill replied, 'it was your own people. The ones blinded by trachoma.'

As soon as he knew that the situation in the palace was calm, Graham got up from his vigil by the radio and walked the 400 yards to Qaboos's house. He was welcomed in by the young man, clearly anxious for news, who ushered him into his small drawing room, where they sat.

'I'm sorry,' Graham told him, 'your father was wounded.'

'I'm really rather surprised,' Qaboos confessed, 'that he wasn't killed.' The heir had never once lost sight of just how badly things could have gone wrong.

'Come out and be seen,' Graham encouraged him.

In Salalah the population seemed stunned. Graham had anticipated euphoria. Instead there was a kind of sullen silence. Two thousand people watched, absolutely motionless, their faces expressionless as Sultan bin Taimur was stretchered out of the palace and placed inside a Land Rover ambulance. It didn't make any sense. As it drove slowly through the crowd, Graham walked alongside, confused about a situation he didn't understand. It was only as the Land Rover approached RAF Salalah that, behind him, Graham heard the first sounds of excitement begin to ripple through the crowd. The noise grew to a roar and then it began to make sense to him. Bin Taimur hadn't left the security of the palace for three years. The people didn't realize it had been their ruler on the stretcher. More importantly, since its inception, SAF had been an instrument of bin Taimur's state. For all its difficulties and disadvantages, the Army, officered by a core of around 150 capable, professional British soldiers, had been the only thing keeping him in power. And the first impressions of the Desert Regiment's participation in the coup suggested that they'd just done it again. That SAF might be involved in his removal was unimaginable.

Until, with his father safe under the protection of RAF Salalah, Qaboos left his house and the crowds saw him for the first time. Then the reality began to dawn on them. That was when the cheering started and didn't stop.

At 1800 hours, 500 miles away in the Operations Room at Bait al Falaj airfield in the north of Oman, Sergeant Malallah received a signal sent by John Graham from Um al Gwarif camp for Hugh Oldman. He was to open the radio telephone link to the Sultan's palace in Salalah. Minutes later Qaboos himself crackled across the line to tell Oldman that he had overthrown his father, who had been injured, but was now safe and in the custody of the British.

That evening, while Teddy Turnill took the document of abdication to bin Taimur to sign in his hospital bed, John Graham and Tim Landon joined Qaboos for dinner in his father's palace on the beach at Salalah. Outside, the cheering continued and bonfires burnt through the night. In the dining room, the three men ate and discussed not just the day's events but what lay ahead. Qaboos was relieved that things had gone as well as they had, but the mood was sombre all the same, acutely aware as they were of the size of the task taken on by the shy 28-year-old. He had to drag his country into the late twentieth century; a 500-year journey that needed to show evidence of progress before there was any hope at all of winning the war in Dhofar. That was his father's legacy. After dinner, Sultan Qaboos left the palace and returned to his house.

At 1530 the next day, an RAF Armstrong Whitworth Argosy C1 transport aircraft took off from RAF Muharraq in Bahrain. On its arrival at RAF Salalah, the former Sultan and four servants were embarked.

Said bin Taimur was never to return to Oman. Nor speak to his son again. He died two years later, aged sixty-two, from a heart attack, while watching television in his suite in London's Dorchester Hotel.

But while the former Sultan lived in luxury in London, those two years in Oman would decide the country's future for the next half-century. And the old man's departure was no more than a beginning; a necessary precondition.

Less than a week after bin Taimur's removal, Operation KIKI began, when, on 29 July, a small team from 22 SAS arrived in Oman to form the new Sultan's bodyguard.

Back in Hereford, Johnny Watts's original Five Fronts plan was revisited.

And at the end of September, a fifteen-man troop from B Squadron flew into RAF Salalah. Their deployment marked the beginning of Operation STORM, the codename given to the SAS deployment to Dhofar in support of the Sultan's Armed Forces.

Chapter 4

October 1970

Trooper Sekonaia Takavesi was at the wrong end of ten days in a swamp in Malaysia when he first heard that the Regiment was on its way to Oman.

Tak's time with the SAS hadn't got off to the easiest of starts. But, as a young 21-year-old infantryman his problems going through Selection were not unusual. His standard-issue leather infantry boots were crippling him. Every day he woke up wondering whether or not he was going to make it through – or whether his blistered, bleeding feet would let him. Unlike the Paras, who seemed to make up two thirds of the competition, he hadn't known what to expect. He hadn't trained. He had embarked on Selection, he realized, with everything against him. An NCO with his own unit, the King's Own Borderers, had told him he would never pass Selection. And the young Fijian was determined to prove him wrong.

The son of a schoolmaster from Vanuabalavu, one of fifty tiny islands that make up Fiji's Central Lau Group, he was an eighteen-hour boat ride from the capital, Suva, to the west. But in 1961 he headed to the capital when the British Army recruiting team arrived. Takavesi was one of 204 men chosen, split into two groups and flown to Britain. He arrived at Heathrow in December with the first group in the middle of a bitter winter. At the airport the young Fijians were handed greatcoats to protect them from the cold. It didn't come close to being sufficient and many of them spent their first British Christmas in hospital. That had been bad enough. Enduring SAS Selection was worse.

Then, barely able to walk and forcing himself to keep going in the face of tasks with names like 'The Sickener', news reached him from Aden that two SAS men, Robin Edwards and Nick Warburton, had been killed and beheaded on operations in the Radfan and Tak began to wonder *just what on earth am I getting myself into . . .*

Now a seven-year veteran with the Regiment, Tak was one of fifteen men pulled aside by B Squadron Boss, Major Keith Farnes, and told they were redeploying. It made sense enough for him and his friend, fellow Fijian Jim Vakatali, to be part of it.

Each SAS Sabre Squadron was split into four areas of expertise, Mobility Troop, Mountain Troop, Freefall Troop and Boat Troop. But as with so much about the way the SAS approached things, these were areas of emphasis, rather than unbreakable rules. Skills were spread wide. And although Tak was part of Mobility Troop, this was going to be a hearts and minds exercise and an intensive five-week course at the military language school at Beaconsfield meant Tak and Jim were both Arabic-speakers.

Tak had found that hard going, but, as ever, he'd pushed himself through to the end. It was simpler just to get on with things. The same principle applied in the jungle. That said, despite the unending wet, the boots that he'd needed to stitch extra leather to so as to keep out the leeches, and an apparently limitless diet of tinned sardines, if forced to choose, he'd still probably go for jungle over desert.

Just a lot easier, he thought, *once you're settled into the routine.* But if the Regiment was sending him to the desert, he'd manage. Tak coped with things that were thrown at him with equanimity. After that first, freezing winter in England, perhaps everything else was a breeze.

The men staged back to Hereford, where they were turned around quickly, briefed and re-equipped, before flying out via

Cyprus to Bahrain, and that, officially, was as far as they went. The SAS may have been travelling to Oman at the invitation of the Sultan, but it didn't make their paymasters at home any less concerned about secrecy.

They entered Oman on visas acquired through the London company of Charles Kendall and Partners, of 7 Albert Court, SW7, that listed their occupation as 'Government Official'. Instructed to wear SAF uniforms, remove any badges of rank, and even leave behind notebooks printed by HMSO – Her Majesty's Stationery Office – they were not, officially at least, in Oman. In country, the SAS were to go by the name of the British Army Training Team, or BATT. That, though, wouldn't necessarily stop them from being recognized. And, in Bahrain, Tak and Jim ran into an old friend: Talaiasi Labalaba.

Tak, Laba and Jim first met in Fiji when, in 1961, they all showed up to meet the visiting British Army recruiters. It's no surprise the three of them were chosen. Laba was a mountain of a man: an obviously athletic 250lb, clearing six foot by a distance, and thick limbs packed with heavy muscle. He moved with the fluidity of a heavyweight boxer. Jim was cut from similar cloth. And Tak, although short of six foot, was nearly as broad as he was tall, a chiselled physique suggesting that he was packing the same power as his friends into less height. He completed the look with mutton-chop sideburns and a thatch of thick black hair.

In Aden the three of them had hunted terrorist bombers together on Operation NINA. Dressed in dishdashes and wearing Arab headgear, their dark skins meant that, in a busy port full of visitors from East Africa, they could move around without attracting attention. The Regiment called this sort of covert operation 'keenie meenie', borrowing from a Swahili phrase describing a snake in the grass. And Tak, Jim and Laba used the new 'SAS Method' to bring down the enemy. It depended on getting close; close enough to distract the target with punch or kick, to give themselves time and distance to draw their Browning 9mm pistols and, instead of firing from the hip, take proper aim, their firing arm straight, and shoot to kill with an accurate double tap: two rounds fired in quick succession. Underneath his robes, around his waist alongside the Browning automatic, Tak hung six spare magazines strapped to a thick belt. Without radios, back-up or body armour, their lives depended on the vigilance, skill and quick reactions of the others. Each had saved the lives of his comrades and in the end, apart from the bullet that mashed the end of Tak's little finger, they'd come through unscathed. Often, it felt that the greatest danger came from the regular British Army patrols. The Fijians watched nervous young squaddies walking the streets with their fingers on the triggers of their rifles. And disguised as locals and unknown to the soldiers, the Fijians were more aware than most of how little it might take. In the febrile environment of Aden, Tak, Laba and Jim had all been kicked, spat at and abused by British troops. Since joining the Regiment, B Squadron's three Fijians had, inevitably, formed a strong friendship. Op NINA brought them closer still.

But Tak and Jim hadn't seen Laba for months. After Aden he'd decided he wanted to return to his parent unit. It was pure fluke that the Royal Irish were stationed in Bahrain as the B Squadron men spent the night before travelling on to Oman. But a night was long enough to catch up. Tak, Jim and Laba talked over beers in the Mess; Laba thrilled to see them again. It didn't feel right to Tak and Jim that they'd be off the next morning leaving their friend in danger of dying of boredom garrisoning an RAF airbase.

'Come back,' they told him, 'we're going on operations.' It was tempting. And the efforts at persuasion got louder and more raucous with each round of drinks. Until someone took offence and all three of them were chased, laughing, from the Mess into the hot Gulf night.

'Come on, Laba!' they urged the big guy, his resistance worn down by beer and friendship. 'Come and join us! There's a war on now!'

But, on this occasion at least, Tak and Jim weren't going to Oman to fight a war at all.

*

The SAS took the training of its medics very seriously indeed. The month-long basic regimental medics course at Hereford brought in outside instructors with hands-on experience. There, apart from stabilizing battlefield casualties, Tak was taught to suture and to diagnose simpler conditions. Then he was sent to St Mary's in Paddington, where he spent a month on attachment. Like a medical student, he'd scrub up, allowed into the operating theatres to watch the surgeons at work. While housemen sat with patients, he'd stand in, listening and taking notes. Tak rotated through different wards and by the end of the attachment he'd learnt to deliver babies, helped treat the broken bodies of road traffic accident victims and was trusted to be left alone to stitch wounds. The medical staff appreciated the assistance he was able to provide. Not least at weekends. When the drunks poured into A&E on a Saturday night, it was never a bad idea to have an SAS operative on hand.

Despite the breadth of what he'd learnt at St Mary's, Tak hadn't been prepared for his first patients in Oman: goats, cattle and camels. There were a lot of hearts and minds to be won before the BATT were going to be trusted with human patients.

On arrival in Salalah, the small BATT team had split into three. At SAF's Um al Gwarif camp one group set up a regimental HQ that included a signals room, armoury and Ops Room. Then they began to work their way through Johnny Watts's Five Fronts list.

The bones of an intelligence cell was set up, and a BATT corporal given the job of developing the Psy-Ops effort. The others formed two Civil Action Teams based in Taqa and Mirbat, small coastal towns east of Salalah, the regional capital. Tak and the rest of his four-man team were despatched to Taqa, setting up shop in an empty house by the main square, overlooked by a stone fort on high ground behind the town. Beyond that, always dominating the plain, was the Jebel; for now, off limits to them. They flew a flag from the roof and erected an information board outside. When the BATT arrived in Taqa, they quickly realized that the little town simply had no civilian governance or administration whatsoever. Taqa seemed to be on its knees, the population mistrustful and, the four-man SAS team believed, frightened of an enemy that walked amongst them, coming and going as it pleased. If making a difference began with treating their animals, so be it.

Nothing to it, Tak told himself faced with his first four-legged patient, *whatever you can do to a human you can do to an animal*. Up to a point. Anything really serious and he called the team's vet out from Salalah, where he was trying to induce two thoroughbred bulls, flown in from Dubai by the RAF, to mate with the small, undernourished Dhofari cattle; 'Beats working with homosexual goats in Harwell,' claimed the vet. And news that the little BATT Civil Action Team in Taqa were doing good spread.

It was the woman brought down from the Jebel who proved to be the turning point. It took her companions two or three days to carry her to Taqa from the hills. In agony. Her original complaint had been toothache. It must have become un-bearable before she sought help for it as she'd have guessed at the treatment. The Jebalis called it *Wazim*. They used pain to kill pain. In the absence of any other kind of medical treatment in Dhofar up on the Jebel, they'd heated a steel rod in a fire until it was red hot then applied it to the source of her pain. The new wound soon became horribly infected and by the time she was brought to Taqa, her mouth was a livid, suppurating map of abscesses and ulcers.

At first, Tak was cautious, sensitive to the possibility of causing offence, but through an interpreter he was given licence to examine her. As messy as it looked it was, it seemed, a straightforward diagnosis. For the next week Tak gave her a strong penicillin injection and the infection cleared up. Her cure was regarded by the Jebalis as almost miraculous. And the next day three or four people came into the BATT for treat-ment. The day after it was twenty. The numbers at what was now a daily clinic continued to grow, with only the most serious cases being sent to Salalah for treatment where, as well as treating medical complaints, SAS medics, appalled by the alternative of rusty knives and dirty dressings, were also performing regular circumcisions. The dramatic effects of the BATT team's drugs were something of a surprise to them too; a fever could be tamed by a single aspirin. But they were treating people who had had no exposure at all to modern medicine. They were having to teach them how to clean their teeth.

'It's pathetic,' one of Tak's comrades reflected, in sorrow and anger at the state of what they'd found. He spoke for them all.

The initial deployment of the B Squadron troop had been something of an experiment: was there a role in Dhofar for the SAS? But just what a difference a tiny handful of SAS could make was being proven daily in Taqa, Salalah and Mirbat. Two months after Tak's arrival, the SAS mission was extended by the MoD to allow them to join SAF patrols. Just tagging along, it seemed, but all the while building the intelligence picture. The BATT men shared what they picked up.

In Taqa and Mirbat, the civilian population warmed to the presence of the BATT teams. As trust grew, so too did the number of snippets about the enemy.

From conversations that began around local preoccupations – *How are you? Your health? Your family? How's the water? How's the camel?* – information about the enemy activity might emerge. All of it was fed back to the expanding intelligence cell at Um al Gwarif, who began to join the dots. By the end of November they had produced the first picture of the enemy's Order of Battle. Between 1965 and the end of 1970 it was believed that just three of the enemy had given up the fight and turned themselves in to SAF. There were now increasing numbers of them beginning to entertain the idea. And the leadership didn't like it.

Tak's BATT team had deployed to Taqa armed for any contingency. For the first couple of months they'd had no cause to reach for their weapons in anger. At the end of November, though, the Taqa BATT exchanged fire with the enemy for the first time. Five months in to Qaboos's reign, the SAS presence in Oman was showing the first signs of provoking a reaction from the rebels.

In the north of the country, from his office in the elegant, whitewashed British Embassy on the waterfront of Muscat's small harbour, Donald Hawley, the British Ambassador, had likened the accession of Qaboos to a modern fairy tale. 'The handsome young Prince did drive out the wicked old King,' he wrote as he drafted his Annual Review at the end of 1970. But the question that nagged away at him was 'whether Said Qaboos will live happily ever after'.

PART TWO

1971
Break-Out

Chapter 5

On the face of it, a few weeks in 1963 spent in Ipswich with Suffolk County Council learning about civil administration probably wasn't as much preparation as might have been ideal before taking over as ruler of an undeveloped Arabian state the size of the United Kingdom. But it was all Sultan Qaboos had had.

But had John Graham had any doubts at all about how radically different Oman would be under Qaboos rather than his father, they were swept aside when he heard the young Sultan's first broadcast to the nation. In light of what had come before, it sounded astonishing. Qaboos changed the name of the country, from Muscat and Oman, a name that enshrined the country's divisions, to Oman. He promised new houses, roads, a national water survey and well drilling, sewerage, a civil airport and a new seaport. He lifted all travel restrictions inside and outside the country, and changed the nature of customs levies, freeing up imports and exports and reducing prices. Health, education, telecommunications and public transport would all receive urgent attention. He would bring control of the country's electricity supply and conduct a survey of Oman's radio and television requirements. The carrying of hurricane lanterns was no longer required.

'These,' he concluded, 'are the first of our plans.'

The trouble was that, as far as the insurgency in Dhofar was concerned, Qaboos was starting too late. The war had already begun and the Communists still had every reason to believe they could win. Whatever military effort his forces made against the enemy would only stiffen their resolve. But Qaboos did, at least, understand the problem. The experience of the B Squadron Civil Action Teams had shown a way forward. The key to success lay with the civilian population. With the intelligence, Psy-Ops, and hearts and minds efforts already gathering pace in Dhofar, the Sultan ticked off the fourth item on Johnny Watts's list of five fronts. He gave his forces a single, simple war aim:

'To make Dhofar safe for civil development.'

The enemy had many names. They were the DLF, the Dhofar Liberation Front. They were POLO, the People's Organization for the Liberation of Oman. They were PFLOAG, the People's Front for the Liberation of Oman and the Arabian Gulf. They were NDFLOAG, the National Democratic Front for the Liberation of Oman and the Arabian Gulf. Unsurprisingly, none of them caught on with those fighting on the side of the Sultan, to whom they were known simply as the *Adoo*, the Arabic for enemy. And by the summer of 1971 the Adoo had become a well-trained, well-armed Marxist guerrilla army, supported, supplied and protected just across Oman's border with South Yemen, in Hawf.

Chinese advisors visited Hawf, where a training camp was established. Further west, the Adoo kept stores at Al Ghaidah. Initially, much of the Adoo arsenal drew on what had been left behind by the British in Aden. But the Chinese ensured that the guerrillas were increasingly well armed with rugged, reliable AK47 assault rifles, 12.7mm Shpagin heavy machine guns, mortars and big 75mm RCLs – portable, recoil-less artillery pieces like Second World War bazookas. With the AKs, particularly, the Adoo outgunned their opponents. In any contact with government forces they were able to lay down a far greater weight of fire, far more quickly. As well as weapons, the Communists brought with them organization, tactics and training. Chains of command were established and Dhofar divided into sectors controlled by different units. Labels like Ho Chi Minh, Lenin and Guevara were used.

They had become a sophisticated enemy supplied with long-range radios that could report back to Hawf, from where their victories, real and imagined, were trumpeted across Dhofar on Radio Aden. But the Communist support came at a cost.

Adoo fighters with leadership potential were transported through Aden to training camps in Beijing and Odessa in the Soviet Union. Alongside military instruction came efforts at political indoctrination and, in some of the men, this took root. They brought it back with them to Arabia, where it provided them with a fast track to power, a way of circumventing the Jebalis' traditional patriarchal societies. In the world inhabited by these young radicals, there was no room for God. There was no room for disagreement. Initially they wanted to take children from Dhofar to Hawf for training and education with their parents' consent. Then they did so without it. En route, children were starved of food by the guerrillas until they denied God. As Qaboos's ally, Buraik, now Wali of Dhofar, reflected: 'Religion is lost on the journey to Hawf.' Parents and elders who protested suffered grievously. One young mother who tried to take back her son from the Adoo was killed when, swung round and round by her feet, her head was burst against a rock. On another occasion, the resistance of two old sheikhs was silenced when their eyes were gouged with a hot knife, before they were left to die slowly.

It all made Mussalim bin Nufl's earlier efforts seem rather innocent. And when bin Nufl himself came down from the Jebel maintaining that, with Qaboos in power, there was no longer any reason to fight, a split was laid bare. Bin Nufl wasn't alone. Other nationalists who had simply wanted better for Dhofar also turned themselves in. The hard-core Marxist leadership had overplayed their hand. By introducing a degree of ruthlessness at odds with a centuries-old Jebali culture, they had alienated many of the very people whose support they depended on. The mistake provided John Graham's hard-pressed forces with a ray of light.

In February 1971, John Graham had to concede that across the whole of Dhofar, an area about the size of Wales, SAF only controlled the Salalah plain ten miles east and west of Salalah, and the road to Midway, an old oil company airfield thirty miles north of the regional capital. But he knew he would lose control of that when the monsoon arrived in April. Even Taqa and Mirbat, where the two BATT teams were at work, did not belong to SAF. Salalah itself, though, circled by coils of barbed wire, was a crucial omission. It was SAF's foothold in Dhofar, the heart of Graham's campaign to take the fight back to the Adoo. And for thirty years it had also been home to a small detachment from Britain's Royal Air Force.

RAF Salalah was proving to be an exhilarating new home. Real, *serious* flying. Whatever plan the Air Force had in mind for David Milne-Smith his posting to Leeming had shown it didn't tally with his own. Perhaps reaching the highest echelons of the Air Force meant ticking all the boxes on the way up. Perhaps a tour as a Qualified Flying Instructor was one of them. But as he had approached the end of his time at Central Flying School, Milne-Smith noticed a circular sent out by RAF personnel about the Sultan of Oman's Air Force. They were looking for volunteers for a secondment to SOAF. Accommodation would be basic; the tour was unaccompanied, but that was OK: still just twenty-five, Milne-Smith was unmarried. And SOAF was at war, flying daily operational missions. DMS signed up, provoking a letter from his Station Commander making it perfectly plain that the young pilot's decision was probably not in the best interests of his career. And at that point the Air Force realized that Milne-Smith was wilful too: more concerned with getting back into the cockpit of a warplane than whatever the politics of his career required. SOAF looked at his record and accepted his application without interviewing him. He was exactly what they were after.

His decision did seem a little perverse. While the arrival of the jet-powered BAC 167 Strikemaster was a big leap forward for SOAF, it was more or less the same as the Jet Provost 5 trainer that DMS had been flying at Leeming. And that was definitely a step down to pilots intoxicated by the prospect of flying Lightnings, Phantoms and, most recently, the new vertical take-off Hawker Harrier. The straight-winged Strikemaster couldn't compete for glamour. *Constant thrust, variable noise*, went the joke about the lack of power on tap. Perhaps not unsurprising, given that the Viper engine that drove it had originally been designed to be disposable, a power plant for the Australian-designed unmanned Jindivik target drone. The Strikemaster gained its impressive-sounding name as a result of a competition amongst the staff at the British Aircraft Corporation factory at Warton in Lancashire, where it was built. It didn't look much like a 'Strikemaster'. Even painted in olive and brown camouflage warpaint, with the red Sultan of Oman's Air Force roundels on the wings, it resembled a tadpole with wings, a bulb of a nose tapering to a slim jet-pipe behind the tail. A Perrier bottle flying fat end first.

It even shared the design of its tail with the original piston-engined Provost. And that, of course, was the bit of the Provost that the original designers had managed to cock up completely. A wrongly positioned decimal point had meant that the tail was about 7 degrees out, making their new aircraft virtually unflyable. The single prototype had its tail nearly sawn off, bent down, then reattached with a splice plate riveted in to close the gap. Initially, at least, the Jet Provost also kept the original Provost main undercarriage, which married with a new nosewheel borrowed from a helicopter made it look as if it was on stilts.

'Oh my God – what a lash-up,' was the reaction of one RAF airman when he first set eyes on the awkward, ungainly-looking new jet in 1955.

By 1970, though, the Strikemaster was a very different beast to the earliest JPs. The initial kinks of the Jet Provost had long been ironed out. It had an uprated, developed Rolls-Royce Mk 535 Viper turbojet, a strengthened wing allowing it to carry up to six times the weapons load of SOAF's old propellor-driven Provosts, and it was over twice as fast. It had evolved into a genuine warplane.

The little jet's potential hadn't gone completely unnoticed

within the RAF. Some had recognized the ground attack possibilities offered by the Jet Provost in 1958 when they sent one of the trainers to Aden for trials. Then in 1965 they'd despatched a small detachment of Jet Provosts to Indonesia to develop tactics for Army cooperation. But in the end, they couldn't quite persuade themselves of the value of a small, simple, cheap, dedicated close air support jet while fixed on the ill-fated pursuit of technological marvels and big twin-engined beasts like the TSR2 or F111, neither of which, in the end, ever actually entered RAF service either.

SOAF's requirements were a great deal more straightforward. When looking for a replacement for the old Piston Provosts, the only serious contenders had been either the Strikemaster or the new North American OV-10 Bronco, a twin-turboprop designed specifically for counter-insurgency operations that had since proven its worth in Vietnam. But in the end it was the little British jet that shaded it. The Strikemaster's rugged simplicity – and Oman's close relationship with the UK – had won the day. Now, just like the Bronco the BAC 167 Strikemaster was battle proven.

It was basic, certainly, and definitely no hot-rod, but it was tough, dependable and straightforward to maintain. And with SOAF it would see a great deal more action than anything coming into service with the RAF in 1970. So David Milne-Smith was going to get shot at too.

But if DMS had disappointed the RAF with his decision to head to Salalah, it was nothing compared to the service's frustration that the remote little airfield was still its responsibility. Before travelling to Oman, DMS had done his homework. He'd read about Oman, about the overthrow of the old Sultan and the war in Dhofar. And about RAF Salalah itself.

The airfield had been established in 1942 by BOAC as a staging post on its Middle East and India Service Five: Cairo to Karachi and all stops in between. Throughout the war it served in a similar capacity for the RAF and USAAF reinforcements flying east via the Southern Arabia route, alongside 8 Squadron's old Vickers Wellingtons. But in May 1945, they left along with the small US detachment. BOAC stopped flying through Salalah two years later.

With that, the RAF ceased to have any real interest in Salalah, but it couldn't leave. It was hooked by an agreement made with Sultan Said bin Taimur, reconfirmed in 1958, that obliged it to 'continue to operate the aerodrome at Salalah'. The old Sultan had made it a condition of a new 99-year lease for the RAF base on Oman's Masirah Island that remained a vital link to Britain's interests in the Far East. Just to rub salt in the wound, bin Taimur charged the RAF an annual rent of £6,000 for the privilege. So, run on a shoestring, RAF Salalah, with its bare-bones facilities and sand runways sealed with oil, simply ambled on as one of the Air Force's strangest postings.

There was brief excitement in the mid-sixties when an American team arrived to assess Salalah as a possible site for a satellite tracking station, but in the end they decided that the Azores offered a more suitable home. Safety could have been an issue.

The roads around Salalah were mined, there were increasingly bold sabotage attacks against the airfield and its facilities, and a month after the US space scientists arrived the Sultan's own guards tried to kill him. Such was British concern for the security of its burdensome outpost that in 1963 a field squadron of the RAF Regiment was sent to protect the base and its people. The Rock Apes, as the RAF's own soldiers had been known since their defence of Gibraltar in the Second World War, had remained ever since as the only fully constituted British unit deployed to Oman.

Since their arrival, sporadic attacks had followed, until 1968, when the airfield had most definitely become a target. By the summer of 1971, 81mm mortar shells and 75mm RCL rounds rained in, along with probes by Adoo foot patrols against RAF Salalah's perimeter defences. In June, three aircraft were damaged on the ground. As the Adoo upped their game, so too did the effort to protect the base.

The RAF Regiment built four forts beyond the wire. Constructed from old oil drums, known locally as burmails, filled with sand and rocks, they were labelled Hedgehogs. And for all their Heath Robinson appearance their thick, layered walls were formidably effective, virtually impregnable to all but a lucky shot from the Adoo. The Hedgehogs soaked up incoming fire. And the Rock Apes were more than happy about that. Every round they absorbed was one less that might otherwise have fallen inside the wire, inside the airbase. From within the forts, the airmen returned fire with their own mortars, GPMGs and, heavy-calibre .50 Brownings. The accuracy of their reply was now greatly improved by the arrival of Royal Artillery spotters working with them inside the Hedgehogs, using Green Archer mortar-locating equipment and ZB298 ground-searching radar. RAF Salalah's ability to counter-attack had also just been augmented by the recent arrival of the Cracker Battery, an expanded Royal Artillery detachment working with SAF's own Omani Artillery, to pound the Adoo positions with high-explosive shells from a big 5.5in howitzer inside Um al Gwarif camp. The other response was from the air.

DMS headed into the Squadron in the morning: a 20 × 20ft room inside the old BOAC terminal with a table and a few straight-backed chairs. It was one of the few permanent buildings on a base mostly built up with prefabs, the routes between them marked by lines of rocks alongside each edge of a track. He greeted those already there and grabbed a cup of coffee. A 1:100,000 scale map of the operational area, sealed with sticky-backed fablon, hung on the wall. What passed for decoration. Admittedly it wasn't much, and it certainly wasn't stylish, but while pilots were on detachment in the Salalah most of them headed into the Squadron. It felt safer, somehow, to be with everyone else. And you knew what was going on. It was that or volleyball on the court outside the Mess. That was more of an afternoon thing, a way of working up a thirst for a sundowner. Next door to No. 1 the transport squadron and helicopter squadron had their own digs. Beyond them was the Ops Room, where the Ops Officer, Doug Dargie, handed out the air taskings. This morning it was Barrie Williams whose name was on the sheet to fly the daily plains patrol. Every morning 1 Squadron launched a pair of jets to skirt round the steep crescent of rock overlooking the base. They didn't expect to see anything. Even if the Adoo were there, it was a tall order to spot a handful of men as you streaked over their heads at 350 knots. All they had to do was stand still and they would be effectively invisible from the air. The Strikeys knew this was an exercise in letting them know you were there; keeping heads down.

Williams, already wearing his khaki green flightsuit, picked up his bonedome helmet, signed for the jet and left the old terminal building for the jet. He passed the old BOAC speed-bird crest still laid in concrete in the ground outside. The *khareef*, the low monsoon cloud that greeted most Salalah mornings between April and October, hung low over the plain, but with the cloud base at 400 feet it was flyable.

The two jets flew in over Rayzut harbour five miles west of Salalah heading north before banking into a turn that would take them round the foot of the Jebel. Then Williams caught sight of them. A group of Adoo, armed with a 75mm RCL, on a hillock inside the entrance of the Wadi Jarsis, preparing to fire on Salalah.

We're lucky, he thought. As he set himself up to attack, Williams thumbed the RT on the little jet's throttle handle to his left to tell his wingman.

'Stream along behind me,' Williams told him. The two pilots spread out, putting in enough separation to make sure the frag from one attack didn't bring down the aircraft that followed. Williams then flew low into the mouth of the wadi. No more than 300 feet. The green walls of the valley rose high above him as he swept in firing rockets and guns. As the bullets churned into the ground around them, the Adoo scattered, dumping the heavy weapons behind them. The two Strikemasters pulled round and set themselves up to re-attack, going round and round, making firing passes on the escaping guerrillas until Williams's wingman called Bingo fuel. He was heading home. Williams acknowledged and checked his own fuel. Enough for one more.

Last run before I go back, he thought as he bore down on the Adoo position in a shallow dive. But it wasn't his lucky day after all. Williams had emerged unscathed from angry black clouds of fire from radar-laid anti-aircraft guns when his Seahawk squadron had attacked Egyptian airfields during the Suez Crisis. This time, a single Adoo bullet severed the low-pressure fuel line to the Strikemaster's Viper engine. And pulling up from the attack, as amber warning lights flashed on ahead of him, he felt the engine winding down. Climbing, he converted a little speed into height, but the cloud kept him low. His gut told him he wasn't going to make it back to Salalah, *but I will try*, he thought. If a crash landing was on the cards, he didn't want to do it with high-explosive rockets on the pylons under the wings. He pressed the pickle button; firing off the remaining rockets low over the Hedgehogs. As the white plumes of smoke raced away, he tried to bring the nose round towards Runway Three Five.

'Mayday, Mayday, Mayday . . .' he began, but he wasn't going to make it.

'I'm clearing the circuit,' called the pilot of an RAF C-130 Hercules as he abandoned his approach into Salalah and pulled the big cargolifter out of harm's way.

'Ejecting,' Williams called over the RT. He was down at 200 feet, a mile and a half out from the runway in a shallow dive towards the ground. He pulled his legs back from the rudder pedals, reached up with both hands, grabbed the yellow-and-black-striped main handle of the Martin–Baker Mk 4 ejector seat, and pulled the blind down over his face.

Nothing.

The seat stayed where it was. In the split seconds it took to realize it was duff, Williams had lost more precious height. But he had an alternative. He released the blind, leaned forward, grabbed for the secondary handle between his legs and yanked it. This time it was immediate. With a huge bang, the seat fired. Down this low, a little over a hundred feet, there was barely time for the seat to separate from the pilot, nor for his chute to deploy, but it did. Just. All the same, Williams hit the ground hard.

Back in the Squadron, news of what had happened to Barrie Williams in Strikemaster 410 spread fast. In the Control Tower, 200 yards away, they'd had a clear view. They'd watched it all happen, and diverted a helicopter, already airborne, to the crash site.

'How is he?' David Milne-Smith asked. No one knew. But the news from the Tower was that he'd got out.

Just a couple of months earlier, Del Moore hadn't been so fortunate. Out west his jet clipped a rock at low level. He'd pulled the ejection seat handle, but he was too low and too fast. The canopy jettisoned, but the little Strikemaster hit the ground and disintegrated before the seat had a chance to fire. He was killed instantly. His wingman returned to Salalah in tears, devastated by the loss of his friend. They raised a glass that evening and decided who would be the one to clear out his room. The month before, a Caribou transporter had come under fire at a strip up at the SAF position in Akoot. The two pilots and the Loadmaster were killed when the big twin-engined DHC-4 transporter stalled and crashed trying to make its escape. Those on the ground had heard the engines screaming as the pilots fought to stay alive. Then another Strikemaster was written off in a botched take-off in June. At least the pilots survived that one.

Now, though, with the shooting down of Barrie Williams in Strikemaster 410, SOAF had lost a quarter of its small fleet of jets in three months. It wasn't a sustainable loss rate. But as long as they were at war, the Strikeys were going to take bullets. They all did. David Milne-Smith had taken his first just a few weeks earlier when a round had cracked through the cockpit glass a few inches to his right. It only took a single lucky bullet. You just didn't think it was going to happen to you. Until it did.

Now they'd got Barrie. And he was never going to fly a jet fighter again. Williams had survived, but, either from the ejection itself, or when he'd smashed into the ground hanging from a barely deployed parachute, he'd broken his back at T7. 'I'm so very, very sorry,' the Commander of the Dhofar Area, Brigadier Mike Harvey, said, when he went to Williams's bedside at the FST field hospital at RAF Salalah.

'Ah, it was a good crack, sir . . .' the pilot replied in his soft Welsh accent; and smiled.

None of the doctors or nurses at the FST mentioned paralysis. And, drugged up to the eyeballs, when the medics had pricked his lifeless legs with pins in search of a feeling, Williams himself didn't make the connection.

Chapter 6

September 1971

The Station Commander at Salalah was in the strange position of running an RAF base that played host to someone else's air force. The only aircraft permanently stationed at Salalah were SOAF's. Worse, Squadron Leader Gerry Honey had been expressly *forbidden* to fly. The RAF's job was only to keep the airfield open and to keep it safe. When Williams was shot down, he was just a few days into a posting he'd been manoeuvred into in return for a promise that it would be followed by a place on the Harrier programme. He'd been fortunate that the Strikemaster had augered in nearly a mile and a half short of the runway. With his firecrews back from the crash site and the pilot safe, he had to get the arrival of air traffic into Salalah back on stream. Starting with that C-130 that had been hauled out of the circuit when Williams called his Mayday.

It was turning out to be hell of a time for a fast-jet pilot, with experience neither of running an airfield nor of the Middle East, to take command of an operational base in Southern Oman.

It had been a record month for the little RAF outpost so far, the highest figures for freight and passenger movements ever recorded. Not a bad effort from a team having to work out of a run-down control tower, with bullet holes in the glass, that had officially been rated as the worst tower in the whole Air

Force. Honey had to draft in extra personnel from RAF Masirah to cope with the exceptional quantity of men and materiel. By the end of the month he'd have absorbed well over 500,000lb of stores.

SAF was ramping up for Operation JAGUAR.

The end of the monsoon at the beginning of October brought with it SAF's autumn offensive. When asked, at the beginning of the fighting season, what his aims were, John Graham's predecessor as CSAF had thought for a moment before giving his answer: 'To keep fit and shoot straight.' With his hands tied by a lack of troops, equipment and political will, his apparently limited ambition was simply a reflection of reality. He was resigned to it. Every year SAF reopened the Midway road and launched attacks into the Jebel, then withdrew. It was a depressingly ineffectual cycle of activity which allowed the Adoo to grow and strengthen their grip. SAF were, at best, holding the line.

Truly wretched, Graham concluded as he took stock of the situation in Dhofar. He was determined that things would be different.

The Jebel stronghold was the Adoo's great strength. SAF could not defeat the Adoo until they cleared the mountains. They had to set up shop where the enemy felt invulnerable. Then stay there. So Graham's aim was clear; but to actually get the job done, he turned to Johnny Watts. He handed tactical command of Op JAGUAR to the Boss of 22 SAS.

The Regiment called it 'Jebelitis'. The symptoms, they said, were SAF's reluctance or inability to establish any kind of permanent presence on the high ground. Since January, the SAS had been deployed in Dhofar in squadron strength. While much of the effort remained focused on civil development on Salalah plain, it mounted small operations up on to the Jebel, the point being to prove it could be done. But it wasn't enough and the civilian population knew it.

'You say you will be here a long time,' one elderly Jebali explained to a Regiment Troop Commander, 'but what is a long time, one week, two weeks? The Communists are here the whole time. As soon as you leave they will come back and punish anyone who helped you.'

The officer's patrol, unable to find water, stayed on the Jebel for twelve days. It needed something altogether more ambitious. And that was exactly what Johnny Watts had in mind. Throughout August and September he planned the operation with the Boss of G Squadron, Major Alistair Morrison, a tall, dark-haired Guards officer. Morrison's immediate preparation for deploying his Sabre Squadron to Oman had been conducting anti-poaching patrols in Kenya, which, in his measured, cut-glass accent, he pronounced 'Keenya'. Morrison realized it had been better preparation than might have been imagined.

John Graham's original plan had been to try to establish a position in the Central Area north of Salalah, to stifle attacks on the base and suffocate Adoo supply lines to the eastern sector, but Watts and Morrison made a case for going into the east from the outset. While it would be a pocket of isolated territory, there was at least a chance of success, and the totemic value of that was crucial. Unlike the vertiginous peaks of the central region, the eastern Jebel was more approachable. Once you'd scaled the intimidating escarpment to get to the plateau, the landscape stretched out ahead in gentle, rolling hills. Movement across the terrain would be easier; rough airstrips for fixed-wing resupply could be built more easily; there was little cover from trees and shrubs so lines of sight were long and arcs of fire clear and wide. It resembled the open savannah of East Africa where Morrison and his squadron had been operating. But if that much was familiar, nearly every other aspect of the SAS operation that Watts and Morrison were planning was unusual. He wanted to use B and G Squadrons as shock troops, a *force de frappe* that would go after the Adoo in their own backyard with an aggression they'd never en-countered before. It would be the first time two full Regiment Sabre Squadrons – 120 elite troops – had ever gone into battle together. And yet the spirit of the Directive to Watts from the MoD's Director of Military Operations was clear:

> You are to take all reasonable precautions
> to avoid direct contact taking place
> between SAS soldiers and the rebel force.

Given what Watts had in mind that was likely to be problematic. But what was deemed 'reasonable' was, at least, open to interpretation.

Laba was back. The big-hearted Fijian had been unable to resist Tak and Jim's invitation to return to the Regiment. Last time the three of them had been reunited inside B Squadron it was Tak who was the new arrival. In 1964, Johnny Watts had been asked to raise B Squadron to give the Regiment the numbers to cope with the demands of the campaign being fought against Sukarno's Indonesia in the jungles of Borneo. The new squadron gave Tak a lifeline after he'd blotted his copybook with D Squadron.

Following a fight in a Hereford pub, the young Trooper was offered a choice: RTU – a return to his parent unit – or a transfer to Watts's new outfit. There was no choice at all. The three Fijians were now part of the B Squadron DNA. Their toughness, strength and endurance impressed everyone. No more so than on the rugby field, where all three of them, when ops permitted, played for Hereford Town. An intimidating sight for any opposition. But it was really their easy-going, good-natured approach to things that won the affection of the rest of the unit. Racism in the early seventies could be pretty overt, but by and large they rolled with it. Tak, the most earnest of the three, tried to make a distinction between ignorance and malice. He didn't raise his voice much; a look would tell you if you'd overstepped the mark. You didn't then want to ignore that warning. Laba drew the sting by clowning around. He'd offer a commentary as he walked across a zebra crossing: 'Now you see me, now you don't . . .' A few drinks down, his *pièce de résistance* was to chew and swallow a sandwich stuffed with cigarettes. The Fijian stomach, he said, could cope with anything. Cigarettes were nothing. His ancestors had eaten missionaries. And come back for seconds.

The desert-camouflaged RAF C-130 carrying B Squadron back into Oman touched down at Salalah on 20 September. Alongside Tak, Laba and Jim, there were a few new faces as they walked down the ramp at the back of the Hercules, stooping under the weight of heavy Bergen rucksacks. In the striking, silver-haired figure of Major Richard Pirie, they had a new Squadron Commander. From the Parachute Regiment, Pirie had made the mistake of admitting that there were aristocrats to be found in the Pirie family tree. He'd been known as 'The Duke' ever since. Pete 'Snapper' Winner was a Lancastrian fresh out of Selection. He'd been to Oman before with his parent unit, the Royal Engineers, but this was his first visit to Dhofar – he could barely contain his excitement at finally being on ops with the Regiment. And, in Mike Kealy, Tak and Laba's Eight Troop had a new Rupert, the term the men used for officers. In his wire-framed spectacles, the 27-year-old Kealy from the Queen's Regiment had yet to earn his spurs. He was a 'Baby Rupert'.

Four of the squadron who'd been part of the first SAS deployment in 1970, Tak, Roger Cole, Pete 'Fuzz' Hussey and Bob Bennett, looked round at the familiar surroundings of Salalah. They were a mismatched-looking bunch. Alongside Tak's bulk or the height of the rangy Devonian, Sergeant Bob Bennett, Fuzz Hussey, at a whisker over five foot tall, was dwarfed. But he made up for it with attitude. Where Tak and Bennett didn't say more than they needed to, Hussey, his hair too long, wearing beads and with a love of beer and rock 'n' roll, was like an enthusiastic puppy. Much the same could be said for Cole. Thin as a whippet and never happier than when he was talking. 'All ribs and cock,' Snapper reckoned.

The monsoon weather had broken four days earlier for clear skies and a light north-west wind. The draining 98 per cent humidity had halved. Dust and haze now hung in the air along with the distinctive smell of burnt Avtur jet fuel. The low-rise buildings, the lines of aircraft tucked behind burmail revetments and the more relaxed approach to uniform – shorts, flip-flops, bare chests and the occasional shemagh scarf wrapped round the head of a British REMF living out a Lawrence of Arabia fantasy – it was the same old scene. And behind it all was the Jebel. That was what they were here for. Them and G Squadron, already in theatre. Two squadrons – 120 men – Pirie had told them as he'd briefed them back at Hereford. But it wasn't an operation they were conducting alone. JAGUAR may have been led by the SAS, but they were going in with two SAF infantry companies from the Jebel Regiment, a platoon of Assault Pioneers – soldiers recruited from Gwadar, the old Omani enclave in Pakistan – and, most importantly of all, the Firqas.

This was the final element of Johnny Watts's Five Fronts plan. The Firqas were units of Dhofari irregular soldiers; tribesmen trained and led by the SAS. Without them, he believed, the war could not be won. Campaigning alone, Watts thought, his men would be as welcome as *Roman legionnaires fighting in Scotland*.

When the 6 foot 5 inch Boss of D Squadron, Major Tony Jeapes, had visited John Graham at SAF HQ and first proposed raising a company of tribal Firqas and arming them with modern weapons, CSAF had sounded sceptical.

'Are you going to train them in GPMG and mortars?' he asked. 'What if they turn against us?' It was one thing throwing them a few ancient .303s that had been liberated from the old Sultan's cache along with boxes of ammunition that had been kicking around since 1942, quite another turning them into an effective military force. But the canny Brigadier had been playing devil's advocate, testing the Regiment's plans for holes.

'Don't worry,' he finally admitted, as Jeapes was losing heart, 'I like it, I like it.'

From T. E. Lawrence in the Middle East and Orde Wingate in Abyssinia, to Tom Harrisson's headhunters in Borneo during the Second World War, the British had long appreciated the value of working with irregular local forces who had both a genuine stake in the outcome and essential knowledge of local conditions. And since Jeapes's first meeting with Graham, a whole squadron of SAS had been deployed to Dhofar to give them the resources to train as many Firqas as they could find tribes who wanted to form them. Since the split in the Adoo ranks between the hard-core Communists and the Dhofari nationalists, growing numbers of what were termed SEPs – Surrendered Enemy Personnel – had returned to the government side. They understood the Adoo: knew who they were, where they were and how they fought. Over 600 had now swapped sides and were welcomed back as prodigal sons, rather than enemy combatants, greeted with a cup of tea and a debrief instead of shackles and an interrogation. Every SEP contributed to the increasingly substantial intelligence picture SAF were building.

Jeapes, the architect of the plan, went into it with his eyes open. It wasn't going to be like working with professional, well-drilled regular troops, but Jeapes took a kind of paternal pride in their roguishness.

The Firqa al Nasi are, he thought, *camel thieves and raiders to a man, motivated by loot* and the belief that Sultan Qaboos had promised them they could keep the land they took from the Adoo. Watts told London that it had been explained to the Firqas that the FN rifles they were given were on loan and that they understood that they were to return them when the war was won.

'I wonder . . .' an FCO official noted in the margin of his report.

Jeapes had broken them in gently with Operation EVEREST. Transported on an armed dhow to the little coastal port of Sudh forty miles east of Salalah, the combined SAS and Firqa force met little resistance as they successfully retook the town. Six months later, when D Squadron was rotated out of Dhofar, there were six Firqas; each was drawn from a single tribe and named itself after an inspirational Arab leader. The first of them, the FSD, the *Firqa al Salahadin*, raised by a senior ex-Adoo commander, was the original and still the best. It had killed more Adoo than all the others put together. The FSD's impact had not gone unnoticed by the enemy either. Name-checked in Radio Aden's propaganda broadcasts, its reputation was travelling beyond Oman's borders.

This, Jeapes concluded in his final report, *is now a straight fight between Communism and Islam*. And the British, on this occasion, had God on their side.

On 30 September, two days before J-Day, the designated date for Op JAGUAR to launch, Captain Shaun Brogan was helicoptered into Mirbat, the home of the FAU – the Firqa al Umri – and the BATT troop led by Sergeant Steve Moores that was there looking after them. From there Brogan, the G Squadron men and FAU were flown north beyond Eagle's Nest, the 3,000ft promontory overlooking the town. Here they joined with the Firqa Gamel Abdul Nasser – the FGN – and their BATT handlers. Brogan, a tall, fair-haired officer from A Squadron, took command of the composite force from Moores.

They're not, he guessed from the looks on the men's faces, *that chuffed about it*, but it was nothing like the sort of welcome he reckoned a strange officer parachuted into A Squadron would have got. However reluctant he might have been to relinquish the leadership, Moores accepted it with good grace. He had no choice. He and the men would just have to get on with it. G Squadron's Boss, Alistair Morrison, like a third of his whole squadron, was out of the picture with hepatitis. So there was no point in dwelling on it. Brogan was the one who had insisted on returning to Dhofar. And Johnny Watts had singled him out for this job.

Oman seemed to be a kind of honeypot for a particular kind of Englishman. Names like Wilfred Thesiger, Bertram Thomas, Ranulph Fiennes and John Blashford-Snell had all been drawn to the Sultanate. It had also continued to offer excitement to a generation of wartime soldiers unable or unwilling to endure the boredom of peacetime soldiering. Colonel David Smiley had run Special Operations Executive operations in Albania and Siam before becoming Commander of the Sultan's Armed Forces in 1958. Johnny Cooper, fresh from running the mercenary war in the Yemen, had organized the honour guard for Qaboos's accession and was now employing his passion for gardening in trying to establish a nine-hole golf course in the desert while running the SAF Training Regiment. Oman still offered a kind of untamed adventure; a romance that was becoming harder and harder to find. Thoughtful and easily bored, Brogan was in many ways cut from the same cloth.

Reading a book as a teenager about the French Parachute Regiment campaigns in Indo-China and Algeria was what convinced Brogan that he wanted to join not just the Army, but the Special Forces. He had to do two years at Sandhurst and put in his time with a Royal Anglian Regiment rifle platoon before being eligible for SAS Selection, but the second he'd completed his three years of commissioned service he was off.

Brogan, the oldest of three brothers, had always felt like the thick one. While he'd joined the Army, both his brothers had gone off to university, where one of them, Simon, was now Entertainments Secretary at Leeds Student Union. That was going well – he'd recently put on a gig by The Who which had become the legendary *Live at Leeds* album. So although he reckoned he'd been written off by his parents academically, Brogan had decided that going to university would be his next move. When he arrived in Dhofar, three days before J-Day, he had with him a set of UCCA university application forms for Johnny Watts to sign, and he asked the Boss as well to write a 200-word reference highlighting qualities other than his usefulness with a machine gun.

Brogan hadn't fired a single shot in anger during his first tour in Dhofar with A Squadron. And they weren't due to return to Dhofar until the New Year. So when, back in Hereford, the CO wanted to send him to Boscombe Down to take part in some high-altitude parachute trials, he said he'd agree to it on condition that he could go back to Dhofar for Operation JAGUAR as a supernumerary officer.

'Right, Shaun,' Watts had told him in the Regiment's tented

lines at Um al Gwarif, 'get in there and make as much noise as you can and create a diversion away from the main force.' Then, grinning, he playfully slapped the young Captain on the cheek. Army orders usually follow a standard format: situation, mission, execution, command signals, administration and logistics all need to be covered. Watts had given Brogan none of those things.

And yet Brogan had known *exactly* what the Boss wanted him to do.

Watts was very nearly late for his own party. He left UAG at 0300 on J-Day for the airfield only to find the gates locked and unguarded. Frustrated, he and his Ops Officer, John Russell, drove round the perimeter to an open entrance on the Adoo side of the base. The hiccup did nothing to dent his anticipation of what lay ahead. He was feeling confident. Watts sometimes told people that he didn't believe violence solved anything. This would have come as a surprise to the Adoo.

'We're going to roll them up like a carpet . . .' he'd told his men at the briefing.

Twenty-five miles to the north-west the B and G Squadrons assault force, tabbing across fifteen miles of rough terrain in full battle order to secure the helicopter landing zone, were on their chinstraps.

Chapter 7

30 September/1 October 1971

The SAS extolled the virtues of the humble desert boot in official reports alongside assessments of the latest weaponry. The simple suede shoes were the Regiment's footwear of choice in terrain like Aden and the Dhofar Jebel. The unyielding, hard soles of the standard army DMS boot were quickly cut to shreds on SAS patrols in the mountains. By contrast, the spongy crepe used for the desert boots stood up better to the sharp rock underfoot and allowed quiet movement by night and better grip and a degree of cushioning. But there were limits to the help a shoe could provide. And given the way the Regiment went about things, those limits were reached quickly.

Tak was No. 2 in the two-man GPMG light-role team. While Paddy, his No. 1, carried the weapon and 500 rounds of ammunition, the Fijian weighed himself down with near 2,000 rounds in chain link draped in figures of eight over his shoulders and packed into his Bergen rucksack: well over 100lb of ammunition. It was a brutal load to add to the SLR rifle, spare magazines, belt kit, three bottles of water and forty-eight hours' worth of rations that each man carried. The GPMG SF – Sustained Fire – teams had to carry tripods too; the signallers the heavy A41 radios with their huge spare batteries, PRC316 HF sets to talk to BATT HQ at Um al Gwarif. Only the 81mm mortars were going to be flown in. It still meant that every four men were carrying a quarter of a ton up through the wadi on to the Jebel. The Firqas, who'd been busily discarding their rations as more than they wanted to carry, christened the SAS 'Donkey Soldiers'. The column had been on the march for six and a half hours.

Nothing to it, it's fun, Tak told himself as he marched, part of a long crocodile line of men, forcing one foot in front of the other, *it's what we've trained for*.

Then, just five yards ahead, Signaller Ginge Rees suffered a heart attack, his body pushed beyond what it could bear.

'If a man is in need of rescue,' the helicopter pioneer Igor Sikorsky once explained, 'an airplane can come in and throw flowers on him and that is about all. But a direct lift aircraft could come in and save his life.' Johnny Watts had wanted a dedicated detachment of four RAF Westland Wessex HC1 helicopters to support his men during Operation JAGUAR. It would be good for morale, he said, to know that the RAF would get his men out if they were injured. He wasn't confident that, with other taskings, the small fleet of SOAF helicopters would always be available to fly casualty evacuation missions when he needed them. But casevac was the very reason the helis had been acquired in the first place. An agonizing ten-hour journey strapped to a mule, endured by a badly wounded British officer, was the catalyst. As the war in Dhofar intensified, SAF's inability to evacuate their wounded men was no longer tenable. And, in autumn 1970, Squadron Leader Neville Baker, recently retired from the RAF, was flown to Italy to pick up the first of SOAF's new Agusta Bell AB206 Jet Ranger helicopters.

Ginge Rees, though, wasn't going to get pulled out. With the presence of the assault force compromised by the clattering arrival of a casevac helicopter, the whole operation would be blown. The signaller was pinned down, the straps of his heavy Bergen, filled with radio equipment, restricting both his breathing and his circulation. The medics raced forward to release him, before laying him flat on the gravel of the wadi floor. No pulse. The medic began CPR, holding Rees's nose and, giving mouth to mouth, filling the signaller's lungs from his own, before pounding at his chest to jolt the Trooper's overwhelmed heart back into life.

Come on, Ginge, for fuck's sake, offered Tak's new Eight Troop comrade, Snapper Winner, from further down the crocodile, hoping his unspoken words would be heeded.

For three minutes the medic continued his desperate attempts to resuscitate Rees. *One, two, three, breath.* Nothing. The lack of a pulse had been the urgent priority in responding to Rees's collapse, but as his attempts at restarting the Trooper's heart seemed to be reaching the end of the line the medic noticed the heat coming off Rees's forehead. The man was burning up. Out of options, he emptied his water all over Rees's face and tried to force it down his throat. And with a cough, nearly five minutes after going down, a startled, disorientated Ginge Rees was back in the land of the living. His kit was distributed throughout the squadron and, drama over, Rees found the will to continue as he and the rest of Watts's assault force tabbed on. They were still four and half hours' march from their objective, the old SAF airstrip at Lympne, one of a number of Dhofar strips named after historic British airfields.

John Graham watched anxiously as, just before first light, Neville Baker, now Boss of No. 3 Squadron SOAF, lit the AB206's single Allison 250-C20 turboshaft and wound up the engine. The twin-bladed rotor began to rotate slowly before disappearing into a threshing, blurred ghost of a disc. The little helicopter lifted a few inches from the ground, the camouflaged fuselage swaying a touch under the rotorhead, then, in the cockpit, Baker pulled up on the collective lever and twisted the throttle grip with his left hand and climbed into the gloom, away from Salalah towards the north-west. Only the return of SOAF's senior helicopter pilot with confirmation that the SAS-led force had secured the position at Lympne would allow Op JAGUAR to continue.

*

The last time Baker had launched an operation involving the SAS – and the first time the new helicopters had been used – he'd been shot at for the first time in over twenty years. He'd escaped unscathed in Israel in 1948 when the Egyptian Air Force had attacked and destroyed his DC3 Dakota on the ground and killed his navigator. He'd spent most of his subsequent career flying search and rescue helicopters. With his correct manner, neat grey hair and raffish moustache he appeared to be the very epitome of an RAF officer, but, when Neville Baker arrived in Salalah to establish the new SOAF helicopter squadron, he was not a combat pilot. And in putting together the new unit, he was immediately flying with people who were.

Defence cuts in Britain sometimes had beneficial knock-on effects for SAF. Faced with an uncertain Army career at home, Nick Holbrook resigned to become one of the squadron's founder members. He was not quite like anyone Baker had flown with before. He was an ex-soldier for starters and, despite operational experience flying little Bell 47 helicopters for the Army Air Corps in Malaya and Borneo and being told that he was exactly what SOAF was looking for, his initial application was turned down. He wrote to Hugh Oldman to ask if there was any point in reapplying. Within days he received a brief reply from the Oman Defence Secretary saying: 'You are accepted.' He assumed that, until coerced, 3 Squadron had decided it only wanted RAF applicants. Holbrook's appearance raised eyebrows too. Deciding that the secondhand Australian lightweight flying suits they'd been issued with weren't up to the job, Holbrook put together his own ensemble: a Denison smock donated by the BATT, Bedford cords, his old gunner's flannel shirt and a bright-red battery scarf around his neck. It earned him a warning from Baker. Holbrook appeared to have got off to a difficult start with his new CO, but that was soon to change.

Baker flew down from Muscat to lead 3 Squadron's first operation. He chose Holbrook as his co-pilot. As the Squadron Boss climbed north from Taqa towards the Jebel, Holbrook assumed he would level off with the top of the 1,500ft escarpment and fly to land giving away as little height – and as fleeting a target – to the Adoo as possible. But Neville kept on climbing. Then, to Holbrook's astonishment, he started his perfect downhill approach into the landing zone from 3,000 feet. The co-pilot bit his lip as the Jetranger descended gently towards the top of the Jebel.

Like he's at bloody training school, Holbrook thought, *not flying head on to the enemy across their bloody front.* Holbrook tensed in the right-hand seat, expecting the worst. Then RT exploding in their headsets.

'You're under fire!' shouted the BATT signaller. 'Get out!' In the background Holbrook could hear the cracks and pops of the Adoo guns through the cans. And Baker continued his approach, apparently oblivious to the danger.

'Neville!' Holbrook shouted, facing the Squadron Boss. *'We're under fire.* Go!' The penny dropped. Finally Baker let the helicopter drop, kicking the rudder and swooping down away from the Jebel to safety below the ridgeline. Furious, Holbrook lashed out, hitting the senior officer hard.

'Don't you ever fucking do that to me again!' he spat. For a moment, Baker sat there, impassive.

Oh shit, Holbrook thought as what he'd just done sank in. He'd just punched his CO. But he quickly realized that he'd come to the wrong conclusions about his apparently ill-equipped Squadron Boss. Baker didn't lack courage; his readiness to strap a shemagh around his head, pick up a rifle and go out on foot patrol with SAF company commanders like Spike Powell and Ranulph Fiennes before SOAF's helicopters were delivered was proof enough of that. It was simply that, in a career dominated by flying search and rescue helicopters, he hadn't encountered this before. And his reaction to the blow from his co-pilot was surprising.

'All right,' Baker said to him calmly, 'you show me how it's done.' Holbrook took him through the bushes without an enemy shot being fired. And two days later Baker called the ex-Army Air Corps pilot into his office.

This is it, Holbrook thought, but Baker was bigger than that. The veteran Squadron Boss knew he had a lot to learn.

'You seem to know what you're doing,' he said, 'I'm off back up north,' and he left Holbrook in charge. Their relationship had changed completely. From then on Baker seemed to embrace his rainbow nation of a squadron. Within it were pilots from the RAF, Royal Navy, Royal Marines and Army, as well as, in Ares Klootwyk, a battle-hardened South African mercenary, whose last job had been flying MiG-17s for Nigeria in the Biafran war. Each of them was able to bring his own particular talents and experience to a unit which, on continuous operations, was finding its pilots flying up to eighty hours a month.

From Eagle's Nest, Shaun Brogan's diversionary force had covered sixteen miles in a day, advancing to contact in a broad arrowhead formation. Or at least the BATT component of it was. On each flank there was a GPMG SF team, ready, if the patrol was engaged, to cover the force at the centre. Brogan, despite having been the one who, with A Squadron, had done much to raise the FAU and FGN and train them, had to admit that they were shambolic. And he wasn't sure how much of a diversion he was actually creating. For twenty-four hours the Adoo seemed unaware of or unmoved by their presence on the Jebel. But Brogan was in no doubt about the necessity of the job they were doing. On a previous patrol on the Jebel he had encountered a group of Jebalis who were in a wretched condition. The Adoo had stolen their food.

'What are we going to eat?' they'd asked. One of the guerrillas had picked up a stone and tossed it towards them. 'Eat one of those,' he said.

Brogan's small force shared their food with them, but arranged for an SAF airdrop of dates and rice. And containers carrying .303 rifles and ammunition.

'Now you are looking after the Sultan's territory here,' Brogan told them, before leaving them, happier than when he'd found them, and continuing west.

Then on the afternoon of 1 October, just as the main force were preparing to begin heading south from Mahazair across the gravel plains towards the Jebel, Brogan finally got the Adoo's attention. Just a few long-range potshots. But with the enemy's focus on his advance, the *force de frappe* were allowed the space they needed. It was just as well.

When Watts arrived on the Jebel just after dawn the next morning he found his men in a shocking state. They may have been willing, but most of them were in no condition to fight, drained by hauling the weight of another man over the length of a half-marathon without adequate water. That they'd made it at all was evidence of what Watts believed was going to make the difference in the operation that followed.

Willpower, he thought, *not firepower*, would, in the end, be the difference between his men and the Adoo.

Following their epic, twelve-hour march, the BATT had secured Lympne without a shot fired. At positions around the 1,000-yard-wide plateau small teams built defensive sangars from drystone walls, using the black rocks strewn around the ground. Others, led by a SOAF liaison officer, cleared the airstrip. And they waited for water. At least the conditions high on the Jebel made that a little easier than in the heat of the plain. The altitude took four or five degrees off the daytime temperature. The real surprise, though, was the greenery of the landscape.

The monsoon – the *khareef* – made Dhofar unique in Arabia. The steeply rising seafloor south of the Arabian peninsula introduces cold water from the ocean depths to the ferocious heat of the summer and, like the steam and condensation that hisses from water dropped on a hotplate, the marriage smothered the mountains of the Jebel in thick mist and cloud for five months of the year. As a rainforest can grow in the microclimate surrounding a waterfall, so the Jebel became lush, with green, rolling hills stretching out to the horizon. A landscape that would, with the end of the monsoon, stay green for another couple of months or so was disarming. It was fertile territory that, as well as to the domesticated goats, camels and cattle of the Jebalis, was also home to exotic species like gazelle, Arabian leopard, lynx, porcupines, wild cats, wolves and striped hyenas.

But if the sight that greeted the JAGUAR force, looking like the South Downs rather than the moonscapes more common in the region, was welcome, it was deceptive. It didn't mean there was water to drink. That was way out of reach. The gentle slopes of the plateaus hid deep-sided wadis that appeared to have been gouged out of the landscape with a chisel. Filled with dense, verdant bush and flowing water, they were sometimes thousands of feet away; Adoo strongholds meant any suggestion that point A, a few hills away, might be easily reached from point B was usually very wide of the mark. The water was going to have to come in by air.

The 22 SAS Boss watched as the first of the big DeHavilland Caribou transport aircraft approached the strip on finals, its heavy undercarriage hanging beneath it. In truth, Lympne hadn't turned out to be much of a strip. None of the SOAF pilots knew it or remembered ever having seen it. They reckoned a pilot had landed there once and entered it in the strip log. But it was flattish, long enough and now clear of rocks.

As the twin-engined airlifter floated down on to the surface and settled on to its oleos, it was immediately apparent something was wrong. The wheels of the main undercarriage broke through the dirt crust covering the strip and pulled the aircraft round towards the side. Were it not for the aircraft's short landing run it could have been disastrous. As it was, it came to a stop with its wing nestling against the only thing worth calling a tree that there appeared to be anywhere nearby. The Caribou wasn't damaged, but the success of Operation JAGUAR depended on SOAF's ability to supply them from the air using its fixed-wing transports that were capable of lifting a great deal more than the helicopters.

The smaller, lighter Shorts Skyvans still seemed to be able to get in, but for who knew how long before the strip crumbled?

There was only one decision to make. Watts turned to his Ops Officer.

'This is no good,' he said, tugging on a roll-up, 'we're moving.' But, until they did, the resupply burden would fall on Neville Baker's helicopters.

Over the next few days 3 Squadron lifted over 300 men from the Jebel Regiment and 30,000lb of stores up on to the Jebel. On J-Day, Baker was in the air for over six and a half hours; Nick Holbrook and his co-pilot for seven and a half. And, as they'd shuttled to and from Salalah, they'd brought water. If there had been any doubt at all, SOAF's helicopter squadron was beginning to make it clear that the war could not be won without it.

Snapper Winner was watching the helis coming in and out when he spotted Laba climbing the hill towards the sangar. The belts of GPMG ammunition around his shoulders glinted in the sun. The big Fijian no longer even seemed to notice he was lugging them around. In one hand he carried the big gun, in the other he was carrying water. Ten gallons of it.

'Come on, Laba,' the SF team encouraged, 'we're pissing air here!' Even Laba was sweating when he reached the position.

'Here's your water, lads,' he said with a grin and loped back down the hill; the economy of his words matched by his easy gait.

The Adoo guns erupted as dusk approached. It was the first time John Russell had seen the splashes of dust from machine-gun bullets walking along the ground towards him.

Just like a Hollywood movie, he thought.

Chapter 8

October 1971

In the early-morning sun, the JAGUAR force prepared itself for the seven-klick advance west from Lympne to Jibjat. It was here that Watts had decided they would make their new home. The mixed-bag battalion of SAS, SAF and the Firqas cast long shadows as they spread out into extended lines, breaking down into action teams and support teams. With the men ready to go, Duke Pirie, the B Squadron Boss, approached Watts with a problem.

'Colonel, we've spotted some movement. What shall we do?'

Looking around at the force of fighting men under his command, Watts didn't take long to consider it.

'We'll go and fucking kill them all,' he told the Duke.

The soldiers skirmished forward, their heavy Bergens again strapped to their backs. Two hours later Jibjat was secure.

'Get your kit,' Nick Holbrook was told, 'you're going up to relieve Chalky White as GLO.' After White had spent seventy-two hours on the Jebel as Ground Liaison Officer and overseen the preparation of two airstrips, SOAF decided that its liaison needed a break.

'Erm, what kit?' Holbrook asked. As far as he could remember he'd only ever been issued with a basic uniform, a 9mm Browning and a shoulder holster. None of what he would need if he was going up to Jibjat to give Chalky a chance for a shit and shower. Holbrook scrounged a water bottle, a tin of lamb stew and a bolt action .30 carbine and climbed aboard the helicopter. It would have to do.

Up on the Jebel, after seeing the last Skyvan off, Holbrook wandered down to the battalion HQ sangar, already constructed from rocks, sandbags and corrugated iron, and introduced himself.

'Where do you want me for the night?' – hoping someone had given it some thought. There were blank expressions and little interest. John Russell pointed to a little wadi just below the airstrip.

'You'd better go off and join the BATT up there.'

The sangar was strewn with kit. Inside, the troopers were trying to clean the day's dust from the weapons, a neverending ritual. Holbrook interrupted the routine.

'I've been told to join you.'

'Oh, have you, Boss? Like a cup of char?'

Typical SAS. Could produce tea anywhere. Holbrook joined them gratefully, forking lamb stew into his mouth as the light faded. The pilot's bed for the night was an isolated eighteen-inch-deep shell scrape outside the main position.

Shit, he thought, *I'm on my own out here*. Like a picquet. He grabbed a pair of Bren guns and positioned one at either end of his trench. He took ten extra thirty-round magazines for the two light machine guns, a box of grenades, and a Verey flare pistol and cartridges.

Right, he thought as he settled down for the night, *if anyone comes near me* . . . But the silence up on the Jebel was unsettling. In the gloom, he listened, straining to hear and identify unfamiliar sounds. A whisper of wind through the grass, perhaps, or the sound of sandals shuffling through the sand. Holbrook raised his head, squinting to see what it was. *People*. But it was one of the Firqa units filing past, no happier than Holbrook about where they'd been laid up for the night and refusing to stay put. Now he was even more alone.

Gunfire fractured the darkness. The Adoo's evening barrage.

But this time the BATT and their guest were able to enjoy the show from a distance. Three miles to the south-west, at Lympne, Adoo mortar bombs thumped into the dirt, lighting clouds of debris that flashed and disappeared. Arcing across the position were tracer rounds from the heavy machine guns, cutting through the fading sky with a deceptive lack of speed that came only when viewed from a safe distance. Smiles and laughing broke out in sangars dotted across Jibjat. The enemy were piling in on Lympne. And nothing. For now, it seemed, the Adoo were struggling to keep up. At least, that was true for the main force.

To the south-west, Shaun Brogan's diversionary force, advancing north-west towards Jibjat, had now well and truly poked the hornets' nest – exactly what Watts had been after.

And while, for the time being, the Adoo might have been making the reasonable assumption that, like earlier SAF operations, the JAGUAR force would spend a couple of days on the Jebel before withdrawing, Brogan's group had been inserted right in the heart of previously uncontested Adoo territory, then brazenly tabbed across inviting trouble. Come and have a go if you think you're hard enough. Initially Brogan had been left alone, but with each day the resistance to their progress towards the main force had grown. First there was hopeful long-distance sniping, but the Adoo were closing in on them. You could tell from the sound of the bullets. From long range, enemy rounds, their velocity exhausted, whined through the air at less than the speed of sound. By day three, though, supersonic rounds were beginning to find their mark, the shockwaves cracking the air in their wake.

At dusk, Brogan's men came under sustained fire. This was more like it. His force skirmished forward. Fire and manoeuvre. It was a well-oiled routine and Brogan urged his group to be as aggressive as they could be; always charging down the source of the incoming fire. There was no doubt at all in his mind that attack was their best form of defence.

'There ain't many gonna get out of this one alive,' one of the troopers drawled in a cod-American accent. Brogan grinned at the familiar, unimpressed SAS response to a firefight. But it was time to call in the jets. Over the A41 radio, Brogan contacted BATT HQ at Um al Gwarif and requested air support. And at RAF Salalah they scrambled the Strikemasters.

David Milne-Smith jumped up from his chair in the 1 Squadron room and ran outside to the hardstanding. The two jets were combat-ready: already pre-flighted and armed, and towed out from beyond the burmail revetments. The straps in each cockpit were already adjusted to fit the two alert pilots. Both 167s were hooked up to an external trolleyacc power supply plugged into the rear fuselage. DMS and his wingman just needed to fire up their engines.

DMS climbed up over the port air-intake and lowered himself into the ejection seat. He connected his leg restraints to the Martin–Baker seat before pulling the four-point harness around him and securing it. He pulled on his bonedome, leaving the oxygen mask hanging to one side. Ground crew connected him to the aircraft's radios and oxygen. Then they removed the five safety pins from the seat.

He switched on the battery, set the instrument switch to START and the inverter switch to NORMAL before checking that his flight instruments had on line. *LP cock on.* Fuel was flowing. Then he reached forward to just beneath the cockpit coaming with his gloved right hand and pressed the starter button, holding it down. The button glowed red. Five seconds later the rpm and jet pipe dials in front of him began to wind up as the engine ignited. The starter button winked off. Ten per cent first; then 40 per cent; the power came up. Milne-Smith clipped on the face mask and, calling the Salalah Tower, checked the radios. Good to go.

He closed the canopy, released the parking brake and pushed the throttle lever forward. The engine note rose as the Viper engine spooled up. *65 per cent rpm.* He started rolling forward, dipping the brakes before accelerating towards Runway Two Two.

In the magazines there were 1,100 rounds of 7.62mm ammunition for the jet's twin FN machine guns. Under the wings were two 540lb high-explosive bombs and, best of all, four racks of 80mm Swiss-made SURA rockets. Sixteen missiles in total; accurate and lethal. It paid to try to be prepared for any contingency when launching in support of troops in contact. And, from the outset, that had been 1 Squadron's overwhelming priority. It was all rather different from the Royal Air Force's uneasy embrace of the close air support role.

The neglect stemmed from the junior service's need to justify its existence as a separate service. After the folding of the Army's Royal Flying Corps and the Royal Naval Air Service into the new Royal Air Force at the end of the Great War, the Air Force had to, in carving out its independence, find roles that were unique and particular to it, such as air defence and strategic bombing. Unless those two roles were demonstrated to be essential to the nation's security, then the RAF was nothing more than an appendage to the Army and Navy. So it was here that it concentrated its resources. The bigger its fleets of interceptors and heavy bombers the more self-evidently necessary it was. By contrast, the RAF view, delivered in lectures in the 1930s at Camberley Staff College, was that the aeroplane 'was not a battlefield weapon'. And so between the wars, unlike in Germany or Russia, the art of close air support was allowed to wither on the vine. While the Luftwaffe used the Junkers Ju-87 Stuka to devastating effect in its Blitzkrieg campaigns and the Russian factories mass-produced the armoured Il-2 Shturmovik, the RAF entered the Second World War with no dedicated ground attack aircraft of any kind, nor any tactics for employing them.

Perhaps unsurprisingly, it took the RAF commanders who enjoyed some operational independence outside the European theatre of battle to devote themselves to it. In North Africa it was the leader of the Desert Air Force, Air Marshal Arthur 'Mary' Coningham who, from 1941, first employed fighters like Kittyhawks and Hurricanes in support of the Army. In

Burma, Wing Commander Arthur Murland Gill led the Vultee Vengeance dive-bombers of 84 Squadron with such success that Mountbatten admitted that the Chindit Commander, Orde Wingate, was requesting them by name.

By D-Day, of course, the message had got through to the Air Ministry. War had forced the RAF to catch up and, while it continued to apply itself to air defence and strategic bombing, the destruction inflicted by rocket-armed Hawker Typhoons in Normandy in 1944 showed that it had learnt its lesson closer to the ground too. It had been a skill forged in war which, were it not for Britain's involvement in a relay race of colonial conflicts following VJ Day, might again have been allowed to slip between the cracks.

But while the Cold War RAF developed all-weather fighters, and, in the Valiant, Vulcan and Victor, three different strategic nuclear bomber designs for a global Third World War which never happened, in Malaya, Korea, Aden, Tanganyika, Indonesia and Oman a motley collection of British aircraft – whatever tended to be available – were flying operations against enemies that shot back. They were flying close air support – often carrying the same 3in rockets that had wreaked so much havoc fired from beneath the wings of the old Second World War Typhoons. And by the late sixties, no British pilots were more well-versed in it than the RAF's three Middle Eastern Hunter squadrons.

And many of them, like David Milne-Smith, had found their way to 1 Squadron SOAF(Tac) where, unlike their counterparts facing down the Soviets in RAF Germany, they were fighting a shooting war. One look at DMS's logbook was a testament to that. RAF convention was that operational missions be recorded in red ink. Milne-Smith's logbook was a sea of it.

As he tucked up the undercarriage of the Strikemaster and climbed away from Salalah to respond to the call from Shaun Brogan's BATT, he took down details of what was required from the Ops radio room. He noted the patrol's callsign, their radio frequency and a grid reference up near Tawi Atair. He marked that on to the folded 1:100,000-scale map he was carrying in the cockpit. The BATT would provide him and his wingman with their targets when they got there.

It was getting dark. The Strikeys would need to get the job done before the light faded. As the SOAF jets rifled in from the west, Brogan made contact with Milne-Smith and his wingman using a SARBE search and rescue beacon. Its designer wouldn't have imagined it being put to use guiding warplanes in against enemy positions, but it was small and light and that had sealed its adoption by the Regiment in both Borneo and Oman. It was a typical piece of Regiment lateral thinking. They needed to talk to the SOAF pilots, but infrequently, they hoped, and in relatively short bursts while the jets delivered the good news. For that the SARBE's battery was adequate.

Contrary to legend, the SAS didn't always have all the answers, but one of the things that marked its members out as a unit was their willingness to learn whatever lessons they could from any situation they found themselves in. The Regiment's lack of trained Forward Air Controllers during the Radfan campaign had been shown to be a weakness. They addressed it. Each patrol now had at least one member with some FAC training and the SARBEs. And the SOAF pilots knew that if they got a call from the BATT, they weren't wasting their time. They'd get accurate control, and they would be needed.

Brogan watched as the two jets dived in on the Adoo positions. On the first pass the leader fired a single rocket to mark the target before hauling off and banking into a tight turn for another pass. As he set himself up, the patrol FAC passed corrections using the impact point of the first rocket as the reference. It was a technique that had evolved through experience and cooperation. Brogan made a point of finding and talking to the pilots at the RAF Officers' Mess at Salalah. They all did. As a result, the BATT Commander's fortnightly sitrep was able to report that his men and the SOAF pilots they relied on were 'very much on the same page'.

Second time round, guns firing and rockets spearing ahead,

four at a time, leaving rippling white plumes behind them, the Strikemasters attacked the Adoo targets. The fire from the tails of the SURA missiles, as they fizzed from the pylons, lit up the pale grey undersides of the jets' wings in a flare, before the view from the SAS position faded back to the grey of dusk. Brogan had been told each scrambled Strikemaster took to the sky carrying ordnance worth £7,000. How satisfying, he thought, as the two Strikemasters, disappearing into the gloom, called in one last time on the SARBE frequency to tell him they were on their way back to base. The rumble of the jets hung in the air long after they'd disappeared from sight. Someone filled the silence.

'Them that dies . . .' the Troop Sergeant piped up in his best Long John Silver accent. Brogan knew the rest. *Them that dies'll be the lucky ones.*

Job done. In dark skies DMS and his wingman returned to Salalah. On the ground there were few of the lights that would be visible at night in the UK. A sprinkling of light from inside the houses that clustered in small towns and villages along the coast. And black. There wasn't a lot of night-flying to be done in the Strikemaster. With unguided weapons and fixed reflector sights there was absolutely no way of delivering ordnance with anything like sufficient accuracy to support troops on the ground at night. There was no point in even keeping the jet crews on alert. DMS pressed the transmit button on the throttle with his left thumb, radioing ahead to Salalah Tower. At least they could light the runway with ground flares. Better than what you got landing one of the piston-engined Beavers in the middle of nowhere after sundown – a couple of Land Rovers on either side of the threshold, their headlights on full beam, pointing down the centreline of the rough strip – a strip that had probably only been judged flyable in the first place by a Land Rover driving down it at speed with loose jerrycans in the back. If it ran the length without losing any the strip was smooth enough to land on.

The powerful landing lights in the nose of the Strikemaster

cut through the dark ahead of him as DMS taxied back to the hardstanding. He twisted the canopy lever and the canopy slid open as he pulled off his mask and helmet.

With the jet shut down and the ejection seat made safe, he unstrapped, clambered down off the wing and walked back to the Squadron. Behind him the ground crew towed the jet back into the relative safety of the revetments. Inside, Milne-Smith pulled out his logbook and reached for the red pen again:

6th October – BAC 167 – Serial No. 408 – OP JAGUAR SCRAMBLE – .45 minutes total flying time – 15 minutes night flying.

That night, Shaun Brogan's group laid up south of a feature the BATT had christened Pork Chop Hill after the scene of a Korean War battle. They occupied three hillocks: the BATT troop in the centre, the Firqas each on the high ground, one to the right and one to the left of them. Unseen in the darkness below them were the forested depths of Wadi Khashayn, but, with the main force established and dug in at Jibjat on the other side of the ravine, Brogan's harassing, diversionary role was complete.

The BATT men sipped at hot tea from tin cups rimmed with black masking tape to stop them burning their lips. Brogan knew that he was in for a cold night. He'd somehow managed to lose his lightweight American sleeping bag in the last skirmish. But it was peaceful now. He wondered what Johnny Watts had in store for them when they rejoined the main force tomorrow morning. *Insha'Allah.*

Chapter 9

8 October 1971

'Steve's been hit!' Brogan cried out to the rest of the Troop, 'Steve's been hit!' Even as he said it he thought it sounded like a line from a movie. The Adoo attack had begun at dawn. Incoming rounds cracked in from close range splintering the rocks around them. As the BATT men grabbed their weapons, Steve Moores went down three yards ahead of Brogan; hit in the gut by an Adoo round.

This was the Troop's first casualty and it was a vicious wound. Brogan recognized the shock in the men's eyes as Moores began to scream out, writhing on the ground in agony. He knew he needed to take control. He had to get Moores stabilized, call in a casevac helicopter and fight back against the Adoo assault. He tried to do it all.

In training, Brogan had rehearsed an aide-memoire using the phonetic alphabet. Each letter – Alpha, Bravo, Charlie, etc. – represented a different, necessary element of what needed to be conveyed. The idea was to save time and clarify directions. There was no need to repeat introduce each subject – grid reference, time, enemy strength, etc. As he reached the end of the checklist he had to decide, did Moores need a doctor on board the casevac helicopter? He glanced at the injured Staff Sergeant, already dosed with morphine from the syrettes carried with his ID disc around his neck.

This man is so seriously injured, he thought, *yes we do*. As

Moores fought the pain, others of the BATT tried to make him more comfortable, to reassure him that help was on its way. Brogan continued to try to direct the battle.

But with a man down, his troop under heavy fire and the cheap Tokai radio he was using being jammed by a stream of excited chatter from the Firqas, he was getting overwhelmed as he tried to direct 81mm mortar fire from G Squadron on the other side of the wadi against the Adoo. But instead of working out corrections mechanically using a compass bearing and plotter, he was guessing at them; trying to imagine what it would all look like from the G Squadron mortar sangar.

Right 200, drop 100. The corrections Brogan was passing on over the walkie-talkie were meaningless. On the other side of the wadi, the Corporal in charge of the mortar team knew it.

'What are you doing?'

'Giving you mortar corrections,' Brogan replied. Then, with a sinking feeling, he realized his mistake. He was making a complete Horlicks of it.

'Shall we start again, Boss?'

A chastened Brogan wiped the sweat off his forehead on a pair of towelling wristbands and began giving the mortar team what they needed.

Neville Baker was the duty pilot. A casevac scramble usually meant a straight line to the casualty. This time, after taking off from Salalah within minutes of the call coming in, he flew a dogleg to pick up Phil the Pill, the SAS doctor, before carrying on to the BATT grid reference. The diversion delayed their arrival for half an hour. After three syrettes of morphine, Moores was on the verge of an overdose. In asking for a doctor to fly in with the heli, Brogan had made another error. Given Moores's condition it had seemed the right thing to do, but, as one of the FST surgeons had once told Baker: 'Never mind the first aid, the quicker we get the meat on the table, the quicker we'll have it back on its stumps.' The first 'golden hour' after an injury is regarded as crucial. Fit young men are capable of surving terrible trauma within that hour until receiving proper medical attention. But only if the wound is survivable. Moores made it into the hands of the 23rd Field Para Ambulance team at the FST alive. They stabilized him, but realized he needed urgent, more sophisticated medical care than they could provide and an RAF medevac was requested. En route to RAF Muharraq in Bahrain, the aircraft flew through such severe turbulence that Moores's condition deteriorated further, forcing the crew to divert to Sharjah. As a last resort he was admitted to the new state-of-the-art Al Maktoum civilian hospital in Dubai, where he died at 0320 local time on 8 October.

It's doubtful that the destruction to his abdomen had ever been survivable. Staff Sergeant Steve Moores was fatally wounded the moment the Adoo fire struck him. And Operation STORM had suffered its first man KIA – Killed in Action.

There were some within the Regiment who questioned whether this was really an SAS war at all. The post-war SAS had built its reputation on operating small four-man reconnaissance patrols behind the Forward Edge of Battle in Malaya and then Borneo. That was their area of expertise, the old hands argued, not going into battle in a company sized unit two squadrons strong. The conclusion drawn by a report into SAS operations in Radfan was that, as well as they performed, they were doing a job that could have been done by a well-trained infantry unit like the Paras or Royal Marines.

Doubts about the way the SAS was being used in Operation JAGUAR were not universal, however. And, in fact, Johnny Watts's second-in-command, Peter de la Billière, was already beginning to appreciate that the reluctance in some quarters to operate as infantry was a weakness that needed to be addressed. The Regiment took in whoever made it through Selection, irrespective of their parent unit. As well as those like Shaun Brogan, Tak or Laba from an infantry background, in its ranks were soldiers drawn from throughout the Army: engineers, cavalry, tankies, signallers, artillery, logistics. DLB realized that the SAS needed to be as adept at fighting infantry battles as it was scouting behind enemy lines or conducting covert keenie meenie operations. In future, with the creation of the Senior Brecon Course, there would be infantry training for all.

There was also resentment from outside the Regiment, which Johnny Watts was sensitive to.

'These sky-diving boy scouts couldn't advise anyone,' one SAF officer moaned. 'They just chunter round the Jebel getting shot at.' While complaints of the who-do-they-think-they-are? variety were perhaps to be expected, there was also a more serious concern amongst some of the British SAF officers trying to turn their regular battalions of Omani and Baluch soldiers into disciplined, cohesive military units. Neither the appearance nor the informality of the BATT was welcome; nor were the apparently preferential treatment and high wages of the irregular Firqa units fighting with them. They were making an important point. The Omanization of the Sultan's Armed Forces was critical to the country's future.

SAF's British officers were an anachronism, but they were a necessary one until Omanis could be commissioned and trained to the standard required to take over. But because Sultan bin Taimur had left Oman with an almost completely uneducated population it was a process, however desirable, that needed time. All the time it left Qaboos vulnerable to accusations that he was in the pocket of the British. The British Foreign Office, too, was anxious about the whiff of colonial influence it gave off, but the young Sultan resisted pressure to 'Arabize' SAF using officers from neighbouring states as an intermediate stage in the process of Omanization. The short-term kudos he might have won locally for doing so would have been outweighed, he believed, by the cost to the quality of his Armed Forces. He wouldn't let the British go until they were able to leave a professional, self-sustaining organization in their wake.

Already the Army was training increasing numbers of young officers through a new training centre and school. The Air

Force lagged behind a little. Staff Sergeant Malallah, who'd manned the radios with the Defence Secretary during the coup, was the first Omani member of SOAF chosen for officer training. After talking to the two other candidates who were interviewed, Malallah realized he'd been the only one who'd told the selection panel what he'd thought, rather than what they wanted to hear. When three senior British officers asked a young Arab his opinions about political hot potatoes like Jordan's links with the Black September terrorists or Egypt's President Nasser, it was perhaps hardly surprising. But Malallah was the only one chosen – a measure of the Sultan's refusal to lower the bar.

And so while the British pilots sent out to serve the Sultan wore shirtsleeves and shorts and enjoyed cold beer at dusk outside the Officers' Mess surrounded by palm trees, Malallah was enduring twenty-five-mile marches carrying a pack, crossing rivers with a rope, and taking cold showers underneath a punctured oil drum in Thetford Forest. There was very little doubt about who were enjoying themselves more.

From the cockpit of the old bush plane, Flight Lieutenant Sean Creak looked down over the spectacular fjords of the Musandam peninsula. This was a different kind of flying altogether. Creak had beaten a familiar path to Oman. After joining the RAF straight from school he'd flown ground attack Hunters before doing an instructor's course on Jet Provosts at RAF Little Rissington. But he hadn't flown anything like the DeHavilland Canada Beaver until arriving in Muscat.

When DeHavilland engineers consulted Canadian bush pilots about what they wanted, the outdoorsmen said power, short take-off performance and the ability to be easily fitted with wheels, skis or floats. It's going to be slow, the engineers pointed out.

'It only has to be faster than a dog sled,' came the reply.

Slow was good, and Creak loved rattling around in the old piston-engined utility plane. It was a perk of the job for SOAF's Strikemaster pilots. The oldest aircraft in SOAF's fleet, they were the last connection to the old flying club days of Atkinson's Air Force. Creak reckoned it was real north-west frontier stuff: putting down at rough airstrips to deliver supplies, mail and medicines to scattered SAF outposts and Oman's more remote inhabitants. The Beavers were still in-dispensable. Most of the time pilots flew solo, but Creak tried not to – and that was another reason he loved flying SOAF's Beavers. There was nowhere else in the RAF that he'd have got to fly around with his dog, Spoon, sitting beside him in the co-pilot's seat keeping him company.

Creak was now something of an old hand. He'd flown out at the same time as Barrie Williams in 1970. He'd then spent the last year of his commission in the RAF seconded to SOAF before immediately re-signing in Oman as a contract pilot. Same job, better pay.

He'd found a niche up in the north of the country doing type conversions and weapons training for pilots coming out to join the Strikemaster squadron. At the same time, he taught them how to fly the Beaver. And it was from Bait al Falaj that the rugged old short-take-off prop-plane flew regular reconnaissance missions over Oman's most remote region.

Beneath Beaver 214's straight, high wings, Musandam offered spectacular views. Dark folds of 5,000ft-thick Jurassic limestone plunged into a blue sea that had carved steep-sided inlets extending up to nine miles inland. The peninsula was an isolated pocket of Omani territory, physically separated from the rest of the country by the Emirate of Ras al Khaimah. It was poor, resourceless and sparsely inhabited, but it was the little spur of Omani territory that was of the greatest strategic interest to both sides of the Cold War.

By land, the only access to Khasab, the main town, was by footpath, too precipitous even for donkeys. Access was by sea, or by Beaver to the airstrip at Khasab. Or by parachute. Musandam had been the location for Operation INTRADON, the first armed SAS action in support of Sultan Qaboos.

Intelligence had been received by British forces in Bahrain that there were foreign dissidents operating in Musandam. An elaborate plan was devised, drawn up in great secrecy under the cover Exercise BREAKFAST, involving a Royal Navy blockade, SAF and the Scots Greys. The SAS were to claim the 3,000ft high ground behind the villages and act as a backstop, blocking exit routes. The SAS leadership team, under Shaun Brogan, were inserted using Zodiac inflatables from the minesweeper HMS *Middleton* before climbing the Jebel through the night. Then Freefall Troop parachuted into a wadi drop-zone from 10,000 feet to test HALO – high-altitude, low-opening – freefalling techniques. Opening their 'chutes below the level of the surrounding 4,000ft mountain peaks, the test was to end tragically, when one of the G Squadron freefallers, Rip Reddy, was killed after becoming tangled in his parachute.

Subsequent searches of the towns and villages uncovered some evidence of subversion, including Chinese textbooks on guerrilla warfare, but, other than reasserting Sultanate control, it wasn't much to show for the trouble and loss of life. The real value of the operation was to follow.

For the next six months, the Squadron's Boss, Alistair Morrison, operated under the title 'Military Governor for the Musandam Peninsula', while he and his men mounted intensive foot patrols throughout the region, building airstrips, setting up clinics, providing civil aid and spreading the word about Oman under Qaboos. Morrison learnt valuable lessons from his time in Musandam, which he knew would prove valuable in Dhofar; most important of all, don't start something you can't finish. People won't thank you for providing medical care for six months, but they'll want to know where the hell it's going when you leave.

As Morrison, now recovered from hepatitis, was flown into Dhofar to rejoin his squadron on Operation JAGUAR he knew that the possibility of setting up a clinic on the Jebel was still some way off. For the time being, the Regiment was taking an altogether more front-footed approach to the problem.

Johnny Watts wanted to move west again to White City and establish this as his HQ and a permanent hub for all subsequent patrols, which he'd send out like spokes in all directions from the centre; pushing out across the plateau, extending the boundaries of the territory he could claim for the Sultan. Relocating again would make the move from Lympne to Jibjat look like a stroll across the parade ground.

It was Snapper Winner's SF team that spotted it first: a tell-tale wisp of blue smoke curling up from the treeline. The Adoo had been careless. Opening up on the JAGUAR positions, they'd set up their Shpagin heavy machine gun without cleaning off the grease used to protect it during transit. As the friction from the stream of bullets heated the 12.7mm barrel the oil burnt off, giving away the Adoo machine-gun team's position. The SF team had them.

'Range 400 metres. One hundred metres right of the rocky outcrop,' came the fire order before describing the target. 'Lay. Rapid fire.' Winner fed belted ammunition into the GPMG as the tracer arced high over the Adoo machine-gun team. He adjusted the machine gun's elevation drum and they fired off another burst. This time they hit their target. Inside the SF team's sangar, the belt 7.62mm ammunition ripped through the receiver of the gun from the left. Spent brass cartridge cases spewed, the metallic ring as they rained into the ground drowned out as the muzzle of the gun barked. NATO standard rounds travelling at nearly 3,000 feet per second churned out in a relentless, irresistible rattle. The Adoo position was obliterated; each ten-second burst from the BATT team's gun delivered a lethal cluster of over one hundred rounds on the target.

Winner's team had already christened the gun the 'Master Blaster'. It was turning out to be a spectacular success. Finally, the SAS men were coming round to the Gimpy.

Perhaps they'd taken exception to the Belgian-designed gun's original French name: the *Mitrailleuse d'Appui Général*. Perhaps the Regiment just didn't want to say goodbye to the tried and tested Bren light machine guns that the new HMGs were being bought to replace. But even when the MAG became the GPMG L7, manufactured under licence by the Royal Small

Arms Factory in Enfield, it had almost dismissed the GPMG out of hand. 'Not suitable,' the SAS said on returning from the Radfan. And in the thick jungles of Borneo that followed, the Bren was unquestionably the right weapon to choose. But the Regiment seemed to be suffering from tunnel vision in compiling its list of complaints. The GPMG was slow in and out of action compared to the Bren. The M13 ammunition belts caught the light when slung across the shoulders and were difficult to carry when wearing a Bergen. It was heavy and, when only limited amounts of ammunition could be carried, the rate of fire was considered to be *too fast*. The GPMG *was* heavy compared to the Bren, but in such a comprehensive trashing of the Army's new machine gun, the Regiment was showing an unhealthy reluctance to embrace change; sticking to what it knew. But, in Oman, those on the ground were warming to it. Fast.

On the Jebel, firing across wide-open wadis, the Gimpies were proving to be war-winners. The L7s were devastating area weapons that created a beaten zone from which nothing could emerge. A handful of them firing in harness could bring a massive weight of fire to bear, destroying walls of rock in their path from nearly a mile away.

Until the arrival of the GPMG in Dhofar, the Adoo had held the advantage against SAF troops armed with FNs and SLRs. They were good weapons, accurate over much longer ranges than the Adoo AK47s, but they couldn't keep heads down; they couldn't lay down sheets of covering fire. The GPMG changed the picture and the Adoo knew it. As one SEP confessed, since it had been brought up on to the Jebel by the SAS, 'the war isn't fun or fair any more'. The GPMG just chewed up whatever it was fired at.

It is, Tak thought, *the best machine gun in the world. There's nothing to touch it.* And he, Laba and Jim were more than happy to sling belts of the ammunition around their shoulders. It made all three of them prime targets.

Tak and his No. 1, Paddy, walked side by side as the JAGUAR battle group advanced down the hill to contact; one of four GPMG action teams advancing through the middle of the string of prostrate Firqas. The irregulars were supposed to be leading the way; to be the ones taking the position, but an instinct for self-preservation had got the better of them and they were horizontal, waving the BATT men forward through their lines. To Tak's right, Paddy had the Gimpy's bipod extended and gripped the left-hand leg as he held the gun at his hip, cocked, ready to react to the first sign of trouble. He and Tak both squinted ahead, scouring the route for movement, paying attention to the faintest glimpse in their peripheral vision. Loose shale crunched underfoot. In a contact, Tak was ready to direct Paddy's fire and feed the gun, clipping 200-round belts on to the chain link they fed through. Each gone in twenty seconds' worth of sustained firing. But that was usually enough.

Without warning, Adoo rounds cracked into the right flank from below the treeline 600 yards away. Then bullets raked in across the line. Eight or nine GPMGs opened up in reply.

Let's do what we have to do, Tak thought, *saturate the place with hot sauce*. To his right, Paddy's frame juddered as the Gimpy shot back, before it suddenly bucked in his arms as a Kalashnikov round nailed it, splitting the butt of the heavy machine gun.

On the right of the formation, Jim and his No. 1 made for the high ground, to try to get above and round the enemy attack. The Adoo let them come. Waiting. Letting the two BATT men bring themselves close enough to be sure of hitting them. The action team closed the distance. Then the Adoo opened up.

An AK47 round pierced Vakatali's left leg a few inches north of his knee. It smashed his femur like a hammer on china. The Fijian's No. 1 turned the Gimpy on the Adoo position before dragging him into dead ground and jabbing morphine into his damaged leg. This was one of the injuries that most worried members of the Regiment. After similar hits in Malaya and Borneo, it was reckoned that you might lose a couple of pints of blood into the cavity created by shattering the big thigh bone. Vakatali needed to get off the Jebel and into the hands of the FST.

Under the irresistible weight of the battlegroup's GPMGs the Adoo melted away again, taking their dead, but leaving behind them the detritus of the engagement: shell cases, blood and flesh. But they'd had their say.

Vakatali was quickly casevaced out on board a SOAF heli. He'd live. And he held on to the idea that medical techniques developed in Northern Ireland to treat IRA kneecappings would save his leg. Word passed round quickly through the BATT ranks that Vakatali was going to be all right. But Tak and Laba couldn't help feel his removal more acutely than the rest. Of B Squadron's three fighting Fijians, they were now down to just two.

Chapter 10

October 1971

At White City the SAS prepared their third airstrip in a week. It was work they were well prepared for. Earning less than £10 a week back home, the Regiment supplemented their income with whatever jobs they could get around Hereford. It built quite a CV. To SAS corporal, Arabist and medic, Tak could also add tarmacking roads, work in a mushroom farm and baker. Even the Regiment paymaster worked in the bakery; bread, buns and doughnuts: the SAS were nothing if not flexible. But soldiering they did for the love of it.

As they set up the new position, White City, as Johnny Watts's new permanent base, John Russell, the Colonel's Forward Ops Officer, sat alongside the new Battalion HQ sangar trying to catch up on some admin. Hunched over the paperwork, he was distracted by a conversation between two of the men. He listened in to hear Trooper Chris Loid admit: 'We're not fighting this fucking war for the Sultan, we're fighting it for Johnny.' The lads' tails were up. And they'd have run through walls for their scrapping, chain-smoking Boss.

Then Operation JAGUAR stalled. Despite special dispensation from both the Sultan and the Imam, the Firqas gave up the fight for Ramadan and at exactly the point where Johnny Watts had planned to press home his advantage. He had, thus far, endured their whims and unpredictability as part and parcel of working with the Dhofari irregulars. The benefits of their local knowledge outweighed their military limitations. But with their refusal to fight, he lost not only half his fighting men, but the only part of the JAGUAR force who knew the ground, the enemy and the civilian population. They were the most important tool he had in cajoling and persuading a frightened civilian population to place themselves under the protection of the Sultan's forces.

Without them, he thought, *we're nothing more than a big fat white hand on a map. A waste of time and effort.*

His strategy in taking on the Adoo had been to give no quarter, to keep on going at them, confident that his men could dig deeper. Now, because of the Firqas' withdrawal, he was being forced to take his foot off their throat and let them breathe. When, two days later, Firqa leaders asked for more rations to replace those they'd discarded rather than carry them as they abandoned positions that had been fought for just days earlier, Watts exploded. What was the point, he asked, of his men losing their lives for this?

The Colonel's frustration was fuelled by his understanding of the reality of his situation. This was the Firqas' war. And, ironically, few things could have been more damaging to the self-confidence and sense of identity of the country emerging under its new young ruler than a crushing British victory in Dhofar.

'Do not try to do too much with your own hands,' T. E. Lawrence argued. 'Better the Arabs do it tolerably than you do it perfectly. It is their war, and you are to help them, not win it for them.' Ironically, it was a point lost on both Saudi Arabia and Iran. Both King Faisal and the Shah shared with Sultan Qaboos their conviction that the British had the ability to finish the war in Dhofar at any time. By stringing it out they were just using Oman as a training ground.

Their view was complicated, though, by Britain's imminent withdrawal from the Persian Gulf. While the government in London knew that the British public would not take kindly to the violent, drawn-out retention of 'another Aden', in Saudi Arabia and Iran, they simply regarded the British withdrawal from Southern Arabia as the presentation of South Yemen to the Communists. By misunderstanding the nature of British involvement in Oman, they feared the same might happen again.

Sultan Qaboos was vigorous in defence of the British, though. And he was enjoying an increasing number of opportunities to rehearse his arguments. While his father had allowed Oman's international relations to languish to the point of extinction, Qaboos was doing the opposite. In doing so – by establishing proper Omani diplomatic relations – he was cauterizing accusations that Oman was no more than an appendage of the British.

Even as the JAGUAR force moved up on to the Jebel, Qaboos had successfully steered his country to membership of both the United Nations and the Arab League. And after visiting Iran for the 1971 Persepolis celebrations he secured offers of material support from Jordan, Iran and Saudi Arabia. For the time being, though, only King Hussein of Jordan had delivered anything concrete. And, as welcome as it was, his initial gesture – three intelligence officers and a pair of thoroughbred Arabian stallions – was not going to significantly affect the outcome of the war.

It was as if Oman's putative Middle Eastern backers wanted to be certain, before committing themselves, that they were backing a winning horse.

As things stood, JAGUAR wasn't the breakthrough it needed to be to reassure them. With most of the Firqa absent, the BATT and the Jebel Regiment still patrolled out of White City. Mixed teams went out inviting contacts and searching for Adoo arms caches using intelligence from increasing numbers of SEPs who were turning themselves in. There were successes. They variously found tea, rice, sugar, ghee, blocks of Russian TNT, detonators, fuse, 60mm mortar bombs, 2in mortar bombs, 3.5in rockets, 7.62mm ammunition, antibiotics, blood plasma and even, on one occasion, the tied-up body of a long-dead civilian. Sometimes they got lucky.

Shaun Brogan watched as Tak, a scarf wrapped loosely

round his neck, headed off on his own into the dead ground. Still wearing his belt kit. Still carrying his SLR.

Off for a crap, thought the A Squadron Captain. Five minutes later Tak was back brandishing a Chinese SKS assault rifle he'd found in the cave he'd chosen for a bit of peace and quiet. Brogan got him to pose for a photograph. Tak held the Adoo weapons in the air and grinned beneath his impressive handlebar moustache. It all helped. Anything they seized meant one more thing their opponents had to replace by transporting it across nearly one hundred miles of punishing terrain.

But it was all a little lacking in the required punch.

As respectable a beginning as JAGUAR had got off to, and Ramadan notwithstanding, John Graham and Johnny Watts knew that liberating an area around White City in the east was militarily no more than clearing and holding a pocket of ground. But it was important because of what it represented – SAF's first permanent presence on the Jebel – and it had been chosen because it was doable, but if the Adoo were to be beaten, the Sultan's forces needed to impose themselves further west. They needed to go for the Adoo supply lines crossing from South Yemen.

Operation LEOPARD represented Graham's first attempt to do so. Alistair Morrison and elements of G Squadron were helicoptered into positions on high ground running north across the Jebel from the coast west of Salalah. The LEOPARD line quickly became porous as the Adoo found routes through the wadis that were hidden from view. But, initially at least, it led to one of SOAF's more unwelcome jobs.

After the Second World War, one of the perks of the job of Station Commander at RAF Salalah was the opportunity to go out hunting gazelles with the local sheikhs. The job of killing animals in the desert was now a good deal less sporting. When one of the LEOPARD line positions called it in, the Strikemasters were launched to strafe the Adoo camel trains. It took a lot of 7.62mm ammunition from the jet's FN machine guns to bring down a camel. A Strikemaster might return to base with the magazines empty, having killed just twenty out of a total of one hundred animals. The big beasts seemed to stay disconcertingly upright for a long time. And there was always a risk. At least one RAF Shackleton crew in Aden had been shocked to watch a camel explode as they'd attacked it. Ammunition and explosives were mixed with camel feed to smuggle it past checkpoints. And for one or two of the young RAF pilots it created a real crisis of conscience, but the loaded camels were pack animals, as critical to the Adoo's ability to wage war as a column of three-ton Bedford trucks. Every single bullet that made it through might be the one that hit a Strikemaster fuel line or smashed through the floor of a helicopter into a pilot's foot. Or which killed one of the BATT men.

Johnny Watts carried the injured man back up the hill himself. Trooper Chris Loid, an ex-Guardsman whom, just a couple of weeks earlier, John Russell had overheard professing his unswerving loyalty to the 22 SAS Boss, was now being cradled in the Colonel's arms with terrible gunshot wounds to his head and shoulder.

With the end of Ramadan the Firqas had once more been persuaded to rejoin the fight, but for all the bravery they displayed in hunting the Adoo, they were still ill-disciplined. This time, exhibiting only a loose grip on their orders, the Firqa Salahadin got themselves caught descending into a wadi. And Chris Loid had gone in after them to provide covering fire while the FSD withdrew.

The problem was the topography. The convex curves of the high ground tightened as they swept down into the wadis, which meant you were dangerously exposed. It was like being permanently on the ridgeline. As Loid descended, what lay ahead of him was out of sight, as masked by the solid background as Loid was exposed by the sky behind him. So the enemy was always going to see him before he saw them; then there was nowhere to go, but back up the hill. From the villages beneath the treeline, Loid was fired on. And, typically,

Watts, the Lieutenant Colonel, went in after him. The Adoo opened up. Watts took whatever cover he could.

They shot the rock away from in front of my head! he observed to himself as he tried to get down the slope to his man. *Shit, you don't want to do that too often.*

Watts got Loid back to BATT lines, but he was too badly wounded and the Colonel knew it. The SAS was a small unit. Fewer than 250 fighting men and they took losses hard. None more so than Watts. The thought of his men dead and dying made him weep. With Loid casevaced out, Watts, still stained with his Trooper's blood, sought some solace. He sat down with G Squadron's Boss, Alistair Morrison, in his sangar and, with tears in his eyes, shared the burden. He smoked fiercely. Whatever comfort he drew from time spent with his squadron commanders, he was acutely aware that responsibility for life and death lay with him; as it did for success or failure. He couldn't let the former jeopardize the latter. As devastating as each loss was, there was no other way. His strike force had to keep on pushing and pushing.

As Watts gathered himself on the Jebel, Loid died of his wounds on the operating table of the FST. His only next of kin was informed that her 24-year-old stepson had been killed in action.

The men of B and G Squadrons were tired now. There was the nervous exhaustion from being constantly alert; physical fatigue from patrolling out from White City night after night; and there was the crap they were eating and drinking. They were getting calories from their rations, augmented when 'The Fresh' arrived by helicopter, but none of them were drinking enough water and that caused problems of its own. Lack of water limited their ability to digest proteins so they lost weight; a couple of stone after a month or two's fighting. And then that protein went straight through you, causing piles.

It wasn't an issue for Watts as he'd practically stopped eating altogether. He seemed to be functioning on a diet consisting solely of tea and roll-ups. It wasn't what doctors recommend for pleurisy. Inflamed lungs caused him pain when he coughed or breathed heavily. Given that he was leading a guerrilla war in mountains 3,000 feet above sea level, the latter was unavoidable. But people knew better than to do anything other than let Watts make his own decisions about what was good for him.

If the Colonel was blind to his own condition, he could see signs of his men's weariness.

They're knackered, he thought, *and getting cautious*. Hardly surprising, he knew. The BATT had already lost 10 per cent of the men they'd brought up on to the Jebel. Two of them were dead and another had taken a bullet through the spine. But this was the point at which he knew he had to drive them on. He sat next to Duke Pirie in the B Squadron Commander's sangar. The two of them leaned against the drystone wall drinking tea. It was midday. Even high on the Jebel the heat was punishing.

'Right, Duke,' Watts told him, 'I want the Squadron out tonight with the Firqas.' Pirie stared ahead through the smoke curling off Watts's cigarette, thinking.

'I'm not going to.'

'Duke, I'm not asking you, I'm telling you. You get out there tonight and I'll come with you and we'll give them a hammering and, you know, we'll come back. But this is a battle of wills and we've got to keep at them.'

Pirie was unmoved. 'I've lost enough guys,' he told Watts, 'enough's enough.'

Watts spun round, stuck his finger in Pirie's face and locked eyes with the Major. 'If you don't take your squadron out tonight you're fired. Now.' Watts understood the Duke's concern for his troops, but this was the way it had to be.

Pirie's face was tight with barely concealed fury. 'All right,' he said.

Chapter 11

November 1971

The patrol left White City under the cover of darkness, fifteen BATT men in arrowhead formation leading the Firqas. The SAS element were top-heavy. As he'd promised, Johnny Watts had joined Duke Pirie's men for the tab to Shahait, a village five miles to the south-east of them. Ops Officer John Russell was with them. Shaun Brogan too.

Brogan got it; understood what Watts was doing and instinctively agreed with him. Over mugs of tea in the sangars he and the Duke had debated the merits of the tactics they were using on the Jebel.

'We have to give them the impression that they're up against a force with unlimited ammunition and skill,' Brogan told Pirie. 'Then they'll bugger off.' Brogan set off from White City determined to chase the enemy down. He chose not to carry a standard army-issue SLR as a personal weapon. Instead he had an ArmaLite AR-18 assault rifle. It was lighter than the SLR and, with smaller 5.56mm rounds, it had less stopping power, but it could be fired on automatic. It would mean Brogan could give the impression that he was returning fire with a machine gun. But not for long. With a rate of fire of 700 rounds per minute, each of the thirty-round magazines was emptied in less than three seconds. He was wearing a combat vest borrowed from the Regiment's Operational Research department that carried six spare magazines.

The first sign of trouble came just before dawn. The Firqas melted away, leaving the Regiment men alone in wild terrain. It had been a difficult march with little moonlight, slowed down by the danger of mines and the difficulty of navigating using bad maps and compasses. Rocks, their edges sharp and jagged through erosion, cracked their shins and harried their footing. They had failed to reach Shahait still cloaked by darkness. As they picked their way forward, the light was coming up on their left. To the right were rocks the size of double-decker buses. From the cover of the boulder field, the Regiment were no more than targets silhouetted against the early morning sun.

Their anxious progress was halted by an intense burst of fire spraying across them from the rocks. As Brogan dived to the ground he felt something lance through his thigh.

God, I've been hit, he realized as rounds zipped through the air and slapped into the dust around him. No pain yet. But Brogan felt for the morphine syrettes hanging round his neck on paracord with his ID discs, trying to work out how badly wounded he was. Keeping low, he tried to twist his head round to look. There was a hole in the pocket of his combat trousers. He could wiggle his toes.

Can you still wiggle your toes if your leg's broken? He couldn't remember. The Duke dived down into the dust beside him.

'We've got to pull back,' Pirie shouted. 'We've got to pull back!' This was exactly what he and Brogan had been arguing about for days. Brogan wasn't having it.

'We're going *that* fucking way,' he told Pirie and pointed forward at the source of the enemy fire. And the Duke, once he'd realized that Brogan wasn't going to listen, didn't argue. Instead, he let the A Squadron Captain take charge.

To his right Brogan could see one of the action team's two GPMGs was already laying down fire. He could see the tracer zipping into the rocks. He shouted across to make sure they kept up the onslaught. Ahead of him, the other GPMG pair were firing high, not hitting a thing, their tracer arcing harmlessly into the sky. The butt of the Gimpy was too low on the No. 1's shoulder. He was young; new to the Regiment and inexperienced. The man next to him feeding the ammunition belts into the gun was not.

'Get a fucking grip on yourself,' Brogan shouted at the No. 2. 'Get the butt up!' Jolted into usefulness, the No. 2 intervened and Brogan watched as tracer began chewing into the boulder field. Now they had to make their aggression pay.

'We're going to skirmish forward,' Brogan shouted to the Troop, 'Pete and I will go first.' *Either my leg's going to collapse when I stand up or it'll work.*

Brogan and Pete Spicer scrambled to their feet and moved forward. The lame Captain was soon falling behind as he limped, favouring his good leg. Fifteen yards forward, Spicer, masked from the Adoo behind some scrub, turned back.

'You're going to have to run fucking faster than that, Boss!'

'OK,' Brogan conceded, redoubling his efforts to hobble forward weighed down by ammunition and water. Behind them, two more BATT pairs skirmished forward in their wake.

Now we're motoring, Brogan thought – to his surprise, he found he could put weight on the injured leg – *showing these guys what real soldiers are like.* It was intoxicating. Every time one of the GPMG teams packed up and moved forward on the flanks, Brogan fired the ArmaLite into the rocks on automatic to try to maintain an unbroken hail of fire. Cartridge cases sprayed out of the gun around him. As he drained each magazine he snapped it out of the assault rifle and stuffed it down the front of his smock, ripping a replacement out of the combat vest and clipping it into the receiver of the gun.

Ahead, he saw one of the Adoo in a green uniform, kneeling and firing at him. All round them now, the bush was burning, tinder-dry grass ignited by the firefight. He raised the assault rifle and pulled the trigger. *Click*. He'd gone through all six spare magazines. A couple of hundred rounds. Twenty seconds of trigger time. Pete Spicer was close, firing M79 grenades at the Adoo positions. His rifle was slung over his back on paracord.

'Pete, throw me your rifle!'

Spicer pulled it off and threw it but it fell short and hit the ground. Brogan scooped up the weapon and, not wasting time to take careful aim, fired one round from the hip at the Adoo fighter. He fired again and the gun fell apart, breaking in half at the body-locking catch. The 'rat's tail' at the rear of the bolt carrier flew back. If he'd been holding the SLR up against his shoulder it would have blinded him. As the Adoo continued to fire, Brogan held the mistreated gun together with his left hand and pushed the top cover back with his right.

All fingers and thumbs, he raged, forcing himself to work more carefully. Finally, fix complete, he raised the rifle and pulled the trigger. Then the magazine dropped out of the bottom of the receiver.

This is like 'Carry On Up the Jebel'. Brogan jammed the clip back in, cocked the rifle, chambering a round, and fired ten times at the luckless guerrilla. The Adoo knew they were beaten; their dawn ambush, where they'd held every advantage over the isolated SAS patrol, had failed. Now they were running for their lives, but the Regiment hadn't finished with them.

Brogan set up a defensive position back on the hill from where he could direct mortar fire on to the Adoo from White City 2,000 yards away, as they withdrew. He reached into his pocket for his map so that he could direct the mortar team. Protected from sweat inside a plastic sheath, the map of Dhofar had a hole where a bullet had travelled right through it on the way out of his leg. His blood had seeped inside it, staining the paper. With the adrenalin of the contact and firefight he'd almost managed to forget he'd taken a bullet.

'You've been hit, Boss . . .' the Signal Sergeant pointed out.

'It's nothing.' But the leg was beginning to stiffen up. Any kind of bullet wound was simply too violent and traumatic to get away with.

'Come on, Shaun,' Johnny Watts said grinning, already smoking a roll-up, 'let's have a look. Get your pants down.' The Kalashnikov round had entered from behind him, high on his leg before exiting his thigh. There were two crimson holes. Watts shook his head.

'That's a Blighty wound if ever I saw one,' the Colonel laughed. 'They've shot your bum off. The girls are going to love kissing that . . .'

Sitting in the back of the helicopter as they casevaced him off the Jebel, Brogan was transfixed by the purple, yellow light of the early morning. It was beautiful and he felt elated. He had been tested and he had not been found wanting. And he remembered the words of the legendary American Civil War general, Robert E. Lee: 'It's fortunate that war is so terrible, otherwise men would love it too much.'

Men cried in the night. On one side of Barrie Williams's bed at Stoke Mandeville hospital was an old man who'd broken his back falling out of a plum tree while pruning it. Same break: T7. On the other was a young rally driver who'd broken his neck rolling a car during a hill climb. He was recently engaged when he became quadriplegic. Williams felt desperate for him; unable even to feed himself. Visits from the paralysed driver's fiancée, Wendy, used to brighten all their days. She was one of the most attractive women Williams thought he'd ever seen. Then one day the driver told Wendy that their engagement was off. He said he didn't want to see her again. Williams could only wonder at the man's bravery. They all had their battles to fight.

After a week on the ward, the consultant had finally levelled with Williams.

'Don't even think about flying again,' the doctor told him, 'you're not even going to walk.' The injured pilot was distraught.

This cannot happen, he thought, unable to imagine life without the use of his legs. He strained to move them, to feel anything. *Nothing*. Then Barrie Williams cried too.

Chapter 12

November 1971

Nick Holbrook still thought of himself as a soldier rather than an airman; a gunner who happened to have ended up flying helicopters for a living. His father, Brigadier Julian St C. Holbrook, had been a gunner too. Back home the son had a treasured photograph of his father, then commanding 6 AGRA artillery formation, with Winston Churchill in 1944 overlooking the River Arno north of Florence while Holbrook's artillery pounded German positions on the other side of the river. Earlier in the day Churchill had written a message on one of the British shells before it had been launched across the water.

'Rather like sending a rude letter and being there when it arrives,' remarked the Prime Minister, clearly enjoying himself. Nick Holbrook's print was signed and dated by Churchill.

In Holbrook, John Graham's Army commanders recognized that they had a helicopter pilot who spoke the same language as them. And while he'd been up north with the Desert Regiment conducting SAF's first pre-deployment training the helicopters, he'd struck up a rapport with the unit's new Commanding Officer, Lieutenant Colonel Nigel Knocker. Knocker was pleased to have found a kindred spirit.

'How do you feel about going out to Oman to command a battalion?' Knocker was asked after being pulled out of a Staff course he'd been on for less than a week. 'It'll be two years unaccompanied; there's a war going on. Talk to your wife about it. I want to know by Friday . . .'

Told that there was no hope of anything with his own Queen's Regiment, Knocker and his wife decided that Oman was too good an opportunity to be missed. After a course in Arabic to prepare him for command of a unit that was 80 per cent Omani and 20 per cent Baluch, he flew out with little more than a vague idea about what he could expect. On his arrival in country, John Graham had left him in no doubt about what lay ahead.

'This,' CSAF explained, 'is a very tough infantry war.' From the UK, Knocker simply hadn't appreciated the intensity of what was happening in Dhofar. It was a world away from trying to keep troops sharp on exercises back home. And yet Knocker quickly began to have doubts about some of the decision-making in the South. Before leading the Desert Regiment down to Dhofar with the next roulement, he took the time to get a feel for the lie of the land from the Commander of the Northern Frontier Regiment he was replacing. He was not overly inspired by what he found. It was nothing to do with either the leadership or the men of the NFR, but with what they were doing holding their firebase at Akoot in the first place. It was a view shared by his predecessor, the outgoing Commander, who, when told to move there, asked: 'To do what?' He had three rifle companies; at any given time he needed one to defend the position and one to fetch water. That left him with a single company of around one hundred men to conduct operations. It wasn't much with which to carry out the orders from Dhofar Area HQ to 'dominate' the area. The best that could be said for it was that it was soaking up Adoo ammunition, manpower and effort. But that was where he was going and he'd do his best to make something of it.

After he rotated south to Akoot with his men, he began to understand the situation on the ground with a little more clarity.

The Commander of the Dhofar Area, Colonel Mike Harvey,

was a remarkable man. As a young Company Commander he'd been one of the heroes of the Glosters' famous last stand at Imjin river during the Korean War. After mounting a fierce defence of their positions, the 1st Glosters, overwhelmed and surrounded by thousands of Chinese soldiers, were authorized to break out. Warning his men that they could not stop for casualties, he led the survivors of D Company to the safety of US Army lines. He was awarded the Military Cross for his actions. Harvey, a distinctive figure sporting a moustache and horn-rimmed glasses, was also a martial arts expert whose party trick was tearing up books with his bare hands.

Harvey's personal courage was beyond doubt, but he'd been in Oman since 1967 and it appeared that, to some extent, his vision of the war was conditioned by what he'd found when he arrived. Like John Graham's predecessor as CSAF, Harvey had been forced by circumstance to pursue a strategy of hold the line and, when the opportunity presented itself, 'kill them all'.

At Knocker's first briefing from Harvey, the Colonel drew two circles on a map as he explained his vision for Akoot to the new Battalion Commander.

'Here's you; here's the Adoo. Take them out.'

Knocker realized that it might fall to him to try to come up with something more imaginative. And useful.

Much to Neville Baker's annoyance, Nigel Knocker began to request Nick Holbrook by name; to the point where it was starting to become awkward.

'Tell that bloody colonel,' the helicopter Squadron Boss told his pilot, 'that we'll send him who we have available in whatever aircraft we have.' Baker's frustration was understandable, but at this stage he didn't know what Nigel Knocker, along with his 2ic and Ops Officer, was cooking up. Knocker valued Holbrook's insights into what was being planned and his willingness, if need be, to say: 'That's rubbish, we can't do that.' And he was the only member of the heli squadron whom Knocker had brought into his confidence.

'Not a word about this to anybody,' he'd told Holbrook.

Over a period of a few weeks, Holbrook and Knocker flew

together six times. The two of them sometimes attributed meaningless operation names to their sorties. On authorization sheets and in his logbook, Holbrook entered only the vaguest details of where he'd flown.

On each occasion, Holbrook would take one of the little AB206 Jetrangers up to Akoot, pick up the Colonel and then fly south down over the Jebel al Qamar mountains – the Mountains of the Moon – that straddled the border with South Yemen. Knocker was looking for a position from which SAF could cut the Adoo supply lines as close to the point at which they entered the country from Hawf as possible. The two men flew recces over the high ground overlooking the Adoo's Ho Chi Minh coastal routes. This was virgin territory for SAF. Despite their being aware of the area's critical importance to the enemy, it was simply out of SAF's reach until the intro-duction of the helicopters made airborne operations a possibility.

In the end they found what they were looking for almost by accident during a shoot-and-scoot mission. The target was a rumoured Adoo training camp just inside Oman on the enemy's 'Chinese Road' resupply trail. While another helicopter set up the mortar team on high ground near the border, Holbrook took a little AB206 down to the coastal plain in a tight spiral, looking for a landing spot where they'd mark a position with a smoke grenade. The soldiers set up the 81mm mortars, waiting for directions from Holbrook. It was during their fleeting stay on the plain that Knocker and Holbrook looked up to see the way the escarpment behind them dominated nearly down to the sea. As they pulled the pin on the smoke and climbed to height to direct the mortar attack, Knocker felt sure he'd found the position he was after. The problem now was to try to establish whether or not he really had hit the jackpot without letting his interest telegraph his intentions to the Adoo. He did not want a welcoming party.

Then, at Brigade HQ in Um al Gwarif camp, Mike Harvey shared his own plans for a new offensive in the west.

'What?' Holbrook blurted out almost involuntarily. 'That's the Adoo stronghold!' The Dhofar Area Commander wanted him to take two Desert Regiment rifle companies, reinforced by two from the Northern Frontier Regiment, and take out the Shershitti Caves. It was aggressive, there was no doubting that, but Knocker was horrified. After months spent at Akoot he understood more about how the Adoo operated: their strengths and capabilities, and the speed with which, on home ground, they were able to take advantage of the slightest mistake. What Harvey was proposing – while its intention was laudable enough – was likely to be a catastrophe.

This operation, Knocker thought, *is going to be suicidal.* But Harvey was about to go on leave. Knocker decided to take advantage of his Commander's absence, sidestep him and talk directly to John Graham when CSAF visited Salalah in December.

'I think we should rethink this, sir,' Knocker told the Brigadier. 'I do not think it's going to be practical to try to take Shershitti with four rifle companies.' And then he outlined the embryonic plan he'd been working on with Holbrook and the senior Desert Regiment officers. Whatever unease Graham might have felt about Knocker circumventing his Commanding Officer, he heard him out. But he gave little away, asking questions only, it seemed, to be certain of the detail of what Knocker was suggesting – a plan that benefited from Holbrook's appreciation of what the helicopter could do and how fast.

'Would you like to tell Colonel Harvey,' Knocker asked hopefully when he'd made his case, 'that this is what we're going to do?'

'I need to think about it,' Graham said, 'and discuss it further.'

Knocker wasn't thinking big enough.

As Graham listened to the detail of the operation Knocker was proposing and, in particular, the location his and Holbrook's Jetranger flights had revealed, he realized that if he gave this the green light, it had potentially massive implications not just for the progress of the war but for the future of the Sultanate. It might just be the game-changing operation he needed. And he knew he needed *something*.

Chapter 13

SAF's headquarters, the 200-year-old stone fort at Bait al Falaj, had once been the scene of a battle that ensured the survival of the Sultanate. It was here, in 1915, that an alliance of tribes from the interior were repulsed by the 700-strong garrison of British Indian troops. The force was just one of large numbers of British military units dotted throughout the region to try to keep the peace.

Until the discovery of oil, London's interest in Arabia had always been in the area's value as a stepping stone to other places. By 1954 over ninety separate agreements and amendments had been concluded with local leaders to formalize the British presence along the peninsula's coast. But the accusation that Britain had been 'backing into Arabia' was a legitimate one. Britain's interest really extended no further inland than it had to. RAF bases at Khormaksar and Falaise in Aden, at Muharraq in Bahrain, in Sharjah, Masirah and Salalah, were all there primarily so that Britain could go about her business elsewhere. Now Britain was pulling out at a time when, ironically, the vast quantity of oil flowing out of Arabian wells meant that her national strategic interest in the Persian Gulf itself was perhaps greater than it had ever been. But the decision to leave the region by the end of 1971 had been made. Now John Graham and the Defence Secretary, Hugh Oldman, had to deal with the consequences of it for Oman's future security.

The two men had first met in Oman in 1963 when Graham

had led 1 PARA on joint exercises with SAF. Hugh
Oldman had been CSAF at the time. Graham had immediately
found common ground with the Colonel from the Durham
Light Infantry. Oldman had spoken enthusiastically about
leading the Sultan's forces and it was those conversations that
had planted the seed of Graham's own interest in taking up the
post of CSAF.

The UK's presence in Arabia had given them both the opportunity to see and understand the issues peculiar to the region
for themselves. They feared that with the end of British Forces
Persian Gulf and the pulling back of command and control to
Cyprus, nearly 2,000 miles away to the north-west, an
appreciation of their concerns would be lost.

Much responsibility lay on the shoulders of the two
expatriate Britons.

While, over his first year in power, Sultan Qaboos had
grown in stature as a leader, it had been wrong, as the British
Ambassador, Donald Hawley, had pointed out, to expect him
to replace his father and arrive as a fully fledged 'philosopher
king'. Over his first eighteen months in power, the young
Sultan, as he gained confidence and experience, had relied
heavily on Oldman not just as Defence Secretary, but as
advisor, treasurer and diplomat. Oldman was, the Foreign
Office believed, 'more overburdened with problems than any
man should have to bear'.

Now, in the old fort at Bait al Falaj, Hugh Oldman and John
Graham were having to contemplate life without the reassurance of a permanent British presence nearby. While SAF
had been holding the line in Dhofar, if there were any military
pressure in the north of Oman then the Army would be
stretched beyond breaking point. The British pull-out from
bases in Bahrain and Sharjah created uncertainty, and that
only increased the likelihood of a new insurgent front in the
north.

As Graham anticipated the British withdrawal, an increasingly clear picture had formed in his mind of what needed
to be done. In his last visit to Oman, the Chief of the General

Staff, the head of the British Army, General Mike Carver, had told CSAF: 'The military in Whitehall will back you thoroughly, but the buggers are in the Treasury and we are having the devil's own job convincing them that Oman is still a case worth fighting for.' Graham managed to secure a commitment from Carver to keep two squadrons of SAS in Dhofar beyond Christmas, but when he asked about new kit, about spares, Carver seemed unable to answer, before finally offering: 'We'll try to help you as much as we can.' It was easy to read between the lines.

Oman is on her own, Graham thought. And, alone, she simply didn't have the resources for a long attritional grind west from White City, especially when the extension on the deployment of two SAS Sabre Squadrons expired. CSAF made the decision that his priority in 1972 had to be to persuade Oman's neighbours – those countries like Saudi Arabia, Iran, UAE and Jordan who had most to lose if Oman fell – to provide her, as he put it, *with the sinews of war.*

Just, he thought, *as aid from Roosevelt's America kept Churchill's beleaguered Britain in the field in 1940.*

He had, at least, managed to secure an extension on the temporary deployment of two SAS squadrons to Oman until April. Beyond that point, the MoD said, only one could remain because of commitments to NATO and exercises in the Far East.

That meant that the forces Graham had in country right now engaged in Operation JAGUAR he had for another four months. If he couldn't achieve some kind of break-through before the departure of that second Sabre squadron, it would then only get more difficult. This was as good as it got.

The officers and men of the Regiment, of course, had no say over whether or not they were sent to Oman or whether they could or should stay. But they weren't the only Brits required by Graham to fight the Adoo. He needed pilots too, albeit flying with the Sultan of Oman's Air Force rather than under their own flag. But, from his office at the Ministry of Defence in Whitehall, the RAF's Chief of the Air Staff had complained that he was struggling to find the required number of volunteers for secondment to SOAF. For most, it seemed, the spartan conditions at Salalah weren't much of a draw for a posting that, on top of hardship and a lack of facilities, wasn't believed to be the smartest career move either. Not *everyone* saw it like that though. For a handful of RAF pilots, Oman represented the last chance to sample the kind of lifestyle that was about to disappear for ever from the modern Air Force. RAF Salalah really had more in common with Air Vice-Marshal 'Mary' Coningham's Second World War Desert Air Force than with the NATO war machine in Northern Europe. And while the RAF may have found it tough to fill the slots, those who volunteered to go to Oman tended to be the kind of people SOAF was after.

December 1971

Flight Lieutenant Denis 'Nobby' Grey had been stuck with his nickname since school. A few weeks in shorts at the beginning of the second year after his contemporaries had all changed into long trousers and he'd been Nobby ever since. When he joined SOAF on secondment from the RAF, Grey continued to stand out from the pack. He was probably the only Strikemaster pilot in the country not to have come from a background flying fighters. Instead, straight out of basic training, Grey had been streamed on to the Handley Page Victor B2, the last of Bomber Command's three V-bombers. As an eighteen-year-old co-pilot on the big four-engined strategic bombers, he and the rest of the jet's five-man crew trained to launch Blue Steel nuclear stand-off missiles against targets in the Warsaw Pact countries. But a subsequent tour at the Central Flying School introduced him to David Milne-Smith. And DMS had gone out to Oman. Like his friend, Nobby Grey applied for secondment to SOAF in search of operational experience and an overseas posting that had become the last of its kind.

Grey was met off the C-130 Hercules by Sean Creak. For the

next month Creak was his constant companion in the cockpits of the Strikemaster and the Beaver. For the first time in his life Grey learnt how to deliver bullets, rockets and conventional high-explosive iron bombs as he and Creak dived in against targets on the Hajar ranges. But, for the first couple of months in Oman, Grey mostly flew the little propellor-engined Beavers around northern Oman. He was away from the war in the south, flying a single-engined utility plane off rough strips in the desert. And, to his surprise, the first red entry in his log-book was not recording an attack from a Strikemaster in support of SAF troops in Dhofar, but a mortar bomb dropped out of the bottom of a Beaver over the Musandam peninsula. It was all very different from the hours spent practising the simulated launch of a 'bucket of sunshine' from the belly of a Victor.

By the time he made it down to Salalah in December, he was one of the few British servicemen heading south. With the British withdrawal from the Gulf ramped up, the traffic was all in the other direction.

As Admiral Anson, the last Commander of British Naval Forces in the Gulf, sailed over the horizon in his flagship, HMS *Ghurka*, he sent a signal to John Graham. CSAF read it and smiled:

THERE CAME A MAN WHOSE NAME WAS JOHN . . .

The biblical reference to John the Baptist may not have been entirely appropriate in Muslim Oman, but Graham certainly appreciated the sentiment. It was at once encouraging and appreciative of the daunting task facing him in Oman at a time when, privately, he was forced to admit that, without out-side help, there was a real possibility that SAF might have to give up Dhofar altogether.

Graham had to change the game. The British had been persuaded to keep 120 BATT in Oman for a few more months, but he got a clear impression from London that, beyond that, he would have to rely increasingly on the Sultanate's own resources. And the effort that had gone into Operation JAGUAR only underlined how limited they were. That had been the largest, most capable force Graham could muster and its success had been entirely dependent on an extraordinary SAS deployment. How could SAF's small Air Force and four infantry battalions finish the job in the east, then hold the ground and keep it resupplied and even contemplate conducting similar operations in the Central and Western areas? Dhofar was the size of Wales. It just wasn't possible.

And time was on the side of the Adoo. They could be supported indefinitely by the Chinese and Russians from beyond his reach in South Yemen. However much SAF were able to disrupt enemy operations they couldn't stop them. Nor could they protect the civilian population the Adoo forced to support them.

Graham realized that he needed a showstopper. He had to do something that brought Oman's desperate situation to wider attention. And which persuaded sympathetic Islamic neighbours to turn words of support into men, money and materiel.

He didn't know what reaction putting a boot down right on the South Yemen border might provoke. It was a political strategy not a military one, based on very little more than, he admitted to himself, *see what happens*. But Nigel Knocker's plan might just be his best chance of provoking *something*.

7 December 1971

David Milne-Smith was tasked with flying Top Cover for a VIP visit to White City. Things seemed to have calmed down up there a bit now. Safe enough to take Beavers in and out now. The only thing you had to watch out for was the crosswind that tried to push you off the east–west strip centreline. That was a problem for another day. Today he was overhead in a Strikemaster, out of harm's way and the range of small-arms fire – and quite capable of fighting back should the need arise.

Routine stuff, he thought, but every time the helicopters flew up to the Jebel the Strikemasters went too, circling overhead, ready to stamp on any trouble. When the scramble bell rang, both the helis and the Strikeys reached for their flying kit. That was standard stuff, but of late there had been one or two tasks that had come in from leftfield.

First there had been Operation TAURUS. This was the only occasion anyone could think of when armed jet fighters had been used to escort a herd of cattle. But this was a hearts-and-minds campaign. The Firqas encouraged the Jebalis to bring their livestock to the sanctuary offered by White City. There, they told their families, the animals would be fed and watered. But with all supplies still being brought in by air, animal numbers soon outstripped SAF's ability to cope. Then the Firqas made it clear that unless the government provided a market for their cattle, they would again lay down their arms. As frustrating as it was, it once more made it clear that without swift action on civil development the BATT's efforts were pointless. So 500 head of cattle were driven down from the Jebel to Taqa guarded by SAF picquets and escorted by armoured cars. The Strikemaster pilots watched the great migration from the air as the dust cloud kicked up by the cattle's progress moved south.

Now there was Operation AQUARIUS. The name had been well chosen and, DMS understood later, had he given it more thought he'd have realized that the VIP flown up to the White City to visit the government's new civic centre was Sultan Qaboos himself. The opening of the new building was, in the end, what Operation JAGUAR was launched to bring about: to create a safe haven for civil development. Safety around the Jebel was still relative though. It was fortunate that the new clinic and store, a prefab flown up to White City by SOAF, was in dead ground as, white against the dirt and sporting the new red, green and white national flag, it would otherwise have presented a tempting target for Adoo mortars.

But the fact it had been built at all was hugely significant. It allowed the Jebalis to believe that this time round SAF really were here to stay. That conviction was the most powerful weapon in the war against the Adoo.

It meant greater numbers of SEPs defecting from the Adoo to the government side and that brought with it intelligence. One of the men had been an armourer trained for a year in Russia. Another, straight after changing his colours, was flown over a wadi where he pointed out the rest of his unit eating their lunch; until a SOAF Strikemaster killed them in a rocket attack. Known as 'Hawkeye' or 'Flying Finger', these operations, mixing as they did betrayal and airpower, were reported by SEPs to be one of the SOAF weapons most feared by the rebels. And captured documents written by the Political Commissar of the Adoo's Ho Chi Minh unit in the Central Area revealed how the Adoo realized that their doctrinaire approach to the insurgency had alienated the population. Their observation posts were always three-strong so that any guerrilla tempted to defect was in a minority. They announced that they too would welcome back any Firqa who decided to return to Adoo lines. And that religious freedom would be tolerated. But it was civil development to which the Adoo had no answer. Without military victory, all they could do was take and give nothing in return. By the end of the year over 600 SEPs had been welcomed back to the government fold.

Throughout the rest of the country, too, Qaboos had acted on the promises of his accession broadcast. There were new roads being built and a new international airport. Ten thousand children were now in school, with two 700-capacity schools in the north working double-shifts to try to cope with demand. A year ago there had been one American Mission hospital near Muscat, but now there were 120 hospital beds and plans to open another six forty-bed hospitals over the year ahead. And, during Operation SCOOTER, the British Army's Royal Engineers had drilled eleven wells in Dhofar, and built a school and a new clinic in Taqa. But while it was impossible to criticize the usefulness of the Engineers' contribution on the ground, it did provide the opportunity for spectacular penny-pinching in London.

The Sultanate was sent a bill for £48 for 'Linen Converted to Rags'. Apparently poor laundry facilities had meant the Royal Engineers' sheets, pillowcases and teatowels had deteriorated to such an extent that it was deemed cheaper to bin them than to bring them home. That aside, the Sappers' three-month deployment to the country seemed to be about the only aspect of the British military's involvement in Oman that London wasn't tying itself in knots over. That was certainly true of the uneasy relationship Whitehall had with the deployment of the BATT.

First there was what to do with the SAS regional HQ once it was forced out of Sharjah with the British withdrawal. There was really only one possibility and that was at RAF Masirah, the island airbase which would be all that remained of the permanent British presence in the Middle East. Even with the obligation to maintain the outpost at Salalah, Masirah remained a bargain at an annual rent of just £15,000. A Twynham hut and a small radio hut were arranged for the Regiment. In order not to raise too many questions, though, it was suggested the fourteen-man SAS detachment disguise themselves in RAF uniforms. It was quickly realized this was likely to attract far more attention than it deflected – as well as upsetting the SAS. And probably the Air Force too. In the end, the SAS HQ became 670 Signals Troop and wore Royal Signals uniform and insignia. Then there was unease about the number of visas being processed presenting a security risk. It was one thing a handful of applications from 'government officials' passing through the offices of Charles Kendall and Sons; quite another when whole squadrons of men were rotating through. The numbers alone offered some sort of smokescreen, the Foreign Office concluded. But with B Squadron's tour coming to an end at the end of the year, Charles Kendall and Sons were braced to deal with another rush rubber-stamping A Squadron's visas.

Just another sixty civil servants flying out to the Persian Gulf to fight in a secret war against the Communists.

*

Tak and Laba were going home. After their gruelling three-month tour on the Jebel, they looked forward to being back with friends and family. And Laba had a young son to return to. Then there was the rugby. While the cold and wet of the English winter didn't appeal much, they would, at least, be arriving back right in the middle of the rugby season. They were going to welcome the runaround as much as Hereford Town RFC was going to welcome having them back. The rugby club enjoyed membership from across all four squadrons of the Regiment and it was through the club that Tak had got to know one of the D Squadron officers, a laid-back, pipe-smoking South African called Patrick Phillips. Laba had written to him asking for his help. The British Army didn't seem to be displaying the same enthusiasm for recruiting Fijians that they once had, but Laba wanted to try to get his brother in. The Army had changed his life and he wanted his little brother to enjoy everything he had.

Before shipping out, there was just one last thing to do: burn their clothes. Like the Royal Engineers' troublesome linen, the fatigues B and G Squadron brought down with them from the Jebel were wrecked; the only safe thing to do was destroy the well-worn garments.

So it was up to A and D Squadron to take Operation JAGUAR forward. And Johnny Watts expected to lead them; to finish the job he had started. The prospect alarmed those around him. Despite his ability to drive himself there was increasing concern about him. By day he was spending more time confined to his camp bed. He had a hacking cough. And any quiet word in his batman's ear urging him to get the Boss to eat something was greeted with fury.

Watts, like Graham, knew that the job of JAGUAR was only half done. While they'd established a liberated pocket of ground at White City it was still only as secure as the strength of its defence. At the point at which he'd wanted to destroy the Adoo in pitched battles over White City – when they were still trying to take his men on – he was unable to. He lost the initiative. By the time he was able to restart the offensive, the Adoo had learnt to adapt. Now they saved themselves, attacking from long distance, in ambushes and in small numbers, then melted away into the safety of the wadis. White City wasn't going to be free until the wadis themselves had been cleared of Adoo.

During Op JAGUAR so far, Watts had lost a fifth of his deployed fighting strength to death and injury. He owed it to those men to finish it off, whatever state he himself might have been in.

Then suddenly Watts's command of 22 SAS was cut short and he was promoted to an instructor's job at Camberley Army Staff College. Given just twelve days' notice of his new appointment, he returned to the UK from Oman bitterly disappointed and frustrated at not having achieved what he set out to do. And far more alarmed at the prospect of a teaching position than anything the Adoo had thrown at him.

In place of Johnny Watts, the Regiment had a new Commanding Officer, another veteran of the 1959 Jebel Akhdar campaign in the north of the country and a man equally unsuited to the classroom: Lieutenant Colonel Peter Edgar de la Cour de la Billière.

Just days before Britain finally left Bahrain for good, the Imperial Iranian Navy seized the Tunb islands that sat in the Straits of Hormuz. It was evident that whatever else happened, Iran was not going to allow anyone else to control the oil route. She was prepared to use force to insulate herself from the potentially destabilizing effects of the vacuum left by Britain; a clear statement of intent. And it provided John Graham with a firm indication that Britain's withdrawal did indeed change the outlook for Oman. Just perhaps, though, Graham allowed himself to believe, in a good way.

It's shit or bust, he thought. Operation JAGUAR had been a success as far as it had gone, but it was also now a drain on his already limited resources. He needed to roll the dice again. His mind made up, Graham told Knocker to forget about Mike Harvey's hoped-for assault on the Shershitti

Caves and start detailed planning for his operation in the South.

'Will you tell Colonel Harvey?' Knocker asked.

'I think it's best,' Graham said, 'if it comes from you . . .'

PART THREE

1972
Sucker Punch

Chapter 14

January 1972

'You're the one who's responsible for me being here, Sean,' Squadron Leader Bill Stoker said. He greeted Sean Creak with a broad smile and offered his hand. Once more, Creak was up north, receiving the new 1 Squadron arrival. This time it was a little different though. Big Bill Stoker was the new Squadron Boss and he was telling Creak that it was all his fault he'd come out to Oman at all.

'Why's that?' Creak asked.

'Well, you remember we met back home when you were on leave?'

'Yes . . .'

'I followed it up!'

The two men had been introduced back in August when Creak had caught up with old friends, fellow Hunter pilots. When Creak talked about flying Strikemasters in Oman, Stoker's eyes had lit up.

'I'd give my right arm to go out there and do that,' he'd said.

'You can do it,' Creak told him. And while Stoker had said he was going to, that wasn't unusual. A lot of people seemed to think a tour with SOAF sounded glamorous, but not many actually made the jump.

Stoker was a bit different though. He was 6 feet 2 inches – tall for a fighter pilot – and married to Kay, a model who'd fronted big brand campaigns for Lifebuoy Soap and Players

Cigarettes. They'd met at the Farnborough Air Show while he was flying Hunters with the RAF's premier Blue Diamonds aerobatic display team. After regular competition on the Cresta Run, the big man was also a life member of the St Moritz Tobogganing Club. Glamour was something of a stock in trade for the new No. 1 Strike Squadron Boss.

On arriving at Bait al Falaj in January, Bill Stoker immediately became the fastest man in Oman. There were ex-Lightning pilots like Russ Peart in amongst the Strikeys, but no one else who'd taken a Lockheed TF-104 Starfighter up to Mach 2.3 over Arizona. Stoker was no stranger to thrills, but even he had thought, after climbing out of the cockpit of the needle-nosed 'missile with a man in it', *that was quite a trip*.

A two-year exchange posting with the USAF at Luke Air Force Base in Phoenix, Arizona, had provided an opportunity to fly some of the latest American hardware like the McDonnell Douglas F-4 Phantom and the Northrop F-5 Freedom Fighter, but that Starfighter ride had been the best of them.

Stoker's day job had also offered its own excitements and challenges. As an instructor preparing young American pilots to fly North American F-100 Super Sabre fighter-bombers in Vietnam, he bantered over a beer with his American colleagues, his job 'was to teach you Yanks how to do ground attack'. And after his tour flying Hunters with 43 Squadron in Aden during the Radfan campaign he certainly had plenty of real live experience of that.

When he returned from Phoenix, Stoker squeezed in a course that earned him his parachute wings before taking command of his own Hunter outfit, 8 Squadron, David Milne-Smith's old unit, based in Bahrain.

Bill Stoker had the perfect credentials to take command of SOAF's Strikemaster squadron. And it was evident to Creak that he was relishing the prospect of what lay ahead.

The Strikeys had been a little rudderless since the early departure of their previous CO. It hadn't stopped them from delivering the good news to the Adoo, but a hard-charging new

Brigadier John Graham in his office at the HQ of the Sultan's Armed Forces (SAF) near the capital, Muscat. Seconded from the Parachute Regiment, Graham was the latest in a line of officers to command SAF while on loan from the British Army.

The oldest and newest aircraft in the Sultan of Oman's Air Force (SOAF) fleet, a DeHavilland Beaver and BAC Strikemaster overfly the palace at Salalah. From here, Sultan bin Taimur, isolated and reactionary, had allowed an armed rebellion to take root.

Colonel Hugh Oldman, one of Graham's predecessors as Commander of SAF, was in 1970 Oman's Defence Secretary.

North of Muscat, Blackpool Beach was the resort used by Western oil workers and off-duty SAF officers. And it was where Oldman first asked Graham how he'd feel about the prospect of a coup to depose Sultan bin Taimur by his son Qaboos.

John Graham greets Sultan Qaboos off the plane on his first visit to Muscat following the successful palace coup that deposed his father.

Operation INTRADON. Acting on intelligence of insurgent activity in Oman's Musandam peninsula, Qaboos was quick to invite support from the SAS. This rare photograph shows members of G Squadron, 22 SAS, in Musandam disguised as troops from the Trucial Oman Scouts, a local unit based in what was to become the UAE.

Operation STORM. As well as the operation in the north, the SAS was also deployed to Dhofar province in the south of the country to help combat the rebellion. Working in secrecy under the cover of the BATT (British Army Training Team), they were not, initially, there to fight. Although, of course, they were more than capable of doing so.

The focus of the initial Op STORM was to win 'hearts and minds'. Provision of medical care in a country almost completely lacking in it was a priority. Here, A Squadron's Troop Commander, Captain Shaun Brogan, inoculates a Jebali.

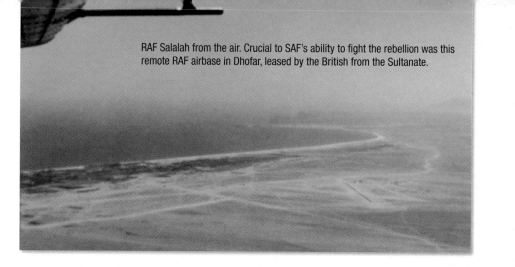

RAF Salalah from the air. Crucial to SAF's ability to fight the rebellion was this remote RAF airbase in Dhofar, leased by the British from the Sultanate.

Made in China. The enemy were known as the Adoo and armed and trained by China and the Soviet Union. This picture shows Adoo leaders in Peking, in 1971, where they were receiving instruction in guerrilla warfare.

First used as a wartime staging post by Britain and America, RAF Salalah gained its own station crest in 1964.

Facilities at Salalah were basic. As well as the 'putting green' there were a swimming pool and an open-air cinema. Otherwise, there was the Officers' Mess.

No. 1 Squadron, SOAF(Tac). Based at Salalah and equipped with the Strikemaster light attack jet, the unit was responsible for providing close air support for SAF and SAS operations in Dhofar.

Housed in the old BOAC terminal, the headquarters of SOAF(Tac) was responsible for all SOAF air operations in Dhofar.

Shot down. The wreckage of Barrie Williams's Strikemaster. Although there was no threat from the air, low-flying SOAF aircraft were at constant risk from ground fire. The ejection seat in the foreground provides evidence of how late Williams escaped from his aircraft.

Squadron Leader Neville Baker with an SLR rifle. The Boss of SOAF's helicopter squadron, and a veteran RAF search and rescue pilot, Baker had to quickly adapt to combat flying in Dhofar. Baker's 3 Squadron pilots always flew with a personal weapon.

Flight Lieutenant Sean Creak with his dog Spoon. Seconded to SOAF from the RAF for two years, Creak joined the Omani Air Force as a contract pilot after leaving the RAF. Flying the piston-engined DeHavilland Beaver was one of the perks of the job for 1 Squadron's Strikemaster pilots. Spoon sat next to him in the co-pilot's seat.

Flight Lieutenant David Milne-Smith. Bored by a posting as a flying instructor, Milne-Smith ignored the advice of his Station Commander to volunteer for two years' loan service with SOAF. Two months after arriving in Oman the bullet that smashed through the canopy nearly killed him. The temporary perspex patch is so that the jet can be flown north for permanent repair.

Flight Lieutenant Denis 'Nobby' Grey. Grey volunteered for secondment to SOAF to experience a lifestyle he knew was on the verge of disappearing for ever from the RAF.

Nick Holbrook in the cockpit of an AB206 helicopter. An ex-Army Air Corps pilot and experienced artillery spotter, Holbrook had operational experience in Borneo before joining SOAF as one of the first helicopter pilots.

A SOAF AB206 helicopter lands at Mirbat. The day before the launch of Operation JAGUAR, Shaun Brogan was flown into the little fishing port before taking command of a G Squadron troop on the Jebel. Their role was to divert Adoo attention from the main operation.

The Jebel. Operation JAGUAR was launched to establish a permanent presence on this high ground, until this point dominated by the Adoo, who used the cover from the thick bush in the wadis to act with impunity.

Lieutenant Colonel Johnny Watts. The hugely popular Commanding Officer of 22 SAS, Watts was the architect of the Regiment's campaign in Dhofar. This unique picture, taken on the Jebel during Operation JAGUAR, shows him surrounded by all his essentials: map, cigarettes, cup of tea, personal weapon and a paperback of Elizabeth Byrd's bestseller, *The Immortal Queen*.

The SAS prepare to go out on patrol on the Jebel during Operation JAGUAR. Note the M79 grenade launcher tucked into the top of the Bergen of the trooper on the right.

By day, the SAS patrolled in long crocodiles with ten or fifteen yards between each man. The patrol commander led from a couple of places back in order to give him time to react in the event of a contact.

SAS trooper carrying a GPMG on the Jebel. The powerful 7.62mm General Purpose Machine Gun proved to be a hugely popular, war-winning weapon for the Regiment in Dhofar.

Shaun Brogan takes a break with his troop during Operation JAGUAR.

Briefing the Firqa. The SAS led and trained local irregular fighters known as Firqas, fulfilling its role as the BATT.

A 3 Squadron AB205 Huey helicopter is guided in by a Regiment soldier in what could almost be an image from the American war in Vietnam.

Delivery of 'The Fresh' was eagerly awaited by SAS units throughout Dhofar. Here Regiment troops unload the spoils.

Resupply by the SOAF Hueys was the crucial prerequisite for SAS and SAF operations on the Jebel.

Goats wrapped in plastic prepare to board a SOAF Skyvan. Great efforts were made to pay, equip and feed the Firqas well. Fresh meat was an important part of this. Live goats were flown to the Jebel wrapped in plastic so that they didn't soil the aircraft's cargo hold.

Squadron Boss like Stoker, Sean Creak knew, was welcome news. Creak had stickered the cover of his logbook with the legend:

FIGHTER PILOTS DO IT BETTER. No. 1 STRIKE
SQUADRON SULTAN OF OMAN'S AIR FORCE DOES
IT BEST

Confidence was a vital part of the arsenal of any military flyer and it was clear that Stoker, fizzing with enthusiasm, had that in spades. Creak thought he'd let the new Boss discover for himself that one of his pilots down in Salalah flew close air support wearing flip-flops.

Lieutenant Colonel Peter de la Billière probably wouldn't even have noticed. The new CO of 22 SAS had a similar disdain for sartorial elegance as his predecessor. Nor was he any less eager to lead from the front, but he was a more severe, less lovable character than Johnny Watts. He dealt with anger by racing up and down Pen-y-fan, and faced with the birth of his first child warned his wife that he only planned to push a pram at midnight on a moonless night when there was no one around. While Second-in-Command of the Regiment to Watts, DLB had frequently had to mind business back at Bradbury Lines, the Regiment's Hereford Headquarters, while Watts was in the thick of it during Operation JAGUAR. But, in order to be an effective Commanding Officer of 22 SAS, DLB realized he would have to delegate. With regret, he knew that while responsibility for the BATT squadrons in Oman lay with him, it was, for him, war by 'remote control'. He was able to set the direction, but then had to leave his men to it.

Arriving in Oman for his first meeting with John Graham, DLB had a clear idea in his mind of the strategy that lay ahead. Following Operation JAGUAR in the east, the BATT and the Firqas should move west to the Central Area north of Salalah. He'd told his own superiors that he believed the job could be done before the arrival of the monsoon. CSAF, though, had become convinced that that route would lose them the war. And in Oman, while the BATT remained under the command of the British Army, they were subject to the operational control of CSAF. John Graham outlined the new plan.

Instead of trying to take and hold the tortured landscape of the Central Area, where impassable, monstrous combs of rock plunged down into bottleneck wadi bottoms, he wanted to leapfrog it completely to put a foot down in the Western Area, right on the border with South Yemen; really get in their faces. Graham pointed to the position, sitting on top of the escarpment north of a village called Sarfait, on a map. Initially the SAS Commander demurred. Johnny Watts too had expected, once the Eastern Area had been pacified, to clear the Central Area. But, Graham explained, the Sultanate simply didn't have the time or the resources to do that. He had to do something to try and break the stalemate and avoid a long attritional war which SAF, fighting alone, could well lose. So Nigel Knocker's operation in the west at Sarfait was a political move as much as it was a military. By establishing a position so close to South Yemen there was chance of focusing international attention on Oman's struggle.

Just to mount the initial assault presented a formidable logistical challenge. Holding it would demand an even greater one. The location could only be resupplied by air, and if water couldn't be found then that too would have to be brought in by SOAF. It was, Graham had to admit, a military risk. But the greatest risk of all was that once he had rolled the dice, no one noticed. He'd then be stuck with a conspicuous, worthless position at the end of his supply chain that cost him the use of an infantry company and half his Air Force flying hours. And from which it would be politically disastrous to withdraw.

He had arrived favouring a move west from White City, but when Peter de la Billière left the Bait al Falaj fort he too was convinced that the plan in the west was the only way of digging Oman out of the hole. While two squadrons of his soldiers remained in country the BATT would concentrate on finishing the job in the Eastern Area from White City down into wadis to clear the Adoo from their strongholds below the treeline, and SAF's Desert Regiment would take Sarfait.

In the last week of January, intelligence reached Dhofar Brigade HQ that heavy guns had been reported at Hawf, the Adoo's cross-border sanctuary in South Yemen.

Chapter 15

February 1972

Nigel Knocker had been reluctant even to *ask* the Firqas what the place was called for fear of giving the game away. Since identifying the feature at Sarfait, he and Nick Holbrook had been assiduous about not returning; instead they mounted their shoot-and-scoot mortar attacks from new, different positions each time they went out. They wanted to keep the enemy guessing.

Heavy cloud delayed their departure, but at ten o'clock in the morning on 2 February Holbrook and Knocker took off in Jetranger 603 and pointed the nose south towards Sarfait. They'd called it Operation SANDCLOUD and, as usual, they carried a pair of mortars with them. For appearances' sake, they'd lob a few bombs in the direction of the Adoo trail, but that was never the point of this sortie. Instead it was a reconnaissance. And this time they'd been joined by one of the No. 2 Squadron fixed-wing transport pilots.

Crucial to the success of the operation was the ability to resupply a battalion of over 300 men, and to absorb that kind of commitment SOAF had to be able to get the Skyvans and Caribous in, not just the helicopters. In order to cut off the Adoo supply lines they needed clear sight from the high ground all the way down to the sea. And they had to have a reliable local source of water. If it fell to SOAF to fly in water as well as food, personnel and ammunition, then the position was unsustainable. It was also obvious that, invisible from the plain, there was a feature that rose 500 feet above them to the north without which the position was untenable. They'd have to occupy that before anything else was possible.

Two weeks later Knocker flew down to Salalah, where he finalized the plans for the air assault on the Sarfait position with CSAF.

'This is going to draw attention,' John Graham told Knocker, 'the enemy reaction is bound to be severe.' Both men hoped so for rather different reasons. As far as Knocker was concerned it would simply be the clearest evidence that he'd spoilt the Adoo's day. For Graham it could hardly be severe enough. The date was brought forward to early April. And the plan was given a name: Operation SIMBA, the Swahili for lion. The SAS had taken the lead on the first two of the big cat operations, JAGUAR and LEOPARD. SIMBA was down to SAF alone.

All very exciting, Knocker thought as he returned to his battalion HQ at Akoot; a dreadful place, surrounded by mine-fields, that he and his men weren't going to have to endure for much longer.

Privately, Holbrook had his doubts about the whole thing. He was acutely aware of the enormous strain it was going to place on SOAF, and not just the helicopters. But at this point he was the only member of the Air Force who knew anything about the plan. In his determination to keep any discussion of SIMBA within as small a circle as possible, John Graham had somehow neglected to include one of his two next-door neigh-bours. While Defence Secretary Hugh Oldman had discussed and supported Graham's belief that SAF needed to mount a spectacular, the head of the Sultan's Air Force, Wing Commander Curly Hirst, whose aircraft were so central to any possibility of success, had not even been told they were think-ing about it.

Donald Hawley, the British Ambassador, had been brought into their confidence, and, like Holbrook, he predicted a heavy burden on SOAF and Airwork, the civilian operation that supported it. And that meant more work for Andy Dunsire.

*

A bearded, unhurried radio engineer with a soft Scottish burr, Dunsire described himself as an armed hippie. He was the proud owner of both a huge collection of jazz LPs, bought in a fire sale from a soon to be nationalized record shop in Aden, and a more modest assortment of automatic weapons from a variety of sources. It was a fair description of the kind of lifestyle a job with Airwork made possible for people who, like Dunsire, left the RAF, Fleet Air Arm or Army Air Corps, but were after a little more of the same, though with fewer regulations.

Little known back home, it sometimes seemed as if Airwork were responsible for keeping most of the world's airlines and air forces in the sky. The company had helped establish airlines in Egypt, India and Rhodesia and supported air forces in Saudi Arabia, Abu Dhabi, Ghana, Qatar, Singapore, Nigeria, Sudan, Kuwait and Jordan, as well as taking part in the Berlin Airlift and running charter flights carrying pilgrims to and from Jeddah for the Haj.

Dunsire had been one of the Airwork personnel whose jobs disappeared when Airwork was pulled out of South Yemen. But he'd been there long enough to see the increasing number of Russian pilots and ground crew who'd arrived after independence to keep the People's Democratic Republic's MiGs flying.

Oman was the next opportunity that presented itself and now, like the rest of his colleagues, he did whatever it took to keep SOAF's small fleet of aircraft flying and fighting. It often required improvisation, common sense and a little discretion over which rules were important and which could happily be bent.

As an accomplished photographer, Dunsire had been called on to set up a cine camera in a Strikemaster cockpit and wired it to the gun trigger. He'd filmed weapons release trials from the co-pilot's ejection seat while filling sickbags from air-sickness and still been commended by the jet's manufacturer, BAC, for his efforts. He'd repaired bullet holes and he'd fused

20lb bombs using gaffer tape and string. And when one of the Strikeys came in asking if there was any way the foot-long radio aerial, which he'd managed to rip off the bottom of the jet as he flew too low over a ridge, could be fixed without a fuss or paperwork, he'd managed that too. Airwork had even developed a sideline in milling wooden legs on their lathe for victims of the Adoo anti-personnel mines.

But for all Airwork's ingenuity, there were sometimes only two or three helis serviceable. For Operation SIMBA, it was going to try to make sure every one of SOAF's collection of Agusta-Bell helicopters was flying. It was going to mean working round the clock to get them ready. Dunsire anticipated that it would take a lot of jazz and whisky to wind down from this one. But SOAF's big AB205s, at least, were nothing if not rugged.

'Almost soldier-proof,' one of Neville Baker's pilots joked, and that was no accident. Baker agreed wholeheartedly.

The best helicopter ever made, he thought. Although built under licence in Italy, SOAF's AB205s were essentially the same as the Bell UH-1H helicopters used by the US Army in Vietnam. The aircraft's official name, Iroquois, was hardly more well known than its Italian designation though. Instead, it was known simply as the Huey. And the slap of its two-bladed rotor and its distinctive silhouette had come almost to epitomize America's war in South-East Asia.

Vietnam was where Neville Baker had first encountered the Huey for himself. He'd flown them from the co-pilot's seat on operations with the US Army's 51st Air Cavalry out of Da Nang. During a two-year posting with the Royal Hong Kong Auxiliary Air Force, Baker was despatched to South Vietnam to write a report on what he found. He was overwhelmed by the scale of it. The massive US base had fifty or more Hueys supported by squadrons of heavily armed fighter-bombers. From Da Nang alone, he thought, *they could splatter an area half the size of Sussex.*

The 3 Squadron Boss knew that in the Agusta Bell AB205 he had an exceptional aircraft; coach-built in Italy like a Riva speedboat rather than churned off Bell's own Fort Worth production line like a Model T-Ford. But assembled in Milan or Texas, either way, the Huey was a serious contender for the title of 'most successful military aircraft of all time'. And the big difference between the Huey and everything else in the SOAF fleet, bar the handful of Caribous, was that, from the outset, it was designed specifically as a combat aircraft.

During the Korean War in 1952, the US Army developed plans for an entirely new kind of air mobile warfare. The generals wanted twelve battalions of troops that could be air-lifted into battlezones, supported and resupplied by their own fleet of helicopters. In developing their plans the US Army studied not only their own experience with helicopters in Korea, but also that of the French in Algeria and the British in Malaya. As they refined their ideas for what they soon labelled 'Air Cavalry' it was clear that no existing helicopter offered anything like the necessary capability. So in 1955 they contracted the Bell Aircraft company to develop a design that did. At a time when many helicopters still used piston engines, Bell opted for something new: a gas turbine engine. Developed by a team led by a German scientist, spirited out of Nazi Germany at the end of the war during Operation PAPERCLIP, who'd helped design the world's first production jet engine, the new engine offered many advantages. It was lighter, more powerful and less bulky than the piston engine. For its size, the Huey would be able to carry more, further and faster than its rivals.

But another, less obvious but no less important, consequence of the Huey's military genesis was that it was designed to take battle damage and keep going. Unlike SOAF's Strikemasters, Skyvans and Jetrangers the Huey's flight controls were linked using rigid tubes rather than wires. If a bullet hit a wire to the rudder in a Strikemaster it cut it; if it hit one of the Huey's tubes it put a hole through it, but the chances were that the tube maintained its integrity. As robust as they were, though, the Hueys were not indestructible.

Baker was under constant pressure from SAF to mount US

Army-style Air Cavalry missions like the ones that they saw on footage coming back from Vietnam. They wanted all the 3 Squadron helicopters coming in at once, delivering a whole hundred-strong company of troops in one go. SAF commanders wanted to arm them like the Americans too. So intense was the fire they were laying down, one US Navy Huey Squadron had, in four months in 1968, burnt out 275 M60 7.62mm machine-gun barrels. That sort of firepower would have been equally welcome in Dhofar. Baker understood the strong appeal of both possibilities, but every time either was raised, he had no choice but to bat it back.

Without the 3 Squadron helicopters, SAF's ability to wage war stopped dead in its tracks. Baker simply could not risk putting too many helicopters on the ground together in one place and at one time, nor mount machine guns in the doors in order to deliberately fly them into harm's way. The US Army received well over 8,000 Hueys from Bell. SOAF had just eight. Between 1961 and 1971, the US helicopter fleet suffered 2,066 combat losses in Vietnam. For all the tragedy represented by the loss of each individual aircraft, it was a numbers game. The US military could afford to lose aircraft. Neville Baker could not.

Nothing in a military career that included D-Day and the invasion of Europe, command of 1 PARA and a mission to the Congo at the height of the mid-sixties savagery there caused John Graham more anxiety than the prospect of launching Operation SIMBA.

Mike Harvey had suggested bullishly that – as he had with the Glosters in Korea – the Battalion, if stranded, 'can always walk out', but that missed the point completely. In giving the Op the go-ahead Graham was committing nearly 50 per cent of SAF's resources to a strategic operation that depended for its success on the response of the enemy, and which, once undertaken, he could not leave without holing civilian confidence in SAF and the Sultan below the waterline.

It all boiled down to a feature called Capstan. From the top of the escarpment at Sarfait, Nigel Knocker realized that the lines of sight didn't extend all the way to the sea. The final 800 yards or so, over which the coast descended through the last 400 feet to sea level, were dead ground. The Adoo could still pass from Hawf east into Oman without being seen. Only Capstan, an isolated rock pinnacle that rose out of the slope to the sea to dominate the thick vegetation of the coastal plain, could do that. Without seizing Capstan, there was a danger that Operation SIMBA would amount to little more than an invasion of the enemy's personal space: annoying, uncomfortable and unwelcome, but hardly terminal.

More importantly, it was Capstan where the Firqas had said there was a source of water. Irrespective of the political and military impact seizing the Sarfait promontory might have, only finding water would bring SOAF's resupply effort down to a sustainable level and release the helicopters for mobile operations throughout the rest of Dhofar. Because whatever happened in the west, operations in the east had to continue and they too relied on the Hueys.

The position at Tawi Atair – Place of Birds – ten miles southeast of White City, should have been the one that didn't need water flown in. Sited just south of a massive limestone sinkhole 150 feet across and over 200 feet deep, its pitted rock walls were home to nesting Rock Doves whose songs echoed around the cavern and gave it its name. There was plenty of water at the bottom, but when BATT men had first climbed down to fetch it, the route was so arduous that they'd needed to drink all they could carry to get back to the surface. That first experience of Tawi Atair had only highlighted the reliance on helicopters of any SAF operations on the Jebel. When 3 Squadron was called on to resupply the patrol, Neville Baker's only available helicopter had run out of flying hours. He couldn't help them.

'I've got men up there pissing treacle!' the BATT Squadron Commander had shouted, but, as Baker had explained before, aircraft aren't like Land Rovers; when they're out of hours they don't fly. After just twelve days on the Jebel the Regiment men had been forced to withdraw.

Now Shaun Brogan was back in Oman, with Two Troop, A Squadron, and up at Tawi Atair trying to make the resupply of the hard-won position a little easier. He knew that resupplying Simba position was going to use up a lot of heli flying hours. Trying to use his initiative, he decided he was going to build an airstrip; then, at least, the Skyvans could resupply his men alongside the Hueys. He had to admit, though, the boulder-strewn slopes didn't look too promising.

Probably best, he thought, not wanting to waste his or anyone else's time, *to get someone to come out from Salalah to size it up.*

Chapter 16

January 1972

While he had recovered from his bullet wound in hospital, Brogan had to get the Regiment to ask if he could postpone his interview at Oxford. His qualifications for studying Politics, Philosophy and Economics at Lincoln College were barely even marginal. He was lucky, though, that the admissions tutor turned out to be an ex-Para who knew all about the SAS. The don smoothed the way by arranging for an interview that meant Brogan never had to reveal he'd only got 5 per cent in his Maths 'O' level. To the astonishment of his parents and brothers, he managed to win a place as a mature student to study PPE starting in autumn 1972. Before the dreaming spires, though, he still had another six months with the Regiment. And, to kick off, there was his return to Oman with A Squadron.

When Brogan returned to the Jebel in early January, its appearance had changed dramatically. Gone was the thick grass that had greeted the BATT when they'd launched Operation JAGUAR at the end of the monsoon. Instead it was dry, yellow scrub. The post-monsoon greenery had been deceptive. This was the stuff that the Jebali cattle really lived on for most of the year; the reason they were smaller than any the BATT had ever seen before.

It was quieter now too. There'd been one major daylight attack from the east, but the Firqa and their three-man BATT contingent beat them back with everything they had. Up on the Jebel, the major job was building the airstrip.

'If you remove the rocks,' the liaison from Salalah had said without too much enthusiasm, 'we could use it.' So Brogan asked for 400lb of plastic explosive, 10,000 feet of detonation cord and safety fuses.

'You must be joking,' came the reply. But he wasn't.

'Speak to the bloke who's just been up here to recce the area,' Brogan told them. What he needed was flown in from the UK. Over the next three weeks, the Two Troop packed explosive around the base of boulders buried deep into the ground like icebergs at sea and blew the tops off them until they had a tolerably smooth strip.

Intelligence coming back from SEPs suggested that the Adoo were feeling the pressure in the Eastern Area. The military effort to drive them out of the wadis was only one part of it. Equally important was the effort to reduce their contact with the local population and shut down their food supply. Right at the end of the supply chain from South Yemen, the Adoo in the east had always been more dependent on food from the Jebali supporters. The less they were able to rely on the local population the more they had to carry at the expense of ammunition. The Development Board drilled wells on the high ground so that Jebalis didn't need to descend into the wadis for water. At the same time there was discussion about the possibility of chlorinating the wells used by the Adoo; a temporary measure that would ultimately purify the water but, in the short term, render it undrinkable. For a while only cooked rice was allowed through checkpoints. And strict controls on food passing in and out of Taqa and Mirbat had gradually been tightened. In February a total ban was put in place. The lack of sustenance from the locals became a self-perpetuating problem for the Adoo. If there was reluctance from locals to support them, they were driven to take what they needed. And coercion only alienated those they purported to be fighting for. At the same time, the BATT made sure that they spoiled the

Firqas with rations that even regular SAF units found difficult to match. Live goats were flown in, their hindquarters enclosed in plastic sheeting to ensure they didn't soil the aircraft, so that the Firqas could enjoy fresh meat, while the Adoo had to watch their food disappear whenever another few hundred head of cattle were driven off the Jebel to market.

'It will be lack of food,' Peter de la Billière and Johnny Watts told the Chief of the General Staff in London, 'rather than military operations which will be the deciding factor.'

Now that the Adoo no longer had the Jebel to themselves, they were finding their rebellion more difficult. But they had not gone away. By night, the BATT hunted for them in the Wadi Darbat and Wadi Kashayn with the Firqas.

Shaun Brogan carried a small notebook with him. In the front were notes relating to military concerns; in the back the names and phone numbers of girlfriends. They soon met in the middle and his troop's patrols acquired some familiar and fondly remembered names: Operation KATE, Operation LAURA and Operation ENID, named after the African-American Peace Corps volunteer Brogan had met in Kenya while training the President's bodyguard. He enjoyed the thought of the girls' names being treated with proper seriousness when they appeared in official reports.

Offensive patrols below the treeline would have been suicidal before Christmas, but with each passing week the thick jungle in the wadi became thinner, offering less cover to the Adoo. There were still efforts to accelerate the process, though. Incendiary rounds were fired from mortars to start fires and clear undergrowth and crops used to feed the Adoo. And Nobby Grey got the chance to follow up his ground attack debut dropping mortar bombs from a Beaver with something even more pyrotechnic: burmail bombing from a Skyvan. SOAF had been enthusiastic partners in an effort to try to concoct a kind of home-made napalm. At Salalah, fuel drums full of Avgas were mixed with washing powder and broken-up polystyrene, taken from the packing material in deliveries of SURA rockets, that acted as a gelling agent. These burmail bombs were then loaded into the back of a Skyvan and rolled out of the back over the target area. Attached to each was an unpinned phosphorus flare placed carefully inside a jam jar to hold shut the lever. Seven seconds after the glass shattered on impact with the Jebel, the grenade went off and lit the home-made Avgas gel. The fires could sometimes be seen from Salalah.

Another Strikemaster pilot got involved in BATT operations rather more directly after Shaun Brogan, down from the Jebel for a couple of days' R&R, walked into the 1 Squadron crew room, told them he had a target for them and that, if they were interested, he'd show them where it was.

During the attack on Pork Chop Hill in the opening rounds of Operation JAGUAR Brogan had called in the jets to hit enemy positions six times on a single day. When, during this tour, the Firqa had insisted on permanent Top Cover from the Strikeys, he'd made sure they got it. He'd been fascinated and impressed by what he'd seen. And he wanted to try it for himself.

From the right-hand ejection seat of Strikemaster 404, Brogan asked David Milne-Smith to circle out of earshot at 20,000 feet above Tawi Atair. He didn't want to warn the enemy that they were on their way. Below them, the remaining green vegetation down in the wadis appeared to be spreading across the brown of the plateau like a creeping vine. Then DMS raised Brogan's Troop Sergeant on the SARBE. The SAS Captain smiled behind his tight-fitting oxygen mask as a familiar voice came back over the RT. The BATT man on the ground directed the Strikemaster on to the location of a village the Firqas confirmed had been taken over by the Adoo. That made it fair game. Brogan watched as Milne-Smith reached forward and armed the rockets. He pressed the transmit button and told the A Squadron sergeant that they were diving in. Then Brogan spotted a red flash whizz past the cockpit glass.

I think, he realized, *we're being fired at*. It hadn't occurred to him that this might be part of the experience.

The jet's two machine guns covered them as they dived in on the position. Four SURA rockets streamed out ahead of them before Brogan was pushed back into the seat as DMS pulled back on the stick and hauled them out of the dive on the Adoo position.

Do I tell the pilot or just not worry? He didn't want to come across like a panicking backseat driver, but he felt he had to say something.

'We may have received some ground fire on that strike,' he told DMS in the most unflustered, calm-sounding voice he could manage, 'I think I saw a red thing streak past the window.'

There was a click over the radio.

'You received ground fire on that strike . . .' It was the voice of his Troop Sergeant.

'Roger,' acknowledged Milne-Smith without apparent concern as they banked steeply, coming round again to re-attack. Good shooting and sang-froid.

Brogan was coming to the end of an extraordinary year in Oman during which, as he contrived to move from one squadron to another to make sure he was deployed, he'd spent more time in the country than any other BATT officer. Over his last four months in Dhofar, Two Troop had retaken Tawi Atair and secured it, extending the liberated areas on the Jebel further east than they had ever been. When they were told that in order to relieve the helicopter squadron they needed an airstrip, they built one. They'd got things done. But they'd also paid a heavy price for it.

The 26-year-old Ronnie Ramsden was a 2 PARA Sergeant who'd just joined the Regiment as a trooper. Brogan saw in Ramsden some of the same eagerness to get ahead that he had himself. Ramsden always wanted to learn more, understand more and get better. Brogan tried to encourage that.

'If you want to take the patrol out tonight,' he told Ramsden, 'you do it.' Brogan could see the Trooper was thrilled to be entrusted with it. He'd been watching the way Brogan did things and he'd learnt the lesson that, unlike a standard SAS patrol, moving with the Firqa at night, the BATT Commander needed to lead from the front in order to be able to control things. More normally, the leader would walk second or third in the crocodile. It provided a split second more time to react, but in Dhofar, especially at night, Brogan believed control was more important. With Ronnie leading the way, the patrol set out. About five yards separated each man from the next. Then, walking up a little pimple hill barely 300 yards from the Troop's HQ, the patrol was ambushed by Adoo hiding in an old stone sangar. Ramsden was shot and killed instantly.

Did I know what was going to happen? a voice nagged away at Brogan. But that was ridiculous. He tried to push the haunting, insidious little thought to one side. But thoughts of death had a habit of creeping up on a soldier. Even the bravest and the best.

The Royal Air Force C-130 Hercules descended towards RAF Salalah, its four Allison turboprops throbbing beyond the poorly insulated fuselage. It was the end of a long, noisy journey from Cyprus for the men of B Squadron, endured in canvas seats rigged along the edges of the cargo hold of the big transport plane. Jim Vakatali and Laba sat next to each other. Jim had recovered from the leg he'd had broken by an Adoo bullet six months earlier. Laba was uneasy. Since getting back from jungle training in the Malayan jungle with G Squadron in Exercise JACOBIN, he'd told a few friends around Bradbury Lines that he wasn't going to be coming back from the next tour in Oman.

As the camouflaged aircraft bounced lazily through thermals rising from the baked ground below, Laba leaned over to Jim and nodded towards the distinctive southerly curl in the Dhofar coastline from which the little fishing harbour of Mirbat faces west. Over the buzz of the engines Laba told his friend: 'That's where I'm going to die . . .'

Chapter 17

March 1972

'Are we,' asked Sir Alec Douglas-Home, 'leaving Qaboos in the lurch?' The British Foreign Secretary had just read a signal from his ambassador in Jordan asking whether or not Oman's efforts to secure military help from King Hussein should enjoy the blessing of Her Majesty's Government. It served to highlight the tightrope London was trying to walk as both the FCO and MoD played tag with the financial cost of the Dhofar campaign. Whitehall's ambivalent commitment to Oman continued to reflect a paranoia that the UK might be drawn into her own 'mini-Vietnam'. There was little danger of that happening given the obsessively tight rein exerted on Britain's support for Oman.

Throughout February and March, Sultan Qaboos and his representatives visited Arab capitals and received delegations in Muscat in pursuit of help for the campaign in Dhofar.

Alongside the Sultan's enthusiastic diplomatic initiative, the reduction of the SAS commitment to a single squadron, Britain's withdrawal from the Persian Gulf, and her continuing spin over how best to get off the Salalah hook and release herself from the burden of running the airfield in Dhofar, it was not hard to see how some might question Britain's appetite for supporting Qaboos. And that speculation gathered momentum.

Then Britain's ambassador in Saudi Arabia was asked to

attend a meeting with his American counterpart. He had received a report from a source he could not reveal that SAS support was to be withdrawn along with British personnel serving with SAF.

'I don't know whether the report was authentic,' the American explained mildly, 'and I've no wish to create a stir about it, but this is surely not the moment for any reduction of British assistance.' Despite the measured delivery, Britain's Man in Jeddah was in little doubt that the conversation was a reflection of *a rather anxious enquiry from the State Department*. At the same time, the US Defense Attaché told his opposite number at the British Embassy that he had heard from a secret source that Britain was withdrawing all her military forces from Oman.

'You seem to have an unhappy knack,' Colonel Fifer told the British officer, 'for bad timing.' In case there was any doubt, the American Colonel then wondered aloud what impact the news would have on Britain's standing in Saudi Arabia. Since, in the eyes of King Faisal, the British had gifted South Yemen to the Communists, there was only one answer to that.

In a series of diplomatic signals classified SECRET & ECLIPSE, Britain pursued the origins of the story through contacts in Washington and the Middle East. The US State Department was prepared only to admit that they came from Saudi sources. London's conclusion, in the end, was that it may well have been Sultan Qaboos himself who, in meetings with King Faisal, had encouraged Saudi fears – inadvertently or otherwise.

While that could only be speculation, it was evident that Qaboos was emerging as an increasingly shrewd and confident advocate of his country's interests. He was dismissive of British references to Vietnam as 'not really valid' and he was well aware of the leverage he enjoyed from Britain's requirement for the RAF base on Masirah Island. He knew that the continuing presence of the Regiment in Dhofar was crucial.

'Without the assistance of the SAS in particular,' he told Lord Carrington, the British Defence Secretary, 'our forces could not have achieved the success they have.' And the SAS commitment, although reduced, remained.

April 1972

Laba and Tak weren't going to Mirbat after all. Instead, on arrival at the BATT's tented lines behind SAF's Um al Gwarif Brigade HQ, they were told that Captain Mike Kealy was taking Eight Troop up to the position at Tawi Atair, where they'd be replacing Shaun Brogan's A Squadron men.

'Looks like you got it wrong,' Jim told Laba with a grin. It seemed that his friend's premonition of his own death was no more than a nightmare. Laba hoped so and, with Tak, looked forward to getting up on to the Jebel again.

Brogan was on the flight-deck, standing between the seats of the pilot and co-pilot for the first fixed-wing landing on his airstrip at Tawi Atair. As they approached on short finals, the big Caribou, flying slowly, nearly hanging, nose low, on its full-span, double-slotted flaps, he got a better idea of the challenges the SOAF pilots would have using it. Carved into rising ground from the threshold, the rough runway created the impression in the cockpit that they were simply going to fly straight into a hill.

'By Christ . . .' subsequently emerged as the general consensus among the 2 Squadron transport pilots.

But the arrival of the Skyvan carrying B Squadron in April offered further confirmation that, however hairy it might have been, it was good *enough*.

The outgoing men, Bergens packed and ready to ship out, greeted the new team. Brogan spotted the broad-shouldered figure of Tak as the Fijian unloaded stores from the hold of the aircraft down the ramp at the back. They acknowledged each other in recognition; the last time Brogan had seen him was six months earlier on patrol from White City during Op JAGUAR.

Brogan didn't know Mike Kealy, their young Troop Commander, well, but, behind a pair of wire-rimmed spectacles, the 27-year-old Captain seemed switched on. And there was vast experience spread throughout the rest of Eight

Troop: troopers, corporals and sergeants who'd fought in campaigns with the SAS stretching back ten years. This combination of hard-earned, long-term corporate knowledge and experience in the ranks together with new blood and fresh thinking, as officers were drawn from throughout the Army on two-year attachments, offered the Regiment one of its unique strengths.

Brogan briefed Kealy on the Firqas, the defensive set-up and the state of the Adoo. And how to repair the airstrip if it needed it. He wanted Kealy to understand what he and his Troop had done and why.

Reject it if you like, he thought, *but don't reject it before we've explained why we did it*. Kealy listened.

The handover complete, they shook hands and Brogan climbed into the Skyvan alongside his men to fly out of the position for the last time. Eight Troop would be OK. There was no particular reason to think that they wouldn't have a relatively quiet time of it at Tawi Atair.

This was not, in the end though, how things played out for them.

Nigel Knocker's Op Order for Operation SIMBA had been meticulously prepared: thirty-four pages of neatly typed instructions distributed on 5 April, twelve days before L-Day.

He began with an estimation of enemy forces in the area and finished with the codewords for different positions. There was a deception plan to mask SAF's true intentions which was reproduced in blue. Attached to the main document were annexes covering fireplans for his two 75mm RCLs and ten 81mm mortars, details of the stores and logistics, signals instructions and three different contingency plans for dealing with civilian refugees and SEPs.

The operation was split into two parts: Phase 1 covered the seizure and reinforcement of the main position. But it was Phase 2, the assault on Capstan, that remained, to a large extent, the focus of the whole effort. With Capstan under SAF control, the expectation was that they could both supply the main position with water and build a blocking line all the way to the coast. To do that, Knocker planned to relieve the Desert Regiment's Red Coy with a company from the Northern Frontier Regiment, the Op Order noted, 'on about 1 May for offensive ops on coastal plain and construction of a barrier'. 1 May, he thought, gave them a little leeway; but Knocker hoped they might launch Phase 2 as early as the 27th.

For weeks, stores, water and fuel had been flown or driven into the Desert Regiment's base at Akoot. This would then act as a forward base for Neville Baker's helicopters. The plan required seventy flights by six Hueys over three days. Until there was an airstrip built on Simba position at Mainbrace, the codename given by Knocker's Op Order to the runway's location, the helicopters were the only way in.

Even though the only space available for briefing was inside an old canvas tent held up with bent poles, Baker's helicopter squadron tried not to let standards drop. The obligatory map of the operational area was attached to a board with drawing pins and there were trestle tables and camping chairs. The solitary light bulb hanging from the ceiling was given a proper shade. A coolbox for evening beers was brought in; pub ash-trays were put out; and the rough gravel underfoot was covered by a patchwork of handmade Persian carpets. On L-Day −1, pilots stood around in a motley collection of variously sourced military clothing, smoking, anticipating the moment at first light when they'd start their engines and engage the big two-bladed rotors of their Hueys.

All the pilots and aircrewmen were briefed by Baker after he'd returned from Nigel Knocker's Orders Group. At that, once again, Baker had been forced to explain that, as much as the Army might like it, it was madness to take all the helicopters in together. Instead he set up a kind of relay race. A pair of Hueys would land every two minutes, unload and head back to Akoot. The next pair would follow. 3 Squadron could keep that up all day for them.

With the exception of Stan Standford, Baker's ex-Royal Navy aircrewman leader, the rest of 3 Squadron's aircrewmen were Omanis. Most were barely in their twenties and often without any kind of formal education, but they were responsible for loading and unloading the helicopters, ensuring they were safe to fly. At the first sign of shooting or serious injury some had decided they'd prefer something a little less exposed to the frontline, but those that remained were learning fast.

Hamed Nasser was the youngest of them, just seventeen, although his age was recorded as twenty for his application to SAF. Nasser had been brought up in Tanzania, where his father was a merchant, the family only returning to Oman after the accession of Sultan Qaboos. Since climbing trees as a boy in Africa to watch the missionary aircraft land, he'd only ever wanted to fly. He loved being on the squadron and had come to regard Baker and Standford as father figures. But despite their calm assurances that all was going to go without a hitch, Nasser was nervous now. This was the first time the squadron had mounted an operation on this sort of scale. And to add to his disquiet, the Adoo knew something was up; they'd watched the build-up at Akoot and delivered their verdict today against Akoot in the form of twenty-six mortar rounds.

But the enemy did not know what was being planned. Nor did they know that nearly sixty men from Red Coy and 2 Coy had been dropped well north of Sarfait and were already tabbing in on foot through the night to secure the SIMBA landing zones.

It was probably as much of a surprise to the crew of the Sultanic Naval Vessel *Al Sa'id* as it was to the enemy that the SAF operation to take Simba appeared to begin from the sea. But that was the whole idea.

Since the glory days of the eighteenth-century diplomatic missions to New York City the Sultan's navy was rather reduced in circumstances. It was certainly in no position to gift a warship to anyone, let alone the Royal Navy. Instead, the help was travelling in the other direction. Replacing a retired RAF group captain who hated the smell of fish and got seasick, this now came in the shape of Lieutenant Commander Jeremy

Raybould RN, the British officer seconded to run Oman's Coastal Patrol. Known to some simply as the Ginger Pirate, Raybould must have been the last RN officer to enjoy command of an operational wooden warship. The CP's two wooden booms, eighty-ton motorized dhows which, it was claimed, were two knots faster than any other dhow in Oman, were limited in the contribution they could make to the war in Dhofar. They had a pair of Browning .50 HMGs – heavy machine guns – to harass the Adoo from the sea, but that was about the extent of it. They were often in more danger from what might be fired back at them. But while the two vessels, SNV *Nasr Al Bahr* and SNV *Al Muntasir*, soldiered on, the arrival of a new royal yacht, the SNV *Al Sa'id*, in 1971, was a step into the twentieth century. Armed with a 40mm Bofors gun, the ship, while hardly a battleship, could at last offer more worthwhile naval gunfire support to operations ashore. And so she was drafted into Nigel Knocker's plans to open SAF's account during Operation SIMBA. Since early April, she'd been firing on different positions along the coast. A few more rounds landing ashore to divert attention away from Sarfait on L-Day itself could only help.

But it was Neville Baker the Adoo should have been keeping their eye on. It was becoming something of a habit when SAF launched an operation, for the helicopter Squadron Boss to go in first. And, as it had been for Op JAGUAR, so it was for Op SIMBA.

Chapter 18

17 April 1972

In the dark blue just before sunrise, Neville Baker, wearing a baggy khaki flying suit, walked out from the Ops tent at Akoot with Nigel Knocker. A line of camouflaged Hueys squatted on their skids, tied down and grey in the pre-dawn. But today Baker and Knocker were taking the little Jetranger; their job, to fly south to establish that the position was secure. Only then would Baker release the big troop-carrying Hueys to begin their day-long shuttle to and from Akoot.

The helicopter pilots all flew with personal weapons in their otherwise unarmed machines. The government-issue FNs weren't ideal. They were too long to fit easily beside the seat and impossible to strap down. Hard manoeuvring – and that was to be expected – could always send them scuttling across the cabin. So most chose AK47s handed in by SEPs or captured from the enemy. A thirty-round magazine seemed more than adequate; except for Royal Marine Bill Bailey, who liked to fly with a handful of grenades strapped to his chest for good measure. The 3 Squadron Boss carried his AK47 and had a 9mm Browning automatic strapped to his waist.

The ground was damp underfoot, the suede of the men's desert boots darkening at the toes as it absorbed the water. For days the skies had been clear. Men and stores had been shuttled into the Forward Operating Base at Akoot without delay or complication. Then, on L-Day –1, before the men of Red Coy and 2 Coy prepared to move south to take the high ground, that all changed when thick, low clouds rolled in on storm fronts from the Indian Ocean, smothering southern Dhofar – and the route into Simba – in low, clinging mist.

Akoot camp was woken by the hiss of a jet turbine as, in the cockpit, Neville Baker's hands danced across the control panel of the little 206, bringing Jetranger 603 to life. So familiar was the routine that the veteran pilot's eyes almost scanned the instruments without conscious instruction, searching for anything out of place, a needle or light that didn't fit the picture. Above him, the two main rotor blades, turning slowly at first, their tips drooping below the level of the rotorhead, gathered speed. But as the revolutions accelerated they straightened, made taut and rigid by the centripetal force. The blades beat at the damp air, generating visible vortices and streaks of condensation as they whipped the still sky into eddies of differing pressures. Those in their camp beds who hadn't been woken by the engine now stirred at the sound of the thumping rotor blades. L-Day began here. And Hamed Nasser tried to ignore the knot of anxiety in his stomach at the prospect of the Adoo's reaction to the op. He had a job to do. What would be would be. *Insha'Allah*.

As Baker and Knocker flew south, the cloud cover deepened. From the cabin of the 206, the two men could barely see the massive Simba promontory, let alone get in to establish the security of the position. Knocker had watched as the weather clamped down with a sinking feeling. After months of careful, detailed planning, it was possible the whole thing could be derailed by an act of God. His mood hadn't been helped by the news that one of his company commanders had managed to wreck his back and had to be casevaced out and back to Salalah. 'Bomber' Bembridge was the best of his mortar men too.

Just what you need the day before a big operation, he'd thought, frustrated at his bad luck. Now they just needed the enemy to make an appearance and he'd be resorting to the codeword 'Bugle' and abandoning the airlift altogether. But the initially bleak picture improved. After an hour, Baker managed to scoot in at low level under the cloud to put the Jetranger down at Yardarm, where Red Company had success-fully established a picquet covering the whole Simba position; although they'd lost their Firqa en route after the irregulars had baulked at the arduous overnight yomp. That was par for the course though. The Firqa may not have conformed to normal military standards, but BATT and SAF commanders learnt to live with that because they were also invaluable. They provided options that regular SAF troops simply could not. And under the FTZ's second-in-command, they'd been tasked with perhaps the most crucial task facing Knocker's assault force once Simba itself was secure: finding water.

The improving cloudbase that had eventually allowed Baker and Knocker to get in continued to lift. It was far from ideal, but it was good enough. The helicopter Boss gave Knocker the go-ahead. And Operation SIMBA, two hours late, got under-way. If you were looking for a silver lining, the damp and drizzle would at least keep the dust clouds churned up by the Hueys' rotor downwash at bay. Fog or dust: they could both end the life of a helicopter.

By dusk, Nigel Knocker was satisfied that Op SIMBA had got off to a good start. For nearly nine hours he'd been air-borne with Baker directing the stream of men and materiel flowing on to the plateau by helicopter from Akoot. Thirty-five Huey loads brought in over one hundred troops, ammunition, mortars, rations, sandbags, wire, water, explosives and digging equipment. The last of these meant that construction of an air-field that would relieve the burden on the overworked helicopters could begin immediately. In the afternoon, thirty-three civilian refugees arrived asking for sanctuary from the Adoo. SAF's first permanent presence in this corner of south-west Dhofar had been established for less than a day and the local population were already demonstrating how welcome to them it was. Late that evening, as he finally had a chance to reflect on what had been achieved, Knocker noted in his diary that it had been a 'very tiring day, but most successful'.

And 3 Squadron had got away with it by the skin of their teeth. The low cloud had nearly nailed one of them.

Helicopters have always been vulnerable to ground-fire. Both their flying characteristics and the nature of the job they do mean they fly low and slow, presenting a relatively easy target. So in Dhofar, 3 Squadron did whatever they could to keep the time they spent down in the dust, where they were a target for Adoo AK47 rounds, to a bare minimum. Unlike most military helicopters, the SOAF fleet spent much of their time cruising at 6,000 feet or more out of range of gunfire from the ground. This in itself could unsettle pilots who'd spent entire careers using the ground as a touchstone for keeping the aircraft where they wanted it. At 10,000 feet that was taken away and one or two pilots who signed up for Neville Baker's squadron simply weren't able to adjust to the strange world at altitude without familiar visual references. They had to leave. But if the journey from A to B alone could be disorientating, the 'SOAF Spiral', the tactic used by the helis to get to the ground once they'd arrived at their destination, held its own challenges. And it too could cause a pilot to lose his bearings. The idea was to drop from cruising height to the ground without ever leaving the narrow column of air above the position you knew was defended by your own troops on the ground. First of all, the pilot pulled off all the power. From that point on the main rotor was auto-rotating, driven, like a wind turbine, by nothing more than the flow of air passing through it. When the speed had fallen to 60 knots, the pilot let the nose drop and tipped the helicopter into a steep 45 degree turn, then held it in an accelerating, descending spiral using cross-controls. If the aircraft was spinning to the right the stick was pulled left and vice versa. A normal descent using auto-rotation – a technique taught to all helicopter pilots in case of engine failure – lost height at around 1,700 feet a minute. In the SOAF Spiral, rates of descent in excess of 7,000 feet per minute were sometimes achieved. The Hueys were falling towards the ground at nearly 90 mph. It needed careful handling, but it was coming out at the bottom that provided the most scope for error. The trick was to do one thing at a time: rack off the rate of turn, *then* let the rate of descent decrease, *then* start applying power. Try to do it all at once and it would provoke a leading-edge stall of the main rotor that meant the helicopter really would fall out of the sky – without sufficient altitude to recover. In Dhofar, when Neville Baker's pilots misjudged it, there was sometimes the possibility of using the depth of a wadi to regain control. But not always.

Flying the SOAF Spiral into Simba would eventually destroy two Hueys and claim the lives of two pilots and two aircrewmen. But, on L-Day, Neville Baker's squadron escaped with no more than a badly bent skid on one of the Hueys after a hard landing on uneven, rock-strewn ground. After having it replaced, the aircraft quickly returned to the frontline. The skid ended up hanging on the wall of the Officers' Mess as a blank canvas for graffiti from the Strikemaster and transport pilots, all eager to compliment their rotary-winged comrades on their evident flying skill. The heli pilots, of course, gave as good as they got.

Bill Stoker loved the banter and enthusiasm of an uninhibited, smoky RAF Mess and he knew that the right atmosphere was good for morale. No one in SOAF(Tac) was left in any doubt about Stoker's conviction that work hard, play hard was the only way to go. And while it was an outlook that, inevitably, had been tempered a little by seniority, he'd certainly done enough in his time to be able to claim that he led by example.

As a young fighter pilot flying Hawker Hunters out of RAF Gütersloh in West Germany in the late fifties, Stoker had thought nothing of driving his tax-free Alfa Romeo Spider to Düsseldorf, one hundred miles away, for a no-holds-barred night out in one of the city's most expensive and exotic nightclubs, then racing back through the night against friends behind the wheels of equally seductive sports cars like the Austin Healey 100/6, only to report for flying in the morning.

As one of the gang pointed out: 'Drink driving was unknown as a crime and no one crashed their Hunter.'

Standing with a beer in the RAF Salalah Officers' Mess watching Nobby Grey try to stop a ceiling fan with his head without scalping himself, or Charlie Gilchrist holding court with his accordion surrounded by drinkers bellowing along at the top of their lungs, it was clear that not much had changed. Pilots will be pilots. The insistence that shirts and ties be worn seemed to make no difference. And the volume of empty beer cans generated by the Mess was a testament to that.

Beer enjoyed a disproportionate importance in Salalah; Amstel, Tiger and Heineken being the preferred brands. When the head of the NAAFI had visited Salalah he'd asked Station Commander Gerry Honey if there was anything he could do to help make life on the remote RAF base a little easier. More Tiger beer was the only request. When, two weeks earlier, the naval resupply vessel RFA *Hebe* had anchored in Raysut harbour to offload 250 tons of beer, the RAF officer compiling the Operations Record Book felt it was worth mentioning not just the quantity, but also the reverence with which an unusual number of volunteers treated the cargo. In fairness, 250 tons of beer seems a lot, but it was going to have to see them through the monsoon, as the rough seas it brought with it made Raysut inaccessible for much of the year. And Oman *was* hot. But the bottom line was that there wasn't a great deal else to do. Even the literature sent out by Airwork to try to entice contract pilots to Oman was forced to acknowledge that. It suggested swimming, fishing, sailing and snorkelling, which it called 'goggling'. And, when it had run out of water sports, pointed out that 'photography is a worthwhile hobby'.

Inside the base there was the open-air cinema, where, with no account taken of the fact that Salalah was an un-accompanied tour, the Forces Cinematographic Society sent a steady stream of Disney cartoons alongside more suitable new releases like *Butch Cassidy and the Sundance Kid* and *Zulu*, a movie that seemed so realistic to the Firqas invited to watch it that they tried to return fire. And there were no women. In the north there was the possibility of an encounter with a bored PDO wife looking for company while her husband was working the oilfields. Such opportunities were few and far between though. And so, clustered round the coral limestone bar in the Salalah Mess, there was a great deal of talking about it instead. It hadn't taken SOAF pilots long to realize that the opening of Oman's new international airport at Seeb, one of the Sultan's range of infrastructure projects, would bring with it air hostesses who would need entertaining during stopovers in Muscat. But that tantalizing prospect was, for the time being, no more than a topic of conversation. For now, beer in a smoke-filled prefab with a few trophies and trinkets on shelves, a picture of the Queen hanging on the wall and cheap curtains remained the number one form of rest and relaxation for the pilots of SOAF(Tac).

The 'father' of the SOAF helicopter force, Neville Baker, made allowances for the fact they were fighter pilots. Always a little more boisterous, he thought. But he was as enthusiastic a member of the RAF Mess as the Strikeys. To some of the younger pilots he could seem like a figure from a bygone age, but anyone who'd caught sight of Baker, believing he was alone, dancing a happy little jig to himself before entering a room, knew he was a man who also enjoyed the lighter side of life. And at least, as far as Baker was concerned, in the Officers' Mess, unlike the nearby Sergeants' Mess, he was unlikely to be subjected to regular renditions of his name, sung football chant style, to the tune of 'Bread of Heaven'. That might have got irksome.

The atmosphere in the Mess tonight though felt claustrophobic. The roof fans that survived their encounters with Nobby Grey's head struggled to deal with 100 per cent humidity. It was noisier than usual too. While the pilots drank, smoked and put the world to rights they had to raise their voices to be heard above the heavy drum of thick raindrops on the corrugated tin roof. They were grateful to be inside. Salalah plain was getting hammered by violent thunderstorms, funnel clouds and gale force squalls that dumped 90 per cent of the month's rain in a single night. While the base escaped relatively lightly, the storms spread destruction throughout Dhofar Province.

What vaguely raised an eyebrow at Salalah was an inconvenience at Akoot, where pilots sat on camp chairs placed on top of tables to escape the water flowing through the tents. But on top of the escarpment at Simba position, Nigel Knocker's Desert Regiment were hit ferociously hard. It was nightmarish. Weather of biblical intensity attacked the men on the Jebel at Sarfait so hard it looked like it might jeopardize the success of the whole operation. The sky flashed and roared as torrential rain filled bunkers, washed away stores, wrecked the command post. Anything paper was history.

Knocker had set up his Battalion HQ in a shallow, open-mouthed cave, quickly christened 'The Grotto'. From inside, where the Colonel and some of his senior officers crowded in, praying for the weather to ease, they heard moaning. Outside, a Baluch Lance Corporal – normally fearless in the face of Adoo fire – was curled in the foetal position at the entrance, wrapped in a blanket.

'I'm going to die . . .' he complained, before being dragged into the tent and warmed with a small tot of medicinal rum. But the soldier was right to be frightened. Up on the 2 Coy position a soldier was struck by lightning and killed. When news came through on one of the little hand-held radios, it seemed scarcely believable. It was a bleak night, made worse by anxiety about the scene that would greet them in the morning and by the brutal collapse of the high spirits that had followed the landing of the first fixed-wing Skyvan on the new airstrip at Mainbrace. It had been cleared and made safe just forty-eight hours after the Desert Regiment's air assault had first claimed Simba for the Sultan and cheers had greeted the squat little cargo plane's arrival.

It was a milestone worth celebrating, but it was not the most remarkable achievement being enjoyed by the transport squadron. In April 1972, there was another good news story that was verging on the miraculous.

Chapter 19

Strangely enough it was a thrombosis that provided the first glimmer of hope. Barrie Williams woke up in Stoke Mandeville after another night of sleep disturbed by the crying and screams of the other patients and he was uncomfortable; there was a funny sensation in his leg. He called Sister Humphries to his bed.

'There something wrong here,' he told the nurse, 'something's hurting.' And he shouldn't have been able to feel a thing. Sister Humphries gave him pills to thin the blood and, with the blood clot gone, Williams was, once more, dead below the waist. But he *had* felt something; he knew he had. It wasn't long afterwards that he woke up again with an ache in his legs; different this time. There was no doubt about it though. He looked down, tried to wriggle his toes and watched them move. His excited relief was almost uncontainable. He was going to walk again.

When he broke his back, Williams severely traumatized his spinal cord, but he didn't sever it. Recovery and repair were a possibility. With that prospect he was quickly moved to the military's rehabilitation centre at Headley Court. By Christmas he was on a strict regime of exercise in the gym and swimming pool alongside as much walking as he could manage; even archery. At first it felt as if his legs weren't his own; like a newborn foal struggling to exert control over unfamiliar limbs. But they got stronger and stronger. He didn't wait to get back to being 100 per cent right before asking whether he could fly again. The answer was yes; providing that he didn't strap himself back into an ejection seat. That meant the fast jets were out of reach, but there was nothing stopping him flying commercially for an airline. Or even returning to Oman. Throughout his time in hospital, Williams had remained in contact with SOAF's Commander, Curly Hirst. Hirst had offered him a choice: the ex-Fleet Air Arm fighter pilot could choose to end his contract with SOAF or, if it was what he wanted, he was welcome back to fly Skyvans or helicopters. The arrival *en masse* at Headley Court one day of a troop of the BATT who'd driven from Hereford loaded with booze to wish him well only seemed to seal the deal. Inspired by their bonhomie and war stories from Dhofar, Williams chose Oman. And he agreed with Curly Hirst that, as soon as he was ready, he could return to Oman to fly the Shorts SC7 Skyvan with 2 Squadron. After a career flying jet fighters, the little transport plane was going to take a little getting used to.

The Skyvan was called many things. While for Williams it was a lifeline, it was also the Six-Ton Budgy, the Flying Wind Tunnel, the Whispering Nissen Hut. But it was never, ever called pretty. In the history of aviation there are a small group of aircraft that will always make the shortlist for ugliest aircraft ever built. The Skyvan barely looked like it would fly. Instead, it resembled a camouflaged freight container with a giant ice lolly stick taped on top for wings and three wheels sticking out of the bottom to remove any last vestige of anything that might be mistaken for streamlining. It was once suggested that a Skyvan had been delivered in a box by men who, job done, returned home taking the aircraft with them and leaving behind the box. But already in service in eighteen different countries around the world and winning a 1972 Queen's Award to Industry for Export Achievement, it was an unlikely modern sales success for the oldest aviation company in the world.

Perhaps most famous for making large flying boats like the elegant Imperial Airways Empire Class or the Second World

War's 'Flying Porcupine', the famous Sunderland, Short Brothers were first registered as a balloon-maker in 1898 in Hove, on England's south coast. After moving to workshops in a Tottenham Court Road mews, then railway arches in Battersea, in 1909 Eustace, Horace and Oswald Short were awarded a licence to build the Wright Brothers' Flyer in the UK from their new home on the Isle of Sheppey. But by the 1950s, ten years after his company had been nationalized during the war, Oswald, the last surviving brother, was working as a British Rail station master while Short Brothers and Harland, as it now was, was based in Belfast as an adjunct of the Bristol Aircraft Company; little more than a production line offering spare capacity for the rest of the UK aircraft industry. It seemed unlikely that Shorts would ever independently develop another aircraft, let alone a private venture that turned out to be a machine customers actually wanted. But in 1959, after rejecting an approach to collaborate on developing the similar in concept Miles Aerovan, design work began on the new Skyvan.

In designing the unusual, boxy-looking utility plane, Short Brothers knew exactly what they were after. They wanted a simple, rugged, short-take-off aircraft that could operate off 300-yard-long unprepared strips in some of the roughest parts of the world carrying loads that were big enough to actually be useful. The square fuselage cross-section may not have looked as elegant as an aerodynamic cylinder, but it meant you could drive a Land Rover into the back.

The Skyvan won friends because it was good at what it did and didn't let people down. Pilots developed great affection for the little twin-prop. And those on the ground whose lives the aircraft had changed for the better were similarly appreciative. One heavily pregnant Dhofari woman, on her way to hospital with 2 Squadron, gave birth en route and named her daughter Skyvan.

Before flying out to join the Metal Box Company in Oman in April, Barrie Williams completed a ground school conversion course with Shorts in Belfast. There he learnt all about what the ODM, the Operating Data Manual, said the Skyvan could and couldn't do; what had been tested and approved as within safe limits and what was not. In the hands of 2 Squadron in Salalah, the ODM was an object of interest, but little more than that. Operational demands meant that it was so often completely ignored that the Skyvan pilots were often flying genuinely 'outside the envelope'.

Barrie Williams might not have been flying jets any more, but that didn't mean for one second that the flying was going to be any less hairy. There were short, rough airstrips supplying SAF positions throughout Dhofar that were terminated with precipitous drops from the top of the Jebel and took no account of prevailing winds. The British military attaché in Muscat likened using them to flying off the deck of an aircraft carrier. Shaun Brogan's lovingly dynamited strip at Tawi Atair was one of them.

Now Brogan's strip kept B Squadron's Eight Troop and their Firqa in food, water, mail, money and ammunition. For Tak, Laba, Snapper and the rest of Mike Kealy's men things were proving to be no more testing than they had been for Brogan and A Squadron before them. But that was the idea. The network of defensive positions spreading out like spokes of a wheel from White City were supposed to be permanent, a clear signal to both the Jebali people and the Adoo that SAF were on the Jebel to stay. The further from White City they extended, the greater the area enclosed that they could legitimately claim to have pacified.

But within ten days of L-Day, Operation SIMBA was already beginning to place an almost impossible burden on SOAF. Even with Brogan's heart-stopping airstrip opening up Tawi Atair to fixed-wing resupply, the gravity exerted by SAF's new commitment at Sarfait was beginning to tell. The position in the west was already proving to be the drain on resources that pilots like Neville Baker and Nick Holbrook had expected it would be.

Every week, it was Baker's job to provide the Dhofar Commander, Mike Harvey, with the flying hours available so that Harvey could allocate these to his units in the field. Once unavoidable resupply commitments had been catered for, what was left could be used to support air mobile infantry operations. It was these hours that enabled SAF to fight a dynamic, unpredictable campaign that kept the Adoo off-guard and uncertain. This was the war Baker wanted to fight, but, as he jumped into his heavily sandbagged Land Rover – numberplate SOAF 1 – to visit Harvey, he felt crippled.

Every soldier, every particle of food, every drop of water, every bullet, Baker reminded himself as he drove the short distance to Um al Gwarif camp, had to be flown into Sarfait.

'These are the hours I've got available for the week,' he told the bespectacled Dhofar Commander. 'Most of them are for SIMBA, which will leave about ten hours for everything else.'

For his own reasons, Harvey had always had an ambivalent view of Knocker's Sarfait operation. It didn't, perhaps, suit his enthusiasm for front-footed aggression. But he had been brought onside by John Graham and he knew that, now it had been seized, Simba could not be relinquished, whatever the cost. But something had to give. Reluctantly, Harvey decided he had no choice but to abandon positions on the eastern Jebel, taken during Operation JAGUAR. Tawi Atair was one of them.

Each SAS Sabre Squadron was made up of sixty fighting men. There were four of them. During the campaign to clear the area around White City of Adoo and make it safe for civil development, four of the BATT had been killed, one had been paralysed and at least another twenty had been casevaced off the Jebel with injuries, some serious. In seven months of fighting, the casualties suffered by the Regiment amounted to 10 per cent of its total fighting strength. It was little wonder that, with Harvey's decision to pull out of Tawi Atair, SAS commanders protested that they were losing confidence in Mike Harvey. It felt like a kick in the teeth for everyone involved in Operation STORM.

And despite his friend Jim Vakatali's cheerful observation on arrival in Salalah that, with the decision to send Eight Troop to

Tawi Atair, Lance Corporal Talaiasi Labalaba no longer had to worry what fate might have in store for him in Mirbat, there had now been another twist. When they came off the Jebel, Kealy's men were heading for the coast. Laba was going to Mirbat after all.

John Graham and Mike Harvey flew into Mainbrace together. In the face of complaints from the BATT, CSAF had endorsed the Dhofar Commander's decision over Tawi Atair. The priority had to be Op SIMBA.

Since the night of the storm, Simba position had been rebuilt. The damage Knocker had anticipated as the wind howled around him in the darkness had been too pessimistic. The Sarfait moonscape was now bone-dry again and there was impressive evidence of industry all around them. There were khaki-green tents and well-organized storage areas. Drystone-wall sangars, built from the black rocks that littered the gravel surface, lent the enterprise an air of permanence. Men moved purposefully around the plateau to a soundtrack of slapping Huey main-rotors and the Garrett turboprops of the Skyvans screaming in full power on take-off, or reverse thrust to bring them to a halt before reaching the limit of the Mainbrace airstrip.

There was something imperious about the way John Graham carried himself. With his swept-back hair and strong nose he had the dauntless bearing of a bird of prey. But as he surveyed the job done by the Northern Frontier Regiment, his manner masked his anxiety. CSAF's concern lay beyond the boundaries of Simba position itself. Because, for all Knocker's success in securing the position, anxiety over whether or not the gamble would pay off continued to gnaw at the ex-Para. The operation needed to succeed on two counts to justify the enormous logistical requirements necessary to sustain it.

While there had been long-range attacks on the position, SAF's descent on Simba seemed, so far, to have failed to provoke any significant reaction from either the Adoo or their sponsors in South Yemen. But it was vital that the operation punched above its weight. If, after the NFR's bold move to seize the position, things continued to grind on as before, then SIMBA had failed to achieve the objective upon which Graham believed the outcome of the war depended. It needed to provoke a reaction.

And even at a tactical level Operation SIMBA appeared to have fallen behind. A week after he'd first expected to complete it, Knocker hadn't, despite recces, even been able to attempt Phase 2 of the operation, let alone complete it. Apart from skirmishing around it by the Firqas, Capstan remained in bandit country. Knocker was able to reassure CSAF on this front. The assault on Capstan would be launched the following evening. The trouble was, it proved to be beyond them.

Nearly vertical cliffs separated Simba from the gentler reliefs hundreds of feet below. Other than abseiling there was no easy way down them but ropes offered no option at all. It simply wasn't a remotely practical way of moving the best part of 200 soldiers. There was just one potential route down: a steep sloping fissure in the escarpment that ran diagonally along from the rock face descending from the boulder-strewn cleft at the top to the foot of the limestone wall. Knocker called it a wadi, but that was definitely a glass-half-full description. To consider the massive geological scar that cut the cliff as any kind of valley simply might have made it feel more approachable, but it sold it short. In comparison to the *alternatives* though, it did seem almost benign. It was anything but, though. And, at night, on 4 May, it crushed the hopes of the two companies of NFR troops that attempted to make their way down it. Knocker was forced to call it off.

Must think again, he realized. It was going to be some time, though, before he was going to get a chance to. The enemy were about to cast their vote.

Chapter 20

5 May 1972

It all began with shouting across a dry river bed. Roughly fifty-five miles north of Sarfait, Habrut was little more than a point on a map where there was known to be water, and yet it had been a focus for tension between Oman and South Yemen since the mid-fifties. The border there was only vaguely defined but widely accepted to run along the middle of a wadi that separated two *Beau Geste* forts, reflections of each other, 300 yards apart, one on the Yemen side, one in Oman, the latter built by the Desert Regiment between 1967 and 1968.

For a week the garrison of sixty Dhofar Gendarmerie guard troops manning the Omani fort had watched as the Yemeni fort was reinforced. Alongside them in the Sultanate fort were a Firqa and their BATT training team. B Squadron were spread thin throughout Dhofar, but Trooper Martin must have thought working with the Firqa in Habrut really was the back of beyond. And he was from Peterborough. There was none of the fresh seafood and football with locals that greeted Tak, Laba and the rest of Eight Troop when they flew into Mirbat. Martin had definitely drawn the short straw in being sent north-west to Habrut. Like the rest of his BATT troop, Martin was intrigued by the build-up across the wadi. As with anything out of the ordinary it was reported back to BATT HQ at Um al Gwarif.

But on the morning of 5 May a group of Omani Firqas crossed the wadi to challenge a small party from the Yemeni side who were walking along the frontier. It wasn't appreciated. The shouting didn't last long before the shooting started. Three of the Firqa went down with gunshot wounds. From the BATT position 800 yards east of the fort, the Regiment men heard the popping sound of small-arms fire and wondered whether it should be any cause for concern. It was. What none of the men on the Omani side knew was that the build-up of troops and stores across the wadi had been directed by the leader of the Adoo Ho Chi Minh unit. By stopping the Adoo patrol in the wadi, the Firqa had played into his hands. The confrontation appeared to have provided him with the trigger he wanted.

At 0830 local time, from positions in and around the Yemeni fort, the barrage began.

82mm mortar rounds rained down on the SAF fort, supported by small-arms and heavy fire from Shpagin 12.7mm machine guns. At one point, sixty bombs fell within the space of an hour and a half. Each of them throwing up a dust cloud and launching a lethal expanding ring of splintered metal and stones from the centre of the blast. But not all the Adoo fire was targeted on the fort itself. One of the early rounds landed in the centre of the Firqa camp.

This was the bomb that killed Trooper Martin.

Jagged shrapnel, a piece of shredded iron torn from the round's casing by the explosive within, ripped through his abdomen. Despite the attention of his comrades, he died within two or three minutes. A further five soldiers were killed throughout the attack, which continued unabated for the rest of the day. The Dhofar Gendarmerie, garrison troops rather than combat soldiers, were in no position to fight back. But for the next thirty-six hours, under the command of Lieutenant Hassan Ehsun, they held on. And Ehsun had to do so without the assistance of the surviving BATT.

Getting directly mixed up in a firefight on the border was just a little too conspicuous for a war the Regiment wasn't even supposed to be fighting, and the small SAS Troop were withdrawn.

*

173

Oh, bugger was John Graham's first thought when he received reports of what was happening on the western border. And not just because it was clear that it would further disrupt and delay Operation SIMBA. The Brigadier had been looking forward to leaving for a well-earned holiday the next day. He and Rosemary were visiting the Far East for the first time. And after the intensity of directing the war effort without a break since the launch of Op JAGUAR eight months earlier, the prospect of a chance to unwind felt as necessary as it did welcome. But as the situation in Habrut deteriorated it was clear that CSAF was going nowhere.

Nigel Knocker had as clear an impression of what was happening to the north as anyone outside of Habrut itself. As Hassan Ehsun's men resisted the attack from Yemen, Knocker's own Simba position was acting as radio relay for messages. Already disappointed by the previous night's failure to reach Capstan, Knocker knew he'd lost any immediate chance to try again when orders arrived from Um al Gwarif to have an expanded half-company ready by 0800 the following morning to reinforce Habrut's defence. That stuck a stick in the spokes of his plans. There would be worse news to come when, at midnight, all RT from Habrut ceased.

In his office in the old whitewashed fort at Bait al Falaj, CSAF considered the situation. He sipped at coffee, the red tabs on the collar of his khaki uniform the brightest colour in the room. After his initial gloom at news of the attack on Habrut, John Graham began to see the problem in a slightly different light. There was no doubt that the Adoo had succeeded in diverting the SAF effort away from Sarfait by forcing them to respond in Habrut. And the loss of men from Simba was a serious blow, putting at risk SAF's ability to hold on to the stranglehold position through the monsoon. But there was just a *chance* that the Adoo had failed to properly measure the long-term consequences of their action. If SIMBA had so far failed to capture the world's imagination, then SAF's response to the bombardment of the Habrut fort might provide a fresh opportunity to draw global attention to Oman's plight.

Graham discussed Oman's reaction to the cross-border assault with Sultan Qaboos and Hugh Oldman. The Sultan's initial decision was that, for now, there should be no retaliatory action. A display of restraint could only serve Oman's cause diplomatically. But that did not mean doing nothing. And as well as ordering the reinforcement of the Habrut fort by the Desert Regiment, John Graham also put SOAF on standby to act.

Nick Holbrook flew one of the three Hueys carrying the DR troops north to Habrut. After the abrupt end to RT communication with the fort's defenders, it was hard not to fear the worst. About six miles out, Holbrook reduced the power with the twist grip in his left hand and simultaneously eased down on the collective lever to adjust the pitch of the rotor blades. The soldiers in the back felt their stomachs lurch as the big 206 utility lost height, swooping down to low level for the run into Habrut. Then, through his headphones, Holbrook began to pick up Ehsun's voice. The young Omani had never stopped transmitting. But he hadn't been sure whether anyone was picking him up and, since his aerial had been shot off, he certainly hadn't expected a reply. But Ehsun and his men had survived the night; pulling back into the cover offered by a shallow wadi behind the fort. Hidden from the Adoo in the Yemeni fort by a ridgeline, Holbrook kicked up a dust storm beneath him as he put the Huey down on the wadi bed by Ehsun's position and disgorged the troops.

Two hours later, at 1115 hours local time, a DeHavilland Canada Beaver from 1 Squadron flew up the border towards Habrut. As the aircraft approached the fort, the co-pilot unstrapped his harness and climbed back into the cabin of the little piston-engined utility from the side door behind the wing, and the hastily copied leaflets were shovelled out of the back over the Adoo positions. They required a ceasefire within three hours or warned that the Sultanate would, reluctantly, reserve the right to retaliate to protect their sovereignty.

There was a little part of John Graham that was beginning to hope fervently that the Adoo would ignore the warning.

*

The official Soviet news agency, Tass, reported Trooper Martin's death with barely disguised glee. 'This soldier,' they said, 'belonged to the Special Air Service, which usually carries out various sabotage and terrorism acts.' Thoughts of anything as exciting as that were far from the minds of Eight Troop. As the situation in the west deteriorated, Tak, Laba, Snapper and the rest of Mike Kealy's men were settling into their sleepy new home, more worried about keeping busy than the prospect of being mortared.

Although it was one of a handful of towns along the Dhofar coast that justified automatic inclusion on a map, Mirbat was a sleepy backwater that made Salalah seem cosmopolitan by comparison. There had once been money in Mirbat, but it was long gone. Large merchants' houses with intricately carved wooden doors, built from stone, Omani limestone mortar and long-serving timber joists, originally from East Africa and moved from house to house because of a scarcity of home-grown replacements, were a testament to that. Their once impressive bearing was now chipped and fraying. Mirbat had been a centre for both the old frankincense trade and the breeding and export of Arabian horses, but was now reliant on a small fleet of wooden fishing boats. The population of a few thousand lived in a tight warren of unpaved roads and narrow alleys that provided the town's circulatory system.

When the Regiment first arrived in Mirbat in 1970 there had been no civil administration at all, no school and no medical care. The Wali – the local governor – was back now, living in a fort at the north-west corner of the town overlooking the beach and harbour.

Circled by wheeling gulls and still within range of the smell of the sea, the SAS lived in the BATT House, a hundred yards to the south of the Wali's residence. A noticeboard outside and sandbags on the roof were the only real evidence from outside that this was the Regiment's home, but inside they had made it their own. The stairs to the roof were built from stacked metal ammunition boxes. There was always a pan boiling for the next brew. Well-thumbed copies of *Penthouse* and *Playboy* counted as a library of sorts. The men slept on camp beds, their Bergens leaning up against the wall nearby. Reach in any direction inside the rooms and there was a choice of weaponry to hand. As well as responsibility for a GPMG, Tak also had an SLR and a liberated AK47 to his name. Each man carried a Japanese Tokai walkie-talkie to communicate with the rest of the Troop, non-military equipment, but cheap and effective. Inside the radio room was the PRC 316 for encrypted transmissions to and from BATT HQ at Um al Gwarif, surrounded by notepads and codebooks. Ammunition, medical supplies and boxes of compo rations were neatly stacked, easy to find and use. Making sure the admin got squared away was endemic within the Regiment; good work for idle hands. And after dark, over a drink, there was the sound of classic rock played on a battered old Philips cassette recorder running off six batteries. The *Easy Rider* soundtrack was played on near-permanent loop – audibly worn it had been played so much. But there was something about the album's spirit of rebellion that appealed to the BATT men and songs like Steppenwolf's 'Born to be Wild' had assumed an almost totemic place in their affections.

The trouble was that in terms of what needed doing in Mirbat much of the heavy lifting was already done. Things like the barbed-wire cattle fence surrounding the town had been built during B Squadron's first deployment while Tak was based in nearby Taqa. It couldn't be built again. And so much of the BATT's time was spent simply trying to fill it. Each of the Eight Troop men found his own way of making himself useful.

During Operation JAGUAR, Laba had amused himself and entertained the Firqas by giving them drill instruction. Explanation, demonstration, imitation and practice.

'Squad, 'shun!' Laba was grinning from ear to ear as he barked orders like a parade ground sergeant major. Watching the big Fijian and the Firqas – soldiers nearly as far from army discipline as it was possible to be – make like they were trooping the colour prompted peals of laughter from an enthusiastic audience. As an exercise in discipline, square-bashing with the Firqas was pointless, but it was another way of fostering the all-important bond between the Dhofari irregulars and their Regiment mentors. And while his friend Snapper fought to find the motivation to stay sharp, Tak, the Troop's Arabic-speaker, focused on hearts and minds in an effort to build the strongest possible relationship with both the Wali and the civilian population. If the Regiment weren't in Mirbat to fight – although God knows it would have broken the monotony – then making sure that it was doing an effective job as a Civil Action Team was the priority. As well as involving a lot of tea and conversation, the hearts-and-minds effort could, sometimes, take a slightly more dynamic form.

Games of football with the local kids were taken seriously. Boys like the permanently grinning Salim looked no match for the big, mutton-chopped Fijians and their team mates, but they had spirit, enthusiasm and agility on their side. Salim became a regular fixture around the camp, fascinated by the BATT men who'd been sent to his little town from countries beyond his imagination. Eight Troop liked having him around, but he also kept them well fed.

Salim announced his arrival at the BATT House with 'Fresh crayfish, Mr Tak!' At first the SAS men were greedy for it, exchanging sweets and chocolate with the boy for the shellfish to supplement the regular diet of British Army compo rations. They took it in turns to cook, benefiting from the skills of the Troop's newest recruit. Barely through Selection, 24-year-old Tommy Tobin was quiet, shy even in the company of some of the bigger characters in the Troop like Snapper, Fuzz and Roger Cole, the talkative West Country medic. But Tobin was well liked; that he'd made it into the Regiment from the unlikely starting point of the Catering Corps meant he could cook. That was never a bad way to win friends on operations. But you could have too much of a good thing. Even Tak's legendary fish curry, a spicy miracle cooked up on a roaring gas stove, became over-familiar. The weekly delivery of 'The

Fresh' at least meant there was steak and chips to look forward to. The weekly slab of beef became a way of marking the passing of time. As Snapper said: 'Nothing ever really happens in Mirbat.'

All the same, Tak couldn't help but fill hessian sandbags just in case something did.

'We're going to Habrut,' Bill Stoker told his men. Gathered in the squadron room, the announcement had an electrifying effect on the assembled pilots.

'I want you, and you . . .' Stoker pointed at four of the pilots he wanted to take with him on the raid. David Milne-Smith, Sean Creak, Taff Hinchcliffe and Nobby Grey all got tagged. The news sunk in: a five-ship bombing mission into South Yemen.

God, I hope this has been cleared at the right level, thought DMS immediately, *this is a big deal; definitely a departure from our normal operations.*

'Are you sure we've got clearance for this?' he asked, in disbelief that the thing had actually been approved. SOAF was usually so careful not even to approach the border. Now, suddenly, DMS was acutely aware that he was a Royal Air Force officer first and foremost. He could just imagine the heyday the press would have with the idea of serving British military pilots mounting unauthorized airstrikes against a sovereign country.

Stoker told him that the clearance came from the top.

This isn't just Joe Blow saying: 'No problem; go and do it', thought DMS, *this is an international border*. He couldn't help but wonder whether Stoker, having only been in country for a few months, had quite grasped the gravity of what he was asking them to do. And he wasn't sure that, necessarily, Stoker had chosen the right team.

'You haven't got Nigel Wilkinson,' DMS told him, 'you need him; Spoon's a bloody good weaponeer.' If they were going to do this they had better make a decent fist of it. Stoker demurred. He was perfectly happy with the four pilots he had chosen, but DMS pressed his point: Wilkinson should be included in the formation.

'You're right,' Stoker conceded, 'we should take him.' But before briefing the mission the next morning, and even as the Beaver prepared to fly north to Habrut to drop leaflets, both he and his boss, the Commander of the whole SOAF operation in Dhofar, Peter Hulme, had to take a pair of Strikemasters on a mission quite unlike any they had flown in SOAF colours before. Before 1 Squadron crossed the border, Stoker and Hulme were going to try to establish whether or not South Yemen was expecting them, by taking a pair of Strikemasters way beyond Oman's borders to take a closer look. It wasn't the first time Stoker had flown a solo reconnaissance mission into the enemy's backyard. In fact, he had form.

While stationed at RAF Gütersloh in West Germany, Bill Stoker had become acquainted with a small British intelligence operation called BRIXMIS – the British Military Exchange Mission. Based in Berlin, this tri-service unit, working under-cover as liaison officers, spied on the Warsaw Pact war machine ranged in East Germany against NATO. At the 1945 Potsdam Conference it was agreed that air training flights could be conducted in airspace within a twenty-mile radius of a point in the centre of the city. The RAF argued that, unless pilots serving ground tours in Berlin took to the air every ten days, they'd lose their flying pay. A single DeHavilland Canada Chipmunk, recognizably a sort of monoplane Tiger Moth, was kept at RAF Gatow to allow them to do so. While they did, the back seat of the little propellor-engined trainer was often occupied by a passenger from the Intelligence Corps with a long-lens camera taking pictures of the Soviet 24th Air Army and the East German Air Force. In the summer of 1960, Stoker, then a 25-year-old flight lieutenant, flew eleven BRIXMIS sorties out of RAF Gatow in Chipmunk WG313. One sortie over Eastern Bloc territory, with a US Army colonel in the back, lasted one and three quarter hours – the BRIXMIS intelligence 'take' was known to have found its way on to President Eisenhower's desk within days; they had letters thanking them for it – and, on another, WG313 suffered an engine failure. On that occasion he was able to bring the little Chipmunk safely back into Gatow for a deadstick landing. That wasn't going to be an option out over the Indian Ocean if either he or Peter Hulme lost the Strikemaster's single Rolls-Royce Bristol Viper turbojet as there was no possibility of that this time. Nor even of being picked up.

After dawn on the morning of 6 May, Stoker and Hulme took off from Salalah and turned towards the Yemeni border armed with nothing more than full fuel tanks and hand-held 35mm cameras. Staying low they flew seventy miles along the South Yemen coastline before Stoker turned back just beyond Al Ghaidah, an old British airstrip where it was feared the Yemeni Air Force could have forward-deployed their MiGs. Hulme continued alone before turning back at Thamud, another old military strip. He returned half an hour after Stoker, following his marathon three-hour mission. Neither pilot had anything to report. For now the Yemeni Air Force remained at Aden. It was negative intelligence, but it provided 1 Squadron with the knowledge they needed to launch.

As the SOAF Ops Room waited for news of the Adoo's re-action to the leaflet drop at Habrut, Stoker briefed his pilots. Since joining the Omani Air Force, none of them had ever sat and listened to a formal pre-strike briefing like this. DMS could feel the tension in the little squadron office as Stoker spoke. They'd be going in twice. Two formations of five. On the first raid they'd concentrate on the gun positions surrounding the fort. With them neutered, they'd go back for the fort itself. Nobby Grey pulled on a cigarette, drew the smoke into his lungs and exhaled.

Outside, a line of five Strikemasters sat on the apron. Andy Dunsire and the Airwork engineers prepared them for the raid, jacking 540lb high-explosive iron bombs up on to the outer wing pylons on heavy yellow bomb trolleys. On the inside ones, they clipped two vertical racks of SURA rockets under each wing. Loaded with two 540lb bombs and sixteen SURA rockets, the five little attack jets sat waiting for the pilots to come out of the old BOAC terminal building to bring them to life.

Wearing yellow Mae West life-jackets over their flightsuits, with 9mm Browning automatics and water bottles strapped to their waists, the five pilots signed for the jets and walked out together, carrying their silver flying helmets in their hands.

Chapter 21

6 May 1972

Neville Baker was already on his way north, gaining a head start on the faster jets so that he was on station, providing search and rescue cover for when the strike began. Given the belligerence of the Adoo at Habrut, 1 Squadron were not expecting their attack to be unopposed.

David Milne-Smith and Nobby Grey strapped in next to each other in the two-seat cockpit. They'd agreed that first time out DMS would fly while Grey recorded it on the cine camera, then they'd swap places for the second sortie. Always a fan of anyone willing to display a little flare, Bill Stoker gave their plan the nod. The Squadron Boss was also taking a second pilot, Russ Peart, in his right-hand seat. Sean Creak, Nigel Wilkinson and Taff Hinchcliffe flew solo.

The five jets taxied out to the runway hold in line astern, an unusual sight for a control tower that rarely despatched more than two at a time.

At the threshold of Runway Two Two, with his feet holding the brakes, DMS gently advanced the throttle lever to full power. He checked the rpm, temperatures and pressures. All good. He released the wheel brakes. 3,410lb of thrust poured out of the Viper engine's jet pipe below the tail, blurring the air, pushing the aircraft forward. At 40 knots the rudder started to bite the air.

The fully loaded Strikemasters were a little reluctant to get airborne, but, accelerating through 95 knots, DMS gently raised the nosewheel. At 110 knots the jet flew itself off the runway. Milne-Smith dabbed the brakes and reached forward to press the 'Undercarriage Up' selector. Then he held the aircraft low, gathering speed along the white-painted runway centreline as they flew north towards the Jebel escarpment, before, hitting 180 knots, he raised the nose and reached for the wheel to his left to gently trim the jet into a best-rate climb. He kept the Viper turbojet at full throttle as the little 167 climbed towards cruising height.

It was the perfect day. Deep-blue skies offered seemingly limitless visibility as the formation, a loose balbo of five, cruised to the north-west. Up above 300 knots the sluggishness displayed by the heavy jets on take-off disappeared. But for a gentle rising and falling relative to the other aircraft as each jet responded to the peculiarities of its own particular route through the air, there was barely even a sensation of speed.

Below them the desert displayed infinite variety, from powdery tan, pink, ochre and grey to stationary waves of rock rolling out of the sand and jagged ridges appearing like the spine of an animal broaching the surface of a lake. There were echoes of rivers and ghosts of surface water and camel trails crossing the ground like veins on a leaf. It all stretched to an indistinct horizon where only haze marked the point where the land met the sky. From the air there was some sense of the processes that formed the landscape.

Newcomers to SOAF found it difficult to navigate using such unfamiliar landmarks, but each was, in its own way, as distinctive as the features that confirmed a pilot's position in Northern Europe. It just took adjustment.

Fifteen miles out from Habrut, Bill Stoker made contact with the Desert Regiment, now occupying the ridge behind the abandoned Omani fort. The plan was simple: rather than try to mount a section attack, which was not a tactic SOAF had previously had any cause to master, Stoker decided that the five Strikemasters would attack as a singleton and in two pairs, while those jets not directly involved in the attack circled in a racetrack in Omani airspace at a height of 5,000 feet.

The Yemeni fort itself was only the focus of a target area that ran 2,500 yards north to south and 1,000 yards east and west. Adoo positions were peppered throughout but concentrated in the north-west of the box. The Squadron Boss went in first.

At 1350 hours local time, Stoker reached past the control column to the instrument panel and flicked the armament master switch from SAFE to ARMED and switched on the two FN gas-operated machine guns. Then he crossed the border and rolled into a 25 degree dive against one of the Adoo machine-gun positions.

The Strikeys normally pulled out of a dive attack at 2,300 feet, but Stoker had briefed the squadron to go lower, attacking from between 1,500 and 2,000 feet to give a greater degree of accuracy. It was less of an issue with the straight-shooting SURA rockets, but the Strikemasters' ability to put a bomb on target was a problem. Without smart bombs, or laser guidance or even the most rudimentary bomb-aiming computer carried by more sophisticated attack jets, they were relying on fixed depression sights and their own eyes. It was Second World War technology.

As he dived, Stoker kept the stick forward, careful not to let the rising airspeed raise the nose and throw his aim, and he waited for the pipper on the reflector glass in the gunsight to move over the target. He kept his index finger clawed tight on the trigger on the handgrip of the control stick, providing his own covering fire with a hail of 7.62mm rounds. Then he pressed the pickle button to release the bombs and pulled back hard on the stick and thumbed the RT switch on the throttle, as the ailerons clawed into the air over the wings.

'Bombs gone,' he called over the radio as he strained against the mounting G-load. He and Peart were squeezed back into their seats as the nose pitched up through the horizon. Limited to just 3.5G with half a ton of bombs hanging off the wings, Stoker was now free to pull up to 5.5G to get the jet out of harm's way. Because this was the most dangerous time. No longer protected by their own gunfire and presenting the whole plan form of the aircraft to the ground, over half the hits taken by the SOAF Strike Squadron came as they pulled out of the dive in search of safer sky. As he climbed he felt a dink as something seemed to hit the jet. But there were no warning lights. His instruments indicated all was as it should be. No problem with the flight controls. He opted to go round again and ripple off the rockets. As he hauled the little 167 round in a tight banking turn, he adjusted the depression angle of the gunsight. There was no shortage of targets to choose from. And he wondered just how much of an impact his five Strikemasters were going to be able to make. He armed the four SURA rocket pylons. What was down there, he thought ruefully, *was suitable for the whole RAF . . .*

As he came round again, the ground-fire seemed to be finding its range. And there was no way any jet could do more than protect itself from a single machine-gun position. Diving in to take out one he unavoidably exposed himself to the others. There was also an unexpected threat in evidence. The Adoo had chosen to bring a new weapon to the battle: a twin-Shpagin 12.7mm heavy machine gun modified as an anti-aircraft gun.

Uncomfortably accurate, he thought. Sooner or later one of his pilots was going to get tagged by it.

'Two and Three, you're in,' Stoker said over the radio after he emptied his wings and pulled out for the last time, 'we're going east.'

Then DMS, Sean Creak, Taff Hinchcliffe and Nigel Wilkinson had their turn.

Of the planned five-ship second wave, a pair of jets were diverted en route to other tasks, leaving just three Strikemasters to return to Habrut. And while their aircraft were being refuelled and rearmed back at Salalah, Bill Stoker had made it clear to his pilots that more of the same was not enough. Stoker had been given the clear message that the Sultan wanted 1 Squadron to bring down the walls of the fort:

visible, undeniable damage. That meant that putting an accurate salvo of SURA rockets with their little 2lb warheads through the straw roof wasn't going to cut it. One of them needed to score a direct hit with a 540lb high-explosive iron bomb. With three jets they had just six bombs between them. And by the time Spoon Wilkinson tipped into his 25 degree dive after Bill Stoker and Nobby Grey and DMS, again sharing the cockpit, four had already missed. Two lights on the instrument panel blinked on as Wilkinson switched the two outboard pylons to bombs and dived down the chute towards the target. As he passed through 2,000 feet, with the gunsight pipper on the fort, he pickled his bombs. The jet bucked as one of the ejector release units fired to release a bomb. Then, without warning, the Strikemaster dropped a wing, rolling hard to one side. Instinctively, Wilkinson countered with the control column, pulling the stick to the side to level the wings. He had a hang-up: only one of his two bombs had separated. Now, with one wing heavy, the Strikemaster was out of trim. As he rolled out over the top, he looked down through the canopy glass to see the dust plume from his bomb. And then, over the RT, came confirmation that his first had failed to hit the fort.

Wilkinson still had one more option: the Pylon Stores Jettison button. Designed to release the underwing stores in an emergency, it was protected beneath a hinged black-and-yellow guard just beneath the coaming. Throwing off the remaining bomb using this override meant Wilkinson would be doing little more than saying to himself: 'That looks about right,' but there was no point in not giving it a go. It proved to be worth his while too. And with the last bomb of the day, Wilkinson, diving in an unstable, asymmetric jet, managed to do what had eluded them all before and put his bomb right into the side of the fort. Exploding in a dense, superheated cloud of rock and shrapnel, throwing dust high into the air, the deep stone wall of the Yemeni fort came tumbling down.

As well as the destruction of the fort wall, reports filtered back to Salalah that one of eight Adoo killed inside the fort had been the Commander of the Ho Chi Minh unit who had instigated the cross-border attack against Oman. The rugged little Strikemaster had shown again that it could be a frustrating compromise. It was unfussy, willing and tough. Day to day it was perfect for the war in Dhofar. But for anything beyond its vital role as a sort of airborne artillery, it was hugely limited. With the attacks on Habrut and the positions around it, 1 Squadron had enjoyed mixed results. There had been some success, but they had failed to completely suppress the mortar assault on the Omani fort. The Squadron Boss was sure that the Adoo had evolved a successful system for dealing with air attacks that meant similar efforts from his men would have diminishing effects.

And, as a final insult, it was Stoker who, during the second wave of attacks, took a hit from the twin-Shpagin machine gun. But after getting fragged by a ricochet during the first raid he was fortunate again to come through without serious damage. The big 12.7mm bullet missed anything vital. This time.

When the Reuters bulletin reported that SOAF had bombed positions inside Yemen, the Foreign Secretary's first thought was of who, exactly, had flown the mission. Sir Alec Douglas-Home signalled Donald Hawley, the British Ambassador in Muscat:

GRATEFUL FOR . . . CONFIRMATION THAT NO BRITISH LOANED OFFICERS INVOLVED

Sir Alec requested a reply by FLASH telegram. But while the Ambassador tried to gather details about the SOAF raids, the Foreign Office was already hedging its bets and hoping for the best.

'We have no reason to believe,' an FCO spokesman said, 'that seconded personnel would be involved.' As British newspapers picked up on reports from the wires, Sir Alec signalled Hawley again. His tone was a little more urgent:

WE ARE ANXIOUS TO RECEIVE EARLY POSITIVE
CONFIRMATION THAT NO BRITISH SECONDED
PERSONNEL WERE USED IN THESE AIR STRIKES

The answer he received was not the one he'd hoped for. Of the eight pilots involved in both raids, only Sean Creak, since leaving the RAF the previous summer, was a contract officer. Otherwise, the raids against targets in South Yemen had been flown exclusively by serving members of the Royal Air Force.

Unlike the arrangements made with other states like Saudi Arabia or the United Arab Emirates using seconded British personnel, there were formal territorial restrictions on the use of those in Oman, only a recent exchange of letters agreeing that there would be consultation. The news in London became more alarming still when Hawley signalled to warn the FCO that Sultan Qaboos had decided to order a retaliatory attack against Hawf, the South Yemeni town close to the Omani border long used by the Adoo as a safe haven and HQ.

John Graham and the Sultan's Defence Secretary asked Hawley to a meeting in Bait al Falaj fort to explain Oman's position. The bottom line, they told him, was that the incident at Habrut and the resulting diversion of resources meant that it would no longer be possible to hold Simba position through the monsoon. To the Sultan's dismay, SAF would have no option but to mount a humiliating withdrawal. The only way to prevent the situation becoming politically corrosive and maintain a modicum of respect was to take the fight back to the Adoo. And the only effective means SAF had of doing that in the short term was to launch a strike against Hawf.

The truth was that the British Ambassador had a good deal of sympathy for the Omani position. He urged London to do more than simply urge restraint. He and his Defence Attaché believed what was needed was the blocking position running along the Sarfait escarpment to the sea that Phase 2 of Operation SIMBA was designed to achieve. But even taking Capstan, a prerequisite for achieving this, had so far been beyond SAF's capabilities. With the diversion at Habrut it was now likely to remain so.

'Could we consider some further help to the Sultanate to enable them to establish this position,' he asked London, 'or some other form of military assistance – as a quid pro quo for calling the Hawf venture off?'

But the Foreign Office was unimpressed. 'The Sultan,' complained one FCO official in an internal memo, 'has much of his father's stubbornness.' The Foreign Secretary was more emollient, but to no great end.

'We sympathize,' offered Sir Alec, promising to do what he could to speed up the delivery of two more Skyvans from the Shorts factory in Belfast. And he asked the Prime Minister, Edward Heath, to put his name to a personal message, to be hand-delivered by Hawley to the Sultan in person.

'We shall continue to do whatever possible to support you in your efforts to bring peace and stability throughout the Sultanate,' explained Heath's letter. 'It is because of my concern for Oman's interests that I have felt bound to ask you to consider the very real dangers which I believe would arise.'

In drafting the letter, the possibility of threatening to withdraw all seconded personnel from Oman was considered, but decided against. Instead, the MoD produced a new Directive to be read and initialled by all British officers appointed to the post of Commander, Sultan's Armed Forces.

And, in Muscat, Hawley received a copy of the Prime Minister's letter to Qaboos, which, he feared, *would not be very well received*.

Chapter 22

May 1972

For now, pilots seconded from the RAF were still crossing the border. There were further strikes against Adoo targets on the 7th, 8th and 10th. And while the Desert Regiment company flown in to reinforce the SAF position at Habrut were able to report that an attack with ten SURA rockets and a pair of 540lb bombs had succeeded in knocking out one of the twin-Shpagin anti-aircraft guns, 1 Squadron – as Bill Stoker had realized on day one – had been unable to bring an end to the firing from inside Yemen. When one Strikemaster pilot returned to Salalah reporting a sighting of a Toyota pick-up truck with a recoil-less field gun mounted in the back, the decision was taken to pull SAF forces out of Habrut. At 10.15 on the 11th, while Bill Stoker, David Milne-Smith and Nobby Grey flew overhead in frustration providing Top Cover, the helicopters flew in beneath them.

Three days earlier, after days of bombardment from the Adoo, the small Desert Regiment contingent at Akoot had also been withdrawn. Simba was now SAF's only position to the west of Dhofar.

Within the concrete and glass of the United Nations headquarters in New York, the South Yemen Representative to the UN lodged a complaint with the Secretary General, Kurt Waldheim. It rather overstated things.

'A British aircraft carrier violated our territorial waters in an act of provocation which was followed by a landing operation of mercenary forces. The carrier was used as a base for fighter aircraft to hit our positions . . . British aircraft used incendiary bombs resulting in the burning of farms and palm trees at Wadi Habrut. At the same time, British helicopters landed followers of Agent Sultan Qaboos of Oman and other mercenaries in the Habrut area in an attempt to besiege the post and occupy it. However, our forces gallantly repelled the invaders.' It continued in a similar vein, concluding that 'preparations for a large-scale invasion of our country appear to be progressing'.

Alec Douglas-Home was unimpressed, pointing out that HMS *Ark Royal*, the Navy's only aircraft carrier, was in refit in Devonport Dockyard. And in any case, the Foreign Secretary asked, 'If a British aircraft carrier had bombarded PDRY would they really have waited almost four weeks before protesting?'

Sultan Qaboos again summoned John Graham to see him. He was furious. While the British had been dismissive of the statement from South Yemen, Qaboos was extremely angry that, with his country now a fully signed-up member of the UN, the inexperienced Omani delegation in New York had failed to make any attempt to counter his neighbour's claims. Graham had every sympathy for the Sultan's dismay. The diplomatic exchange had so far been very one-sided.

The hoo-ha at the UN, the Brigadier thought, *where the wretched Omani delegation has hardly unpacked, is staggering.* And yet, despite its exaggerations, the Yemeni statement was the only version of events that existed. It was inevitable that, initially at least, opinion began to accept South Yemen as a victim. Qaboos asked the Commander of his Armed Forces to draft a response that redressed the balance. Graham was only too happy to. Because in doing so he had a chance to further stir up the hornets' nest.

And it served to highlight two completely different agendas.

John Graham and the British Foreign Office may both have wanted Oman to defeat the insurgency, but from that point their view diverged. The British were desperate to avoid anything too pungent. Graham, on the other hand, had reached the conclusion that only by stirring up as much trouble as possible would he have any chance of changing the game in Dhofar. He had wanted the world to notice. Now he'd been given a loudhailer.

When South Yemen's UN Statement had argued: 'It is not accidental that the British Colonial Forces and their lackeys are attacking the People's Democratic Republic of Yemen at a time when American Imperialism is desperately escalating its war of aggression against the heroic people of Viet-nam,' the head of the British mission in New York had noted drily that 'some of the language has a curiously Chinese flavour about it'.

When Graham returned to SAF HQ and began to dictate the Omani statement to his typists, Sergeants Davis and Page, he very much hoped that the Chinese were listening. His words, delivered to the Sultan in English before being translated into Arabic, were unvarnished.

'The PDRY Government,' Graham charged, 'provides the necessary facilities on its territory for PFLOAG to receive weapons and warlike stores from foreign countries, mainly China.'

When, as the diplomatic war of words escalated, the Omani mission to the UN pointed out that China's official news agency had openly reported the Chinese government's support for the Adoo, and in doing so acknowledged that China had 'interfered in the internal affairs of another state member and . . . actively supported sedition and aggression directed against another state', a surprised Yemeni mission asked: 'Does this mean that Qaboos wants to wage war with them, too?'

'The Chinese,' reflected the UK mission after reading the Omani assertion that China had broken both the letter and the spirit of the UN Charter, 'do not normally take this kind of thing lying down.'

Graham's words had started a dangerous game, the repercussions of which were uncertain. But, he had concluded, he could not win the war without outside help. SAF and the Adoo were at a stalemate. And he was banking that whatever reaction he provoked from China or any other antagonist,

Oman would not be allowed to fall. Greater, more direct support for the Adoo might prompt Oman's supporters to do more than promise moral support, send the odd shipment of SURA rockets or arrange for early delivery of a couple of transport aircraft.

Oman's position just had to get perilous enough.

The British response to that was contained in a SECRET – UK EYES ONLY document describing Operation ROBIN. Its purpose was very clear:

```
Should the security situation in Oman
deteriorate seriously, it might be
necessary to give the Sultan open military
support with forces based in the UK. This
plan, Joint Theatre Plan (East) Number 20,
covers the provision for this support.
```

If there were any existential threat to Oman, the MoD was prepared to use a fleet of over thirty transport aircraft to fly in a full infantry battalion, Royal Engineers, Army Air Corps helicopters, armoured cars, artillery and up to eight battlefield support helicopters. A pair of Royal Navy warships would patrol the coast.

For now, though, embarrassed by the involvement of RAF pilots in the raids on Habrut and nervous at the prospect of an attack on Hawf, the Foreign Office simply asked Donald Hawley to remind the Sultan and the SAF Commander that there were conditions attached to the use of British personnel seconded to Oman's Armed Forces. It was the last thing they needed to hear.

Neville Baker was struggling. Keeping Simba position resupplied was proving to be a critical drain on helicopter hours. It had also cost him one of his precious Hueys when the terrible twins, Royal Marines Dave Duncan and Steve Watson, had crashed on their return from Akoot. Baker was having to say no to BATT taskings. It wasn't quite as bad as it was a year ago when he'd had to contend with just two serviceable helis, three pilots resigning and two medevaced out, but it couldn't carry on like this indefinitely.

From the outset, he'd known that Simba had the capacity to do this to him, but he'd been promised that the retention of the position was contingent on the discovery of a water source. Within the first week. But there was no sign of it yet, and no sign of abandoning Simba as a result. In making the gravity of 3 Squadron's situation clear he had an ally in CSOAF, Wing Commander Curly Hirst.

Nigel Knocker had produced thirty-six copies of the Op Order document for Operation SIMBA. Beyond those for the Desert Regiment, three were for SAF HQ, three for HQ Dhofar, three for the Navy, one for the file and three spare. While he'd made sure SOAF had copies down in Salalah, he failed to specify a copy for the SOAF HQ at Bait al Falaj in the north. As a result, Hirst had been presented with a *fait accompli*, one which was now driving his little air force into the ground. In making his feelings felt, Hirst had had a stand-up row with Knocker when he'd first visited Simba. But it did nothing to solve the problem – now exacerbated by the number of Skyvans closing in on the moment they'd need to leave Salalah for a major hangar service up at Bait al Falaj.

With the monsoon imminent, White City was the only position that Hirst felt absolutely confident he could keep supplied. The restrictions on flying hours though meant that SAF had no choice but to run the gauntlet on the ground. And, in doing so, Captain Hugh Jones was killed.

Every two weeks, a convoy known as the Taqa Road Opening left Salalah to resupply SAF outposts to the east, including the BATT in Taqa, Mirbat and, beyond them, Sudh. SAF took care to reduce the threat from mines by using a heavy roller attached to an armoured car to clear the road to the harbour at Raysut, twenty miles to the west, and were equipped with British Mk 4 mine detectors, but the route to the west was impossible to make safe. A report by the Mine Warfare Branch of the Royal Armament and Research Development Establishment discounted almost entirely 'the chance of visually detecting a "mine-sized" disturbance'. So instead, as the fleet of three-ton Bedford trucks and Land Rover escorts drove east, they fanned out, each vehicle avoiding existing tyre-tracks in the soft sand of the coastal plain. Ahead of them Land Rovers were armed with powerful .50 Browning HMGs in an effort to ensure chokepoints were clear of potential ambushes.

When the Soviet TM46 anti-tank mine detonated underneath the Bedford, Hugh Jones was blown out of the three-tonner's cab, landing on rocks yards from the truck and suffering a depressed skull fracture. Unconscious as his comrades bound his injury with field dressings, he was flown out by helicopter – the casevac alert, at least, was something 3 Squadron never dropped however restricted flying hours became – to the FST, but the trauma to his head was too serious. Although the surgeons performed a craniotomy, opening his skull to relieve the crushing pressure from the sub-cranial oedema, the damage they discovered to the thirty-year-old officer's brain was severe. Jones never recovered consciousness.

After running into the brick wall of Operation JAGUAR, the Adoo's appetite for tackling SAF in force in the east had diminished. At a point where it had seemed they were on the verge of being strong enough to fight more conventional infantry battles, they were now once more operating in small patrols, mounting long-range stand-off attacks with mortars and RCLs, as well as ambushes, and laying mines: classic guerrilla warfare. But the change in Adoo tactics was greeted with regret by many fighting for the Sultan. When the enemy attacked *en masse*, they just presented a bigger target.

There had been an open invitation to the Adoo to return to Mirbat since spring of 1971, when they'd attacked the town with mortars. On that occasion they had probably expected to launch more than three 60mm rounds, but accurate return fire from the BATT Civil Action Team's GPMG against the mortar baseplate came quickly. Followed by bombs from the Regiment's own 81mm mortar, the Adoo withdrew.

Firqa guerrillas on the Jebel during Operation JAGUAR.

A rare picture of Trooper Sekonaia Takavesi taken towards the end of B Squadron's Operation JAGUAR deployment.

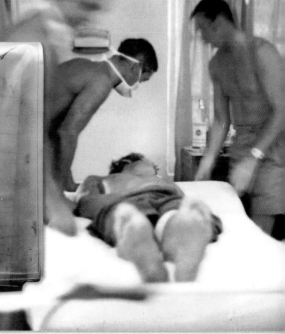

Shaun Brogan's map. It was in his pocket when he led an assault on the Adoo unit that had ambushed them. The bullet that hit him in the leg passed right through the map. His blood can still be seen to the left of the bullet hole.

On the operating table. Brogan's wound was treated in the Salalah field hospital. Note the medicinal bottle of whisky on the side. After coming round from the anaesthetic, Brogan was carried to the Officers' Mess on the stretcher and propped up so he could join in with the revelry.

Lieutenant Colonel Nigel Knocker with Neville Baker at Akoot prior to launching Operation SIMBA to take the high ground dominating Sarfait near the Yemen border.

Under canvas, Neville Baker pins up a map of the operational area prior to briefing his pilots for Operation SIMBA.

Unseasonal heavy thunder storms threatened to scupper the SIMBA operation. Unperturbed by the resultant flooding, Neville Baker gets on with things.

Short Skyvan from an escorting Strikemaster. Two days after being helicoptered in, Nigel Knocker's Desert Regiment opened the airstrip at Sarfait that allowed fixed-wing transport to come in. Strikemasters provided Top Cover for all aircraft movements in and out of Simba position.

A DeHavilland Caribou takes off from Salalah. As well as the Skyvans, 2 Squadron SOAF also had a small fleet of these larger short take-off and landing transports. Although effective, they were also unreliable.

All food, ammunition and water had to be flown into Simba position. The need to fly in water, particularly, placed an almost overwhelming burden on the SOAF helicopter squadron.

Capstan, the codename given to the shark-tooth-shaped feature, left, below the Sarfait escarpment at the right of the picture. SAF control of Capstan was necessary in order to interdict Adoo supply routes along the coastal plain.

Into Capstan. After a rumoured source of water at Capstan could not be found, it too had to be resupplied by helicopter – a job that almost got Nick Holbrook shot down.

Attack run. Repeated efforts by the 1 Squadron Strikemasters to take out the Adoo heavy-machine-gun position that dominated Capstan were unsuccessful.

Runway building SAS-style. In order to relieve the helicopter squadron Shaun Brogan decided to build a runway at Tawi Atair, his position in the Eastern sector. His troop used high explosive to decapitate buried boulders.

Take-off from Tawi Atair. Because of the slope, aircraft would land uphill to aid braking and take off downhill to speed their acceleration.

Browning .50 machine gun. A consignment of these heavy-calibre machine guns was distributed to SAS positions at Tawi Atair, White City and Mirbat. Their destructive power leant weight to Brogan's reports to HQ that any Adoo on his position were met with 'massive retaliation'.

Shaun Brogan prior to joining David Milne-Smith for a dusk rocket strike against Adoo positions near Tawi Atair.

Squadron Leader Bill Stoker. The Strikemaster squadron's new Boss joined the unit in January 1972 and quickly established a reputation for leading from the front.

1 Squadron pilots; from left: Bill Stoker, Taff Hinchcliffe, David Milne-Smith (crouching), Nobby Grey and Sean Creak, prior to launching SOAF's first cross-border strikes against Habrut fort in South Yemen.

Walking out to the jets before the raid against Habrut. The mission would see serving RAF officers bombing a sovereign country without London's prior knowledge.

Pre-flight inspection.

Nobby Grey runs through his cockpit checks.

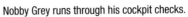

Heavily armed Strikemasters climb away from RAF Salalah.

The five bombed-up Strikeys flew in a loose balbo towards the target at Habrut on the border with South Yemen.

Strikemasters launched high-explosive and armour-piercing 80mm SURA rockets in a 20 degree dive.

The target. As well as the fort itself, Bill Stoker's pilots also attacked dispersed gun positions that surrounded it.

By spring 1972, nearly two years after deposing his father, Sultan Qaboos had grown into the role of ruler, displaying increasing confidence at home and abroad. He was certain that SOAF attacks against South Yemen would not damage Oman in the eyes of other Arab countries.

Armourers load a 540lb bomb on to the pylon of a Strikemaster. The yellow band around the nose indicates that it's live.

'Maximum destruction' was the order given by the Sultan. The cross-border attacks against the South Yemeni town of Hawf were the biggest operations yet mounted by SOAF. Serving RAF officers were banned from taking part by Whitehall – much to the frustration of the Squadron Boss, Bill Stoker.

Throughout the combined Strikemaster and artillery attacks, Nick Holbrook hovered above Hawf in a little AB206 helicopter acting as AOP (Airborne Observation Post) directing the SAF artillery barrage from Simba.

Stickers produced by the 1 Squadron pilots.

I SQN. SOAF(TAC) BY APPOINTMENT PEST EXTERMINATORS FOR THE SULTAN ALSO SLUM DEMOLITION SPECIALISTS IN DHOFAR

Beyond the wingtip of Sean Creak's Strikemaster, smoke rises from targets hit by the attacking SOAF jets.

In their haste, they left behind a camel, their mortar sight, a cup with its owner's name painted on the side and a small red notebook containing more names. Over Radio Dhofar, the men of the Firqa Salahadin gleefully invited the named Adoo to return to Mirbat to pick up their belongings whenever it was convenient. The FSD had since been moved out of Mirbat to avoid what the BATT Squadron Commander had described as an 'Aldershot situation' developing: the trouble caused by the Firqa, Dhofar Gendarmerie and the Wali's Askar guards, all chasing the same local women. For an army officer, there really was nothing new under the sun. Running the Firqa was just a variation on a theme.

In Mirbat over a year later, Sekonaia Takavesi, who as Eight Troop's Arabic-speaker had responsibility for the local Firqa al Umri, or FAU, didn't have to deal with the same problem.

After internal disagreements in 1971 led to a split that reduced the numbers of the FSD from one hundred to thirty, idealistic attempts at raising pan-tribal Firqas were abandoned. Now each was drawn from a single tribe and operated within that tribe's territory. That tempered the men's interest in the local talent. But it also meant that, now always operating in defence of what was theirs, the Firqas were committed and courageous; the effective counter-revolutionary force that Johnny Watts had first imagined. But much was still dependent on how the Firqas were led; that meant the strength of the relationship between the Firqa Commander and the BATT.

There was a big difference, one Squadron Boss had said, between 'go on and come on'. And Tak wasted no opportunity to go out on patrol with the FAU, under their commander, Bahait. The Fijian Trooper liked the impressive 25-year-old tribesman. At 6 feet 2 inches in his plimsolls, a sarong-like cloth called a *futta* around his waist matched with an army shirt and an AK47 in his hand, the handsome young Dhofari had the bearing of a leader. More importantly, the SAS man knew that he could trust Bahait with his life – the Firqa leader would have shared his last drop of water. That was how it worked in Oman; personal relationships were the key to it all.

As he did with the Firqa and the Wali and his Askars, Tak also befriended the small platoon of Dhofar Gendarmerie who'd only recently arrived in Mirbat after being withdrawn from Habrut. Following the trauma of the Adoo attacks on their previous home, it was felt that a spell garrisoning the fort in Mirbat would give the shell-shocked guards a chance to settle their nerves. It certainly seemed likely. The Adoo felt far away. Although the Jebel north of Mirbat was spectacular, an imposing escarpment rising from 4,500 to nearly 6,000 feet as it climbed to the west, it was also distant, separated from the town by six or seven miles of open ground and the Jebel Ali, a 300ft hill a mile ahead of them. On top of that, the DG maintained a small picquet, a tripwire for any trouble threatening the town. On most days in Mirbat, the loudest noise was the sound of the seagulls cawing as they circled above the fishing dhows.

But Tak was a cautious man by nature, a worrier who wanted everything as it should be. If he got a thought in his head it nagged away at him until he'd dealt with it. And so, since arriving in Mirbat, Tak had been building up the BATT House's defences, piling heavy sandbags one on top of the other around the GPMG sangar on the roof. Like Noah building the Ark, Tak built a structure so substantial it took him over two weeks, working alone, to build; and so apparently over-the-top that the rest of Eight Troop enjoyed great sport taking the piss.

'One day you'll be grateful,' he told them quietly in his slow, sonorous voice, never once letting them put him off his stride, 'it'll save your life, eh?'

They were more grateful for the fish curries. Singlehandedly, he'd built sandbag walls several feet thick that he knew would stop a heavy-machine-gun round, and all he got was abuse for it.

Chapter 23

May 1972

So far the Sultan had listened to those who'd urged restraint. As he'd weighed the pros and cons of an attack on Hawf he'd been encouraged by support from Arab neighbours although none – including Saudi Arabia, who he'd been hopeful might contribute directly with their powerful Air Force of Hunters and Lightnings – were prepared to offer more than words. And yet Qaboos's courting of potential allies was a key point of difference with the British. He had been assiduous in keeping them informed through both cables and diplomatic missions to the capitals. He was confident that support for Oman was far more widespread than was being broadcast publicly – or shared with the British, who were convinced that by retaliating Qaboos would alienate potential Arab supporters. And so it had been *tempting* to act, but as time since the Habrut attacks elapsed, it became harder with each passing day for him to order SAF to mount operations against Hawf in direct retaliation. And Qaboos now regretted that conversations with Hugh Oldman and Donald Hawley had dissuaded him from acting earlier.

Hawley, who each time he had visited the Sultan had carried with him the Prime Minister's letter to Qaboos in his jacket pocket, felt the need to present it had passed. Although, he reported back to London, the Sultan was 'still rather hankering after doing the operation', the

Ambassador believed that the crisis had been averted.

'I am not as steamed up as I was a few days ago,' Qaboos confessed to Hawley. He told the Ambassador that he had been persuaded. 'You can rest assured that the operation will not take place.'

After receiving the news from Muscat, Alec Douglas-Home telegraphed Hawley with just two words in reply: 'Well done.'

It was to prove a very short-lived diplomatic triumph.

After an absence of eleven days, on 22 May, SAF returned to Habrut to restore the Sultanate's presence in the area. After being helicoptered in, C Company, Northern Frontier Regiment, established positions on high ground overlooking the wadi. Their arrival was unopposed by the Adoo, but this turned out to be no good omen. In 120°F heat, the Company Commander led a patrol down from the ridge to the Omani fort. While SAF had been gone it had been reduced to ruins by the Adoo using carefully placed explosive charges.

Sultan Qaboos summoned John Graham to the palace in Muscat. It seemed unlikely that both men might be hoping for the same outcome from their conversation. As they spoke they cut very different figures: Graham, the athletic, stiff-backed scion of an old military family in his pale, tailored khaki drill uniform, brass buttons, medal ribbons and parachute wings; and, still just thirty years old, the doe-eyed, fine-featured young monarch. With his black beard and flowing Arabic robe, Qaboos could have an almost mystical appearance; his gentle manner and composure only reinforced the air of serenity around him. But for all his civility there was no mis-taking his anger now. The destruction of the fort at Habrut was the final straw. There was a limit to how much provo-cation he was prepared to take. He'd become convinced that doing nothing was no longer an option. And with Hugh Oldman, his Defence Secretary, now out of the country, he wanted to pin Graham down.

'This question of Hawf,' the Sultan enquired of his senior military commander, 'I've been told by so many people that it's beyond our capability; that it will cause no end of trouble. I want to know your opinion.' Over the preceding week, Graham, like the Sultan, had thought hard about the wisdom of a retaliatory strike. And his conclusions were much more in tune with Qaboos than with Oldman and the British Ambassador. At the same time, he was careful; the Brigadier didn't simply want to announce that he disagreed with his friend and boss, Oldman. But he did know which side of the fence he wanted the Sultan to come down on.

'Looking at the military factors,' Graham began, 'there is really nothing to be gained by an attack on Hawf and a great deal to lose. They could send their Air Force and could cause a lot of destruction against RAF Salalah and who knows what else.' He paused before continuing. 'But, in these matters, the political factors nearly always outweigh the military and no one is better able than you to weigh up the consequences on the political side.'

'I quite understand,' Qaboos said.

'Well, Your Majesty,' Graham added, 'all I can say is that if you decided to retaliate against Hawf, I, the Army, the Air Force and most of your people would, I think, be delighted . . .'

The Sultan nodded, before telling his commander that he was 'resolved on Hawf'. Graham, buoyed that Qaboos had been sufficiently bold to take the riskier decision, controlled his reaction.

'Would you like,' he asked, 'a token or a maximum-destruction attack?'

'Maximum destruction.'

Graham drove into Muscat that evening to talk to Donald Hawley at the British Embassy. Behind brass-studded gates, the British mission looked out to sea over a natural harbour flanked by cliffs on which visiting sailors had painted their ships' names in white. At the top of the cliffs were two forts; on the left, Fort Merani, built by the Portuguese, towered high above the Embassy, and further away, to the right, was Fort

Jelali, still used as a prison. In the early evening, the clanking of the prisoners' chains as they descended the steep steps to the water to perform their ablutions could be heard by the Ambassador and his staff.

The Sultan had already informed Hawley of his decision, which the Ambassador relayed to London. Privately, he told Graham, he was sympathetic towards it, although worried about the reaction it might provoke both in Parliament and abroad, but none the less he was obliged to share the new Directive for CSAF drawn up by the MoD. Graham read through the two-page document as Hawley sipped at his drink:

```
YOU ARE TO ENSURE NEITHER YOU NOR ANY
BRITISH SECONDED PERSONNEL UNDER YOUR
COMMAND ARE EMPLOYED OUTSIDE OMAN
```

It came as no surprise to Graham, who had already made arrangements to spare London's blushes. He'd asked his Deputy Commander and SAF's most senior contract officer, Colonel Colin Maxwell, to sign six blank sheets of foolscap paper. He would then take these with him to Salalah to dictate the Op Orders for Operation AQOOBA – Punishment – over his 2ic's signature. All thought of a ground assault was now behind them. SAF were going to hit Hawf with successive waves of attacks from the Strikemasters and artillery shells from a battery of 25 pounders at Simba position.

Bill Stoker was fuming. Not only did the order from Muscat exclude him from the most significant operation in his squadron's history, but of the pilots whom he'd led on the raids against Habrut only Sean Creak could be considered for the Hawf. But he had no choice. Responsibility for leading 1 Squadron SOAF(Tac) across the border into South Yemen passed up the chain of command to one of Stoker's predecessors, now head of the whole Omani Air Force operation in Salalah, Peter Hulme. Hulme was no more happy about the situation than

Stoker. The tough little contract officer had managed to mould an outfit in Salalah that drew from every branch of the UK Armed Forces and beyond and made no distinction whatsoever between seconded personnel and those on contracts. That could only be divisive. But he asked Stoker to gather the whole squadron so that he could explain the situation.

David Milne-Smith listened, Hulme's discomfort evident to all in the room. Bill Stoker stood with him, his jaw clamped. DMS had been surprised that RAF pilots had been allowed to go to Habrut, so officialdom finally catching up didn't add to it. Hulme had a well-earned reputation for fearlessness and skill as a pilot – and he knew the Strikemaster inside out having overseen its introduction into SOAF service – but, DMS couldn't help thinking, *he isn't particularly current*. Milne-Smith kept his mouth shut, but they were sending the B-Team, he thought, *not choosing the best pilots*.

But 1 Squadron weren't the only ones involved. A pair of Neville Baker's men had also been given the nod.

Hovering north of Hawf at 0830 hours on 25 May in one of SOAF's little Bell 206 Jetrangers, Nick Holbrook and Dave Duncan waited for Peter Hulme to roll into the first of the dive-bombing attacks. They were very firmly inside South Yemen's airspace. Neither of them carried ID or badges of rank. And as well as the AK47s they usually carried strapped to the back of their crash-resistant seats they had also been issued with Goolie Chits, so named because they offered the hope of saving the bearer's balls in the event of capture by the enemy. In English and Arabic, the typed notes set out the terms and conditions:

```
SAFE CONDUCT PASS
The bearer of this document is a pilot of
the Sultan of Oman's Air Force fighting
the communists in the name of God. This
pilot  is  a  contract  officer  of  the
Sultan's Armed Forces.
```

```
If you assist him in reaching the nearest
SAF unit you will be immediately rewarded
with R2000, and you will be given all
assistance   for   safe   conduct   to   any
location you wish.
R2000 REWARD
IN THE NAME OF GOD AND SULTAN QABOOS
```

While his co-pilot, Duncan, took the controls, Holbrook held a pair of binoculars. For the next five hours, stopping only to refuel, Holbrook's job was to act as AOP – Air Observation Post – an airborne spotter, watching and directing the jet attacks and the Omani Artillery guns. During the briefing the night before Holbrook had studied photographs of the targets along with the jet pilots: the Adoo HQ, a tented training camp halfway up the slope and masked by trees, a motor transport complex and a stores depot. The challenge was to take out the targets without causing collateral damage to the main town or mosque.

Holbrook watched the five Strikeys streak in below him, tiny camouflaged gnats against the impressive drama of the landscape. Bombs first, followed by SURA rockets sketching thin straight white lines of smoke that hung in the air after the jet had hauled off before dissipating on a trace of sea breeze. Thin toadstools of dust rose near vertically in the calm air where the bombs hit. And, all the while, Holbrook felt rather redundant.

They've got their targets, he thought, *if they're missing them there's not much I can do about it. It's because their aim's rotten.*

During the first wave the jets were going for the camp and the MT complex. Holbrook was saving the stores depot, closer to town and demanding the greater accuracy of the artillery, for himself.

Dark smoke and flames began to rise from the transport depot. Beyond beaches fringed with white, the low morning sun twinkled on the surface of the blue sea.

'Last pass,' he heard crackle over his headset as the Strikemaster formation turned back to Salalah to refuel and rearm. The plan was to maintain an unbroken assault on the Adoo. Holbrook pressed the transmit button.

'Hello, One Zero,' he introduced himself, 'this is SOAF chopper.' He passed on the grid reference and line from the guns. As an AOP moving around the sky he had to give them a gun to target line, rather than the Observer to target line a ground spotter would pass on. With permission to fire on the stores complex, Holbrook gave the guns the command to fire. There were practically shells in the air before the jets had returned to Omani airspace. That was the idea anyway.

Holbrook watched through the binoculars, frustrated to see the shot land short of the stores building. The line was accurate though. Holbrook gave the artillery crews a correction, adding twenty-five yards to their range – the smallest correction possible – and gave the command to fire again. This time the explosions, eerily silent from the air, puffed beyond the building. He took twenty-five yards off again and tried giving it five rounds, hopeful that a spread of shells would mean one of them would hit the target. But to no avail. Each shell appeared to be landing exactly where it was supposed to. It was uncanny.

I've never seen a gun shoot so accurately, he thought. Then, over the RT, the jets announced their return.

For the rest of the morning, the guns and the jets passed the baton between them. But then, halfway through the morning, Holbrook hit bingo fuel and swooped back into Oman to refuel. Back on the ground he finally got to the bottom of what was going on with the guns when he checked in with the Artillery Command Post. On hearing that this was a destruction shoot, senior British officers seconded to the Omani Artillery, keen not to miss out, had elbowed their way up to Simba. When Donald Hawley had asked London for clarification on whether or not seconded officers – particularly the artillery – might act in an advisory capacity, Sir Alec

Douglas-Home had, after discussing it with the MoD, given his approval. That advice was now being stretched to breaking point. As far as Holbrook was aware, gunners seconded from the Royal Artillery were doing the job themselves: taking every bit out of the backlash, constant ram, everything double-checked. And they were good; putting the shells on the same spot over and over again.

It wasn't the first time that British soldiers, faced with Hawf's use as a base for operations against Oman, had tried to stick a finger in it.

Both Tak and Laba had been part of the SAS snatch squad that went into Hawf in 1966 during Operation FATE. While Bill Stoker's old Hunter squadron flew Top Cover overhead, soldiers from the 1st Battalion Irish Guards were flown in at first light aboard Wessex helicopters from the Navy's newest assault ship, HMS *Fearless*. After the infantrymen had established a cordon around the town, the Regiment went ashore in Gemini dinghies. As dawn broke the heavily armed SAS squad slipped through the perimeter into the town. Working from house to house, they arrested any rebels fingered by an Arab informer who went into Hawf alongside them. Twenty-two Adoo were later delivered by the British to SAF at RAF Salalah. But it was no more than a last sticking plaster while Hawf remained, as part of Aden Protectorate, a British responsibility. Since then, the border town had continued to be a thorn in the side of the Sultanate. Now, more than ever.

When Holbrook returned to the skies over Hawf, he put the binoculars to his eyes again. Smoke appeared to be pouring from the stores depot he'd been targeting.

But I didn't hit the bloody thing, he thought. The 25-pounder shells had been so accurate, though, that, falling each time into the same hole, they'd penetrated deep into an underground store, causing a fire that spread throughout the facility. Then Holbrook picked up smaller puffs of smoke from the 4,000ft-high ridgeline behind Hawf. *Putt, putt, putt*; the tell-tale spoor of a heavy anti-aircraft cannon. Holbrook and Duncan's Jetranger was the only thing in the sky.

You cheeky buggers. Departing from the list of pre-planned targets, Holbrook passed new grid coordinates to his gunners and fragged the Adoo guncrew with airburst shells. As they ran down the cliff the AOP brought high-explosive rounds down on the Triple 'A' position to put it out of action for good. That was one of the dangerous ZU-23 cannons removed, but there were others.

SOAF Strikemasters had dropped twenty-five iron bombs and fired 180 SURA rockets. Of the latter, Sean Creak had been responsible for firing nearly half of the day's total. For each sortie, the Airwork armourers mixed and matched the warloads carried by 1 Squadron. Creak had flown two carrying rockets alone; others carried a full bombload of four 540 pounders. It didn't seem much compared to the heavy payloads carried by bigger, dedicated attack jets, but it was hardly insignificant. Each of the little Strikemaster bomb trucks was delivering a similar haul to that carried by early models of the B-17 Flying Fortress, Boeing's legendary Second World War heavy bomber. The trouble was that the *accuracy* of the bombing was comparable too. Despite the weight of ordnance expended against Hawf, Creak was disappointed. Eight of the twenty-five bombs had gone into the sea. If he was honest with himself, he didn't think that they'd made a terribly good job of it.

An early assessment of the outcome of the raids was sent from SOAF(Tac) HQ, recorded on an RAF signal pad in the radio room at Bait al Falaj and given to Curly Hirst. Reports suggested that the results of the day's attacks had been 'satisfactory', but that the main Adoo headquarters building had escaped any serious damage. Curly Hirst wanted his attack jets to go back in.

Late on the evening of the first day the Commander of the Air Force told Graham: 'I want to complete properly the job we've started.' Graham was tired after the tension of following the progress of the day's operations against

Hawf. Without proper consideration, he approved Hirst's request, but he soon had a nagging feeling that it had been a mistake.

Chapter 24

26 May 1972

The previous day, Peter Hulme had been lucky. During the raids on Hawf his Strikemaster had been hit four times by the Adoo anti-aircraft fire without sustaining serious damage. Now, at 0930 the next day, he was back overhead South Yemen.

On a successful first pass, Hulme dropped his two 540lb bombs. After pulling up and carving round out to sea he then flew down the slide again in a 30 degree dive to empty his wings of sixteen rockets. With his finger on the trigger emptying the machine-gun magazines, he pickled the rockets, his thumb pulsing on the button to fire four salvoes of four in quick succession. His last attack of the day.

He knew as soon as the thump of the rounds hit the airframe that it was bad. Amber warning lights lit up on the instrument panel and the radio went dead. He'd lost the electrics. At least it wasn't the red warning system lighting up and screaming in his ears indicating a fire. Hulme pulled the nose up, to convert his speed to height; that would buy him time. Established in the climb he banked and pulled to bring the nose round to the east – and the direction of friendly territory. If he was going to have to abandon the aircraft, he didn't fancy testing the usefulness of a Goolie Chit in a town he'd spent two days bombing.

The needle on the fuel gauge ahead of him was winding

down – white on black. He was losing fuel. Hulme looked out over the wings to see a thick plume of white streaming from the starboard side. Still climbing, Hulme thought his best option might be to try to eject over Simba position. He'd be overhead in seconds, and he knew Neville Baker was on search and rescue standby. Chances are he'd be picked up quickly.

Then fuel began to spray into the cockpit, spreading a dark stain across his cotton flying suit. And he realized there was no way out of the jet. If there was fuel – and fuel vapour – in the cockpit, then triggering the ejection seat would ignite the fumes and turn the Strikemaster into an airborne fireball. There would be nothing left but falling, smoking wreckage spreading out across Dhofar. Search teams would be unlikely to find much of him.

With fumes in the cockpit he selected 100 per cent oxygen. Alongside him, he saw the reassuring sight of his wingman, ex-Navy pilot Bob Ponter. Ponter stayed on his wing as Hulme continued to climb gently to altitude. The SOAF(Tac) Boss was going to have to try to bring the jet home. Using hand signals, he tried to convey his intentions to Ponter. And he kept flying east towards Salalah.

Hulme cancelled the amber flashers, switched off all non-essential electrics and flew on, waiting for the engine to fail.

When the fuel-starved Viper 535 turbojet cut, Hulme closed the throttle, reached forward to the centre pedestal with a gloved hand to close the HP cock and switched the LP cock to off. He was now at the controls of a very simple flying machine: a two-and-a-half-ton, all-metal glider. Whether he lived or died was now down solely to whether or not he was good enough with the stick and rudder.

Staying on his wing as Hulme lost height, Bob Ponter radioed ahead to warn Salalah Tower that Hulme was inbound. Air Traffic put the fire crews on standby. But they weren't needed. Hulme was up to the job. The stocky little fighter pilot brought the battle-damaged jet in for a perfectly judged dead-stick landing. He'd saved one of SOAF's precious jets, but he'd not been alone in picking up ground-fire.

Following the raids on Hawf there were now four Strikemasters being patched up. Airwork were hopeful of bringing three of them back on line within a week. The last would take a month to sort out.

The Strikeys had got away with it over Hawf. But a few miles to the east, the Adoo's big 12.7mm Shpagin machine guns were about to swing a wrecking ball through SAF's plans. And, most particularly, to those of Nigel Knocker at Simba.

It was nearly 3 a.m. before a combined assault approached Capstan itself. Nearly a month after it had first been planned, Nigel Knocker had finally managed to successfully despatch two companies from the Desert Regiment and Northern Frontier Regiment to seize the all-important feature.

They had set out at dusk, led by the Firqas. Behind, Captain Graeme 'Smash' Smyth-Piggott led half of B Coy, NFR. Despite weeks of recces to establish the route down off the escarpment it had still been extraordinarily hard going. Even as they started climbing out of the gap separating Capstan from the cliff face, it still seemed unlikely that 200 men, carrying their water, food, weaponry and ammunition, had managed to make it down unscathed. They had moved slowly through the dark, led by the Firqas, using ropes and often holding tight the shoulder of the man in front. Now, nearly nine hours later, they were closing on their objective. And Smyth-Piggott was pretty certain they were going to find Adoo when they got there. He was dreading it.

The worse contacts of all, he thought, *are the night contacts; you can't see; you don't know what's going on.*

Yet Smash revelled in soldiering in Oman. On ops he cut a wild-looking figure: tanned, bearded and sporting a shemagh over long, sandy hair; rarely seen without a cigarette and, in the evening, a can of Heineken. His ebullient manner suggested he approached the war like public school with guns but it went hand in hand with a coolness under fire. And when he suddenly saw the Firqa soldier ahead of him drop, he hit the ground. His platoon followed his example.

Smash crawled forward across the rough ground to find out what was going on. Eventually one of the Firqas returned. They'd seen a camel; it wasn't one of theirs, so they'd killed it. The assault force was going to enjoy fresh rations on day one on Capstan. They took the feature without a shot being fired.

Knocker's troops had taken the Adoo by surprise. And the next morning, instead of a dawn chorus of incoming fire from enemy mortars and machine guns, the worst the men on Capstan had to contend with was the hard ground, which made it difficult to dig positions. Instead, they built sangars up using rocks. And as the sun came up Smyth-Piggott looked down over an unbroken view across the coastal plain all the way to the sea and he knew that Capstan had the potential to deliver all that was expected of it. But in order to make it stick – to both hold the position and mount aggressive patrols down to the Adoo camps and supply lines – they needed men. And they needed water.

Each soldier's daily allowance was one gallon of water. With that he had to drink, eat and wash. Unless they found water on Capstan at least five 40-gallon burmails of water needed to be delivered to the position daily.

For the time being, Knocker tried to supply them with the 'Indian Rope Trick'. Using ropes and pulleys, around one hundred men were lowering Capstan's resupplies down the 2,000ft rock wall of the escarpment. And they were using helicopters. Neither was any kind of long-term solution.

Smash and the rest of the men on Capstan enjoyed about forty-eight hours' grace before the Adoo made their displeasure felt.

From the airstrip up at Mainbrace there were two wadis that might have offered a measure of protection to a helicopter flying into Capstan. One of them, though, was overlooked by a feature called the Finger, a massive spur that extended south of Simba position and dominated Capstan itself. That had recently become home to a Shpagin operated by a gunner SAF had christened the Khadrafi Kid. The second, down a fissure in the face of the cliff itself, was great until halfway down, when there was no choice but to fly into the Kid's sights to reach either of the two Capstan LZs.

Flip a coin, Nick Holbrook thought; *which route am I going to take today to resupply Capstan?*

Holbrook took the Huey down the escarpment wall and made it in and out of the eastern LZ. Then he brought the big 206 round to the south-west and swooped down, hugging the ground. Beneath the camouflaged belly of the helicopter, visible through the glass panel in the nose just ahead of his feet on the rudder bar, the dense green vegetation of the coastal plain passed in a blur. Covered from the high ground by Capstan itself, the short journey between the east and west LZ offered a brief moment of relative safety. Never lasted long enough.

Holbrook pulled on the power, altered the pitch of the rotor and the blades and climbed up to the western LZ, correcting the torque with a touch of pedal. The aircraft, her cabin full, shuddered; the instrument panel ahead of him vibrated to a slightly different rhythm to the fuselage as if not quite bolted down. Ten thousand rivets in loose formation. Just as it should be. Find a helicopter that didn't shake as if its components wanted to do their own thing and Holbrook would have been worried.

Ascending over the lip of the LZ he tried to put her on the ground fast. Outside, the thick rotor blades smacked at the air, a Huey idiosyncrasy recorded on a thousand news reports from Vietnam. It was usually enough to bring the army running out to pull their stuff off the heli. Holbrook thumped it down on the skids, keeping the rotor spinning as his aircrewman unloaded. But today none of the soldiers had run out to help. It was taking too long and the western LZ was vulnerable: shielded a little by the main feature, but, from the east, only by a low bank crowned with shrubs. They blocked the line of sight, but that wasn't the same thing as cover.

'For Christ's sake, Sali,' he called back to his aircrewman, 'Get that bloody stuff off.' And as he spoke he saw the scrub to his right begin to dance. The Khadrafi Kid. They had seconds before the Shpagin had cut down the bushes and had a clear shot at them.

'Get a move on, Sali!' The scrub was being shredded, turned to dust and debris by 12.7mm rounds rattling in at 600 rounds per minute. Then it stopped. Holbrook guessed he'd got a window while the gunner changed the belt. Time to get out. But to take off forwards and plumb into his sights just as the new ammunition belt began to chug through the receiver was madness. Holbrook decided to attempt a manoeuvre he'd had no cause to try since flying training, when it had been taught as nothing more than a coordination exercise: a backwards take-off.

A helicopter normally takes off on a cushion of high pressure air underneath the main rotor. As the pilot pushes the stick forward to tilt the rotor forward, some of that pressure is lost as the column of air is deflected backwards. More power is fed in to compensate, along with rudder to prevent the extra torque from spinning the helicopter fuselage around its own axis beneath the rotor. As the cushion of air is left behind even more power and more rudder is needed until sufficient forward speed and airflow along the length of the fuselage mean the helicopter begins to actually want to fly in the direction it's pointing rather than being forced to do what it's told by the pilot. Only with forward speed can a helicopter pilot relax a little; until then, he's spinning plates. It all became a little trickier when you tried to do it backwards. Not least because you couldn't see where you were going.

Holbrook glanced at his gauges. 6,600 rpm through the Lycoming T-34 turboshaft. He twisted the throttle grip on the collective stick with his left hand, increased the power and pulled. Hanging beneath the main rotor, the aircraft rose vertically. Feet on the pedals and left hand on the collective stick, Holbrook kept the Huey stable, pointing straight ahead. He had to gain height before pulling back on the cyclic to push the heli backwards; rush that last move and he'd stuff the tail rotor into the ground.

Leaving the cushion of air below him he began to pull back, fighting the helicopter's inclination to weathercock with heavy boots of rudder as his backwards airspeed built up. As he reversed out of the western LZ, the ground dropped away below him. Without an airspeed indicator, which only worked in forward flight, he had to estimate the right speed at which to swing the Huey round on her axis – and not exceed the 30 knot limit set by the manufacturers on backwards flight. As he kicked the rudder and whipped the heli round into the direction of travel he dropped the nose and built up speed, diving towards the relative safety of low level. He took a deep breath and exhaled slowly.

All better left, he thought, *to the wide-open spaces of Salisbury Plain than the tree- and boulder-studded slopes of Capstan . . .*

From the top of the escarpment, Nigel Knocker had watched it all; relieved to see Holbrook swoop away from Capstan intact. But he knew it was only a question of time.

The writing's on the wall, the Colonel realized; *without a safe route in for helicopters, eventually one's going to get shot down.*

Just seven days after B Coy and Red Coy had climbed through the night to take Capstan, Knocker took the reluctant decision that he was going to pull them out. Without its own water supply which, despite their assurances, the Firqa had failed to find, Capstan was untenable.

Three days later Smash Piggott was off Capstan and back in the familiar surroundings of a Simba position sangar at dusk with a beer and a cigarette, enjoying what he called the Farnborough Air Display. Every evening, Nigel Knocker called in the jets to circle overhead, ready to dive in on the muzzle flash of an Adoo machine gun, or the smoke rising from a mortar tube. But the Strikeys didn't have it all their own way any more than the helicopters did. As they dived on their targets, the Khadrafi Kid would open up on them. And every night they'd try to place a bomb on his position on the Finger only to be fired on as they pulled up. Neither the bombs nor the rockets seemed to have any effect at all.

As the rock escarpment glowed pink and orange in the setting sun, Smash listened in to the RT between the pilots on his SARBE radio beacon. He recognized their voices: Bill Stoker and David Milne-Smith. He knew them both. DMS got the first bite.

'I've seen the flash,' he told his Squadron Boss, 'I'm going in.'

'No you're not,' Bill Stoker replied, 'this man is mine!' But the result was the same as ever.

The Khadrafi Kid had set himself up in a cave covered by a boulder across the entrance. Behind it he was invulnerable to the Strikemaster attacks. The Kid was able to nip in and out of safety to fire on SOAF at will. And, providing he was hidden round the back of his rock before the bombs and rockets struck, the jets couldn't do a thing to stop him.

Back in Salalah, on forty-eight hours' R&R, Smyth-Piggott made his way to the RAF Officers' Mess. The only place to be. Showered, shaved and wearing a shirt and tie, he was a good deal more presentable than the shaggy creature he'd been up at Sarfait. He ordered an ice cold beer and sat down next to Bill Stoker. He pulled out a cigarette and lit it, sending a cloud of smoke into the room.

'That bloody Shpagin's getting up your nostrils, isn't it?' Smash teased. The Strike Squadron Boss let out a brief laugh, his thoughts flashing back to his frustration in the skies over Simba. He looked at Smash with a glint in his eye.

'Do you know what I'd like to do, Graeme?' Stoker said, smiling. He sipped at his drink. 'I'd like to bring him in here, buy him a beer and shake his fucking hand . . .'

Be that as it may, Smash realized, Big Bill Stoker was still fuming about being stopped from leading his squadron in against Hawf.

And at Mirbat, too, the talk was all about guns.

Chapter 25

May 1972

At last there was something new to sink their teeth into. In Mirbat, the BATT had been given an impressive new piece of kit.

After SAF's withdrawal from Akoot following the launch of Operation SIMBA, it was decided to airlift one of the Desert Regiment's 25 pounder field guns to Mirbat. After changing the gun's carriage axle so that it could be rolled into the back of a Skyvan, the two-ton artillery piece was flown into the airstrip east of town.

It was hardly state of the art. Designed in the 1930s, the Ordnance QF 25 pounder was the mainstay of all the British and Commonwealth artillery units throughout the Second World War. From Norway to New Guinea it was used in every theatre of war. In the hands of the Australians the 25 pounder had been fierce in defence of El Alamein. When the United States entered the war, the first artillery shell fired against the *Wehrmacht* was launched from a 25 pounder. There was good reason for its ubiquity, though; it was believed by many to be the best field artillery piece of the war. In the hands of a good crew it was capable of firing 25-pound, 3.45in shells at such a rate that during the Allied invasion of Europe the Germans believed they were under attack from an automatic gun. And in 1972, despite its age, it remained in frontline service across the world.

At Mirbat, Troop Commander Mike Kealy decided that responsibility for their new gun would go to Tak and Laba. Neither of the two infantrymen had had any previous experience of a big field gun. To bring them up to speed the two Fijians were given two days' intensive training by Royal Artillery gunners on secondment to SAF. There was plenty of ground to cover. There were two different sights for direct and indirect fire. The latter, unlike the mortars, used range rather than elevation to find the target. Tak and Laba were introduced to the mechanics of the gun; as well as firing it they were going to have to maintain it. They learnt how to operate the breech and ram the shells; were shown how the brass cartridge case carrying the propellant charge and the high-explosive projectile were packed separately and had to be joined before being loaded. Then the gunners left them to it.

After the monotony of their deployment to Mirbat so far, Tak and Laba revelled in the new challenge, Laba exuberant and his friend Tak working methodically through what needed to be learnt. They positioned the new gun next to the Dhofar Gendarmerie fort – alongside the men flown out of Habrut – 400 yards or so inland from the sea. The handsome DG fort, with its red Sultanate flag fluttering above a fifty-foot-high turret, was on a small hill at the furthest north-east corner of the town ringed by a cattle fence of vertical poles and barbed wire. From here Tak and Laba could see the BATT House and Wali's fort by the beach and had an unbroken arc of fire across the whole of the plain between them and the dark wall of the Jebel six miles to the north. The sandbagged fort, with three-foot-thick walls and metal ladders linking the floors, was also home to Gunner Walid Khamis, a young soldier from the Omani Artillery, who was the third member of the Mirbat guncrew.

Shirtless, wearing shorts, khaki baseball caps and leather Jesus sandals, the Fijians built their position. As well as lavishing attention on the 25 pounder, they dug into the baked earth; two holes, one for the gun and another, twenty yards behind in the dead ground where the hill sloped away from the fort, for an ammunition dump.

The two friends talked in Fijian as they worked, enjoying the physical toil of building up the stone walls and sandbags around their pits. There was a palpable sense of achievement and ownership. This was *their* work. And, with Gunner Khamis, it was *their* gun. The price to be paid was the inevitable banter from the rest of the BATT troop. Never likely to miss an opportunity to take the piss, they ribbed the two Fijians for their infidelity – abandoning the Regiment for their new love: the Artillery. As ever, it was water off a duck's back. It took a lot more than that to rile them.

And so life in Mirbat ambled on, apparently removed from the growing tension further west.

Until now, SOAF had conducted its operations in Dhofar without a thought for any possible threat from the air. There wasn't one. And it was only the benign air defence environment that allowed the unsophisticated little Strikemaster to do an effective job. But when, on 29 May, following the cross-border raids against Hawf, a cluster of contrails were spotted high overhead RAF Salalah, it was assumed to be a reconnaissance in strength from South Yemen and it prompted a rapid reassessment of the air threat to the vital airbase.

Ironically, were it not for Britain, there might barely have even been one. Not only had the British Aircraft Corporation supplied the embryonic South Yemeni Air Force with Strikemasters, but it had also managed to help the Soviet Union provide the balance of its fleet.

When the USSR, needing an engine for its new swept-wing Mikoyan/Gurevich MiG-15 fighter, asked the UK to sell her the latest Rolls-Royce Nene turbojet, to the probable surprise of the Russians and the astonishment of the Americans, Britain had said yes. So now, two days after the incursion over Salalah, when Curly Hirst produced his report on the air threat to Oman, the MiG-15's successor, the MiG-17 'Fresco', and the Ilyushin Il-28 'Beagle' bomber, just entering service with South Yemen – and also powered by the Nene – were at the top of the list; flown by the Russians. He couldn't help but wonder whether British and Soviet airmen, albeit flying under the flags of other nations, might meet in the skies over Southern Arabia.

When Bill Stoker and Peter Hulme had conducted their reconnaissance missions along the Yemen coast before the attacks on Habrut, there had been no evidence that South Yemen had moved jets within range. But it didn't mean they couldn't. The British Joint Intelligence Committee maintained that South Yemen had the theoretical ability, at least, to launch 'a serious air attack on Salalah airfield with little or no warning'. Hirst's own report came to the same conclusion; should it want to, the South Yemen Air Force was quite capable of launching the MiGs from Al Ghaidah, armed with a pair of heavy 23mm cannon, on strafing attacks against both the base and the Shell Fuel Farm. And there was absolutely nothing SOAF could do about it.

Determined to do *something*, Russ Peart and Taff Hinchcliffe, both ex-Lightning pilots with long experience flying air defence missions, launched in their Strikemasters to fly a handful of Combat Air Patrols up by the border, but more in hope than expectation. They knew better than anyone that it didn't amount to much more than flying around going: 'Grrrrr.' Slow and, with two 7.62mm machine guns, less heavily armed than the Spitfires and Hurricanes that won the Battle of Britain, the Strikemasters were next to useless as fighters.

It was a fact of which Sultan Qaboos was only too aware. Since February, when intelligence reported that South Yemen had moved MiGs forward to the airfield at Al Ghaidah, he'd been pushing Hawley to enquire about the possibility of defending Dhofar's air space.

'These crazy people,' he told Hawley, 'might do anything.'

But every study showed that a credible, effective air defence system would be ruinously expensive. Oman, Hawley's Defence Attaché concluded after discussing the issue with Bill Stoker, 'cannot afford the entrance fee even, let alone the annual subscription'.

And so in May, as a formation of six Royal Air Force

McDonnell Douglas Phantom FGR2 fighter-bombers staged through RAF Masirah on their way to the Far East – each one equipped with a powerful long-range radar as well as air-to-air missiles and capable of delivering more firepower than the entire Omani Strikemaster force – Salalah Station's Commander, Gerry Honey, could do little more than pull a pair of Browning .50 heavy machine guns back from the Hedgehog forts inside the base, dig slit trenches and switch off the NDB beacon when it wasn't needed. A fierce-looking weapon resembling one of the RAF's big Bloodhound surface-to-air missiles appeared to guard over the base, but it did no such thing. Like so much else at Salalah it was just built from old burmail oil drums, just a facsimile of a missile. A lick of bright paint and the addition of a couple of RAF roundels didn't make it any more real.

At Bait al Falaj, Curly Hirst recommended to John Graham that the Sultanate request the despatch of an RAF Regiment Bofors gun battery, and the return of the RAF's Canberra spy planes, last used to take photographs of South Yemeni facilities the previous September.

Throughout June and July, one or two English Electric Canberra PR9s of 13 Squadron – a dedicated photo-reconnaissance unit based at Malta – became an almost permanent presence on the pan at RAF Masirah. The Canberras were no strangers to the island base. Since 1970, Operation MASLIN had seen them monitoring the border between Abu Dhabi and Saudi Arabia, in dispute over oil rights, a few more jets taking pictures in what was one of the most spied-on regions on the planet.

American pilots flew Northrop RF-5As out of Iranian bases on daring missions across the Soviet border until 1971. The missions continued, codenamed DARK GENE, with RF-4C Phantoms for another seven years after that. The legendary glider-winged U-2 operated out of RAF Akrotiri. The Soviets flew MiG-25 Foxbats out of Egyptian bases across Sinai at Mach 2.5 and 70,000 feet. The USAF trumped that, flying Lockheed SR-71 Blackbirds across the same area at over three times the speed of sound and 80,000 feet.

Not all the secret stuff happened in the air, though.

In March, Alec Douglas-Home had asked his Middle East Department whether or not it was possible for SAF to mount commando raids against targets deep inside South Yemen. Sultan Qaboos was asking himself the same question. After the attacks on Habrut, the Sultan had agreed to arm Mahra tribesmen, unhappy with rule from Aden and whose territory straddled Oman's border with South Yemen. Like Topsy, the idea grew and grew until, using the principle of the Firqas, Qaboos had persuaded the British to agree to support what they were now calling the Mahra Operation. Reluctantly, the MoD eventually agreed to provide 'an extra team of six SAS personnel to direct and administer a clandestine operation in PDRY [South Yemen] . . . on the condition that the operation remains deniable and that the SAS itself does not cross the border into PDRY territory.' If rumbled, the plan was to use the same cover story as for the regular BATT: that Britain was simply providing training for the Sultan's forces. But there was a difference between doing so for operations within Oman and running a force specifically raised to conduct guerrilla operations inside the territory of another state.

Donald Hawley appreciated the potential political embarrassment if the Mahra Op was discovered but, he thought, *if it were launched, we should probably get the blame anyway . . . might as well be hanged for a sheep as a lamb.*

It is, thought Neville Baker, *a sinister, secret war mentioned in whispers in dark places.* The veteran, silver-haired pilot was a stickler for decency, for doing the right thing. He didn't like crudeness or boorishness. And he hated having to lie to friends and senior officers about what he was up to, but he'd been sworn to secrecy by his superiors. He was one of a handful of pilots roped in to support some of the war's off-the-books activities. It seemed to him to be a hydra-headed conspiracy involving the palace, the Defence department, SAF HQ, the SAS and the British government. The CIA appeared to have an interest around the fringes too. At least the spooks were easy to spot.

Especially when they were married to film stars. When Charles Alden Black arrived in Oman with his A-list wife, Shirley Temple, on a fisheries advisory mission, it was not, Baker suspected, his *only* reason for being in the country. And although Black was undoubtedly a respected marine consultant, he also had form as a spy, having served with distinction in Naval Intelligence in both the Second World War and Korea.

As Baker flew him along the Dhofar coast, Black used a massive long-lens camera to take detailed line overlaps of the Jebel. Baker watched it all with interest. He'd already had some unusual experience flying men with cameras when, while flying Westland Dragonflies with the Royal Ceylon Air Force in the fifties, he'd flown David Lean's film crew while they captured the final long-distance shots of *Bridge over the River Kwai*. But at least that lot had filmed what they'd said they were going to film.

Not a bit interested in the fish, Baker noticed as he glanced back at Black. To the best of the veteran pilot's knowledge, the American didn't once look out to sea.

When senior officials of any of the agencies involved needed covert trips to the operational area, they called on Baker to take them. The usual routine was to fly first to a BATT position at Shisur, about fifty miles north of Midway, then into the Empty Quarter beyond to meet with heavily armed troops and their vehicles. Supported by Saudi Arabia, the outfit appeared to be packing more firepower than both the SAF battalions in Dhofar put together. It could get hairy. On one occasion Baker and his Crewman Leader, Stan Standford, ferried a palace official out to a rendezvous point well beyond Oman's border. They carried with them a heavy cargo of gold bars lashed down to the floor of the Huey's cabin. On putting the heli down on the skids, they were met by a group of armed tribesmen. Met by the official, shouting quickly turned to shooting before the gold was eventually handed over and they were able to take off and scuttle south back into Oman.

As instructed, Baker put in false records and omitted flights from official logs, but it made him uneasy. Unlike the day-to-day flying from Salalah, he was never clear exactly whose interests he was serving with this off-the-books stuff.

All very difficult, he thought. Although Baker wasn't the only one trying to avoid a paper trail.

Curly Hirst ordered the Strikeys to fly daily recces using hand-held cameras along the coast to Al Ghaidah airfield in South Yemen. It was a job from which, following the new Directive on seconded officers, Bill Stoker might have excluded himself, but listing the flights as 'Recce west' in his logbook seemed sufficiently vague. Technically he was not actually flying over South Yemen, only along her coast. And by using generic callsigns, Hirst had told him, Salalah's RAF controllers, while they may have recognized his voice, would not be obliged to enter a written record of his name in the Air Traffic Log.

But while the Omani Air Force did their best to be alert to the possibility of an air strike against their airbase, when the attack came, it did so from a more traditional direction.

Chapter 26

8 June 1972

For a week after the overflight from the west, RAF Salalah had felt as if it had the Sword of Damocles hanging over it. But tonight there was something to celebrate. For his heroics in bringing back his shot-up Strikemaster from Hawf, Peter Hulme had been decorated with Oman's highest military honour, the Sultan's Gallantry Medal. The pugnacious little SOAF(Tac) Commander was the first European to be awarded it. And so the Officers' Mess was using the occasion of its summer barbecue to raise a glass.

Outside, kebabs sizzled over hot coals piled in half-burmail drums, infusing the gathering with the inviting smell of cooking food. People streamed in and out carrying rounds of drinks. It was going to be a busy night for the men behind the bar. From sundown a large crowd had descended on the Mess. Most of the SOAF pilots were there, still outnumbered by the number of RAF officers in Salalah to keep the base running. Tables were spread across the patio, all heavy with glasses and food. Mingling in between, people stood chatting, putting the world to rights. For this special occasion, bright sodium lights had been rigged up outside and shone through the tall palm trees like spotlights.

Barrie Williams was sitting on the edge of a sofa, his back to the Jebel, talking to the man of the moment, Peter Hulme. With a drink in his hand, the SOAF(Tac) Boss gestured up at the arc lights, illuminating the courtyard like a beacon within the perimeter of the airbase.

'This is a bit silly,' he said. Williams looked around at the scene. But they both felt safe enough. Neither of them dwelt on it.

It was 8 June, the anniversary of the formation of the People's Front for the Liberation of Oman and the Arabian Gulf, to give the Adoo their official title.

One hundred and fifty yards away, sitting in the Salalah Ops Room smoking his pipe, Flt Lt Paul Ryan was the Duty Officer in charge of the air station's defences. While his Squadron Commander completed a jungle warfare course in Malaysia, Ryan, his 2ic, was leading the deployment of 2 Squadron RAF Regiment to Salalah. He was linked by radio to his men in the two Hedgehog forts out on the plain, and to the Cracker Battery guns. It had been a relatively quiet tour so far. There had been regular mortar and RCL attacks on the Hedgehogs themselves, but that was what they were there for; so far, nothing had landed within the perimeter of the base. Ryan's job was often just to try to keep his men occupied.

2 Squadron considered themselves to be the RAF Regiment's elite; parachute-trained infantry whose instinct was to get up and at the enemy. To their great frustration, the rules of engagement set by the MoD, determined not to allow British units to be drawn deeper into the war, prevented them from doing so. They could return fire from the Hedgehogs using their mortars, Gimpies and Browning .50 HMGs. And they could call in the jets and the artillery. But if they picked up Adoo contacts on their ZB298 ground-looking radars, they could only send SAF's Z Company out to hunt down the enemy.

Perhaps the greatest excitement so far had been intercepting Chinese voices speaking over the Adoo radio net.

Ryan was also aware that there was a hole in their defences. His men had two systems for picking up enemy attacks, the radar, which picked up movement on the plain, and Green Archer mortar-locating equipment. The latter detected the movement of the mortar bomb as it climbed and as it fell. What it couldn't do was pick up anything fired on a flat trajectory, like a round from a 75mm Recoil-less Rifle.

David Milne-Smith had just walked into the Mess building when he heard the crump of the explosion. The first round came in fast at a shallow angle on target for the patio before being stopped by a plant tub which absorbed much of the energy and debris. Then the second round speared in.

Barrie Williams flinched instinctively as he heard and felt the shockwave punch out from the second round detonating behind him. *Bloody close.*

The RCL round, the size of a tube of tennis balls, skidded into the hard ground and exploded with a flash, spraying serrated, uneven shards of iron in a shockwave low over the ground like the blade of a scythe.

Helicopter pilot Charlie Gilchrist had been sitting on a chair next to Bill Cooper, one of the RAF's Air Traffic Controllers, when the bomb blew up. All around people hit the floor, or tried to bottleneck in through the Mess door. Gilchrist ran for the air-raid shelter at the other end of the patio, diving into a tangled bundle of six or seven others.

Underneath the umbrella of palm trees, the air was thick with smoke and dust churned up by the explosion, a choking cloud settling in the glow of the sodium lights.

David Milne-Smith ran back outside to a picture of carnage. Injured men lay amongst broken glass and upended furniture. Red wine from smashed bottles puddled on the ground along with the blood beginning to pump from terrible shrapnel wounds. DMS saw his squadron comrade Taff Hinchcliffe, his ankle wrecked, in a heap on the ground. He picked the big man up and carried him into the relative safety of the Mess.

When Charlie Gilchrist emerged from the shelter, over the sound of people calling for help and shouting directions, he heard someone say: 'Russ has got it in the knee.' Russ Peart was a friend of his. A piece of shrapnel had cut into the side of the Strikemaster pilot's leg, just missing his kneecap. Nearby,

Bill Cooper, the RAF man Gilchrist had been talking to, was lying bleeding heavily from his left heel, much of which he'd lost. All the injuries were to the legs. The frag from the RCL round had cut through like grapeshot.

Then Barrie Williams caught sight of Peter Hulme. A chunk of shrapnel had ripped right through the Squadron Leader's left leg, taking much of the muscle with it, leaving both tibia and fibia smashed and visible through the hole. Across the front of his shin, his foot was attached by an inch of unbroken skin.

From across the base, those that had escaped converged on the Mess to do what they could to help. Men grabbed rifles and manned defensive positions around the edge of the airfield in case the RCL attacks marked the beginning of something bigger.

Neville Baker and Stan Standford ran from the cinema where they'd been watching a movie before planning to join the party. While Baker went to the Squadron to tell the Ops Officer to establish radio contact with SOAF HQ in Muscat, Standford, the Aircrewman Leader, went straight to the Mess to administer first aid and help get the injured men to the Field Surgical Team. They were lucky there was someone there to receive them. Just five minutes earlier one of the surgeons and the anaesthetist had left the party after being called back to the FST.

The first job was to prioritize the patients in order of clinical need. And Air Traffic Controller Bill Cooper, badly shocked and vomiting beer and kebabs, was first. He was given two pints of blood and a pint of clear Hartmann's solution before they put him under.

55FST was the latest surgical team to rotate through Salalah. Surgeons Major Joe Johnston and Captain Nick Cetti, and their anaesthetist, Captain Bill de Bass, had been out in Oman since the end of March. Establishing a proper field hospital had been a precondition for Johnny Watts sending the SAS to Dhofar. He wanted his men to go into battle reinforced by a confidence that, if injured, they'd get the prompt expert medical attention they needed.

The benefits were mutual. For Army, Navy and Air Force surgeons the FST provided an opportunity to hone their skills on genuine battlefield injuries, experience that no amount of practice on sheep, shot for their benefit at Porton Down, could reproduce.

But only about one in eight of the patients treated by the FST were British servicemen and an even smaller percentage of them were BATT. Working shirtless, in shorts, out of a tented operating theatre straight from M*A*S*H, the surgeons treated anyone who needed it, British and Omani, male and female, military and civilian, friend and enemy, based on clinical need alone. The FST became a vitally important component of the civil development effort in Dhofar.

As well as gunshot wounds and blast injuries, they dealt with haemorrhoids, hysterectomies, caesarian sections, appendectomies, toothache, the obvious complaint of a patient listed only as 'Mr Tight-Anal-Ring' and even a breast reduction. And it wasn't just people: the FST had no qualms about delivering Sean Creak's dog Spoon's litter by C-section either.

Johnston, Cetti and de Bass treated Bill Cooper using a procedure called delayed primary suturing. When fast-moving bullets or shrapnel enter the body, first they tear the flesh apart before letting it crash back against itself, killing the surfaces and sealing in whatever they've dragged through behind them: dirt, clothing, shoe leather, dead skin. Then anaerobic bacteria go to work causing infection and gangrene. In the FST, the first job was debridement, cutting away the dead flesh along the path of the bullet, before packing the hole with clean gauze and wrapping it with bandages. This allows oxygen to percolate through the wound and prevents it becoming septic. Five days later the patient is anaesthetized again, the gauze is removed, and providing the wound is pink and healthy looking it's sutured up in layers from the inside out. The procedure worked outstandingly well and, even in the rough-and-ready conditions in which the FST operated, post-operative infection rates were low.

The team cleaned up Cooper's wound and wrapped it up, but even as they did so they could see there was a strong chance that he'd have to lose what was left of his foot. Just after midnight they got to work on Peter Hulme. The compound fracture to his shin and the loss of flesh meant he too would be lucky ever to be quite the same again.

To an outsider, the conversation in theatre didn't always seem to reflect the gravity of the situation the surgeons were facing. As Bill de Bass struggled to get a tube down Hulme's short, bull neck, Joe Johnston raised a questioning eyebrow. De Bass knew he'd be presented soon enough with an opportunity to joke about the surgeon's competence. The irreverence kept the show on the road. After six hours in theatre, Canning, de Bass's Anaesthetic Technician, piped up.

'Can I go out of the operating theatre, sir?'

'Why?'

'Need a shit, sir . . .'

'So do I,' de Bass replied as his hand pumped away at the Haloxaire apparatus delivering the anaesthetic to Hulme's lungs, 'you're staying here . . .'

And for some time. There were nine serious injuries inflicted by the Adoo that night, including four Strikemaster pilots, a helicopter pilot and one from the Skyvan squadron. At a stroke, the enemy had inflicted a serious blow on the SOAF operation in Salalah. It was a hell of a way for the Adoo to celebrate their birthday. The FST surgical team didn't get out of theatre until well after sun-up the following morning. Nor did the luckless Canning.

Salalah was not alone in being on the receiving end of an apparently fierce enemy reaction to SAF's seizure of the plateau in Sarfait. The Adoo had already displaced the Army from Capstan and, in June, Simba position itself was hit by over 150 incoming mortar rounds over a period of ten days. And while the South Yemen government had been curiously mute in response to the attacks on Hawf, it had admitted for the first time, in a statement in the UN, that its own forces had been engaged in operations against Oman. As the monsoon set in, Donald Hawley's assessment of SAF's position was gloomy in the extreme.

'SAF,' he cabled London, 'are stretched in every respect – deployment, planning capability, aircraft hours and combat administration . . . A coastal block is beyond SAF's capability. I would not be surprised if events eventually required SAF to move back to the plain, the coastal towns, perhaps White City and some location near Habrut.'

That corrosive thought nagged away at John Graham too. It would mean that, for all the massive effort that had gone into launching Operation JAGUAR with the SAS in the east and Operation SIMBA in the west, he would be withdrawing to more or less exactly the position he inherited when he took over in 1970. Such a retreat would be catastrophic.

Yet despite Hawley's assessment, the British government remained as reluctant as ever to commit itself further. Just six days before the RCL attacks on the Salalah Officers' Mess, the MoD had refused a request for another ZB298 radar to help the RAF Regiment detachment defend the base.

When John Graham visited Hugh Oldman at his house in mid-June, the Sultanate's Defence Secretary was despairing. He had returned from London where, in meetings with Lord Carrington and the Chief of the Defence Staff, he had again argued the case for Oman. As the two men talked over early-evening drinks, Graham noticed that the distinguished, dark-suited Defence Secretary had tears in his eyes.

'Bloody British!' Oldman said. 'They express good wishes, but there is no plan to help us financially.'

Same old thing, Graham thought as Oldman aired his frustrations, *vague promises and fuck-all action.*

'It's disgraceful,' Oldman continued, 'the Arab nations must help Oman, but the UK and US should take the lead. After all, the British started the rot here when they left Aden . . .'

But there was a glimmer of hope. And John Graham had put his finger on it early. British fears about a hostile Arab reaction to the raids against Hawf proved unfounded. The Sultan had been right. And South Yemen's cries of foul in the UN brought the kind of attention to the war in Oman that Graham had gambled SAF's provocation might achieve. The diplomatic initiative had swung firmly back in Oman's favour. Qaboos continued to receive expressions of support from Saudi Arabia, the Gulf States, Tunisia, Syria and Egypt, but it was the delivery of a battery of twelve 25 pounder guns from Jordan that marked the beginning of anything more tangible. Jordan and Iran had both just established diplomatic missions in Muscat and Graham was doing his very best to court both ambassadors. With apparently no hope of further twisting Britain's arm, the advice sent home by General Khalil and Mr Zand to their respective countries might prove crucial. The Jordanian general travelled around the country visiting SAF positions, while Graham helped Mr Zand and his wife find a flat. And when the Sultan provided Graham with a new air-conditioned Datsun, CSAF gifted his Land Rover to the Iranian Ambassador. It was upon this foundation that Graham built his relationship with the Persian diplomat.

If SAF could hold the line a little longer – if he were able to show that Oman was a cause worth backing – then his efforts might just have the opportunity to bear fruit.

Meanwhile, the monsoon was beginning to hamper air operations. The new Vickers Viscount turboprops used by the Air Force to shuttle between Dhofar and the north were forced to refuel at Masirah en route to Salalah in case the coastal plain was clamped by low cloud. If they couldn't land they needed the range to reach a diversion. And, unable to see the airfield, Nobby Grey had been forced to bring a Beaver in using the NDB beacon and QGH radar advisory service from Salalah Tower. He was lucky. Just a few weeks earlier, neither the beacon nor the radar were serviceable. And the standby radar was offline too.

At that point, disabled and blanketed under the *khareef*, Salalah really ceased to be a functioning airfield, leaving troops on the ground out of reach of fixed-wing air support. The margins remained desperately slim; the war in Dhofar always seemed to be fought on the very limits of what was possible. And ultimate responsibility for the prosecution of the war, successful or otherwise, remained with one man: John Graham.

Summer in Muscat was exceptionally hot. Temperatures of 120 degrees sapped a man's energy and blurred the clarity of his thinking. And after months without a break, John Graham knew he was beginning to feel the strain.

Not up to the mark, he worried, as he forced himself to keep a tight grip on the many tactical, strategic, logistic and diplomatic strands of the campaign. He knew he was tired; that he needed a break. He didn't even have his wife Rosemary to talk to. After she had returned to the UK for the children's holidays, there was no one to help him either share the burden or take his mind off the pressure of a job that was relentless. There was Hugh Oldman, but the Colonel, increasingly ground down by his own responsibilities, was hardly in a position to lift anyone's spirits. It wouldn't be long before even the Sultan himself admitted to Donald Hawley that he was concerned about Oldman's health. Then there was Hawley himself, but Graham didn't feel able to confide too deeply in the Ambassador, who he knew was duty-bound to report back anything of interest to London. So that left Graham to drive himself on alone.

Loneliness of command, he told himself. It was just the way it was.

Then, on 17 June, Graham collapsed in his office.

He was found by one of the Omani Artillery Staff Officers lying on the wooden floor. And after a few days in bed in his Bait al Falaj home, Flagstaff House, the Brigadier was ordered home by SAF's Senior Medical Officer to recuperate. Graham felt thoroughly ashamed, but he tried to hold on to the thought that, in the condition he was in, *to go on in a critical job at an important time is wrong*. For the next month, though, as he recovered his strength back home, war was in the hands of those left in Oman.

He left feeling in his water that, following the combination of Operation JAGUAR, Operation SIMBA and the raids on Hawf, the Adoo were going to attempt something down on Salalah plain to even the score. Taqa, he thought, where the sanctuary of the Jebel sat closest to the town, was the obvious place.

And, unknown to Graham, or indeed anyone in SAF's intelligence operation in Dhofar, that thought was at the forefront of the minds of the Adoo leadership in the Eastern Area. SAF were not the only ones who were struggling to maintain the intensity of the last nine months of fighting. JAGUAR and SIMBA had damaged the Adoo's standing and credibility; they too needed a breakthrough. And, like Graham, their commanders appreciated that the military and political effects of their actions were inextricably linked. After 1 Squadron's cross-border raids against Hawf, Graham had written in his diary that the game had changed from 'volley ball to rugger'. Now the Adoo, in order to regain the initiative, needed a last-minute drop goal. Taqa, defended by just a handful of BATT troopers, looked like a good bet.

PART FOUR

1972
Counter-Punch

Chapter 27

June 1972

In May, Jim Vakatali's troop in Taqa had had to deal with the deaths of two civilians killed by an Adoo RCL attack. Like Eight Troop, the BATT team there were heavily armed, but there was no effective defence against hit-and-run attacks like that. They were, fortunately, just sporadic now. In June, while two B Squadron men were casevaced to the FST with gunshot wounds as fighting continued on the Jebel, Taqa and Mirbat had been quiet. There were a few hopeful Adoo potshots on the night of the attack on the RAF Salalah Officers' Mess, but nothing to frighten the horses. The Eight Troop Gimpies shot back against the Adoo mortars, but it was kneejerk stuff. The Adoo were likely to be long gone before the machine-gun rounds sliced in.

The only person medevaced out of Mirbat was Jakey Vaughan and, painful as it was, that had been nothing more serious than toothache. With just a few more weeks to run, thoughts there were beginning to turn to home. Laba looked forward to seeing his son; Tak had a girlfriend to return to; they all anticipated a night out in Hereford; and, best of all, they could lay off the seafood for a bit.

Perhaps it was all as it should be. The Regiment Civil Action Teams in Taqa, Mirbat and Sudh weren't there to fight. And yet it would have been a grave mistake to imagine that they were neither prepared nor capable of doing so. Like the

Incredible Hulk, you didn't want to make them angry. This was not a point lost on Adoo military planners. They knew that if they moved against Taqa, the BATT, despite their small numbers, posed a serious barrier to success. Time and time again on the Jebel they had come out worse against small teams of SAS fighting with persistence and firepower that suggested opposition from a much larger unit. The Adoo knew that something a little different was required.

Barrie Williams brought her in steeply. With full flap and the throttles pulled back to the flight-idle stop, the snub-nosed Skyvan descended sharply at a rate of nearly 2,000 feet per minute towards the airstrip. Through the cockpit glass he could see the limits of the little town, the dhows anchored off the beach and the two forts standing guard between the town and the Jebel escarpment ahead. Williams kept the speed between 80 and 85 knots by gently altering the aircraft's pitch using the control yoke. At flare height, he pulled back to level off and check the descent. The aircraft buffeted a little as the elevators bit, before riding a cushion of air under the flat fuselage until the main wheels thumped the rough ground. With his right hand he manipulated the two throttle levers to engage reverse thrust. The pitch of the propellors changed and Williams was pushed forward against his harness as the Skyvan rolled to a halt halfway down the strip with an angry buzz. As he applied the brakes and shut down the two Astazou engines, he saw figures crossing the rough ground towards him; men from the Mirbat BATT.

'Animal, vegetable, mineral or a mixture of all three. There's just no end to the jobs you can do with a Shorts Skyvan.' The manufacturer's advertising set great store by the box-shaped turboprop's ability to carry two tons of bulky freight. As a supermarket makes 'serving suggestions' on its grocery lines, their ads for the freighter illustrated the '2 grand pianos and players', '1 elephant and mahout', '6 eskimos, 2 reindeer and a sleigh' or '1 bull, 3 cows, milkmaid and cowman' the aircraft's owner might want to load into the back.

But when Barrie Williams brought his Skyvan into Mirbat on 7 July, he was carrying nothing so exotic; lashed down in the cargo hold were rations, medical supplies, mail and wages for the Firqa al Umri. He was also carrying heavy metal boxes of ammunition. Eight Troop were stocking up before leaving, making good what they'd used during their time in Mirbat. In a little over a week's time, they'd no longer be around to make use of it, but they were going to leave their replacements with a full three-months supply: hundreds of mortar shells and tens of thousands of rounds of 7.62mm GPMG ammunition.

G Squadron's Commanding Officer, Alistair Morrison, could have done without the diversion to Gan, the RAF's remote island airbase in the Indian Ocean. But an unwelcome trip to the Maldives was the price paid for the MoD's refusal to recognize Dhofar as an operational area. While the war in Oman remained a secret one, the RAF felt it was fair enough to reroute the flight carrying the SAS out to Salalah to deliver a spare Conway jet engine to a broken down VC10. The big transport jet had been carrying families out to the Far East, and until the engine arrived was stranded amidst the coral reefs and palm trees of Gan.

Going out for an Op, Morrison thought, *we should have priority*. But the unscheduled diversion took them with it and, as a result, Morrison's advance party were four days late arriving in Dhofar. There was barely the time to disperse them to the various BATT positions to ensure a seamless handover before the main body of G Squadron men arrived.

Since leaving Oman six months ago, after the Squadron's participation in Operation JAGUAR under Johnny Watts, Morrison had taken his men on exercise in Malaysia, but it was Oman where, despite the MoD's view, the Regiment was actually engaged in operations; where it was doing its job. It was good to be back; and good to see Duke Pirie again. The blond B Squadron Boss, who'd fought alongside Morrison out of White City during Op JAGUAR, took him to BATT HQ, where they were sharing a room. Morrison dropped his Bergen alongside a camp bed. They wouldn't be doubled up for long. Pirie would soon be on board an RAF C-130 flying him home. This time round, G Squadron were replacing B Squadron in theatre, rather than fighting alongside them. When Morrison's main body of men arrived, there'd be just twenty-four hours where both Sabre Squadrons were in country together.

With a couple of days before the balance of G Squadron arrived, Morrison, the elegant, well-spoken Guards officer, despatched the men of his advance party. He was sending Jeff Taylor, a Corporal who'd left the Republic of Ireland to join the British Army's Irish Guards, to Mirbat.

Tak and Bahait, the leader of the Mirbat Firqa, met every day. Today, though, the young Firqa leader was uneasy.

'Something strange is going on,' he told the Fijian Trooper. Although he didn't know it, the FKW – the Firqa Khalid bin Walid – operating out of Taqa, was also reporting to Jim Vakatali that something wasn't right. Tak pressed the young Firqa leader for detail. Bahait and his 2ic and Quartermaster, Salim, could tell him nothing more. They just knew all was not as it should be. It was impossible to glean any corroborating information from informants within Mirbat. Since the BATT and the Firqa had rounded up the Adoo support cell in the town a year earlier, there weren't any. Mirbat had been ringfenced. Tak decided to send Bahait's guerrillas north to investigate.

'Do you want me to come too?' he asked, grateful for an opportunity to break the boredom of the final countdown to the end of B Squadron's tour in Oman. 'No,' Bahait told him. He wanted to take the Firqa up towards the Jebel on his own.

Two days later Bahait and his men returned. The Firqa Commander seemed even more exercised than he had been before. Again, he told Takavesi: 'Something strange is going on.' He and his men had seen movement in the mountains, but the Dhofari wasn't able to pin down what it might mean, if anything. Despite pushing, the Trooper couldn't get any more out of him, but it was clear that Bahait was unhappy.

Tak didn't like it, but he trusted Bahait. He felt sure that if the Firqa leader had known anything, he'd have shared it. Takavesi shared what he knew with Mike Kealy, who passed it back to BATT HQ at Um al Gwarif, but it was pretty tenuous stuff. And it was met with an assertion from the intelligence cell that large numbers of men simply weren't able to move unnoticed in the mountains.

In any case, it wouldn't be Eight Troop's problem for very much longer. The changeover was in full swing. Tak's replacement, G Squadron's Trooper Jeff Taylor, had already been flown into Mirbat. The difference in the two men's appearance was striking. Taylor was fresh out of the box; his OGs, the light cotton uniforms the BATT wore, not yet matted with dust and frayed. Like the rest of the Troop, Tak had done what he could to stay clean and healthy, but by the end of the tour things were getting ragged. His black hair was thick and long, dirt had become ingrained and the shorts that had practically become his only item of clothing until the end of the week before had to be incinerated with the rest of B Squadron's dirty laundry.

Tak talked Taylor through the local situation, everything the Irishman needed to know to pick up seamlessly. Tak explained who was who within the Firqa, told him who he rated and where the faultlines lay. And he introduced Taylor to Bahait and to Salim, who also distributed the Firqa's pay.

Tak also warned the G Squadron man that something had got Bahait rattled, that Bahait was a good guy, and that it was worth paying attention, whatever the Green Slime back at BATT HQ were saying.

Chapter 28

17 July 1972

Almost exactly a year earlier, on 21 July 1971, seven Jebalis and their seventy goats were flown down from the Wadi Maseer to Mirbat. As the BATT unloaded the Skyvan with the help of the Wali's Askars and the Dhofar Gendarmerie, a mine laid beneath the airstrip exploded, killing a small boy and ripping off the leg of one of the DG guards. Ensuring that the strip remained safe demanded constant vigilance. From a pilot's point of view it was one of the better ones: long and flattish and running north–south. But it lay beyond the town's perimeter wire, so every time an aircraft was expected, the airstrip needed to be inspected before SOAF was given the all-clear. After checking the landing strip, Laba and Mike Kealy waited at the side, watching the little piston-engined DeHavilland Beaver descend. It was a familiar sight to the Fijian. These little aircraft had followed him round Arabia, supporting ops in Aden with the Army Air Corps before being donated to the Sultan's Air Force when the British left the crater in 1967.

Sean Creak set the pitch to full fine and mixture to rich from the auto-lean position and set full flap. He pressed the transmit button.

'Just landing at Mirbat,' he told Salalah over the VHF radio as he brought the aircraft in on short finals. That was the trick to flying the Beaver around Dhofar: letting them know where you were. And if you at least let Ops know when you were arriving and departing it gave them a chance of narrowing the search if you didn't come home.

Laba had made sure there was nothing unexpected buried beneath the surface to spoil the pilot's arrival. Alongside Creak in the cockpit was the G Squadron Boss, and it definitely wouldn't have been good form to allow him to go up in smoke. Morrison was flying round all the various BATT locations in advance of his men coming in, talking to the troop commanders to gain a clearer appreciation of the situation on the ground in a country that was changing with dizzying speed. What he learnt from conversations with the B Squadron teams he could disseminate to his own men in the tented BATT lines at Um al Gwarif before sending them out.

All the same, there was no point in using any more of the runway than he had to. Creak tweaked the throttles for the round out and placed her near the runway threshold at just a shade over 60 mph. A point of pride.

He'd won the spot-landing competition in the Beaver earlier in the year. Admittedly, so had two other people when the judges couldn't separate them, but joint first wasn't too bad. It was still first.

A perfect three-pointer in the first half of the Mirbat strip meant he could pull to a halt at the parking area halfway down and take off from that point using the second half. No need to backtrack. As the Beaver trundled down the gravel he sensed his feet on the rudder pedals, careful to prevent the torque from the propellor causing the tail wheel to swing out.

Alistair Morrison jumped into a Land Rover with Mike Kealy and the two of them drove off towards the BATT House, leaving Laba and Creak behind to talk over a brew. Creak was struck by the big Fijian's size.

About as wide as he is tall, he thought, as he looked him up and down. But despite his imposing appearance, there was a complete absence of fierceness on display. Creak was charmed as they talked about Dhofar and about going home. Laba didn't say much, that's true, but then, Creak thought, *they're not the most loquacious people, the SAS.* Instead, Laba just made the pilot feel at ease.

Nearly an hour later, Morrison and Kealy arrived back at the strip in the beaten-up old Land Rover, the tyres crackling over the loose surface. Before climbing back into the cockpit of the Beaver, Creak risked shaking the big Fijian's slab of a hand and wished him well.

What a very nice man, he thought as the 1,400 horsepower of Pratt and Whitney Wasp radial engine coughed into life, belching smoke into the humid air. When Creak next returned to Mirbat it would be in very different circumstances.

Laba walked back to the BATT House. Once more, Bahait and the Firqa were going out on patrol. Since the FAU had returned from their recce to the north, there had been new reports of some kind of disturbance on the Jebel Samhan. Again, Tak sent the men out to investigate. No one entertained the possibility that whatever trouble the Adoo were causing might have been staged with the sole purpose of removing the thirty-plus-strong Firqa from Mirbat. And from the little town's meagre defences.

Camouflaged in sand and stone, an RAF C-130 Hercules sat fat and squat on the Salalah pan. In the damp of the *khareef*, the bright white panel painted over the roof of the flight-deck to reflect the heat of the fierce Middle Eastern sun hardly seemed necessary. It was Tuesday afternoon, 18 July. Down the cargo ramp at the back, the remaining thirty-one members of G Squadron tramped out carrying their Bergens and belt kit – all they would need bar food, water and ammunition for the next three months – and climbed straight into the back of a pair of Bedford three-tonners for the short drive to Um al Gwarif camp. There they assembled a jigsaw of camp beds and hung mosquito nets overhead, but there was no need to make it home; it was just for the night. And some of them didn't expect to spend much of it sleeping in any case; not with one last chance to raise a glass in comfort.

The hubbub settled as the G Squadron Boss walked to the

front of the group. Alistair Morrison looked around at his men gathered under the thick green canvas of the BATT HQ tent. An unshaded light bulb hung down on a wire from the frame above the men's heads.

The creation of G Squadron from the old Guards Para had been controversial, but these men had since earned their spurs during Operation JAGUAR. He was confident that they would cope with whatever the three-month tour threw at them.

In precise, plummy tones that contrasted with the variety of accents on display amongst his soldiers, Morrison briefed them on what lay ahead, telling them who was going where to join troop sergeants and officers already in position. He reminded them of the good work they had already done in Oman. And the Major, who as the *de facto* ruler in the Musandam Peninsula eighteen months earlier had done so much to demonstrate the contribution the Regiment could make to a hearts-and-minds campaign in Oman, reminded them that this was what their mission in Oman was all about. But, as they all knew, while the MoD reassured Parliament, explaining that SAS 'training teams are required to take all reasonable precautions to avoid direct contact with the rebel forces', sometimes it just couldn't be helped.

Tomorrow morning at 0800 hours, Morrison told them, they'd be driven out to the range at Arzat to check their weapons and zero the sights before dispersing to their locations.

After dinner, most of the men made their way to the NAAFI bar, where they concentrated on enjoying their last cold beers until the end of the tour. They tasted sweeter for that. And so more followed. Joined by men from SAF the NAAFI became more crowded. There were a few faces familiar to veterans of earlier tours, but by and large the BATT kept themselves to themselves. They had their own way of doing things. Even the songs they sang had their lyrics doctored to fit the bill.

'DLB,' went one, 'he tell the nation, have no fear of escalation . . .'

Officer Commanding 22 SAS, Peter de la Billière, back at

Bradbury Lines in Hereford, would have appreciated its grasp of the political sensitivities of the campaign in Oman.

In the Um al Gwarif NAAFI, it looked like it was going to be a late one.

Just a couple of miles away in the Officers' Mess at RAF Salalah, there was a similar picture of smoke and alcohol. It was Nobby Grey's last night in Dhofar before rotating back to Bait al Falaj in the north. None of the pilots welcomed being dragged away from the operational area, but the squadron bosses enforced it. The intensity of life on the frontline was intoxicating, but, unbroken, it ended up being crippling. However reluctant they were to go, Bill Stoker and Neville Baker made sure that their men got some R&R.

As ever, there were a handful who were keeping a tighter rein on things. SOAF maintained alert crews from dawn to dusk. Tonight, four pilots had their names on the authorization sheets for Wednesday morning: David Milne-Smith, Sean Creak, Neville Baker and Charlie Gilchrist. When the sun came up, a pair of armed Strikemasters and a Huey would be sitting outside the old BOAC terminal, battle-ready, waiting for the order to scramble to come through from Ops.

Nobby Grey wasn't the only one anticipating his departure from Dhofar. Forty miles away in the BATT House, Eight Troop sat around talking about home, and playing cards. Whirring away in the background, the little Philips tape churned out *Easy Rider*, from Steppenwolf to the trippy sounds of the Electric Prunes. The BATT House looked as good as it could do. It was never going to look polished, but it was tidy. The men's Bergens were packed, resupplies of stores organized and ordered. Metal boxes of ammunition were stacked neatly and, outside, Bob Bennett's mortar pit was lined with 81mm rounds, unpacked and laid out close to hand, ready for an immediate response. With everything squared away ready for G Squadron to pick up in the morning, Fuzz and Laba were enjoying a drink. Each BATT position was given a bottle of G10 rum to see them through the tour. Over the tour, they'd saved up their ration. So far in Dhofar, Tak had stayed off the booze, but he was looking forward to returning to civilization and seeing his girlfriend, and with the prospect so close Fuzz was finding his resistance to a tot of rum a little easier to break down.

'I don't drink on ops,' he reminded the energetic little Trooper from Oldham. Tak didn't even like rum, but it was their last night. Fuzz and Laba looked at him expectantly, shadows flickering across their faces from the low candlelight.

Why not have a couple, he thought. He held out his tin mug for Hussey to pour, then topped it up with Coke to disguise the strong taste of the spirit.

'Well done,' he said to his friends, 'time to go home, eh?'

Fuzz and Laba raised their mugs and Fuzz pulled on a cigarette. Sprawled lazily on wire and canvas camp beds, the two of them showed every sign that they were digging in for the night. Tak finished his drink and decided to leave them to it. They'd all be back in Hereford by Friday night; there'd be plenty of opportunity for good times once they were back home.

Chapter 29

18 July 1972

On 31 January 1968, the Viet Cong launched an unprecedented series of coordinated attacks across South Vietnam. In one operation they seized the US Embassy in Saigon, forcing a six-hour gun battle with US troops as they fought to reclaim the building. In another they attacked the Presidential Palace. And at Da Nang, the huge US airbase, thirty American aircraft were destroyed. The attacks took US forces completely by surprise and, while they failed to secure any permanent military gains, they were a political triumph for the VC, revitalizing a campaign that appeared to be in danger of defeat. What had been an act of desperation had, despite leading to heavy Viet Cong losses, bought them the time, credibility and support they needed to continue. And by July 1972 they were on the verge of victory. Within a month, the United States would pull out the last of its combat troops from Vietnam after suffering over 45,000 men killed in action over the previous seven years.

While the British were understandably alarmed at the prospect of Oman becoming their own Vietnam, the Adoo leadership were inspired by the prospect. And on the night of 18 July they gathered their own forces, ready to launch an attack which, they hoped, would transform their fortunes in the same way that the Tet Offensive had done for the Viet Cong.

There had been around 400 of them, gathered in the utmost secrecy beneath the treeline in the Wadi Ghazir, twelve miles west of Mirbat, halfway to Taqa. The planners had been careful choosing their target. Razat, on the plain near Salalah, had been considered, until one of the Adoo leaders who was privy to the plans surrendered to government forces. Then White City had been favoured. Snatched by the BATT during Op JAGUAR, it became the location of the first civil development on the Jebel. As the hub of SAF's first permanent location there, it had great symbolic significance. To overwhelm White City would have provided irrefutable evidence that SAF could not stop the rebellion. But the Adoo knew the position too well to risk it. They knew that it was defended in depth by well dug-in positions. And in the last month two powerful new Browning .50 heavy machine guns had been laying waste to their fighters at distances well beyond the range of the GPMGs. And they hadn't enjoyed the Gimpies much either. If they attacked White City they'd suffer unacceptable losses. So they settled on Taqa.

Until their intelligence suggested that Mirbat was less well defended. It was further from the sanctuary of the Jebel, but an attack on Mirbat offered them a greater chance of success. And that might make enduring the terrible biting blackfly that infested the wadis during the monsoon bearable. The Adoo commanders told their men that the target was Sudh, east of Mirbat, to ensure that, this time, the real target would remain unknown.

They tried to make sure that they'd planned comprehensively. They had already created a diversion that had drawn the Firqa al Umri out of the town. They were attacking at the height of the *khareef* monsoon when they knew that, with heavy cloud and drizzle cloaked low over the plain, SOAF's feared Strikemaster attack jets from RAF Salalah would be unable to support the town's defence. The Adoo plan would see them sweep into the town at night, surround it and hold it until dawn. During a few short hours in Mirbat, before SAF had any hope of sending reinforcements, they were going to kill the Wali and all his officials, their families, and any of the population they believed were sympathetic towards the government. They had lists of names and had allocated different squads of men to clear specific streets. After sacking the town they would withdraw to the cliffs and ravines of the Jebel, carrying the town's weaponry as a prize, and once more dissolve into their smaller, harder to find constituent units.

Success, they knew, would provide them with a massive propaganda victory and see civilian confidence in the Sultan's ability to defend his people crumble.

But the Adoo weren't used to operating in such large numbers and that caused problems of its own. Just assembling such a substantial force had been a formidable undertaking. At least five separate units drawn from both the Eastern Lenin Sector and the Central Sector, all used to operating independently under their own leader, had to form a single assault force for the first time. And it was too much for one of the rebel commanders. After clashing over what he believed was an overly complex plan, he abandoned the attack, taking his men – over one hundred of them – with him.

That still left them with close to 300 experienced, heavily armed guerrilla fighters. They were attacking in battalion strength. The force moved out of the Wadi Ghazir after dark and began picking their way east.

Al Tawil, the member of the Adoo High Command's Military Committee leading the operation, had decided that they would launch their attack at 0300 hours. When, they expected, Mirbat's defenders would be fast asleep.

On the first floor of the BATT House, Fuzz and Laba were lying on their camp beds still wearing the clothes they'd spent the day in. Smoke from Fuzz's cigarettes hung in the room. The light was low and the music from the little tape recorder kept on coming. As the rum swam around their heads, they tapped their feet and sang along to the propulsive beat of 'Born to be Wild', leaned back and absorbed the slinking stoner rock of

Jimi Hendrix's 'If Six was Nine'. To the backing of a crying lap steel guitar, one-hit-wonders the Fraternity of Men urged them: 'Don't Bogart That Joint'. Steppenwolf followed 'Born to be Wild' with the plaintive rolling blues of 'The Pusher'. It was music synonymous with America's fight in Vietnam; an ironic, counter-cultural soundtrack to the newsreel footage that had ended up defining that war. Fuzz and Laba drank it all in. Round their necks their ID tags and morphine syrettes hung on lengths of paracord like decorations. Unwashed, wearing frayed clothes, their hair long and stubble shadowing their chins, Fuzz and Laba looked more like travellers on the hippy trail than anything you might expect in a British Army outpost. But their long-barrelled SLR rifles leaned against the pitted wall and by their sides were their belt kits: customized, chopped-down versions of standard infantry webbing; the SAS were never without their belt kit. In it was everything they needed to stay in the fight: ammunition, water, battle dressings, compass and a 24-hour ration pack. Along with their weapon and belt kit, they always carried one more piece of essential equipment: their radio.

The Adoo didn't even wear shoes. Instead, a life lived barefoot in the mountains had toughened and flattened the soles of their feet; an adaptation that allowed them to traverse rough, loose ground with the poise and stealth of mountain lions. But tonight the monsoon, the very thing they were relying on to give them an extra advantage when they attacked Mirbat, was making their journey more difficult. It was the driest July on the Salalah plain since records had begun in 1942. But what rain fell, fell during a thunderstorm on the night of 18 July. The wet ground softened their feet and made the terrain slippery and treacherous. Loaded down with unusual quantities of heavy weaponry, they struggled for grip, moving down from the Jebel with nothing like their normal balance and assurance.

To a man they carried AK47 assault rifles. But as well as their personal weapons, they were lugging large amounts of support firepower. There were mortars and two Shpagin machine guns, all with heavy tripods, Goryunov medium machine guns and twenty light machine guns. As well as two Chinese 75mm RCLs, the assault force had a Swedish-made 84mm Carl Gustav recoil-less rifle anti-tank weapon – apparently inherited from the British at some point – and rocket-propelled grenade launchers. To feed all this, there were also heavy boxes of mortar rounds, 7.62mm short rounds for the AKs, fifty-round chain links of 12.7mm ammunition for the Shpagins and more for the light machine guns. But as well as their not factoring in the difficulty of the wet terrain, even finding their route in the pitch black and rain was uncertain.

With thick, low cloud, there was no light from the sky of any kind. And Mirbat, without electricity, offered no beacon to guide them. Unable to see more than a few yards ahead, they made frequent stops to discuss their position. Were they on track? And as the force got bogged down, they fell behind schedule. The leaders of the different factions began to argue over whether or not their plan, which they'd agreed, depended on being in and out before sunrise. Should they continue or abort? They agreed to continue, confident that their over-whelming numerical superiority would see them through.

An attacking force would normally want an advantage of at least three to one to be confident of success. The guerrilla battalion closing on Mirbat swamped the waiting BATT team by *thirty* to one. And with the Firqas successfully removed from the fray by the Adoo diversion, it was just the nine men of the BATT, the Dhofar Gendarmerie Garrison and the Wali's Askars and their ancient bolt action .303 rifles, relegated, back in the UK, to public school armouries for use by teenage cadets. And neither the DG nor the Askars were combat troops.

Late or not, the Adoo had good reason to feel confident.

Fuzz and Laba heard the rumble of the storm in the distance over the sound of Byrds supremo Roger McGuinn singing Bob

Dylan covers. After some of the druggy psychedelia on display elsewhere, this tune had a little more bite. A ferocious acoustic guitar attack underpinned the machine-gun rap of Dylan's lyrics spat over the riff by an uncharacteristically snarling McGuinn. Harmonica wailed over the top in between the verses. It was 0430 hours. But Fuzz still had energy to burn. Didn't look like he and Laba were going to get much sleep tonight. 'It's Alright Ma,' McGuinn sang in the chorus, 'I'm Only Bleeding'. As the song ended it segued into the roar of a Harley-Davidson accelerating away into the distance.

It was barely an hour after the last of the G Squadron revellers had finally called it a day and made their way back from the Um al Gwarif NAAFI through the tangle of camp beds to get their heads down. At 0500 hours, SAS Quartermaster Lofty Wiseman hauled himself out of his sleeping bag and stood up, 6 feet 4 inches in his bare feet. Wiseman still had time to run before his tour ended and today's changeover only served to remind him of how much he was looking forward to shipping out of Oman. After months in the cloying heat of the Salalah plain, the Hereford climate was looking like a welcome alternative; and home also meant an overdue opportunity to get on the beers and on the pull. The tour, though, hadn't been without its high spots.

The major excitement so far had been the delivery of the BATT's three new Browning .50 HMGs on board an RAF C-130. Unpacking the crates to reveal the greased, unused weapons was like opening a Christmas present. Finished in black and engineered with the strength and precision of a steam engine, they gave off the unmistakable oily smell of industrial machinery. The new guns meant the BATT had a weapon that, unlike the Gimpies, could outrange the Adoo Shpagins.

It was an old design – born in 1855, designer John Browning had test-fired the new gun at the end of the First World War; he did so wearing a jacket, tie and bowler hat – but it remained brutally effective. After nearly two million had been produced during the Second World War, it remained in production still. But it could be a tricky beast. Even mounted on a massive, sprung tripod, it kicked like a mule at the best of times. And if care wasn't taken in setting the barrel then the recoil could be even more violent. Just days ago one of the B Squadron gunners had been flown down from the Jebel with a broken collarbone, cracked by the big gun's blow-back action. Two of the Brownings had been sent up the Jebel to defend White City and Jibjat. The third of them was despatched by Duke Pirie to Mirbat, where Wiseman helped set up the gun and gave Snapper Winner instructions on how to use it. He'd warned the experienced Lancastrian ex-Sapper that for all its bulk and apparent solidity, the five-0's tolerances were low. The heavy machine gun needed a lot of TLC.

It had been more routine stuff of late, though. For the last couple of weeks, Wiseman had been organizing the resupply of the BATT locations across Dhofar; getting G Squadron out on the ranges and into their positions this morning would be one more step along the way, his last major job before he too could begin to look forward to settling into the canvas webbing seats of a Hercules for the long flight home.

After pulling on his clothes, the Quartermaster made his way outside into the morning mist and, still groggy from sleep, walked past the trucks and rows of tents to the armoury.

Forty miles away, Laba and Fuzz were still awake, the pair of them happy and relaxed. They lay back on their camp beds, settled enough even to ignore the uncomfortable metal framework that usually dug into their backs. The punchy little signaller's cigarette packet sat open on the floor, the last few tabs loose in the box. It was hard not to wind down to the soothing twelve-string jangle of Roger McGuinn's 'Ballad of Easy Rider' singing out of the little Philips. Mellow and peaceful, the gentle little song about freedom and escape swirled around them; the only other noise in the pre-dawn, barely perceptible from the BATT House, was the washing of the waves against Mirbat's white sand beach. And while the Byrds' frontman crooned about leaving town, they thought of home.

As the song floated around the BATT men's room, on top of the Jebel Ali, half a mile to the north of the town, the eight men of the Dhofar Gendarmerie picquet were sleeping soundly, wrapped up in their sleeping bags. Lulled into a false sense of security by the pace of things in Mirbat, the guards had neglected to post a sentry. They were effectively blind and deaf; and so the town's early warning was down.

On the coastal approaches to Mirbat, the Adoo assault force split into four companies of men. One was held back to man the support weapons. The mortar platoons set up their weapons half a mile north of the Jebel Ali: an arc of five tubes with the town at the axis. Then a guerrilla platoon began slowly and quietly making their way up the shallow sloping sides of the Jebel Ali. The longer they could conceal their ascent, they knew, the greater would be their chances of over-whelming the DG picquet. They needn't have worried. At around 0515 hours, they found the sleeping men clustered on the ground, their weapons lying uselessly beside them. The men who had survived the Adoo attack on Habrut and been moved to Mirbat to rest and recover away from the action were killed as they slept, bayoneted in their sleeping bags.

On the high ground, the Adoo fighters set up one of their two 12.7mm Shpagin machine guns while the first tints of dark blue began to emerge from within the black of the night sky. From the top of the Jebel Ali, the Adoo now had a machine-gun position that dominated Mirbat's defences.

At Um al Gwarif, Lofty Wiseman removed nine GPMGs and 2,000 rounds of 7.62mm ammunition in 200-round belts from the armoury. He loaded them all quickly on to the flat bed of one of the Regiment's three-tonners, padlocked the armoured front door behind him and went to get a cup of tea and something to eat.

*

It was time to go. Along the ring of Adoo mortar positions, the teams dropped high-explosive rounds down into the muzzles of their weapons. The men ducked away, covering their ears. There was a split second of metal scraping against metal as the bombs slid down on to the firing pins. Then the night sky exploded, the report from each weapon rumbling into the next and echoing off the wall of the Jebel behind them. The first barrage of bombs soared into the blanket of low cloud.

Chapter 30

19 July 1972

Three mortar rounds crumped in to start it. While Fuzz Hussey sat up in bed, Laba barely blinked. It didn't warrant much more than that. This was standard Adoo stuff. Like a crowing cockerel, an early-morning Adoo hit-and-run didn't mean much more than rise and shine.

Three more rounds smashed in in quick succession; the noise of the explosions sharper, closer. Hussey swung his feet off the bed, alert now.

'There's no small-arms fire,' Laba told him, 'they're just stonking us.'

Another triplet of explosions suggested that the Adoo were correcting their fire, walking each barrage closer to the town.

'I don't like the sound of this,' Hussey said. Laba still seemed supremely unconcerned.

'They're just testing the fort,' the big Fijian reassured him. It was nothing to worry about.

'How do you know that? I mean, where did you get that information from?'

'Ah, they always do,' Laba replied, unperturbed.

Tak woke to the sound of the rounds going off. But he was no more concerned than Laba.

Being attacked at first light, he thought, *that's normal. They'll soon get bored and go away*. But the weight of fire

257

continued to grow, getting closer and more accurate. Soon Fuzz wasn't the only one thinking that this wasn't just the normal wake-up call. Snapper and Tak both rolled out of bed, grabbed their SLRs and pulled on their belt kit. Snapper tied the laces of his desert boots and quickly made his way up the home-made bamboo ladder on to the roof – and the five-0 sangar; Tak climbed down towards the mortar pit a few yards beyond the walls of the house. And as Mike Kealy, the quiet, self-contained young Troop Commander, reached for his torch, another bomb from the Adoo mortars landed close enough to shower him with debris shaken from the mud brick walls of the BATT House.

Since passing Selection and being badged, Mike Kealy had given a great deal of thought to how he would fare leading experienced, older Regiment campaigners when the shooting started. Now, feeling both anxiety and relief that it looked like he was about to find out, he slipped out of his sleeping bag. He wiped the dirt from his face and pushed his glasses on to his nose. The dust in the air caught his throat and he coughed to clear it.

Perhaps their nerves were shot after what had happened at Habrut. Perhaps it was simply that the Adoo mortar onslaught that had killed or wounded four of them and forced SAF's withdrawal from Habrut had begun the same way. But, unlike the BATT, when the first falling mortar rounds began to pound along the gravel plain as they marched towards the perimeter fence, the Dhofar Gendarmerie in the fort up on the hill radioed Dhofar HQ at Um al Gwarif to report the contact. At 0530 hours, SAF received their first hint that there was trouble brewing at Mirbat.

At the same time, Mike Kealy glanced at his watch before, wearing flip-flops, he climbed up on to the roof of the BATT House. The Regiment communicated with the HQ via their own radio net and, unaware that there were already reports filtering back to Salalah about the Adoo attack, it hadn't occurred to him to radio this in until he had something accurate and useful to report. Only a couple of weeks earlier BATT HQ had reminded all their locations of the need to be certain. Kealy had to find out for himself what was going on. A thin strip of pastel light on the horizon was raising the indigo curtain of the night. But there was no brightness. Impenetrable cloud hung barely 150 feet above the town. Even as dawn broke it was still going to feel dull and claustrophobic at Mirbat today. A fine drizzle like a Scotch mist hung in the air. It was *driek*.

Tall, thick sandbag walls were built up around the edges of the building. The house groaned under the weight of them. At the north-west corner, Snapper Winner, already at his stand-to position inside the bulky angular black scaffolding of the Browning's tripod, looked as if he was being consumed by a giant spider. On the opposite corner, behind defences built up from sandbags and dirt-filled metal ammunition boxes, Roger Cole and Jeff Taylor prepared the GPMG SF. It seemed likely now that Sustained Fire was going to be required today.

In the slate half-light Kealy saw the tall, rangy figure of Bob Bennett approach from the forward sangar wall. In his quiet West Country burr, the Sergeant in charge of Eight Troop's mortar team pointed out the line of Adoo mortars as they flared in the distance, sending rounds arcing into the air a second or so before the sound of the exploding propellant travelled across the distance that separated them. Closer, firing from the Jebel Ali, Bennett pointed to the muzzle-flashes from the enemy's Shpagin.

Kealy had eight men under his direct command. Between them at the BATT House, alongside their personal weapons, they had a GPMG SF, a single 81mm L16 mortar and the Browning. Like the rest of the Troop he couldn't help but tot up the forces he had at his disposal. And the odds didn't look good.

Over the growing din of the incoming fire cracking and bellowing in, he heard Tak speaking Arabic on the radio. He was talking to Bahait, the Firqa Commander, but the Fijian drew a blank. The FAU leader reported that his force of forty men were still out on the Jebel. A handful of men remained in the Firqa House south of the BATT's position. But the Firqa main force could offer no help.

Kealy flinched involuntarily at the sound of three thunderous blasts, three seconds between them, erupting from just beyond the BATT House walls. Startled at first, he realized it was the sound of his own mortar team throwing ranging shots in search of the Adoo baseplates.

'Where's Laba?' Kealy asked, reminded that he hadn't seen the big Corporal since the shooting had started. Bob Bennett, a little Tokai radio clamped against his ear as he plotted the fall of Hussey's mortar fire, nodded in the direction of the DG fort.

'He's manning the 25 pounder,' Bennett told the Boss before passing corrections to range and bearing over the radio to Fuzz.

While he'd still been able, before the weight of incoming fire made the journey suicidal, Laba had jogged across the 400 yards of open ground to the gun on the hill to get the old artillery piece into the fight on their side. That was a kernel of better news. Kealy was grateful for Laba's presence of mind. And yet the young Captain still didn't know what the Adoo had in store for them. So far, despite the intensity of the attack, the rebels had continued to stand off and attack them from a distance. But something out of the ordinary was definitely unfolding. What if that was just a prelude? Just the artillery barrage before the infantry advance. No way of knowing.

But Kealy felt a stab of apprehension as he realized just how threadbare the Mirbat defences really were. He knew he had to raise the alarm with BATT HQ. A shell whistled in and exploded beyond the walls, shredding the outer layer of sandbags with shrapnel. Kealy ducked and scrambled low across the flat roof towards the Browning .50 sangar.

Snapper Winner was ready to fire on command. He gripped the two handles of the Browning and looked down the thick barrel through the fixed concentric circles of the sight towards the Adoo positions. The powerful machine gun was no rapier. But weighing in at over three times the weight of even the GPMG, it offered a broadsword instead, with explosive-tipped

Returning for a second morning of attacks, Wing Commander Peter Hulme, Commander of SOAF's entire operation in Dhofar and standing in for Bill Stoker, was nearly brought down by ground fire. Here fuel can be seen streaming from his starboard wing as he brings his jet in for a deadstick landing at Salalah.

A Canberra on the pan at Masirah, 1972. During SOAF cross-border raids, the RAF launched 13 Squadron Canberra PR9 spyplanes from RAF Masirah on long-range reconnaissance missions up and down the Yemeni coast.

RAF Salalah was defended against attack from the ground by a ring of improvised forts known as 'Hedgehogs', manned by men of the RAF Regiment. But the 'Rock Apes' could only retaliate against mortar or RCL attacks from the Jebel, not prevent them.

Shrapnel damage to the accommodation block. On the anniversary of their formation the Adoo launched a barrage of RCL attacks against the airfield. Two rounds hit the patio of the RAF Officers' Mess during a barbeque to celebrate the award of the Sultan's Gallantry Medal to Peter Hulme. Hulme and others were badly injured.

The FST. The wounded were treated in the Field Surgical Team's new Twynham hut operating theatre.

Members of the FST inspect damage from the Adoo RCLs. Skidding in on a flat trajectory, the shells threw out shrapnel that cut across the patio like the blade of a scythe.

B Squadron, 22 SAS, returned to Oman in April 1972, landing at Salalah on board an RAF Hercules transport.

Sekonaia Takavesi and Eight Troop were sent to take over as the BATT Civil Action Team at Mirbat. Their home for the tour was the BATT House, the closest to the camera of the three large buildings around the market next to the beach.

Corporal Talalaisi Labalaba, wrapped in bandoliers of 7.62mm ammunition, carrying a GPMG. Takavesi and Labalaba had first met when they both volunteered to join the British Army during a recruiting drive in Fiji in 1961.

The view of the Dhofar Gendarmerie fort from the BATT House. Tak and Laba were responsible for a 25 pounder artillery piece located in a gunpit alongside the DG fort.

Inside the BATT House looking north towards Jebel Ali (just visible at the top of the picture). Top left is the sangar occupied by Pete 'Snapper' Winner's Browning .50 heavy machine gun.

Skyvan with Mirbat fort in the background. As the end of Eight Troop's tour approached, their position was resupplied with three months' worth of ammunition ready for the arrival of their G Squadron replacements.

Aerial view of Mirbat looking south – looking in the same direction that the Adoo attacked across the plain. The line of the wire surrounding the town can be seen. The DG fort is on the low hill beyond the north-east corner of the town, the BATT House and Wali's fort just beyond the north-west limit of the town. Dominating them both and the plain in between is the 300ft-high Jebel Ali, the dark rock cluster at the bottom right of the picture.

Captain Mike Kealy. Just twenty-seven years old and new to the SAS, Kealy was uncertain how he would fair in command of battle-hardened, experienced Regiment troopers.

BATT mortar fire. The Adoo launched their attack in the dark before dawn with a mortar barrage. Return mortar fire from Fuzz Hussey, directed by Bob Bennett, was the initial SAS reply.

After the Huey was beaten back by enemy machine-gun fire, the bullet holes in the fuselage of Neville Baker's helicopter – just visible in the pilot's door at the top right of the picture, and through the perspex window of the cabin door – provide evidence of how lucky the team were to escape after their first casevac attempt.

David Milne-Smith and Sean Creak scrambled towards Mirbat in a pair of rocket-armed Strikemasters as soon as the low *khareef* cloud over Mirbat had lifted sufficiently.

The Strikemaster's reflector gunsight. Because the cloud forced them to attack at extreme low level, Milne-Smith and Creak had to guess at the correct depression angle to feed into the sight that would predict the fall of their shot.

A Strikemaster firing a salvo of 81mm SURA rockets. Unable to safely or effectively drop bombs at such low altitude, Milne-Smith and Creak were limited to using rockets and machine guns.

Strikemaster turning hard at low level. This picture shows how, when Bill Stoker joined David Milne-Smith on the second 1 Squadron mission in support of Eight Troop at Mirbat, the heavy-machine-gun round that hit him entered through the top of the wing and punched a large exit hole in the bottom.

Out of fuel and forced to glide into Salalah without power, Bill Stoker was escorted by his wingman, David Milne-Smith, who handled the RT, allowing Stoker to concentrate on flying.

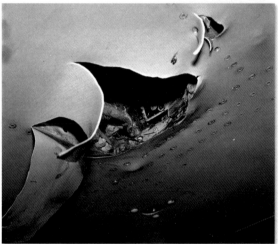

Battle damage to Bill Stoker's wing from the Adoo Shpagin 12.7mm heavy machine gun on Jebel Ali.

The G Squadron relief force were choppered in and dropped on the beach south of Salalah. This picture, not taken at the time, provides a vivid impression of the scene.

Resupplies of ammunition are parachuted into Mirbat on the day of the battle. This picture, never-before-seen, was taken by Andy Dunsire from the back of the Skyvan flown by Barrie Williams.

Casualties from the Battle of Mirbat are stretchered back to the FST from the 3 Squadron casevac helicopter.

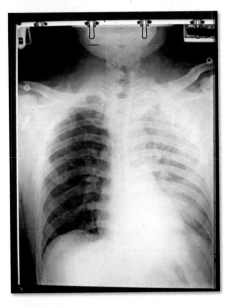

X-ray taken of Sekonaia Takavesi after the battle. The Kalashnikov round that disabled him for much of the battle – and nearly killed him – can be seen lodged in his right shoulder at the top left of the picture. The image also reveals the lack of air in his left lung due to bleeding.

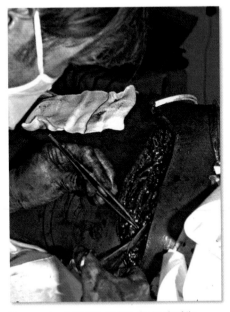

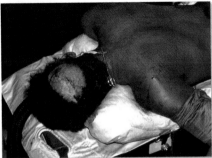

Tak on the FST operating table, his head shaved in order to treat the wound from the bullet that grazed it. The entry wound from the round that passed across his back can just be made out behind his left shoulder.

Surgeon Joe Johnston excises the track of the bullet. A chest drain is visible at the far end of the cut.

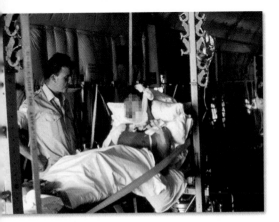

Tommy Tobin is medevaced home aboard an RAF C-130 Hercules two days after the battle, his terrible facial wounds treated and stabilized by the FST surgeons.

Mirbat fort. The extraordinary battle for it, fought on 19 July 1972, proved to be a turning point in the Dhofar war. The action, and the men who fought it, entered SAS legend.

half-inch rounds that could take out armour plate. As Kealy had talked to Bob Bennett, Winner cracked open the top cover of the big .50 and gently placed the chain-linked ammunition belt in the feed tray; a ticker-tape of brass and lead. He flipped the cover down and, pulling back twice on a heavy lever on the right of the receiver like he was playing a one-armed bandit, cocked the gun and chambered the first incendiary round. A piece of the chain link was ejected from the right of the gun and fell to the floor with a light metallic tink, barely audible above the rattle of the Adoo machine guns. Thumb on the V-shaped butterfly trigger, gripping the two spade handles at the rear of the gun, Snapper released the safety catch.

Green tracer rounds from the Shpagin on the Jebel Ali zipped in through the dull dawn. At a distance, they seemed almost manageably slow, only to accelerate viciously as they closed down on their target, snapping in like the tip of a bullwhip.

Tak didn't think that Snapper was scared of anything, but that's not how Winner felt right now. The ex-Sapper's heart was going like a jackhammer, but while a knot of anxiety twisted in Winner's stomach, he felt all right; in fact he *welcomed* it.

Without fear, he told himself, *you do not have that razor's edge of concentration.*

In the distance, he could see Laba working on the 25 pounder in the gunpit outside the walls of the DG fort. Behind him, he heard the ammunition-box stairs clank as someone made their way up to the sangar. He turned to see Mike Kealy clambering over the sangar wall. Kealy dropped down on to his flip-flops and scuttled across to Winner, who cocked an ear to hear what his Boss had to say. Winner hadn't seen Kealy like this before; there'd been no cause for it. But, he thought, the young Captain was calculating the odds. And he looked unfazed by them.

'Go down to the radio room,' Kealy told Winner in a low measured voice, 'and establish communications with Um al Gwarif.' As he acknowledged the order a shell screamed overhead towards the town. The two BATT men flinched in its wake. A split second later they saw the explosion behind them; then, after a beat, the air-sucking cough of the soundtrack. There was already screaming and crying from Mirbat from the destruction caused by long mortar rounds. But this last round, Kealy and Winner both knew instantly, had been no mortar. Clearly the weight of the Adoo attack had not yet reached its peak. Winner made safe the Browning and climbed down to the radio room, pulled on the headphones and began to tap out a Morse code message on PRC316.

The room shook as another Adoo shell blasted outside the wall with a loud crump, showering Winner with plaster and dust. As he choked on the dry, settling cloud, Winner waited for a response from the BATT HQ. In his ears, he could hear only the roll and squelch of the radio static. Then, cutting through the background, the synthesized monotone stutter of the HQ signaller's Morse punched through. Winner glanced again at the tattered old codebook.

In order to protect the security of their communications, all Regiment radio traffic in Dhofar used code rather than plain Morse. But to convert a message from English into code was laborious and time-consuming. And with the crescendo of gunfire outside, Winner hesitated before reaching for the codebook again. Then Fuzz Hussey ran into the radio room and helped him make up his mind.

'Listen, you bastard,' Fuzz spat in flat Lancashire vowels, 'you only need to code a message when the enemy doesn't know where you are. If the enemy knows where you are, then what in the name of hell do you need to code a message for? They're firing at us, for God's sake!'

Hussey was right. They were well past the point where Standard Operational Procedure took precedence over the reality of the situation on the ground.

Fuck the rulebook, Snapper agreed, and with his finger and thumb he rapped out the tap-dance rhythm of his message in plain Morse. Fuzz was right. There was neither the need, nor the time to arse around with codes today.

```
_._. ___ _. _ _. _.._ _ / .._ _. _.. . .__ / .... . ._
...._ _._ / ...._ .. ._. . / ._ _. .. _ / ___ ._ _
```

Contact ... Under heavy fire ... Wait ...
Out

As the weight of incoming fire began to open cracks in the
BATT House walls, Snapper leapt up from the chair to return
to his stand-to position behind the Browning on the roof. A
thought still nagged away at him. It shouldn't have been
possible for the Adoo to have launched a full-scale attack like
this on Mirbat without there being some warning. There was
supposed to be a guard on the Jebel Ali. At the very least an
exchange of fire from their defence of their position should
have raised the alarm

Where's the night picquet? he wondered. *Why haven't they
opened fire? Where are they?*

Chapter 31

We are in the shit, thought Fuzz Hussey as it became clear that, as the day dawned, the Adoo attack was only increasing in ferocity, *we are really in the shit. There's only bloody nine of us.* But from the mortar pit at ground level, as he hovered over the fluorescent sight dial of the L61 mortar inputting Bob Bennett's corrections to range and bearing, while Tommy Tobin and Tak maintained the flow of bombs, Fuzz was one of the last to know just how deep in they were. While the mortar team maintained their steady barrage of 10lb mortar shells on the Adoo positions, on the roof of the BATT House the situation was becoming a little more confused.

Roger Cole saw them first from the GPMG SF sangar on the left. Across the gravel plain to the Jebel, daylight changed the picture. The firefly flare of the Adoo mortar positions was lost as the sun washed away the darkness. The percussive racket of the Shpagins remained; so too the thump and crump of the mortars, but in place of the accompanying fireworks there was a thickening pall of smoke, new plumes emerging and adding to it like blowing geysers from where the Adoo mortar bombs fell. And all around, the surface of the ground, chewed up by machine-gun fire, danced like dry rice on a snare drum. Emerging from it all, at a distance, Cole picked out a group of around forty men advancing towards them. Cole shouted out to get Kealy's attention. But while it may have been Kealy that Cole was addressing, there were six BATT men on the roof and, as one, they turned towards the north, their eyes scanning to get a fix on Cole's sighting.

As his fingers flexed around the spade handle grips, Snapper's thumb pushed down on the trigger of the .50, taking up the first pressure. His eyes narrow, he stared over the long barrel of the Browning, with the distinctive, perforated sleeve at its base. The brass cases of the ammunition feeding from the left of the gun caught the low light of the overcast early morning. He glanced at Kealy expectantly. But the officer was impassive. He removed his glasses from the pocket of his shirt, cleaned the lenses and placed them back carefully on his face. Snapper waited.

'Hold your fire,' Kealy said.

'Let's open fire now,' Snapper urged the young Troop Commander. After months slugging it out with the Adoo on the Jebel during Operation JAGUAR, Snapper had developed an instinct for when the Adoo meant business. And he was sure he was not wrong this time. New to the Regiment and inexperienced compared to his battle-hardened men, Kealy had shown a willingness to take their advice in Mirbat, confident enough to take or leave it on merit, rather than pointlessly assert his authority, but on this occasion Kealy stood firm.

'We've got to wait for the night picquet,' he said. There was a chance it was the DG guard from the position on the Jebel Ali. Despite Tak's earlier RT exchange with Bahait, there was a possibility it could have been the Firqa returning from their patrol. Until the identity of the men was beyond doubt, Kealy wasn't going to risk a blue-on-blue; he was not going to open fire on his own side.

In the Wali's fort ahead of the BATT House, Kealy could see the Governor's Askars lining the battlements with the .303 Martini Henry bolt-action rifles. They too seemed to understand the situation. Tak's daily visits to the fort and his efforts to foster the best possible understanding with the Wali and his militia seemed to be paying off.

'Hold your fire . . .' Kealy repeated, quiet but firm, his eyes fixed on the men advancing across the plain.

Fixed in the sights of the BATT and Askar guns, the

advancing soldiers began to move with more purpose; accelerating and spreading out into an extended infantry line as they approached through the smoke of the mortar exchange. Then, acting together like a First World War attack across no-man's-land, they raised their weapons and began to fire.

And, from the roof of the Wali's fort, the sudden rattle of a single Bren light machine gun became Mirbat's first response to the Adoo infantry's declaration of intent.

B Squadron's Commander, Duke Pirie, was woken up in the time it took for someone to reach him from the BATT radio room. There were troops in contact at Mirbat, he was told, and he needed to get to the Ops Room. On a camp bed in the Duke's room for the night because of the changeover, the G Squadron Boss, Alistair Morrison, couldn't help but get the same precis of the situation as Pirie and he, too, got up and pulled on his clothes. The two majors went straight through to the Ops Room to find out what was going on, but there wasn't much more the Duty Officer could share. But if Mirbat was under fire then, alongside the eight-man BATT troop from B Squadron, Morrison knew that one of his own men, Jeff Taylor, who'd flown in with Morrison as part of the advance party, was already there. The situation was confused, though. There had been a single, brief message from the BATT House less than half an hour ago and nothing else since. But that silence and the fact the signaller had called it in in plain Morse both offered clues as to the seriousness of the situation in Mirbat.

Pirie and Morrison began to organize their response. They had no choice but to plan for the worst and make sure that they mobilized all the resources available. First of all, via SAF HQ, a call was put through to the Air Force radio room. Pirie wanted jets and helicopters. Then the blond Major left to go to find his Quartermaster, Lofty Wiseman, to tell him that the couple of thousand rounds he'd loaded into the back of the Bedford for G Squadron's morning at the Arzat ranges wasn't going to be nearly enough. Not even close. Pirie wanted him to empty the armoury into the back of a truck and drive the load to RAF Salalah.

'Open fire!' Kealy shouted, at last letting his men off the leash.

With relish, Snapper thought as he finally depressed the Browning's trigger with his thumb. The big machine gun immediately began to chug, its barrel pumping forwards and backwards as it spat big .50 cal explosive bullets at the advancing Adoo. Behind it, Snapper's whole body juddered like a navvy with a pneumatic drill as the barely contained recoil from the big gun was transmitted up through his arms from his tight grip on the spade handles. Heavy brass cases churned out of the bottom of the machine gun, piling up on the floor in a rising metallic slag heap. Out of the right of the receiver, the Browning ejected the spent chain links into another corner of the sangar. What the big .50 conceded to the Gimpy in rate of fire, it made up for with a kind of relentless, bassy persistence.

To Kealy's left, Roger Cole and Jeff Taylor fired the Gimpy, its buzz-saw rattle setting up a deafening poly-rhythmic cacophony with the Browning, punctuated by the open-mouthed thump of the mortar lobbing 81mm bombs into the air as fast as Tak and Tommy Tobin could drop them down the tube. But it was the noise Laba was making that really caught their attention.

The deep roaring boom from each shot of the 25 pounder artillery piece had barely rolled across the plain before the next thunderclap began to echo around the battlefield. Enveloped in smoke from the propellant charge, Laba was firing the big gun as rhythmically as a piston in a steam engine, maintaining a steady rate of fire of four or five rounds per minute. It was an extraordinary singlehanded effort. To cover command, loading, laying, the breech, ramming, and preparation of the ammunition, the official size of the guncrew for a 25 pounder was six. A reduced detachment was four men. The big Fijian was doing it all on his own. And the old gun's mechanism was anything but automatic. Keeping the gun firing was like the worst the Industrial Revolution could throw at its workforce: heat, noise, heavy metal, shock and hard, relentless physical labour. With each shot Laba, aiming straight along the barrel of the gun, had to wind it on to the elevation he wanted, marry a 25lb high-explosive projectile to the brass shell case containing the propellant, then pull open the breech lever, slam in the assembled round, ram it, jam the breech lever forward like a mad signalman changing the points, fire, then pull open the breech again to let the spent brass case slide out in a swirl of hot gas and acrid gunsmoke. Each round weighed the same as a full-size family television. And with each shot, the temperature of the metalwork around the breech rose higher.

But the regular bark from the gunpit sounded almost as if the gun were being belt fed. And if Laba's comrades at the BATT House were impressed by the big man's industry, the Adoo, unaware and unable to see behind the thick armour-plate shield that protected him, could only draw the most obvious conclusion: that the old field gun was being manned by a full-size crew. And they would need to take into account the strength of the defence they might encounter as a result.

Neville Baker was woken by a bang on the door from the SOAF Ops Officer. The helicopter Squadron Boss opened his eyes and shouted an acknowledgement.

'Casevac Mirbat,' came the shout back through the door. Baker looked at his watch; just after six o'clock. A couple of minutes later, wearing his flying suit and boots, he was rapping on the door of his co-pilot, Charlie Gilchrist. The young RAF pilot told him to come in. Baker turned the handle and opened the door. Gilchrist was in bed.

'We need to get airborne,' Baker said, 'I'll tell you all about it later.' Baker didn't *know* any more at this stage. Although, if it was Mirbat, it had to be the BATT. Gilchrist jumped out of bed and pulled on his gear as Baker waited, then the two of them jogged outside to the waiting Mini-Moke, reserved for the alert crews to get them from wherever they were on the base to the Squadron as soon as the call to scramble came in.

They jumped into the little beach buggy and sped off towards SOAF(Tac) HQ underneath low, grey-white cloud. A cloud-base of not much above fifty feet didn't make for great flying weather. It wouldn't cause them any trouble, but there was no way the jets were going to get up in it. Fine drops of mist dampened their foreheads as they sped towards the tower.

And yet, despite Baker and Gilchrist's urgency, no one at Mirbat had yet actually made any request for air support, either from the helicopters or from the jets. But, as more Adoo joined the lines of rebel infantry advancing on the BATT positions, that was starting to become the focus of a heated debate.

There's only one way out of this, Snapper thought as he watched the Adoo pour across the plain towards them, *and that's air power*. But, just weeks earlier, a directive had been issued from BATT HQ to locations throughout Dhofar reminding all the troop sergeants and commanders not to call in the jets at the first sign of trouble. When calling for the jets, the BATT needed to be specific about coordinates and certain of their target. They needed to make each jet sortie count.

Now Mike Kealy and Tak were locking horns over it. As it had been with the decision over when to open fire, it was ultimately Kealy's call, but within the Regiment that fact didn't stop his men making their own view felt. And forcefully if necessary.

'Mike,' Tak had suggested, 'why don't you call the jets in?' One look across the plain left Tak in no doubt about the severity of the situation.

It's just like a war movie, he thought as he watched the sections of enemy advancing across the gravel plain. Too many to count, their blood up, confident of success. To his eyes, given the obvious size of the Adoo force ranged against them, the need for air support was a given. But Kealy, possibly conscious that if he jumped the gun in calling in the Strikemasters it might be counted against him by his own superiors, and with less operational experience to bring to bear on what was happening at Mirbat, seemed reluctant to accept the Fijian's view that Fast Air was urgently needed.

'So what!' Tak said, his voice rising in exasperation at Kealy's unwillingness to ignore the instruction from HQ. Right now, as far as the Fijian Trooper was concerned, it didn't matter what HQ said. There were hundreds of Adoo out there. Since the BATT had returned fire, the two machine guns, the mortar and the 25 pounder had forced the Adoo to go to ground, to seek cover and slow their advance. But for how long? To Tak, a veteran of fierce Regiment campaigns in Aden and Borneo, it was clear that Eight Troop remained in grave danger of being overwhelmed.

'Get the fucking jets in!' Tak screamed at him. The young officer had never seen the usually laid-back Fijian sound so fiery, but he stood his ground. Kealy had made up his mind: he was going to wait. Then his Tokai radio crackled. He put it to his ear.

The gunpit, he thought, straining to hear over the din of the firefight. Laba? But, unable to hear the message, Kealy couldn't be sure. Before he had a chance to consider it further, there was a shout from the two machine-gun sangars. Roger Cole and Snapper Winner needed ammunition. Unless they kept the two machine guns in commission any discussion of whether or not jets were going to be able to dig them out of the hole they were in was moot.

Kealy shouted to Tommy Tobin to help him. Then the two of them ferried heavy sharp-edged ammunition boxes up the home-made staircase and ladders from the ground floor to the roof, sliding them along the flat surface to their recipients like a barman sending a whisky in a wild west saloon.

From the cover of the ground floor, Kealy and Tobin had returned to a maelstrom. The noise of the firefight was physical; a staccato assault of sound and violence. Around the sangars, Adoo machine-gun rounds tore up the hessian sand-bags and chinked into the dirt-filled ammunition boxes below. Little waterfalls of sand poured from each of the holes. Below, the big 12.7mm Shpagin rounds chipped into the stone walls of the house. And in the air around the roof chunks of lead criss-crossed, each warping the sky like an express train as it cracked past. Cole, Taylor, Winner, Tobin and Kealy could *feel* each near miss.

Rejoining the fight, Kealy grabbed his SLR and buried himself into the sandbag wall, taking careful aim and picking off Adoo with crisp, targeted double-taps; making each shot count. This is what the rifle was designed for. While the Adoo's fully automatic AKs had the advantage in close-quarter battle, from this distance it was the powerful, accurate SLR that was now weapon of choice. When Kealy's rounds hit their mark, Adoo fighters were picked up and dumped backwards by the force of the 7.62mm round's impact. To the Troop Commander's right and left, the GPMG and the Browning raked right and left across the limits of their arc of fire, cutting down any Adoo who broke cover. But from their relatively recessed position in the BATT House on the edge of town, their view funnelled between the Wali's fort to the left and rising ground to the right, Cole and Winner didn't have a completely unobstructed view of the Adoo advance against the DG fort. Only Laba was witness to that.

The effort at Um al Gwarif was ramping up. While the SAS Quartermaster pulled in men to help him load the contents of the armoury into the back of a truck, in the Officers' Mess, Graeme Smyth-Piggott was being woken by his Company Commander, Tresham Gregg.

After coming down from Simba position, the Northern Frontier Regiment was now the in-line battalion on the plain, manning positions at Adonib along the coast and, alongside the RAF Regiment, one of the Hedgehog forts defending the airfield. Today, though, Smash was the duty officer at UAG, on standby to respond to any sudden incidents with the sixty men of Five and Seven Platoons NFR he had under his command. And it sounded as if what was unfolding forty miles along the coast definitely qualified as a sudden incident.

'All hell,' Gregg told him, 'is happening at Mirbat.'

Chapter 32

'I've been chinned.' It was Laba, transmitting from the gunpit. Tak could hear the strain in his voice over the cheap little Japanese radio. Laba added that he was all right, but from the BATT House it was impossible to know just what the situation out by the DG fort was like. But the forward position had become the inevitable focus of the Adoo attack.

Chinned. Tak considered his friend's choice of words. Laba had been grazed by a bullet either directly or by ricochet. If the big man was really badly wounded then he'd have said so. He was clearly still in the game, but probably underplaying it. Tak tried to find out more, but there was no response from Laba; just the empty hiss and whistle of static.

That's enough for me, Tak thought, *I've got to join him.*

'I'm going out,' he told Kealy, thinking *nothing's going to stop me running up there*. The officer saw the look in the powerful Fijian's dark eyes and nodded his approval.

'Take some extra medical kit,' Kealy added. 'And keep low . . .'

Tak grabbed his SLR, strapped on his belt kit and stood inside the heavy wooden door of the BATT House, steeling himself for a 500-yard dash across open ground. The Fijians had a reputation within the Regiment for being fearless, but Tak was scared. Only a madman wouldn't have been.

I've got no choice, he told himself, *it's either your day or not. It's my day*, he decided and he darted out beyond the safety of the sangars and the stone walls of the BATT House and began an almost suicidal charge up the hill towards Laba.

From his position on the roof, Snapper saw Tak run out under the close, dark, overcast sky that hung over Mirbat, a figure in shorts, legs like pistons, dodging and ducking as he tried to make himself as difficult and unpredictable a target as he could. But from the five-0 sangar, Winner could see green tracer rounds from the Adoo machine guns zipping across his path, ahead and behind him, each one led and followed by another five high-velocity rounds he couldn't see.

He's gonna drop, Winner thought, his heart in his mouth as he willed his friend on.

Rounds whipped around him, snapping and zipping through the air in a seemingly impassable, invisible cat's cradle of inter-secting trajectories. Around his feet he saw plumes of dirt kicked up from bullets striking the ground. Pumping his arms and legs, he charged on, not yet halfway across.

Shit, he thought, *I can't believe I'm doing this*, but as he bobbed and weaved, throwing his fourteen-stone frame from right to left as if he were taking on the opposition back row for Hereford Town RFC, he was covering the ground. And so far his luck was holding. But as he closed in on the fort, so he ran closer to the vanguard of the Adoo attack and as the ground rose underneath him he only became more exposed.

Four hundred yards in – a full circuit of an athletics track – and nearly a minute out in the open, the crepe soles of Tak's desert boots began to bite the gravel slope of the final hill towards the gunpit. His lungs now tearing for breath and his heart drumming, he powered up past the ammunition dump on the back of the knoll, towards the 25 pounder, then dived in over the rock walls and sandbags surrounding the gun and landed in an inelegant heap at his friend's feet. Foot-long brass shell cases were strewn around the floor of the gunpit, kicked away by Laba as they dropped out of the back of the gun after each shot.

Laba, hair damp with drizzle and sweat, his chin streaked with blood where the bullet had hit him and his face and clothes blackened by oil and gunsmoke, grinned widely.

'Bula!' he welcomed his friend in Fijian. 'Watch out! Keep your head down!' Laba barely interrupted his relentless open breech, load, ram, fire, open breech rhythm on the artillery gun. As the triple-base propellant of nitrocellulose, nitro-glycerine and picrite launched the high-explosive shells down the barrel, the gun kicked back on the rubber tyres and split trail of its carriage. Thick, acrid white smoke smothered the gun position as each shot rumbled away under the low cloud. As their desperate last stand continued, each man felt buoyed by the presence of the other. While Laba was joking and laughing, Tak felt invulnerable. But they remained the Adoo's priority target, one which would have profound consequences for the whole BATT defence if it fell.

If the Adoo overwhelmed the two Fijians, they also captured the 25 pounder itself. And with control of the field gun, they had a devastating new weapon they could turn on both the BATT House and the town itself. Under a barrage of accurate shelling from the 25 pounder, it was hard to see the Regiment's resistance continuing for much longer.

Laba gestured towards the 25-pounder ammunition boxes. There was work to do. Laba's guncrew had just doubled in size. With Tak marrying the high-explosive shells and the charge cartridges and Laba just concentrating on loading, lay-ing and firing the gun, maybe they could double the rate of fire. But everything was complicated by the weight of incoming fire. They remained under heavy attack. As soon as either of them put their head up they could hear the bullets whistling by, while the armour shield around the barrel of the gun clattered like a tin roof in a hail storm as it protected the two BATT men from the onslaught.

On scrambles, the alert helicopter always flew with two pilots. The Huey didn't need a second pilot, but casevac sorties usually took them into harm's way and filling both seats in the cockpit provided redundancy. If one of the aviators was shot, the mission continued. It could also make for a quicker getaway. And while Neville Baker was briefed in the Ops

Room, co-pilot Charlie Gilchrist went through a brief exterior check of the helicopter, AB205, serial number 705. He checked that the Airwork engineers had removed all the covers, locks and tiedowns, then walked up and down the fuselage casting an eye over it for anything out of the ordinary. Baker walked out to the aircraft and the two pilots climbed into their crash-resistant seats and strapped themselves into their harnesses. In the back, Aircrewman Stan Standford plugged his headset into the Huey's intercom system, wondering what today's scramble would bring.

'SAS are having a bit of trouble at Mirbat,' Baker told his crew, 'some Adoo have come down off the hills.' As he spoke, Baker looked up and his gloved left hand reached to the over-head control panel, where he checked the electrics were ready for engine start.

Main Generator Switch – ON and cover down.

Starter Generator Switch – START.

Battery Switch – OFF.

Baker's practised eye glanced across the systems instruments, checking their static indications, slippage marks and ranges. On the pedestal panel between the seats, he flicked the two fuel switches to ON and checked he had full and free movement of the flight controls. He twisted the throttle as close to the engine idle stop as he could, wound on a touch of friction, then pushed and held the engine start trigger with his thumb. The Lycoming T-53 turboshaft immediately whistled loudly into life, its grating, powerful whine audible even through Baker and Gilchrist's ear-defending headsets. As the compressor speed reached 15 per cent the big two-bladed main rotor was beginning to turn, flicking across the view forward from the cockpit. As the compressor speed wound up past 40 per cent, Baker released the start button and slowly advanced the throttle to idle.

The main rotor accelerated, beating through the damp air in a disappearing blur. Beneath it the whole helicopter began to throb and shake like a bus travelling along an unsealed road. Baker pulled the RT switch on the cyclic stick with his right hand.

Salalah Tower, the Squadron Boss opened on the Air Traffic frequency, speaking into the mike curled round from his headset, and he requested a radio check.

Pulling up on the collective stick with his left hand he felt the main rotor take the weight of the helicopter and corrected instinctively with a little left rudder. Then he established the Huey in a low hover over the hardstanding before accelerating south through the drizzle towards the sea. Once over water, he banked gently towards the east and settled into an 80 knot cruise, scudding beneath the low cloud barely twenty feet above the Indian Ocean swell.

With the coastline to the left, the crew of Huey 705 flew just far enough out to sea to be sure of avoiding Adoo small-arms fire until, as they approached Taqa, the cloudbase dropped down to the surface of the sea, blocking their route ahead.

Since Tak's departure for the gunpit, Kealy's 2ic, Bob Bennett, had also talked to him about calling in the jets. Unlike Tak, the unruffled, experienced Troop Sergeant had been more successful in allaying the Boss's concerns that it was a decision that might count as a black mark against him. But as he made the decision to request air support, Kealy realized, with a start, that beyond Snapper's initial contact report there had been no further communication between Mirbat and BATT HQ. While for around forty minutes the firefight had raged around them, at Um al Gwarif they were still being forced to make their own assumptions about what was going on. Once again, Kealy sent Snapper down to the radio room. This time Winner's tapped out message made it clear: Eight Troop needed a casevac helicopter and he rattled off another series of dots and dashes:

$$\bullet \bullet \bullet \quad - \quad \bullet - \quad \bullet - \bullet \quad - \quad \bullet - \bullet \quad \bullet \quad - \bullet -$$

STARTREK

– the codeword for air strikes. Mirbat needed Fast Air.

*

From the moment the keys to the Mini-Moke were handed over, the 1 Squadron duty pair were joined at the hip. From dusk till dawn they were inseparable, committed to being airborne in two fully armed Strikemasters within five minutes of the request for air support being received by the SOAF radio room. No one ever took that long.

On 19 July, the names on the roster were David Milne-Smith and Sean Creak. As soon as the call came through to their rooms from the Ops Room, the two fighter pilots were up, in flying suits, and running for the little car. But it was clear to them both, as soon as they left the accommodation block, that the weather was unflyable. The *khareef* was all but down on the deck.

Bill Stoker was already in the small crew room.

'What's going on?' Creak, the nominated Flight Leader, asked the Squadron Boss.

'I don't know; they're under attack from the north and all we're getting . . .' Stoker paused, before admitting: 'It's not terribly clear.' But like his two pilots, he knew that unless the cloudbase improved they were powerless to help. And like them, he also knew that, if the call for air support came from the BATT, it wasn't a request made lightly. Whatever was happening at Mirbat was serious. With the cloudbase outside, though, stubbornly clamped below 150 feet, they were grounded. There were two practical problems. The first was simply that, while it might be possible to take off and climb blind, on instruments, through the cloud to a safe height above it, if the weather was the same all along the coast, then they'd have no chance of descending through the cloud at Mirbat. Even if the BATT reported that there was a 200ft cloudbase above them, it was simply too dangerous to descend through cloud in the *hope* that you would break clear before you hit the ground.

And if, Creak thought, *we can't get back down again, we'll be as much good as a spare proverbial at a wedding.* There was absolutely nothing that the Strikemasters could do to help the men on the ground if they couldn't see them.

There was also the danger of a brief 'Sucker's Gap' appearing over Salalah. If a temporary break in the cloud over the airbase provided an opportunity to take off, it had no bearing on whether they'd be able to get down again at Mirbat. More importantly, it didn't guarantee that, when they returned to Salalah, the cloud wouldn't have closed up again over the station. And ultimately it was this, not a concern that they'd find their hands tied over Mirbat, that was keeping the two pilots, desperate to get airborne and help, grounded.

If the cloudbase over the airfield was below 200 feet even the ACR7 radar and a talkdown from Air Traffic wasn't enough to bring them home safely, forcing a diversion to the old oil company airstrip at Midway which, fifty miles to the north, was beyond the grip of the monsoon.

The two pilots might have been happy to take that chance, but it wasn't any lack of nerve on their part that was holding them back. It was simpler than that. Until the cloudbase cleared the 200ft radar minimum, it was actually illegal for them to leave the ground.

'How's the weather at Mirbat?' Creak asked, still thinking through their options.

'There's cloud, but they're not discussing the weather too much,' the Ops Officer replied, before adding, with an edge of dryness, 'more that they're under attack . . .' Creak ignored it, realizing that they really only had one option.

'We'll have to stay below,' he decided. The instant the Tower could confirm that the cloudbase had reached the 200ft minimum, the Strikemasters could scramble, but they couldn't afford to climb above the clouds. They'd have to fly the whole mission at very low level, sandwiched between the overcast sky and the ground. But being able to get to Mirbat and back was only one half of the story.

'Let's say the cloudbase gets to 210,' said DMS, his thoughts racing ahead to how that lack of airspace would play out over the battlefield, 'what can we do?'

The jets wouldn't have the necessary altitude to set themselves up in dive attacks.

'We've never strafed level before, never rocketed level before and there's no point in taking bombs because the fuses won't arm. And even if they did, at that height they'll blow *us* up . . .'

Meanwhile, in Mirbat, Eight Troop continued to fight for their lives.

Chapter 33

There was only so much two men could do. Tak wasn't sure how many men were locked inside the fort to his right, but if he could bring them into the battle, it might help improve the odds. A couple of the DG guards could help keep the 25 pounder in business. The Fijian realized that, having already survived the race across from the BATT House, he was going to have to expose himself again to the hail of Adoo gunfire. Leaving Laba behind still working the gun, he scrambled flat over the sandbags at the back of the gunpit. The thick wooden door of the fort was just seven yards away. And, from the north-west at least, the gun, between him and the Adoo lines, would still offer a degree of cover. Dropping down on to the gravel, Tak stayed low and moved fast, scrabbling over to the door and trying to get it open. It was locked. Above his head, bullets cracked into the fort walls, showering him with stone chips. Tak tried again to loosen the metal clasp holding the door shut, then shoulder charged the heavy door, but he couldn't move it.

Tak cursed to himself then began banging on the door with his fist.

'Come out!' he shouted in Arabic. 'We need you!' He hoped that the guards inside – men he spent time talking to every day – would know it was him, that they might step up for a friend. He continued to bang and shout.

Then, after the scrape of metal, the door groaned open a touch. Behind it was one of the DG guards, his face washed out and pinched with fear. Tak recognized him and, speaking in Arabic, urged him to join the fight. Taking his courage in his hands, the little guard slipped around the door into the cross-fire. But he was instantly overwhelmed by the intensity of the crossfire and an instant appreciation of his own vulnerability beyond the three-foot-thick walls of the fort. Terrified, he bolted, running and diving straight for the cover of the ammunition dump twenty yards behind the gunpit.

No good at all, Tak thought, as the frightened guard dis-appeared from view behind him. It was no time for indulging in understanding; the big Fijian just needed men. He continued banging on the door and shouting for help.

Inside, the Omani Artillery Gunner, Walid Khamis, forced himself to the door, his loyalty to Tak and Laba helping suppress an otherwise irresistible fear. Like the DG guard before him, even to consider venturing beyond the safety of the fort was an extraordinarily courageous decision to make. He was a gunner, not an infantryman, and nothing in his training or experience had prepared him in any way for the ferocity of the combat outside. But he was part of Tak and Laba's gun-crew and Tak was saying they needed him. From within, he could hear the rattle of the machine-gun fire and the crump of the mortar shells outside. He scraped the bolt across, pulled open the heavy wooden door and stepped outside.

He was cut down almost immediately when a bullet from a Kalashnikov tore into his lower back and ripped into his stomach, causing internal bleeding and nerve injury that paralysed his lower legs. Wheeling first from the force of the impact then staggering as he clutched the gut wound, falling back into the safety of the fort wasn't even a conscious decision. As he tumbled from view, Tak caught sight of his face, contorted with pain. For his bravery, Khamis had been swiftly and violently removed from the fight.

And Tak and Laba were back where they started.

12.7mm Shpagin rounds began to mallet in around the fort door as the Adoo heavy machine guns zeroed in on him. The relentless stream of bullets chiselled smoking, dotted lines along the stone walls. Tak had been out in the open too long. Forced to give up on his efforts to drag anyone else out, he turned and, in two or three strides, ran back to the gunpit and threw himself over the wall.

By flying out to sea, running parallel with the wall of low cloud they'd met abeam Taqa, Neville Baker eventually found the obstacle's limit. As soon as the cloudbase lifted a little, he cut in underneath it and turned east again to run into Mirbat. As Huey 705 flew the final few miles in towards the town, the overcast lifted a little. Baker gave himself a little more height over the waves and nudged the speed up, cruising now at a shade under 100 knots.

Although Salalah had informed them over the radio that the BATT had now explicitly requested a casevac, there was little concrete information. Baker was just keeping his eye out for some SAS, and, he guessed, *a bloke with a bandage on his head*. Just a normal casevac. But it wasn't at all clear; sitting alongside, co-pilot Charlie Gilchrist was expecting to find that the fort had already been overrun. It turned out that neither of them had quite anticipated what lay ahead.

Eight hundred yards out, Baker checked his engine gauges – 6,600 rpm – then he eased back on the cyclic stick to start to slow the big helicopter's forward speed. At the same time he pulled up on the collective with his left hand to keep the Huey flying level and fed in a little power. All the time his feet were sensitive to any corrections needed to keep the nose pointing forward. He was bringing the Huey in fast.

About half a mile ahead, Charlie Gilchrist could see the fort. He scoured the scene looking for Adoo troops, any evidence that the position had already been taken by the enemy.

The main rotor slapped the air as Baker poured the power on, scrubbing off the airspeed as he descended towards the beach just north of the Wali's fort. Then he spotted a figure running out towards the waterline. For a moment he was unsure until the figure threw a green smoke grenade to mark the landing zone. He was BATT. All good; nothing to worry about. The Squadron Commander continued to feed in the power as their speed dropped. As he passed through one hundred yards, the speed over the ground was down to 20 knots.

Next to him, Charlie Gilchrist turned left towards the Jebel Ali, still keeping his eyes peeled for signs of the enemy. Then before he quite grasped what he was watching, Gilchrist saw a line of sharp plumes of water traversing the surface of the sea across the helicopter's nose.

Ahead, the BATT man on the beach who'd been guiding them in began what, from the cockpit, looked like a mad jig, waving his arms, trying to warn off the approaching heli.

'What the bloody hell's going on?' Baker wondered aloud over the aircraft's intercom. Then, ahead of them, the soldier pulled the pin on a red smoke grenade. It billowed crimson in front of them in sharp contrast to the grey weather, mud bricks and white sand in the background.

Their BATT welcoming party was scrubbing the landing.

Baker piled on the power and lowered the nose of the Huey to give him some manoeuvring speed as he squeezed the rudder with his foot to swing the helicopter round to port and away from shore. The Lycoming T-53 screamed as it spooled up in response to Baker's demands on the controls, the sound of 1,400 horsepower digging three tons of helicopter out of a hole. As ever, the Huey did all that was asked of her without complaint. But as the big 205 turned, she presented the length of her fuselage to the beach.

Machine-gun bullets raked along the Huey's camouflaged side, each one piercing the thin skin of the main cabin with a metallic chunk. As they rattled along the big heli, one of the rounds smashed through the window of the sliding main cabin door, crazing the perspex around the bullet hole.

To Charlie Gilchrist, it all felt unreal. Stan Standford behind him didn't have any trouble at all with the reality of what was going on. From his canvas seat in the back of the aircraft, he was looking at the daylight streaming through the holes in the side of the cabin. The enemy machine-gun rounds had missed him by inches.

'Are you OK, Stan?' Baker asked

'Yeah, fine,' came the answer from the phlegmatic, seasoned Aircrewman.

As they accelerated low over the sea away from Mirbat, Baker checked the instruments and warning panels for any sign of damage to the Huey's systems. It looked like they'd got away with it. But they'd taken hits. Baker decided the only sensible thing was to put down in Taqa, ten minutes up the coast, and assess the extent of the battle damage to his helicopter.

As the Huey dipped away to the west, Roger Cole, relieved to have been able to wave off the helicopter and prevent a catastrophe before the Adoo found their range against the defenceless aircraft, ran back up the beach, diving for cover behind a low wall. He scrabbled along behind it on his hands and knees for fifty yards until he was certain he was no longer in the sights of the Jebel Ali Shpagin.

Tak heard the thump of the helicopter as Baker hauled the aircraft out of danger. As the Adoo continued to swarm across the plain towards the fort, he didn't have time to consider what it might mean. He and Laba had no capacity for anything but feeding the hungry 25 pounder.

The artillery piece could be aimed in one of two ways. More normally, it was used, working with a forward observer, to lay down indirect fire. In this role, shells were launched upwards into a ballistic arc. The guncrews, often out of sight of their targets, set the distances given to them into a calibrating sight which translated it into the required elevation angle for the barrel. Much more rarely, the gun was used to provide direct fire, where the guncrew, rather than shooting rounds into the air, aimed straight at their target and fired shells on a flat trajectory. Direct fire was only effective over closer ranges because as the distance travelled by the shell increased, so its speed and energy decreased, allowing gravity to take its course.

Since the Adoo fighters had begun their advance across the plain, Laba had been firing directly at them; cranking the elevation handle anticlockwise, to bring the barrel of the field gun to bear on the enemy below him. Rather than lobbing shells into the sky, he was firing them downhill, taking aim by line of sight along the barrel of the gun.

As each pocket of guerrilla infantry broke cover to cross the featureless last few hundred yards of gravel, they exposed themselves to fire from the GPMG and the Browning from the BATT House, and high-explosive shells from Laba and Tak. But it was impossible to stop them all. And if the rebels made it into the lee of the high ground that carried the fort, then they were beyond the reach of Cole and Winner's machine guns, given cover by the local topography and location of the BATT House.

Once the Adoo fighters made it to the perimeter wire, only Laba, Tak or the DG inside the fort could stop them; and the DG appeared to be keeping their heads down.

So Tak and Laba kept firing, all the time crawling around the gunpit on all fours, to stay out of reach of bullets that were lancing in low enough to splinter the tops of the six-inch-high boxes that carried the 25-pounder shells.

Crawl and load, fire, then crawl back and do it again. And again.

This is ridiculous, Tak thought, *they're almost on top of us.* But Laba, his chin still wrapped in a roughly tied shell-dressing, kept on joking and laughing. And as long as he kept that up, they were both still in the game. And they could hear over the radio that back at the BATT House their comrades in arms were still in it with them. But the shooting was beginning to come from all directions.

The Adoo were trying to flank them. And to the east of the fort and Mirbat town, the SAS, both from the gunpit and the BATT House, their view blocked by both the fort and the edge of Mirbat town itself, were blind.

Tak reached for one of the brass shell cases littering the floor of the gunpit. He heard the crack of an Adoo SKS assault rifle. Before it had had time to register he was knocked off his feet by a bullet that struck him on his left shoulder with the force of a charging elephant concentrated on an area of flesh the width of a pencil. Travelling at over 2,000 feet per second, the 7.62mm round from the Chinese carbine assault rifle travelled straight through his left arm and into his chest, where it ripped across him, glancing off his shoulder blade, then chipping his spine as it drilled a path through to his right shoulder where, pointing down towards his armpit, it came to a halt. As Tak fell back against the sandbags his eyes caught Laba's.

Then another round sliced across the back of Tak's head, jerking it as it burnt past.

Knocked flat by the force of the double impact, Tak lost track of where he was. Then, curled up against the sangar wall, the pain began to surge through him.

'Laba, I'm hit!' he shouted in Fijian. His friend finally left the field gun and crawled across clinking detritus from battle lining the floor of the gunpit towards him to try to dress the wound. His own chin still bleeding through the gauze tied around his face, Laba pulled a battle dressing out of a pouch on his belt kit and helped press it against the neat little entry wound on Tak's left shoulder. The visible damage barely hinted at the extent of the injury. What was certain, though, was that Tak had lost the use of his left arm.

From here on, propped up against the sangar wall and moving around with the greatest difficulty and discomfort, Tak was going to have to rely on his right arm alone to load and aim and to fire the SLR at any Adoo who crossed his sights. As he set up the rifle on the edge of the sangar, blood streamed from the wound to his scalp, matting his hair and mixing with sweat and rain as it ran down his back.

Laba *had* told him to keep his head down.

At Um al Gwarif, Lofty Wiseman passed the contents of the BATT armoury along a human chain leading to the back of a line of Bedford three-tonners parked up outside. He added 20,000 rounds of GPMG ammunition to the 2,000 he'd already loaded for the day at the ranges. The truck's suspension began to wilt under the load of stores being piled inside it. The SAS relief force were going to take the lot.

Just after 0700 hours, another STARTREK request was received in the SOAF radio room from Mirbat. It was clear that their situation was not improving. It only jabbed at the sense of tension and frustration. By now the 1 Squadron crew room was thick with cigarette smoke and suggestions. Word spread quickly that Mirbat was under attack and every jet pilot wanted to be involved. But it was only DMS and Sean Creak who had the leg restraints for the Strikemaster's ejection seats strapped on beneath their knees. Given the obvious seriousness of the fighting in Mirbat, as the Squadron had filled up there had been some discussion of getting more than two jets airborne. Again, though, the limiting factor was the weather. With the cloud down so low, it would be reasonably straightforward to set up a racetrack for a pair of aircraft alternating their attacks, but without a clear horizon, trapped beneath the overcast, trying to deconflict a greater number of aircraft was likely to lead to disaster. So thoughts once more turned to what the alert pair could do.

Sean Creak had taken a Beaver into Mirbat two days earlier, but the town, usually so quiet, wasn't a position that was at all familiar to the Strike Squadron. DMS wasn't sure that he'd *ever* been called east. They knew the basic geography, but not the detailed layout, nor potential lines of attack. The more preparation they could do in advance of flying in the more impact they would have – and it provided a welcome, constructive diversion while they waited for the weather to release them.

On a chinagraph board in the Squadron, Stoker, Creak and DMS drew a sketch map of the headland, marking the positions of the Jebel escarpment, the town, the BATT House and the two forts. They added the high ground around the DG fort and, to the north, the Jebel Ali. Immediately, a clearer picture of how and where they might set up a racetrack emerged. They could coast in over the beach along a line north of the fort before turning starboard out to sea, away from the Jebel wall, to come round again for a re-attack.

They were also certain about how they would attack. Bombs were quickly dismissed as an option. With RAF squadrons, many of the pilots had flown toss-bombing profiles, where they'd released 1,000lb dumb bombs as they pulled their jets into a steep climb from low level. Thrown on to a rising ballistic trajectory, there's time, before the bomb arcs down on to its target, for it to arm and the aircraft to roll off the top of a half-loop and fly clear of the debris hemisphere of the explosion. But, without any kind of recent training in the technique, 1 Squadron were as likely to hit the BATT positions as they were to throw the bombs miles beyond Mirbat to land harmlessly in the desert.

That meant SURA unguided rockets were the weapon of choice, although even they were going to require a little bit of improvisation. In Dhofar, the Strikemasters always launched the little missiles from a 20 degree dive above 2,000 feet. Today they weren't going to be able to go above 200 feet. A dive attack was impossible. Instead they'd have to fly almost straight and level and rely on the rising ground to give them an angle of attack. But that meant that setting the depression angle in milliradians of the gunsight was guesswork. By adjusting the depression, the pilots were trying to make sure that the aiming pipper displayed on their sight calculated the gravity drop of the weapon, allowing accurate shooting at different dive angles. As if shooting pheasants with a twelve-bore, Creak and DMS had to lead the target or their rockets and bombs would fall short.

'What do you think we should use?' Creak asked his wingman.

'I don't know,' Milne-Smith replied, considering the problem, 'a ten-degree dive is thirty mils; let's try fifteen.' Of the two pilots, Milne-Smith had the more recent experience, having done some rocketing from two or three degrees flying Hunters with 8 Squadron in Bahrain.

But we're not talking pinpoint, he thought, *it's harassing fire – heads down – and we've got to do something.*

The two pilots sent an instruction to the Airwork engineers to rearm the Strikemasters. As well as magazines full of 7.62mm machine-gun rounds, the alert pair usually each carried two 540lb bombs and sixteen rockets. Today, the bombs had to come off. Creak and DMS wanted the maximum load of thirty-two SURAs; they wanted rocket ships. Then Creak put another call through to the Tower: 'What's the cloudbase?'

The wait for the weather was agonizing.

While 1 Squadron champed at the bit in Salalah, SOAF's other contribution to the battle raging at Mirbat had been forced to withdraw to Taqa, fifteen miles up the coast, to lick their wounds. Baker brought the shot-up Huey in low over the banana palms lining the beach and, hovering over the landing pad, lowered the helicopter down on to her skids. He shut down the engine and they climbed out to check the damage.

As the three-man crew cast a close eye over the fuselage, lining up the entry and exit holes of each bullet in order to establish whether or not anything critical had been hit, one of the Taqa BATT troop jogged down to the pad to meet them. Huey 705 had arrived at the little fishing village unannounced and he was curious to find out what was going on. Like Eight Troop at Mirbat, the B Squadron men were ready to ship out. But all thoughts of their own departure had been displaced by the news that their comrades, just fifteen miles up the coast, were under heavy attack.

'It's too dangerous for you to return to Mirbat,' the BATT man told them, 'not safe. You need to return to Salalah.' They wouldn't have been going anywhere if the Shpagin rounds had punctured anything vital, but Baker's crew had been lucky; while 705's main cabin had been perforated, the engine, gearbox and flight controls had all escaped the Adoo guns.

The helicopter's exposure, though, had been fleeting.

In the gunpit, with Tak out of the game, Laba needed more firepower. The 25 pounder was running low on ammunition and Tak couldn't make the twenty-yard journey to the ammunition dump behind them to reach more. Laba was also beginning to worry that, as lead elements of the Adoo reached the perimeter wire fifty yards away, he and Tak were in danger of fragging themselves as the big 3.45in shells exploded.

'There's a 60mm mortar outside the gate of the fort,' Laba said. It wouldn't help much over the last fifty yards, but it would be possible to get more rounds down and that might keep those Adoo who hadn't yet made it to the wire from getting that close in the first place. Those already there, they'd have to pick off with their rifles. To reach the mortar, though, Laba was going to have to leave the cover of the sangar.

'Cover me,' he grinned, somehow still able to seem unfazed by the grim situation. This time it was Tak's turn to urge his friend to stay safe.

'Laba, keep your head down,' Tak told him as he laboured to hitch the SLR into position with his right arm, 'watch out.'

'You too.'

Then, keeping low, Laba hauled himself over the sandbag wall.

Chapter 34

The clatter and thump of the machine guns continued to pound his eardrums, but, from the roof of the BATT House, Bob Bennett felt like an onlooker.

At the gunpit, he thought, *they're having their own private battle*. But, somehow, Laba and Tak had managed to keep that 25 pounder going. Bennett was sure, though, that the rate of fire from the Fijian pair had fallen off. He turned his long, sun-baked face across towards the fort and narrowed his eyes to try to focus on the gun position.

Pain screamed across Tak's back. Trying to force it from his mind, he scanned the flat expanse of the gravel plain ahead for any sign of movement. With the semi-automatic SLR he couldn't lay down a hail of fire to force Adoo heads down, but only pinpoint those enemy fighters coming out from cover then try to nail them before they had a chance to take their shot. To his right, Laba crawled along the gravel on his belly towards the door of the fort, the height of the hill affording him the most meagre cover.

Tak glanced over at him and his eyes met Laba's. The look on his friend's face unnerved him. Something in Laba's expression suggested that he knew something was wrong. Tak snapped back and focused on trying to provide cover. Then he heard the report of rifle shot. He turned to see Laba already flat on the ground, his throat punched out and blood pooling around him. Laba's eyes were still open, but the life had gone from him. The bullet wound to his neck had killed him instantly. And now Tak was on his own, shocked and distressed by the sudden death of his close friend, very seriously injured and facing the weight of the Adoo infantry attack on his own.

I need some people here, he thought, as he looked at the walkie-talkie lying out of reach on the floor of the sangar.

He couldn't even grab the radio for help, and yet Laba's death had only made him more determined. There was no time to grieve, he needed to survive.

On the far side of the gunpit, nestled amongst the spent shell cases, the little Tokai popped and crackled. Every few seconds he heard Mike Kealy's voice cut through the static.

'Come in Laba . . . Radio check . . . Over.'

'Come in Laba . . . Radio check . . .'

'I don't like it,' Mike Kealy declared. He'd made his mind up. Unable to reach the two Fijians on the radio and alarmed by the silence from the big field gun, the 27-year-old Troop Commander decided he had to find out what was going on for himself. Like Tak before him, he was going to make the run from the BATT House to the fort. And he wanted a volunteer to join him so they could cover each other as they made the journey. After another STARTREK transmission from Snapper requesting air support, Kealy was flanked by three other men as they clustered around the 316 radio. They all wanted to join him. Kealy silenced them.

Inexperienced when he'd joined Eight Troop, Kealy had earned respect over the course of the deployment by listening to his men and taking their advice. But he had also been reserved, feeling his way as he got to grips with his demanding new command. While he was the officer, the men had felt that through suggestion and debate Kealy would make the decisions *they* wanted made. Today, though, the ex-Queen's Regiment Captain seemed to have undergone a transformation. Any reserve or boyishness had been stripped away to reveal a soldier who they knew belonged alongside them.

Now Kealy had weighed up the situation and he knew who

he wanted to take. While he was gone he needed his Sergeant, Bob Bennett, to take charge at the BATT House and, as a trained Forward Air Controller, talk to the jets when the weather allowed them in. Snapper was necessary to man the Browning and continue to handle their communications with HQ. Kealy chose Eight Troop's newest recruit, Tommy Tobin. The 25-year-old ex-cook was a trained medic and that, depending on what they found at the gunpit, could prove crucial. Fuzz Hussey would have to do without him on the mortar. Tobin's dark, boxer's face acknowledged the decision without demur. He fetched the patrol medical kit and hooked the strap over his back.

The two men staying behind pooled their morphine and handed the syrettes to Kealy and Tobin.

Snapper, biting back his disappointment at not being able to get to Laba and Tak, sat back at the radio and tapped out another sitrep for BATT HQ.

Bennett, as he turned to make his way back up on to the roof, caught Kealy's eye and grinned.

'You won't get far in those . . .' he said as he nodded in the direction of the Jesus sandals on Kealy's feet. In Kealy's brief, embarrassed reaction there was a flash of the fresh-faced young officer who'd so recently joined them. Otherwise today it had been entirely absent.

When Neville Baker and his crew arrived back at RAF Salalah the cloudbase had lifted a little. It still hung heavy over the field, blocking any view of the Jebel to the north. Two Strikemasters had been towed out between the burmail revetments where the Airwork engineers, wearing shorts and flip-flops, prepared them according to the instructions from Sean Creak and David Milne-Smith. Low-riding yellow carts were rolled underneath the 540lb bombs hanging beneath the outer pylons of the wings. The yellow rings around the noses of the weapons indicated that they were live. Winding handles round and round, the armourers raised the cradles until they supported the heavy iron bombs, before they were unbolted and returned to the store. For Andy Dunsire, Airwork's radio specialist, arming the jets wasn't what he'd signed up for, but he'd quickly realized that down in Salalah everyone did every-thing, and that suited him. And while undoing the work they'd already done to set the two Strikemasters up with bombs was hardly welcome, the civilian engineers too had been told that the situation in Mirbat was exceptional. And, at least today, working in the drizzle and murk of the *khareef*, there was no danger of burning yourself on the metal skin of the aircraft. That was the more usual concern.

With the 540 pounders on their way back to the bomb dump, the engineers removed the outer wing pylons and attached two SURA launcher rails instead. Dunsire and the Airwork team then fitted sixteen of the Swiss-made 25lb missiles under each wing in vertical racks of four; each rocket held slotted notches in the stabilization fins of the weapon above it and was secured at the back with a locking flap.

So now, again, it was in the hands of the weather. But if the cloudbase continued to rise, the Strikeys were ready to go the moment it reached 200 feet.

There had been a lull in the fighting. A brief respite. It wasn't just the 25 pounder that had quietened down; the Adoo too appeared to be gathering themselves. In meeting such fierce resistance, the guerrillas had been forced to fight their way towards Mirbat and they'd pushed too fast, emptying their magazines then losing momentum. While their mortar teams continued to lob bombs over their heads at the town's defenders, the rebel infantry regrouped and rearmed wherever they could find cover in broken ground. Like a sprinter getting ready to settle into the blocks before a big race, the bulldog figure of Tommy Tobin stood by the door of the BATT House wearing a black T-shirt and filthy khaki shorts, ready to make the 400-yard dash to the DG fort. His face was impassive; only his hands quietly fussing over his rifle betrayed the anxiety inside. Mike Kealy was crouched on the other side of the room, tightening the laces of his desert boots. Kealy got up, his heavy belt kit strapped around his waist, and picked up his ArmaLite carbine. From the roof, they heard the rattle of the Gimpy.

'OK, Tommy,' Kealy said, 'it's time to go.'

They slipped out of the gates, jogging past Fuzz Hussey, huddled over the 81mm mortar, then accelerated, running hard for the inadequate cover of a two-foot-deep wadi seventy-five yards to the right of the BATT House. So far, the Adoo hadn't seen them.

On the roof of the BATT House, Snapper Winner, covering them with the big .50 Browning, watched them run. His thumb hovered over the heavy machine gun's butterfly trigger, but he held his fire. He didn't want to be the one to alert the Adoo to what Tommy and the Boss were up to any earlier than necessary.

One hundred yards into the wadi, not yet halfway to the fort, Kealy and Tobin reached a mud-brick laundry house on the northern outskirts of Mirbat. Almost unbelievably, the leathery old owner greeted them as they approached, apparently oblivious to the battle raging

As-salaam 'alaykum. Peace be with you. The elderly laundryman proffered his hand.

Kealy and Tobin shook it, forcing their faces to betray neither surprise nor impatience, and returned his greeting. *Wa 'alaykum as-salaam.*

Hearts and minds.

The two BATT men continued their run, until, another hundred yards on, they were split by a train of machine-gun bullets surging past, shockwaves cracking, and splintering into the dirt beyond them. Kealy felt the heavy rounds warp the air as, with every fourth or fifth, glowing green tracer speared across his path. Whatever pause there had been in the Adoo assault was now over. And, in Kealy and Tobin, the rebels had a new target. The two BATT men, caught in the open, with barely half of the 400 yards they had to cover behind them, had been seen. As dangerous to turn back as to continue, they forged on. As bullets spat around them they pepper-potted as they went, each covering the other as he ran, then switching and repeating.

*

'OK, we're going to give it a go,' said Sean Creak, already moving towards the door of the Squadron room. DMS followed, walking past the hastily sketched map of Mirbat. The moment confirmation came through from the Tower that the cloudbase had nudged beyond 200 feet the alert pair were on their way.

As Squadron Boss, Bill Stoker wished them well. As a fighter pilot, he wished he was going with them.

Creak and Milne-Smith climbed up on to the wingroots of the two waiting Strikemasters. Camouflaged in olive and brown, the red Omani shields painted on the tail and a full-load of thirty-two SURA rockets racked beneath the wings, the two little jets were ready for the fight.

Both men then stepped up on to the engine air intake on the side of the fuselage and swung the other leg over the rim of the cockpit. They had folded maps tucked into pockets stitched below the knees of their flightsuits and yellow Mae West life-jackets strapped over their chests. Today, unusually, would involve taking the single-engined aircraft out over the sea. Dinghies and survival equipment were packed into the Martin–Baker ejection seats. Settling down into them, they clipped their leg restraints to the chairs. If they were forced to pull the handle, the straps would whip their feet back towards them to ensure they weren't ripped off by the instrument panel as the seats were fired out of the aeroplane. They clipped into the four-point harness, pulled on their silver bonedomes and connected themselves to the radio and oxygen via the PEC. Flight Leader and wingman both reached forward to the gun-sights above the coaming, and pulling then pushing the angle control knob to fine-tune the sight set a 15 milliradian depression. Soft, grey kidskin gloves covered their hands.

With the starter and ignition switches on, they pressed the red start buttons. Over the three seconds the Viper engine took to wind up, the air behind the jet pipe at the tail began to shimmer. Ahead of the two pilots, the engine instruments flicked into life. Almost subconsciously, Creak and DMS scanned the dials, noting that the needles all hovered within prescribed limits.

After radio check and taxi clearance from the Tower, they released the brakes and advanced the throttles. A prod of power from each of the Viper 535 turbojets and the jets rolled forward slowly, both bowing one after the other and rocking gently as Creak and DMS tested the brakes before continuing. Then the strike pair rolled towards the threshold of Runway Two Two. They were soon airborne.

On any other day, Creak and Milne-Smith would have tucked up the undercarriage and trimmed the jets into a max-power climb to height. But while they might have had clearance to leave the ground, the cloud was still smothered low over the Salalah plain. If they were going to be of any use at all at Mirbat, they were going to have to spend the whole sortie underneath it. It would be like trying to fly through a tunnel, hemmed in above and below. Banking low over the ground, they arced round towards the south-east, rolling out as they approached the limits of Salalah town.

From 150 feet above the ground, the flat roofs of the houses seemed almost close enough to reach out and touch as they rushed past beneath the bellies of the Strikemasters.

Thank goodness, Creak thought, *there aren't a lot of locals who have radios with whiplash aerials and TVs.* Otherwise it would have been like trying to fly through barrage balloons. As they bisected the white stripe of the beach below, it was a relief to cross the coast and get out over the sea. There was a little more sky, but that didn't mean they were out of harm's way.

It was possible, Creak knew well, to become mesmerized by the view ahead. Above them the sludgy clouds whipped over the big glass bubble of the cockpit. Less than a hundred feet underneath them, the waves, always shifting, rolled along. Everything looked the same, but nothing was fixed. And after just fifteen minutes over the sea at low level, it can become hypnotic, the eye confused by the absence of anything relative to take a fix from. It was very, very easy to become disorientated and simply drift down into the sea. And, as the strike pair flew east in a loose battle formation, keeping their speed down to a little over 200 knots, DMS knew that gaining altitude wasn't any kind of solution either.

Creak's wingman was acutely aware of the danger of an uncontrolled entry into the thick layer of cloud above. It was one thing planning to pull up and into the clag – then there's a set routine: wings straight and level, one . . . two . . . three, pull back on the stick, eyes on the instruments and then follow them as you're enveloped. Then treat the story told by the instruments from that point on as gospel. But if a pilot slips into cloud unexpectedly – *before* switching on to instruments – then it's hugely disorientating. Everything's happening fast; there's no fixed point; the semi-circular canal in the ear is confused. And then the temptation is to try to descend back out of the cloud again. But when the cloud's down at 200 feet there's a good chance of that killing you.

DMS couldn't help but consider what lay ahead at Mirbat. It was all very well staying below the cloud as he trailed Creak in loose formation low over the sea. But, at Mirbat, they'd be flying into the lion's den. They knew from the increasingly desperate BATT sitreps that there was a battle raging. Pressed between low cloud and rising ground, he and Creak would be manoeuvring hard at low level, getting fired on, trying to avoid each other, and concentrating on not clipping the ground. It would be only too easy to slide into the cloud. It was a perfect combination of the unfamiliar. Nothing about the scramble conformed to 1 Squadron's normal operations beyond the fact that they were on their way to help troops in contact. There'd never been any option other than simply to do whatever they could to relieve the BATT Troop. But they were making it up as they went along.

If I'm honest, he thought, *if we'd sat down to plan it in advance, we'd probably never have taken on the mission.*

Milne-Smith focused on the job in hand. One eye on Creak's jet, the other on the position of his own, he kept Strikemaster

403 flying straight and level, his gloved fingertips gently gripping the control column.

Behind them at Salalah, Royal Air Force crash crews put out ground flares to mark the approaches to Runway 22/04. Anything that might help bring the Strikemasters home safely.

Chapter 35

From the sangar on the north-eastern corner of the roof, Snapper watched them go.

Any minute now, one of them's going to get zapped, he thought. And he knew he was the only one who could do anything to try to keep them alive. As Mike Kealy and Tommy Tobin pushed on towards the gunpit, they were hidden from the Gimpy's arc of fire. Behind Snapper on the far corner of the BATT House, the GPMG SF covered the northern approaches, but only the big Browning covered the route to the DG fort. From behind it, he watched the Adoo tracer wasp past the two BATT men.

But tracer cut both ways.

As well as describing the course of the bullets from the gun-crew firing the weapon, the burning green tracer that cut Kealy and Tobin's path also drew a dotted line back to them. Shutting out the noise and blast of the gunfire and mortar bombs exploding around him, Snapper followed the Adoo rounds back to their source. And there, to the east of the DG fort, he picked out the muzzle flash of an Adoo machine gun; at over half a mile away, little more than a twinkling against the background. Snapper lined the position up in the concentric circles of the Browning's sight and controlled his breathing. Then, with a smooth application of pressure to the trigger, the .50 chugged into life, as metronomic and inexorable as a steam locomotive. With his left hand he fed the belt in through the receiver. On the other side, discarded links flicked out. Underneath, spent brass cases spilled on to the floor like coins flowing out of a fruit machine. Drizzle hissed and vaporized as it touched the hot barrel of the gun. And as the gun's mechanism pumped angrily back and forth, Snapper, gripping tightly – manhandling the thing – watched his own red tracer fly flat and hard towards the Adoo gun. But it was the four rounds of exploding incendiary ammunition between each tracer that destroyed the enemy machine gun. As the big .50 calibre bullets streamed in, a beaten zone with the Adoo guncrew at its centre disappeared in a cloud of dust and shrapnel, leaving nothing complete, useful or alive behind when the air cleared.

Kealy and Tobin were in no way safe. But Snapper had ensured that, at least, the machine gun that had so nearly tagged them posed no further threat. He watched them sprint forward.

The Browning, always temperamental if you didn't mollycoddle it, was holding up for now.

It was all Takavesi could do to replace one magazine with the next. While the Adoo attack had appeared to stall he'd been given some breathing room. But with his left arm hanging uselessly by his side, he had to remove one spent thirty-round clip from his SLR, pull a replacement from one of the pouches of his belt kit and snap it into the bottom of the rifle. Just a few yards from him, Laba's lifeless body lay in the gravel, blood draining from the neck wound that had killed him. And now the shooting had started again.

Still propped up against the sangar wall, Tak hefted the rifle back on to the sandbags and waited for the Adoo to present themselves as targets, careful not to squander a single round. But, increasingly, there was no shortage of targets. Clearly the Adoo didn't know that, defending their objective, there was no more than a single badly wounded soldier and his rifle. Had they known, they might well have been bolder, but, weighing up the risk of exposing themselves in greater numbers, they continued to advance slowly in small groups. It seemed that only the *impression* of a much larger force generated by Laba and Tak, working the 25 pounder together, was keeping the gunpit from being stormed.

But, even potting them one or two at a time, Tak knew he was running short on ammunition.

He saw Tommy Tobin first. Dodging and swerving, trying to vary his path, the stocky young medic's arms and legs pumped hard as he pushed up the loose rock slope over the final fifty yards to the gunpit. After twenty minutes alone since Laba's death, there was help. Tobin brought with him no heavy weaponry or firepower beyond the SLR, but his arrival was no less welcome for that. Somehow Tobin too had made it to the sangar unharmed. As he began to vault over the sandbags into the gunpit, he made eye contact with Tak, a split-second connection exchanging reassurance for relief.

Then Tak heard a rip of automatic gunfire.

And, simultaneously, before Tommy had cleared the sangar wall, Tak saw him knocked back, his face torn apart by a Kalashnikov round. The bullet hit him on the right-hand side of his chin, instantly removing half of his lower jaw, peeling back the skin of his cheek to expose what was left of his jawbone, rows of teeth and the roof of his mouth all the way back to his molars. As Tobin gasped at the force of the impact, he inhaled chips of splintered teeth deep into his lungs. Four other rounds hit his right shoulder, right chest, abdomen and left hand as he crumpled, falling a couple of yards from where Tak was sitting. The Fijian knew he was powerless to go to his aid. If he even tried to help Tobin, he realized, *we'll both be killed.*

No one can help Tommy, he thought.

As he followed Tobin up the hill towards the sangar, Kealy saw the Trooper flicked back by the force of the bullet's impact and fall to the ground. Barely breaking his stride he made for the medic, grabbed him and dragged him behind the gunpit, where the sandbags and the gun itself would afford him a scrap of cover from the Adoo assault. Despite the bleeding ruin of his face, Kealy realized that Tobin was alive. But, like Tak, he knew that if he lingered, exposed to the rebel gunfire, then soon he would not be. Glancing again at Tobin, Kealy dived for the closest cover. But rather than the gunpit the Captain leapt into the ammunition bunker seven yards behind. His landing, as he came over the sandbags, was a soft one.

Underneath his desert boots was the body of one of the Dhofar Gendarmerie guards. Kealy recoiled as he shifted his weight and stepped off the dead man. Then he noticed that, huddled in the opposite side of the dugout, was the petrified figure of the DG soldier who'd responded to Tak's call to leave the fort. The man's terror was palpable, a primal fear that, Kealy recognized from the man's eyes, he needed to treat with caution.

If I try to tell him to fight, Kealy thought, *I know he'll kill me*. Ignoring him, Kealy raised the Tokai radio to his ear and pressed the transmit button.

'Laba's dead,' he reported, 'Tak and Tommy are very seriously injured.'

Then he heard Tak's deep baritone, strained from the pain of his wounds.

'Boss,' the Trooper said, 'they're through the wire . . .'

Back at the BATT House, reaction to the contents of Kealy's brief sitrep was stunned disbelief. None of them were under any illusions about the situation they were in. They'd be lucky if any of them survived. But Laba; how could Laba be dead? Bob Bennett, now directing the battle from the BATT House in Kealy's absence, found Snapper and sent him back down to the radio room.

'Call for reinforcements,' he said calmly. Bennett's *sang froid* throughout had been remarkable, but the news of Laba's death was heart-rending for him. And he knew it had dragged down the mood of the whole Troop. And as he watched Winner pound down the stairs from the roof, the Sergeant knew he had to keep on going, and yet had to admit to himself that he had *a sinking feeling over whether or not we're going to survive*.

*

At Um al Gwarif, the news of what was happening at Mirbat had not spread smoothly through G Squadron. With the decision made to send them into Mirbat to reinforce the BATT, the Squadron Commander, Alistair Morrison, went to brief his men. While the three-tonners lined up outside the Ops Room, their engines running, warming up, the Major told his men that the plan had changed. They were going to be driven straight to Salalah, where they'd be loaded on to helicopters and flown into Mirbat. As they filed out to the trucks, their faces reflected their mood of determination. Many of them were already loaded with waistcoats of heavy GPMG chain link ammunition wound over both shoulders and across their chests.

Somehow, two of the newest members of the Squadron managed to misunderstand what was being said. And as the driver graunched the old Bedford into gear and dropped the clutch, they still believed they were off to zero the guns.

The first reports from BATT HQ had reached Bradbury Lines in the small hours of the morning. A three-hour time difference meant that the Commanding Officer of 22 SAS was alerted to the reports coming in from Operation STORM long before dawn. For Peter de la Billière, it was a situation that had a painful familiarity. Once more he was on the receiving end of radio reports describing the resistance of a small SAS unit under siege from a larger, more powerful force of guerrilla fighters. And, as in Aden eight years earlier, he was powerless to intervene.

If the Ops Room at Um al Gwarif had struggled to form a coherent picture of what was happening on the ground at Mirbat, it was even worse for DLB. The news he received was sketchy. But what he did know was that if the SAS fell at Mirbat through a failure of training, technique or resolve, then it would be his failure. As in 1964, he had already done all he could. Whatever influence he had been able to bring to the character of the Regiment was already in evidence.

As unpopular as it had been with some of the longer-serving

NCOs, DLB had instigated the 'Senior Infantry' course to ensure that, in embracing more irregular forms of warfare, basic infantry skills were not overlooked by the SAS. After it had been exposed as a weakness during his squadron's deployment to the Radfan, the Regiment now always had trained Forward Air Controllers. And, since his own experience fighting in Korea, DLB had insisted that all his soldiers place a premium on conserving their ammunition. Rounds expended without effect were wasted and irreplaceable. The SAS were only to shoot when they had a target. It was a maxim that was keeping Tak, with only the clips of 7.62mm ammunition he'd carried with him from the BATT House, in the game.

Economy or not, Tak couldn't keep going much longer. He'd been in the gunpit for nearly an hour and a half and he was running out of bullets. The equation was simple: every single Adoo fighter who made it within a hard scrabble of the gunpit had to be stopped before reaching it by a round from Tak's SLR. He only had to fail once and he knew he would be killed and the gunpit would fall. And, with Kealy in the ammunition dump, twenty yards behind, in holding back the frontal assault Tak was still on his own.

The topography that hid Tak's isolation from the eyes of the Adoo also hid them from Mike Kealy. Carved into the descending slope of the hill behind the gunpit, Kealy's bunker was in dead ground. Unlike the gunpit, positioned at the front lip of the hill, the ammunition dump couldn't be seen by the advancing Adoo. But from inside it neither could Kealy see their advance across the plain. Only if the Adoo made it past Tak's rifle to the top of the hill would they drop into the sights of Kealy's ArmaLite.

If they knew, Tak thought, trying to figure out why the rebels hadn't already stormed his position, *they'd just stand up and run round the back. They're frightened.*

That was a sliver of luck. Over the cacophony of the machine-gun fire rattling off the 25 pounder he could hear

Mike Kealy in the ammunition dump speaking over the radio to the BATT House trying to get support.

'Boss,' Tak shouted, 'I'm running out of ammunition.'

Kealy turned to the stunned DG guard quivering beneath the hessian sandbags. If he couldn't make the man fight, he thought, he could at least get him to do something to help the fight. He unclipped empty magazines from two FN rifles and tossed them to the Omani soldier.

'Fill those,' he demanded, leaving no room for objection. The guard worked quickly, stuffing brass and lead into the metal boxes against the magazine's spring. When the first clip was filled, Kealy stood up and threw it hard in the direction of the gunpit. Arcing through the air it landed heavily amongst the piles of old shell cases that carpeted the floor of the position.

Tak put down his rifle and, gritting his teeth against the pain wracking through him, reached gratefully for the resupply. Using his right hand alone, wedging the rifle against the ground to gain some leverage, he removed the magazine from his own gun and tried to jam the new clip into the SLR in its place. But it failed to neatly engage and snap home. Tak checked it and realized it was an FN magazine, and the relief that had greeted its arrival washed away.

When the British adopted the Belgian-designed FN FAL rifle, a few modifications were included before what became the L1A1 Self Loading Rifle began rolling off the production lines of British factories. Amongst the changes were the loss of the gun's ability to fire as a fully automatic weapon, the addition of an enclosed slotted flash suppressor around the muzzle and a folding rear sight. But the redesign was also completed using Imperial, not metric measurements. And while the size of the NATO standard 7.62mm rounds was the same, the dimensions of the FN and SLR magazines were marginally different as a result. And now Tak was paying for it.

With his right hand, he painstakingly thumbed two or three rounds out of the FN clip and pushed them into the SLR magazine, jammed it back into the rifle, and heaved it back on to the sandbag wall. When they were gone, he had to go through it all again. It was an excruciatingly unwieldy way of trying to cover the approaches to the fort, but Tak needed to keep the gun trained on the enemy. He couldn't afford to fill a magazine full of twenty rounds; it would simply leave him vulnerable for too long.

All around him, the incoming Adoo fire continued to shred in, pitting the 25 pounder's shield and splintering the stone and mortar of the DG fort walls to his right.

'Zero Alpha. Zero Alpha. This is 82. Message. Over.' From the radio room at the BATT House, Snapper tapped out the news that Laba was dead and that Tak and Tommy were very seriously injured. They needed help. He ended the sitrep to HQ in a way that left no room for doubt.

'Situation desperate,' he told them. Then he raced back upstairs to climb back in behind the .50 Browning.

From his position in the forward sangar on the roof, Bob Bennett could make out the shape of a figure, nearly 800 yards away, holding down the barbed wire of the perimeter fence, his AK47 raised high, urging the men forward. Standing tall in a peaked cap and belts of ammunition criss-crossing his chest, inspiring and driving his troops on, he reminded Bennett of some kind of an image from a Communist propaganda poster. A hero of the revolution! Even Bennett had to admit it was a stirring sight. *A brave man*, he thought. But the SAS Sergeant was now in no doubt about what was at stake. *Their aim*, it was perfectly obvious now, *must be to take the town. And that must mean taking us.* Then in the back of his mind he remembered Aden; his thoughts paused on what had happened to Robin Edwards and Nick Warburton, the two SAS men decapitated in the Radfan in 1964. And Bennett assumed that if the Adoo were allowed to overrun Mirbat, then the nine-man BATT team would suffer the same fate.

It's a fair distance, he thought. The Adoo commander was on the limit of the SLR's effective range, but Bennett was sniper-trained. He had clear line of sight, there was no wind and he had a static target. He raised the rifle and took aim, squeezing the trigger and . . . *crack* . . . the stock kicked into his shoulder.

Missed, he chided himself, as the guerrilla continued pushing his men forward towards the fort. He took a breath then steadied himself and let the sight settle on his target. With the gentle squeeze from his index finger, the SLR cracked and recoiled again.

Damn. The rebel remained in action; still straddling the wire; still rallying his assault force.

But Bennett wasn't the sort of character to get needled by it. He was too cool, too experienced for that. He'd just take the next shot. He controlled his breathing, shut out the chaos of the battle raging around him and focused. Everything slowed down as he applied the smoothest of pressure to the rifle's trigger; the only part of him that wasn't completely still. Half a mile away, his target was unaware that he'd been singled out. The SLR jerked back as the 7.62mm round was fired down the length of the barrel, ripped into a fine spin by the rifling within. It left the muzzle at a speed of over 2,700 feet per second. A moment later, still travelling faster than the sound of the report from the gun that fired it, the sharp-nosed bullet speared into its target. The Adoo leader buckled and fell; another one of the bodies hanging like washing along the taut wire of the fence.

But there were plenty more to take his place.

Back at Salalah, Lofty Wiseman drove a handful of the G Squadron men from Um al Gwarif to the airfield. The simple leaf springs of the old Land Rover 110 might have been strong, but they certainly weren't forgiving, and the troopers were thrown up and down in the back as Wiseman kept his foot down along the unsealed, graded track. Wiseman had been one of the first men at BATT HQ to discover the gravity of the situation in Mirbat. If any of the men in the back of his Land Rover were still uncertain, they took another step along the path to understanding when Wiseman reached down past the gear lever to the footwell on the passenger side and pulled open a cardboard box. With a shovel-like hand he scooped up a fistful of morphine syrettes and passed them back. As they quickly found their way into pockets and belt kits, Wiseman reached down again for more.

Yet even as the men in the back of the Land Rover prepared for the worst, in one of the three-ton Bedfords carrying the rest of the relief force to the helicopters, G Squadron's two newly badged troopers continued to think they were on their way to the ranges.

Chapter 36

Sean Creak pressed the transmit button on the throttle lever with his left thumb.

'Hello, BATT House, this is Red Leader,' he said. 'Two Strikemasters inbound. Over.' He released the RT button and waited for a reply. Creak and DMS were five miles out approaching Mirbat Bay at nearly 250 knots. Around a minute's flying time. En route, the cloudbase had lifted slightly to around 350 feet, giving the two pilots a little usable airspace. With ground features like Jebel Ali and the fort itself rising to well over a hundred feet above sea level it was a significant extra margin.

There was no answer on the BATT frequency. Creak tried again.

'BATT House, this is Red Leader. Two Strikemasters inbound. Over.' There was nothing but a mush of static in response.

Before departing Salalah, Creak and Milne-Smith had dialled the BATT frequency into the jets' radio sets. Each of the SOAF frequencies was colour-coded for ease of use. The standard frequency for talking to the ground was known as Blue SARBE and used a search and rescue beacon adapted to 240.0 Megahertz instead of the international distress frequency of 243.0 Megahertz. The system worked well. But today, as he ran in towards Mirbat low over the sea, he could raise no one.

In trail, half a mile behind, DMS listened to his Flight Leader struggle to make contact. And with more recent experience than Creak flying in support of the Regiment in Dhofar, it suddenly occurred to him that the BATT, not properly integrated with the SAF communications net, might be on their own frequency. He reached forward to the station box, switched from UHF to VHF and dialled in a new frequency, White SARBE, on 123.8MHz. Then he pressed transmit.

'BATT House, two Strikemasters inbound. Over.'

From Mirbat, Roger Cole acknowledged the call over the Troop's SARBE beacon. Although Cole spoke in measured, controlled tones, DMS could hear the tension and strain in the BATT man's voice.

'What do you want? Over,' Milne-Smith asked him.

'They're on the wire. Anything forward of the fort is hostile. Do *something*,' Cole said, 'and do it soon.'

'How many of them?'

'There are fucking hundreds of them.'

Careful not to let reaching for small switches at the bottom of the instrument panel affect his control of the low-flying jet, DMS switched frequency again to talk to his Flight Leader.

'I've managed to get hold of him,' he told Creak, 'he's on White SARBE.'

Creak quickly weighed up his options. Streaking in towards Mirbat he hadn't yet spoken to the BATT himself. He could keep on going and make this his first pass attack, or haul off and settle into a racetrack offshore, establish communications with the FAC and then take targets from them. But the instructions DMS had passed on from Roger Cole were clear.

On the wire, Creak thought, *OK, I understand that. I've got the element of surprise here. I can do it all in one swoop, low as I possibly can, firing the guns along the wire.*

'I'm going to fly straight in on a strafing run,' he told his wingman.

'I'll follow behind you,' DMS replied, his voice stripped of warmth by the scratch and compression of the radio. DMS watched Creak settle into his attack run.

The Flight Leader pushed the throttle forward to the stops, accelerating to a shade over 350 knots. With his right hand he reached forward in front of the stick and flicked the Armament Master Switch up to ARMED. Beneath it an indicator lamp began glowing red. Moving along the instrument panel to the right he settled on the Guns switch and selected BOTH. The metal toggle switch flicked firmly underneath the kidskin leather of his flying gloves. He chose not to use the rockets on his first pass – the gun run would establish whether or not he was laying down fire where it was needed. Until he had confirmation of that he'd keep the SURAs tight.

Don't want them blowing up in their faces, he thought. A blue-on-blue attack was definitely not how he wanted to open his account in support of the BATT's last stand.

Tracking in towards the north-east, Creak aimed for a stretch of low ground between the rocks of the Jebel Ali to port and the Wali's fort off his starboard wing. Ahead of him he could see the ground slope up towards the DG fort. He could see the Adoo soldiers crossing the perimeter wire.

As the Strikemaster swept across the beach the ground blurred beneath it and Creak's peripheral vision strobed as features flashed by. Ahead, connecting the coastal plain and the low cloud, was the wall of the Jebel. Contained between the ground and the opaque gloom above, it was like flying headlong into an open box. In order to re-attack, there was only one way back to set up for another run and that was the same as the way in.

With deft, near subconscious control inputs on stick and rudder, Creak lined up the perimeter fence underneath the aiming pipper at the centre of the reflector sight glass. Flying almost straight and level down at a height of one hundred feet, he pulled the trigger on the control column and, from just below and behind him, out of the lips of the engine air intakes, bullets spat from the two FN 7.62mm machine guns. Oily gunsmoke streamed back over the wings staining the pale grey paint of the jet's underside a dirty black. From the ejection seat, he could feel the vibration resonating through the airframe as the two belt-fed machine guns discharged bullets at a rate of 950 rounds per minute.

He saw the ground kick and burst as his bullets tore into the plain ahead of him; a line of destruction advancing across the desert at around two thirds of the speed of sound. Adoo in the path of the FN guns either scattered or died. Creak kept his index figure closed tightly around the trigger on the control column.

After fighting alongside RAF Hunters, some of the old, bold SAS veterans had been unimpressed by the firepower offered by the little Strikemaster. And it's true, the machine guns were no match for the destruction delivered by the Hunter's 30mm ADEN cannons. But on this occasion, the less powerful 7.62mm weapons offered an important advantage over the bigger guns: there was little chance of a ricochet damaging the jet firing its guns as it flew over the point of impact. At the altitude forced on the Strikemasters by the weather, the debris hemisphere of rock chips and shrapnel thrown up by each high-explosive 30mm ADEN round would have been a huge risk.

Lower the better, thought Creak. And as he swept towards the fort, his starboard wing was nearly level with the battlements around the top of the Tower.

From the gunpit, Tak watched Creak's pugnacious little attack jet roar past, with smoke puffing from the muzzles of the two machine guns. Empty brass cases and discarded chain link spilled out of chutes from beneath the Strikemaster's belly. The red roundel of the Sultan of Oman's Air Force under the starboard wing flashed past and Tak saw Adoo guerrillas cut down in its wake.

The best sight I could possibly see, he thought, *the best music I could hear*. And he allowed himself just a glimmer of hope.

Behind him in the ammunition dump, Mike Kealy pulled a fluorescent orange air panel from his belt kit and laid it out over the body of the DG guard. With the Adoo nearly on top of them, he wanted the attacking SOAF jets to know *exactly* where they were.

As he lanced past the fort, Creak felt a series of heavy thumps punch along the length of the aeroplane. Immediately, just below the coaming, amber lights of the Standard Warning Panel began to flash on. Seven machine-gun rounds had punctured the fuselage. Some sliced through the jet's skin without causing significant damage. But others hit critical systems. And one had damaged the hydraulics. For now, the red fire-warning light remained off. But Creak knew that a fire tends to take a few minutes to develop. There was no guarantee that it wouldn't follow, along with its attendant audio alarm through the helmet.

So much for the element of surprise, he thought. He had a snap decision to make: either stay in the turn and come round to re-attack, or pull up into the clouds and bug out. He glanced at the warning panel again.

Christmas, he realized, *there's no way*. He levelled the wings, fixed his eyes on his instruments and pulled back on the stick and thumbed the RT button. A split second later he was wrapped up by the overcast, leaving nothing behind but shell cases and the hot rasp of his Viper turbojet echoing around the plain.

Down on the deck, his throttle open, David Milne-Smith was lining up for his first pass, in trail, half a mile separating him from his Flight Leader when he saw Creak's jet disappear into the clouds.

Christ, he's not coming back from that. His first thought was that Creak's departure was inadvertent, but whatever the reason DMS knew his friend had left the stage for good. It was as they'd always known. Once you deserted the thin layer of sky below the cloud offering Visual Flight Rules, there was no way back down through the thick cloak hanging over the plain. The radio clicked in his ears then Creak's voice came through.

'I've been hit with something. Don't know where or what.'

Creak sounded calm though; on top of the situation.

'Do you need any help?'

'No, I'm all right for fuel. But it looks like I'm out of this. I'm heading back to Salalah.'

'OK, I'll stay here.'

Milne-Smith was still in the fight. He switched the Armament Master Switch to 'Armed'. Getting shot at *always* made Milne-Smith angry and now the Adoo had put his friend out of the game. But after firing just 250 rounds Creak had played a crucial role in two ways. First of all it was his arrival that raised the spirits of the BATT defenders. And, more importantly, he'd acted as a pathfinder for his wingman. The success of Creak's strafing run was confirmed by the advice of the BATT FAC: 'Anything out there is fair game.' DMS ran his hand along the line of toggle switches to arm the weapons. And this time, as well as the machine guns he energized the firing circuits to the eight pylons of SURA rockets. He was certain now that he wasn't going to hit his own troops. As he coasted in over the beach, Milne-Smith aimed along the line of the perimeter fence and began firing the guns. A moment later, his thumb pressing down on top of the control column, he pickled the first eight rockets from under his wings. The little SURAs fizzed off the rails at the speed of rifle bullets, leaving straight white trails of smoke behind them. He kept his finger on the machine-gun trigger.

Surging across the forward edge of battle, DMS could pick out the rebels swarming across the plain. Seeing the Adoo at all from the cockpit of a Strikemaster, normally releasing weapons above 2,000 feet, was rare enough. But to see them in such numbers now only rammed home the scale of the action he'd joined. He pressed the transmit button to find out if his first pass was having the required effect.

The answer was immediate: 'We need lots more of the same.'

It was a new voice on the radio. Back at the BATT House, Roger Cole had passed the SARBE to the Troop Sergeant, Bob Bennett.

As he spoke to Bennett, Milne-Smith extended for a second or two north of the fort, then reefed the jet into a hard 60 degree turn to starboard, tipping the Strikemaster on to its wing and describing a tight semi-circle back over Mirbat town towards the sea.

'How long have they been at you?'

'Since dawn.'

Pulling back on the stick and keeping the power on, DMS sank back into his seat as the G loaded up. He clenched the muscles in his legs and stomach to keep the blood from draining from his brain to his feet like the contents of a centrifuge. On the coaming the needle on the accelerometer nudged 4G. As he carved round the turn he kept his boot on the right rudder pedal, careful to make sure he didn't side-slip out of the turn and up into the clouds whipping past just above his wingtips.

The empty, clear skies over Dhofar meant the Strikeys often flew with a relatively comfortable margin for error. There was sometimes room to play things a little loose. It wasn't unusual to ask a wingman for a fuel check and hear 'Bingo plus a bit' in reply. You never heard that at Cranwell. But in the thin wedge of sky between Mirbat and the cloud, David Milne-Smith needed to fly as precisely as if he were part of an aerobatic team. He held the little Strikemaster in a flat turn, keeping her nailed to the height he wanted. Beneath him, the flat roofs of Mirbat blurred past.

Two thousand feet above him, Sean Creak broke out of the cloud and saw the sun for the first time since getting out of bed. It was as if someone had turned the lights on in a dark room. The scene bore no resemblence to the claustrophobic violence beneath him. Vivid blue sky sat above a carpet of soft white cloud that stretched as far as he could see in every direction. Still low in the sky to the east, the sun cast the shadow of the Strikemaster on to the inviting cotton wool below. The bib of matt black paint covering the jet's nose ahead of the canopy glass softened the glare. Creak turned west towards Salalah and continued to climb. With time and space to take stock, briefly, he considered the possibility of trying to return to the fight, but a proper inspection of the warning panel quickly put paid to the idea. Amber lights warning of low fuel pressure and a hydraulic pump failure were glowing.

I've probably got a fuel leak, if not two or three. And if he was streaming hydraulic fluid, then that too was a fire risk. *Sorry about this*, he thought, *but I'd better get home.* Pulling back on the throttle to conserve on fuel, Creak then reached forward and dialled in the frequency for the Salalah Control Tower to warn them that he was on his way back. And that he wasn't sure what sort of shape he'd be in when he reached them.

One thing was certain, though, with Salalah still clamped under the *khareef* he was going to need to be talked down through the cloud to the runway by ground controllers using the ACR7 radar.

He kept a vigil on the battered jet's temperatures and pressures as he nursed her west. And after talking to the RAF controllers to prepare for his own arrival, he changed frequency again to raise SOAF Ops.

'You need to send another pair of aeroplanes,' he told them.

Banking around the headland again, DMS levelled the wings. Unloading, the Gs fell away and he settled into his fourth attack run. His last. He had just eight SURA rockets left on the pylons and whatever was left in the machine-gun magazines after three passes with his index finger hooked around the trigger. As he crossed the coast, the little missiles hissed off the rails and darted towards the plain. 7.62mm rounds chewed up the ground ahead of him as, a couple of seconds later, the Strikemaster bored across the sky overhead, the destruction it had caused beneath its wings. DMS thumbed the RT button.

'BATT House, this is Red Two, I'm out of ammunition. That's my last pass. Over.' Milne-Smith looked down at his instruments and, eyes fixed on the artificial horizon, pulled back on the stick. He was already climbing into the clouds when the reply from Mirbat began with a click.

'Red Two, we need ten times more and we need it very soon. Over.'

DMS trimmed the jet into the climb with his left hand, then set the Armament Master Switch to SAFE. As the *khareef* enveloped him, thoughts crowded his mind. He knew he would be returning to Mirbat. Soon enough to make it count, he hoped. And he wondered what had happened to his friend. The last sight he'd had of Sean was of his shot-up Strikemaster pulling up through the drizzle into the overcast.

Chapter 37

The two Strikemasters had scattered the Adoo attack, but could only keep them at bay while they were overhead. With the departure of the second jet, the enemy were, once more, able to advance. Even losing men to the BATT machine guns and SOAF jets, attacking in such numbers the rebel infantry had resilience; they could absorb casualties and keep on coming. As the Russian Army had shown in the Second World War, quantity has a quality all of its own.

From the gunpit, Tak could see Adoo fighters moving south to the east of the fort. Flanking him. And the angles were all wrong for him. He had a clear view north, but to the east the corner of the fort, just five yards to his right, quickly blocked his arc of fire. From the ammunition bunker, he knew that Kealy couldn't see any of this. But if the Adoo tried to come round the back of the fort, then it would be the Troop Commander who'd see them first. Tak shouted a warning to Kealy.

As Kealy raised his head above the sandbags, he glimpsed a trace of movement, a figure at the far corner of the fort. Then he caught sight of a hand grenade looping through the air towards him. Landing short of the bunker it scratched across the dirt towards him and rolled to a stop on the edge of his position; an orange-sized Chinese offensive grenade, its fuse burning down towards detonation.

'*Grenade!*' he shouted instinctively, alerting Tak to the new danger, as he ducked low, curling himself into the wall of the dugout to shield himself from the blast. Kealy opened his mouth in anticipation of the overpressure. When it came, the concussion thumped across the bunker like a drumbeat, ripping at the hessian sandbags and assaulting his ears. The explosion sucked the oxygen from the air and showered him with grit and stones. But, despite ringing like a bell from the detonation, he was unhurt. Inhaling a lungful of the choking smoke, he scrambled to his feet again and quickly levelled his rifle at the place where he'd seen the guerrilla. The rebel was there, leaning round the wall to see the effect of his grenade attack. Cradled high, the stock tucked into his shoulder, he carried an AK47, his finger on the trigger. Before the rebel could respond to the danger, the SAS Captain took a snap shot; a double-tap to the head. At this range – just a few yards away – before Kealy's trigger finger was done, near coincident with the report from the muzzle, the first round from the ArmaLite had smashed through the front of the Adoo fighter's skull, carved through his brain and torn off the back of his head. In a single frame, Kealy's target had snapped from a threat to a blood splatter pattern on the pale, sand-coloured mortar of the fort wall. A moment later, his lifeless body slumped to the ground. Bone fragments and brain tissue, thrown against the wall, but too heavy for the blood to support, peeled off and landed in the dirt.

'Tak,' Kealy shouted out, 'you take the left, I'll take the right.'

As well as the plain forward of the gunpit, now Tak, his bullet-damaged body protesting in agony, had to crab around the gunpit to cover Adoo emerging from the corner of the fort just yards from his position. But the Adoo weren't just flank-ing the fort. They were flanking the whole town.

'I'm ready to go,' Bill Stoker said from the SOAF radio room, 'what's happening? Over.' He was speaking to Sean Creak. When the alert pair had finally scrambled, Bill Stoker had watched them go with a tug of frustration that he wasn't going with them. That desire to be involved ran through the veins of

any fighter pilot worth his salt. But he'd resisted the temptation to pull rank. As Sean Creak coaxed his jet back to
Salalah, though, it was clear that Strikemaster 409 would be
taking no further part in the battle. But if they weren't going to
be able to rearm Creak's aircraft, turn him round and send him
back, the right operational decision – the best way of ensuring
that they had another fully armed jet over Mirbat as quickly as
possible – was to prepare a fresh Strikemaster. And no one in
1 Squadron had their name rostered against that. There was
never any doubt in his mind that the mission was his.

From the cockpit of his inbound jet, Creak described the
situation on the ground at Mirbat, explained how and where
he'd gone in with DMS, and what had happened with the
confusion over the Regiment's singular approach to SARBE
frequencies.

'Thanks very much, mate. Over.'

Although Bill Stoker now had the benefit of what Creak had
learnt in his single pass across the battlefield, further detail
had also arrived from another source.

While the initial communication between SOAF and the
BATT had been muddled, the two Squadron Commanders,
Duke Pirie and Alistair Morrison, realized early on that close
and successful coordination with the Air Force was critical to
saving the situation in Mirbat. As Peter de la Billière had in
Aden, while trying to save Robin Edwards and his besieged A
Squadron troop, Duke Pirie installed himself at SOAF HQ at
Salalah airfield so that he could manage the flow of information between the Regiment and the flyers. Close air support,
troop reinforcements, resupply and the evacuation were all
dependent on SOAF getting good, early information. While
Pirie, the outgoing B Squadron Boss, set up what amounted to
a Joint Operations centre, his G Squadron counterpart, Alistair
Morrison, preparing to lead a half-squadron of his men into
Mirbat, briefed Bill Stoker on what he could expect to find
at Mirbat. The Guards officer spoke with an unruffled air of
authority. Were it not for the belt kit and olive green battle-
dress he could have been an investment banker speaking to the

board rather than a man fifteen minutes from flying into combat.

For Stoker, the polished SAS Major passed on one key additional piece of intelligence: the Adoo had brought their Shpagins with them. Because, when it came to tussles with the Shpagins over Habrut and Simba, Big Bill Stoker had history. On learning that one of the powerful 12.7mm machine guns was ripping up Mirbat from a position on top of the Jebel Ali, he made it his mission to do something about it.

'Advisory information only.' The words from the Ground Controller crackled through Sean Creak's headset at the moment he emerged from cloud. As a pilot descended through cloud towards the ground it was a lot of faith to place in the man watching the radar screen on the ground. And with the approaching aircraft still a mile out, and just 300 feet from the ground, the controller was obliged to tell the pilot he was on his own. If the approaching flyer couldn't see the runway at this point, there was nothing more the controllers could do to help him down without the strong risk of talking him straight into a burning hole in the ground. But as Creak cleared the cloudbase, holding his speed at 120 knots with 70 per cent rpm from the Viper engine, Runway Two Two stretched out ahead of him. Relief flooded through him.

The threshold flashed past below him. He gradually pulled back on the throttle, reducing the power smoothly as he checked the descent with a little backwards pressure on the control column. As the camouflaged jet flared and settled down through the last feet towards the runway, its wheels feeling for the ground, Creak closed the throttle completely. The main undercarriage skidded as it hit the oiled sand strip. And as the speed washed off below 70 knots he lowered the nosewheel. He was down.

The nosewheel settled on to the runway and he applied the brakes. Then, as the speed dropped off, the Strikemaster suddenly began to veer off towards the left. Creak tried to fight it, booting the rudder pedals and brakes, but it was tugging too hard. And, as he slowed, he was helpless to stop the aircraft pulling off the side of the runway. After surviving the machine-gun attack over Mirbat and bringing his battle-damaged aeroplane back safely to Salalah through thick cloud, he finished up in the dirt. It was the final ignominy. But it was also further evidence of just how lucky he'd been. The jet's refusal to cooperate as it rolled to a halt was because she'd taken a machine-gun bullet through the nosewheel tyre. It was no more than a foot or two from his feet. The other six bullets that had stitched their way down the side of Strikemaster 409 were all behind him. He was still in one piece and the firetrucks, standing by for his arrival, hadn't been necessary. He was just going to need a tow, that was all.

The Bedford trucks delivered G Squadron to the Salalah dispersal. As they climbed down from the tailgates of the three-tonners it was clear that they were loaded for bear. Along with their personal weapons it seemed as if, at a glance, there was one GPMG for every two men. And there were four American M79 grenade launchers. Like the ArmaLite assault rifles favoured by some of the Regiment men, the M79, within the British Army at least, was unique to the Regiment. It was an ugly bulldog of a weapon that resembled a sawn-off shotgun. But, able to fire a 40mm fragmentation grenade over a range of up to 400 yards, it plugged a gap between a hand grenade and a mortar. Dubbed 'Thumper' by the American GIs in Vietnam, the M79, despite weighing no more than an SLR, was like a one-man, miniature artillery gun. But in the rush to load the trucks with ammunition, the grenades themselves had been left behind. One of the Air Despatchers was sent racing off to the ammunition dump to fetch two boxes of the high-explosive projectiles that he remembered hauling off the last RAF C-130 resupply.

'Quickly now . . .' they told him.

That first grenade was no one-off. With the Adoo now advancing around the fort, Tak and Kealy were within range of the rebels' throwing arms. It was a dangerous new threat to their survival. The Adoo machine guns and the AKs couldn't penetrate the sandbagged walls of the gunpit and the ammunition bunker. From the Adoo mortar line behind Jebel Ali, they were safe from all but the luckiest of mortar shots. But from round the edge of the fort, the hand grenades could be lobbed right into Tak and Kealy's positions.

Tak had been lucky so far. Grenades fell short, wide and long, spitting up gravel as they cratered the ground around the gunpit, but for the single grenade that he'd watched, in slow motion, drop with a clank amongst the brass pond of shell cases inside the walls of the 25 pounder position. Unable to move quickly enough to reach it and get it away, he'd only been able to stare at it, braced for a blast that never came.

Then one of the guerrillas who'd skirted around the back of the fort also found his range. The grenade arced in with a sickening inevitability. Powerless to check its progress, Mike Kealy followed its trajectory with a rising dread. The little spherical green bomb fell short, then skidded and rolled towards the edge of the bunker with just enough agonizing momentum to drop over into his rough-hewn sanctuary. At the far end of the dugout, the fuse fizzed, sending a thin plume of dark smoke into the air. Kealy knew he had six seconds from the moment the pin had been pulled. If it had been thrown immediately, perhaps he had three seconds left. If the Adoo fighter had let it cook off a little before hurling it, then he might have no time at all. He tried to bury himself into the opposite wall of the pit, turning his back towards the nearby bomb. He could feel his heart thumping above the crack and thunder of the battle beyond the bunker. But he could do nothing but tense against the inevitable explosion. Contained within the close walls of the bunker, the concussion alone would be devastating. The shrapnel that went with it, though, would shred him.

Kealy waited, eyes clamped shut, curled up as small as he could make himself. Each heartbeat anticipated a painful end. Around him, nothing else mattered. The sound of the battle receded. The Adoo attack faded away. It was just Mike Kealy, the 27-year-old Commanding Officer of Eight Troop, B Squadron, 22 SAS, and the bomb that was going to kill him. He pressed himself further into the wall of the sangar. His heart thumped.

Then nothing.

The fuse of the Chinese-made grenade sputtered out, leaving the little bomb sitting on the floor of the bunker as harmlessly as an avocado on a greengrocer's shelf.

That now he and Tak had *both* survived dud grenades was more than just chance. The drizzle and damp of the monsoon that had encouraged the Adoo to attack when they were sure Mirbat would be shorn of air support had also seeped through their stores. It wasn't just the odd hand grenade that was mis-firing, it was most of them.

All the same, thought Kealy, *that bugger's getting too accurate. I've got to do something about him.* The officer pulled himself to his feet cradling his ArmaLite, hoping to pot the guerrilla who'd thrown the grenade. As he raised the rifle to his shoulder and popped up above the sandbags to take aim, he heard the rattle of an Adoo light machine gun, then an impact to his head.

I've been hit, he thought. But again his luck had held. It was the shockwave of a bullet passing through his hair. Half an inch taller and he'd have been grazed. An inch and he'd have been killed. He felt another bullet warp past his neck, and he dropped back into the cover of the ammunition bunker.

There wasn't a lot more he and Tak could do to hold back the rebel tide. Crouched back down in the trench, he pulled out his walkie-talkie and tried to raise Bob Bennett at the BATT House.

Chapter 38

Forty-five minutes after he'd scrambled from the Salalah runway en route to Mirbat, David Milne-Smith applied the parking brake and shut down the Viper turbojet. He unclipped his oxygen mask, then reached forward to the centre of the instrument panel and held down the switch to open the canopy. As the big glass bubble whirred back on its rails, he pulled off his bonedome. He ran a hand through thick blond hair that had been matted against his head by the tight helmet. Strikemaster 403 was already surrounded by the ground crew.

Instead of pulling off his harness and climbing out once the engineers had inserted the pins to make the ejector seat safe, DMS remained in the cockpit. He knew the situation on the ground and he'd barely burnt through the Avtur fuel in the wingtip tanks. If Airwork hung another 32 SURAs off the wings, he could be airborne again in ten minutes. Back overhead Mirbat in twenty.

But apart from returning to the dangerous skies over the battlefield he had another nagging concern. The last time he'd spoken to his wingman was when Sean Creak had said he was returning to base. Since then DMS had heard nothing. And he realized that, since he'd landed, he'd seen no sign of Creak's jet.

He saw Bill Stoker striding across the dispersal towards him. The Squadron Boss had a yellow Mae West around his shoulders, maps stuffed in his flightsuit pockets and leg restraints strapped above his calves. He was going flying.

'What's happened to Sean?' Milne-Smith shouted, impatient for news.

'Sean's fine,' Stoker told him. The jet had taken a few hits, but Creak was back in Ops. 'I'm replacing him. What's it like?' There was no mistaking the Boss's eagerness to get involved.

He's raring to go, DMS realized. While Bill Stoker stood alongside the cockpit, the 25-year-old Flight Lieutenant tried to paint a portrait of the battle. While they spoke, behind them, the armourers slotted the 81mm rockets beneath the wings.

Milne-Smith was going to lead the sortie, with Stoker as his No. 2.

'We'll just do a racetrack,' he explained. 'Just follow me in. Daisy chain.'

'What's the cloud like?' Stoker asked. It had been a little better at Mirbat than Salalah. It was low, but doable. And it was improving. After scraping past the 200ft minimum for the first scramble, it was up over 380 feet now at Salalah.

'We're going to do the same. Seemed to work,' DMS assured him. 'We need to get back there.'

Stoker agreed and walked over to his waiting jet. Strikemaster 407 was ready to go. As Stoker strapped himself in and pulled on his helmet, the engineers refilled the ammunition cans on Milne-Smith's jet, folding belts of linked 7.62mm rounds into the magazines.

When Mike Kealy asked him to lay down a ranging shot in the wadi, Bob Bennett sucked his teeth at the prospect of it. The depression was seventy-five yards south of Kealy's position, but to hit it, using nothing more than experience and what he could see with his own eyes, Bennett was going to have to estimate distance, mortar elevation and the weight of explosive charge necessary to accurately lob that first bomb in the right place.

But from its point of impact, Kealy could then control the fire mission, by feeding back corrections to the Troop Sergeant at the BATT House. If Kealy could bring mortar fire in close to the fort to the north and east, he could stop the Adoo advancing across open ground and deny the fort itself as cover. The high ballistic trajectory of the mortar bombs meant that, unlike with a gun, it was possible to put rounds right in behind an obstruction.

Bennett passed on his instructions to Hussey, who, with the departure of Tak and Tommy, the rest of his mortar team, to the fort, was now firing the weapon alone. Fuzz acted on Bennett's instructions, increasing the elevation of tube and tucking the bipod legs in closer to hold it upright. The unstoppable little Lancastrian then dropped a round down the muzzle of the weapons. There was a brief scrape of metal on metal before the bomb thumped out of the tube into a high arcing delivery.

Kealy heard it scream overhead only to watch it whump uselessly into the ground nearly half a mile beyond where he'd wanted it. But it did provide the necessary reference to work from. The Captain held the Tokai to his cheek and passed corrections back to Bennett.

'Fire one bomb,' he finished.

Looking out towards the fort, his eyes narrowing to focus, Bennett marked the fall of the first round on his mortar plotter board and gave Hussey the new fire mission. The mortar tube, swinging upwards on a metal joint attached to the heavy metal base plate, was reaching the limit of its elevation. Again the bomb walloped out of the tube. Again it was long. Still calm, Kealy clicked transmit and fed back corrections based on the pall of smoke rising from the explosion.

Fire one bomb.

Long. Corrections.

Fire one bomb.

Still they were falling too far from the fort to ease the pressure on Tak and Kealy in the two dugouts. Faced with a near vertical tube, the legs of the mortar bipod would push it no further, but the corrections from Kealy and Bennett kept coming. Fuzz looked up at Bennett on the roof in exasperation. What else could he do?

*

There were eighteen on board the two Hueys making the first lift. In the back of Neville Baker's helicopter, Stan Standford managed to squeeze his share of the heavily armed G Squadron troopers into the cabin. Although none of them carried the large Bergen rucksacks they would have had with them as they were ferried out to the BATT positions around Dhofar, they made up for it with the weight of weaponry and ammunition they carried. It seemed that those who weren't criss-crossed with belts of GPMG chain link instead wore the bandoliers of M79 grenades that had been brought at the last minute from the stores. The Squadron Boss, Alistair Morrison, was last in. He tucked himself in next to the sliding door behind Baker's seat in the cockpit. To his left, he noticed the bullet hole in the side panel from the aircraft's earlier, aborted attempt to get into Mirbat.

In the other helicopter, Aircrewman Hamed Nasser sat facing backwards. As the young Omani looked across the cabin at the nine SAS soldiers they made for an intimidating sight. There was no chat. Some of them opened and closed their hands around their rifles. Their faces, streaked with camouflage cream and cold-eyed, signalled only determination. The prospect of being on the receiving end of what a motivated group of elite soldiers like the men sitting in front of him might do was an unsettling one.

The B Squadron Civil Action Team at Mirbat hadn't been there to pick a fight. But if that's what the Adoo wanted, then the Regiment was very happy to oblige.

Neville Baker wound on the power and hauled the ever-dependable Huey into the air. For the BATT men, without ear defenders, the whine of the Alison turboshaft in the cabin was total.

Alongside Baker, the Captain of the other helicopter, an ex-Fleet Air Arm pilot, Roy Baylis, twisted the throttle grip and pulled up on the collective stick to his left. The skids became light as the main rotor gripped the air. Baylis kept the aircraft in check with the pedals. The two heavily loaded helicopters hung in the air for a moment, then, their fat blades thumping, they pirouetted towards Salalah town, dipped their noses and accelerated south.

Two hours after Baker's earlier sortie there was more airspace below the clouds, but they still hung heavy overhead. Flying low over the rooftops, the two camouflaged helis coasted out over the sea and into the haze. Flying in loose formation about a hundred yards apart they turned east towards Mirbat. Instead of following the coast as they had earlier, Baker led the pair further out to sea. The Huey was a noisy, distinctive aircraft and the relief force didn't want to announce their arrival to the Adoo.

Behind them, the remainder of the G Squadron men crammed themselves into a third helicopter flown by RAF man Chris Chambers. With their departure, Morrison's force of thirty-one was airborne.

But flying at a hundred feet above the sea at a cruising speed of near 100 knots, the three helicopters were still over twenty minutes away from Mirbat.

Eight Troop's extraordinary defence was beginning to falter. It was nearly 0930 hours. After four hours of the most intense fighting endured by a British Army unit since the Glosters' last stand at Imjin River in Korea in 1951, the edges were starting to fray. Ammunition was running low. Laba was dead. Tommy Tobin was lying in the dirt with most of his jaw shot off. The 25 pounder's contribution was over. And Tak and Mike Kealy were, somehow, holding on next to the DG fort as Fuzz tried to disrupt the Adoo advance with mortar fire. Now Snapper, behind the sandbags and ammunition boxes of the .50 sangar, was struggling with the only other weapon that could cover the approaches to the fort. The mechanism of the big Browning, firing near relentlessly since Kealy's order to open fire, was becoming gummed up with tiny shreds of brass, shaved off the cases as they were pulled through the receiver. As much as possible, Snapper had fed the belt through with his left hand, but without a No. 2 to do the job properly, the chain-linked ammunition didn't feed through cleanly. Now Winner was reduced to firing single shots. After each one he had to recock the gun manually. The effect was not even a poor relation to the steam train chug of the heavy machine gun at full chat.

But, as frustrating as they were, there was some benefit to the stoppages. Without them, Snapper would have been out of the game completely.

At his feet, sitting amongst the clinking metal carpet of spent brass and old chain link, were his last two boxes of .50 ammunition.

'Smash' Smyth-Piggott tried to ignore some of the wilder stories about what was going on at Mirbat. Some were speculating that the town had already been overthrown, but the punchy Northern Frontier Regiment Captain knew that soldiers fighting for their lives rarely have the opportunity to keep HQ fully in the picture.

More important things to deal with, he reckoned. After being woken by his Company Commander, 'Smash' had mustered his soldiers and rushed them from Um al Gwarif to Salalah in a couple of three-tonners. But now the men of 5 and 7 Platoons of the NFR were just hanging around on the dispersal. After screaming to a halt outside the Squadron buildings in his Land Rover Smyth-Piggott had gone straight to the Ops Room. He didn't see the G Squadron men before they boarded the helicopters. But with the SAS men already being choppered into Mirbat he quickly understood that he and the NFR had been usurped. And now, with the slap of the departing Hueys' rotors still hanging below the cloud, 'Smash' was left pacing around outside Salalah Ops in frustration.

'Why didn't they let us go?' he said to anyone who'd listen. 'We were ready.' And they were. But today, for one day only, the Regiment had enjoyed the back-up at Salalah to go out in support of their own. With G Squadron at UAG it was never going to be any other way.

*

North of the airfield buildings, two BAC 167 Strikemasters, their machine-gun magazines full and their wings laden with SURA rockets, accelerated down Runway Two Two. The jets' Rolls-Royce Viper engines roared as the camouflaged aircraft gathered speed, the drizzle of the *khareef* smothering the dust that usually kicked up in their wake. Instead, pale wisps of condensation flared and vanished over the wings as the pilots rotated into the moist air. With Bill Stoker as his wingman, David Milne-Smith was departing Salalah to return to the fight. Staying beneath the cloud, the pair banked together towards the south and flew low over Um al Gwarif camp. As they flew out to sea, as one, they turned east.

It was too dangerous to land in Mirbat itself. Instead, Neville Baker led the formation of helicopters in at low level over the sea to a beach a mile south-east of the town. In the Huey's cabin, battered by the husky whine of the engine and chop of the main rotor, any notion of stealth or surprise seemed unlikely. But with the fighting to the north, by coming from below the horizon they hoped to mask their approach from the Adoo. From the relative safety of the LZ, Alistair Morrison would then lead his G Squadron relief force north towards the BATT House and the fort clearing any Adoo resistance as his troopers advanced through the town. Lashed to the floor of the cabin, Huey 407 was carrying 10,000 rounds of 7.62mm ammunition.

As Baker reduced the speed and pulled on the power to land, Morrison looked ahead through the cockpit windows over the pilot's shoulder. Framed by the vibrating instrument panel below, it was difficult to make out Mirbat ahead through the low cloud and mist. Fifty yards apart, the two helicopters from the first lift settled on to the thick tubes of their skids on the sand. Neville Baker eased down on the Huey's collective lever, to release the aircraft's grip on the sky. But above the cabin on the hinges and rods of the rotor head, the thick twin blades continued to beat the air. Beneath the thumping, blurring disc, shielded to the north by a low ridge his nine lethal passengers de-planed.

Along the beach, Aircrewman Hamed Nasser stood by as the cabin of his own helicopter emptied SAS men on to the beach. Five of them were armed with GPMGs, another carrying the blunt-nosed M79, strapped with bandoliers of bombs for the grenade launcher. Across both helicopters the G Squadron relief force were carrying as much firepower as a hundred-strong infantry company.

Morrison and his men turned their backs and crouched shielding themselves from the stinging sand and sea spray whipped up by the violent downdraught from the two helicopters as they took off. As quickly as they'd touched down, they swung around beneath their rotors and dipped their noses as they accelerated out to sea. As the clatter from the helis receded, Morrison circled his men around the weapons, radio and ammunition. Morrison glanced up at the ridge dominating their position. The first task was to secure the LZ for the arrival of the third Huey. The G Squadron Boss deployed fourteen of his men up on to the ridge to secure it. The men shouldered their weapons and, covering each other, moved north. As they advanced, Morrison stayed back with his signal sergeant and two other troopers to meet the balance of his thirty-one-man assault force.

With one more Huey inbound, Neville Baker and Charlie Gilchrist, instead of returning to Salalah, ducked in again to Taqa LZ, ten minutes' flying time from Mirbat. For all the drama of the morning so far, they remained the duty casevac crew. And they knew that as soon as they could get into the besieged town, there were two very seriously injured BATT men to rush back to the FST. And the body of one of their comrades. It would be no surprise if the number were to rise. They shut down and they waited. Clearance to go would come from the Taqa BATT, in contact with the Ops Room at Um al Gwarif.

From the top of the ridge, the G Squadron soldiers saw a group of five men walking across their front. The men seemed relaxed and unhurried as they moved through the drizzle. From a distance of seventy-five yards it was difficult to be certain of their identity. The fourteen men held their fire. One of Morrison's soldiers raised a pair of binoculars to his eyes and adjusted the focus. Barefoot, dressed in uniformed shirts and *futtas* around their waists. But so far from the fighting, he assumed they were fighters from the Firqa patrolling the southern approaches to the town. Then he noticed the distinctive shape of the weapons all five of the men had cradled in their arms.

'They're Adoo,' the Trooper reported, 'they've got AK47s.'

From where he stood in the shadow of the ridge, Morrison saw two Arab men walking along the beach towards him. Again, their identity was unclear but their manner was easy and unsuspicious. Without any apparent concern, they continued approaching Morrison's little four-man team along the seafront.

They're Firqa, Morrison thought, *out from the town*. The BATT soldiers kept their weapons checked as the two men came closer. Then Morrison realized that the pair were carrying Kalashnikovs. They were enemy. Neither the Adoo nor the SAS expected to find each other this side of Mirbat, so each assumed that the other was friendly. But now it was clear, Morrison invited them to lay down their weapons.

Then, from the ridge, the angry percussion of a GPMG rattled across the beach. The group of five Adoo in the sights of Morrison's defensive line tried to run for cover in the direction of the Jebel, but they were cut down by the SAS Gimpies. G Squadron had opened their account.

On the beach, the two guerrillas marked by Morrison's group of four quickly weighed up the odds and opted for survival. They put down their rifles and surrendered.

As the immediate threat to the position was cleared, Morrison heard the rhythmic wallop of the third helicopter, approaching low over the grey sea behind him. Thirteen men climbed out of the two sliding cabin doors and jumped down on to the beach. With the departure of the Huey for Salalah, the Squadron Commander called a Chinese parliament to discuss their options. To a great extent they'd come into

Mirbat blind. At Salalah they had been able to select what looked like a suitable insertion point. But beyond that they could only react to the situation they found on the ground. It seemed clear.

The only way, Morrison agreed with his men, *we can do anything is to get into town.*

And, the G Squadron Boss realized, they had had one incredible stroke of luck. The LZ they'd chosen had effectively trapped a large group of Adoo between the fourteen men on the ridge, the wire fence around the southern limits of the town, and the sea.

One of those peculiar quirks in battle, he thought. If he left the defensive line on the high ground to cork the bottle, the remaining force of seventeen men could move forward like beaters at a shoot, closing down the enemy. And killing any of them that chose to fight or flee.

Over the radio, Morrison's signal sergeant called in a sitrep to Um al Gwarif. In reply he was passed the latest information from Mirbat: Labalaba was dead.

The big, smiling Fijian was a popular figure amongst Morrison's men. They'd fought alongside him during Operation JAGUAR and, subsequently, when he'd joined them in Malaysia for jungle training, he'd become very close to a lot of people on the Squadron. Where there had been some confusion about what was going on at Mirbat and how they were going to go to work, it was now quickly replaced by barely suppressed anger at Laba's loss. Harnessed to an unusually large collection of GPMGs, M79s and SLRs, it didn't look like being a healthy combination for any Adoo who got in their way. G Squadron were going after the men who had just killed their friend.

The SAS Major instructed his signal sergeant to establish contact with the BATT House.

There was no reply.

Chapter 39

Bob Bennett put the walkie-talkie to his ear. Again, Mike Kealy's measured, clear diction crackled through the little Tokai radio from the ammunition dump. From the *tone* of the young Captain's transmissions alone it was difficult to get a sense of just how desperate a situation he and Tak were in as the Adoo closed, poised to overrun them both. But the content of his message made it quite clear.

'Bring the mortar rounds closer,' Kealy said.

Did I hear that right? Bennett thought. 'Mike, if I bring them closer, they're actually going to fall right on top of you.'

'That's exactly where I want them,' Kealy insisted. 'On top of my position. Just do it *now*.'

But there was logic in Kealy's apparently suicidal demand. The Troop Commander had realized that he was dealing with a straightforward equation. If he did nothing, then he and Tak would die. But if Bob and Fuzz actually aimed *for* him, the inherent inaccuracy of the mortar's indirect fire might spare them.

The principle of getting a mortar round on target was similar to trying to hit a flowerbed with a hosepipe without being allowed to point directly at it. The point where the stream of water hits the ground can be altered by raising or lowering the nozzle of the pipe. If you want to bring it closer you point the pipe higher and simply waste some of the jet's energy on height. But the closer you try to bring the fall of the water jet, the higher you've got to point the hose until, near vertical, water's going straight up and straight down. And at this point it's almost impossible to direct with any real accuracy.

So, as Hussey struggled to bring the fall of shot closer, the odds of him getting the rounds to actually land where he wanted them to got longer. He could no more guarantee to drop a round *inside* the restricted dimensions of either the gun-pit or the ammunition dump than he could be sure they wouldn't fall there. But it was all in the odds. And the two sangars didn't offer a very big target. But unless they defied the odds and dropped a bomb in the bunkers themselves, then the sandbags, as they had with the Adoo grenades that had exploded beyond the sangar walls, would save the two BATT men on the receiving end. None the less, while Bennett and Hussey may have understood the calculations Kealy was making, it was an order that seemed staggering in its gutsiness.

Still, it didn't make Hussey's job any easier. He'd reached the limit of how close he could get the fall of the mortar shot.

'You've got to bring it closer,' Bennett told him.

Oh, God, this has got to be wrong, Hussey thought, resigned to what he was about to attempt. He took a deep breath then he crouched down, grabbed the hot mortar tube with both arms and hugged it close against his chest. As he pulled it back, the two bipod legs swung free, no longer serving any useful purpose. To all intents and purposes, Hussey was now aiming the 81mm weapon like a garden hose.

'Frag them,' came the order from Bennett.

In the mortar pit, twisting his head down and away from the tube Fuzz dropped a bomb into the muzzle. Braced, he felt it grate down the barrel before, with a boom that seemed to resonate through him like a kettledrum, the round was punched high into the air. He was enveloped by acrid white smoke from the charge, another layer to add to the pungent veils of burnt propellant that hung over the battlefield.

Then he waited for the next fire mission to be called down from Bob Bennett on the BATT House roof.

*

It's like Zulu, Tak thought, as he watched the Adoo advance continue across the plain north of the fort, still relentless, still in overwhelming numbers. And he forced himself to carry on with the excruciating process of unloading the rounds from the FN magazines and pressing them into his own. His face was smeared black with gunsmoke and his black hair thick with clotted blood. As well as the choking smell of the battle, the aural onslaught was visceral and unremitting. Like the red-coated, pith-helmeted 24th Regiment of Foot, it had seemed inconceivable that the little SAS Civil Action Team at Mirbat would be the target of such a determined attack in strength. But like the heroes of Rorke's Drift, Tak and Kealy – and their comrades back at the BATT House – had somehow been able to keep the enemy assault at bay. Just. Packed behind the sand-bags of the gun sangar, protected from the shrapnel spat into the air by the dangerously close mortar rounds now raining in from the BATT House, Tak continued to conserve his ammunition. But it was a strategy loaded with risk. Limited to single shots and double taps, the injured Trooper had to allow the enemy close before he could be sure of using the power of the SLR to knock them down. He couldn't afford to miss. The guerrillas were often just four or five yards away when he aimed and fired. But the intervention of Hussey's mortar was slowing them down; keeping the numbers making it round the corner of the fort manageable. Then Tak heard Bob Bennett over the Tokai, still sitting out of reach across the floor of the gunpit. He was talking to the jets.

As Bennett guided the Strikemaster pair in from the roof of the BATT House, relief and gratitude flooding him, he couldn't help but worry that the pilots' luck was going to run out.

This time there was no confusion about the frequencies. After David Milne-Smith called ahead to announce the strike pair's arrival, the reply came through immediately on Blue SARBE. DMS recognized the voice of the FAC he'd spoken to on the first sortie.

'Hello, Red Leader, this is BATT House. Same again. Fire

wherever you can. Enemy HMG on Jebel Ali. Also rear of the fort. Over.'

DMS pressed the transmit button on the throttle.

'Roger, BATT House.'

Behind him, Bill Stoker, tuned into the same 123.8 VHF frequency, heard it all, the voice of his young Flight Leader sounding clipped and efficient over the hiss of the RT.

Taking a hand off the control column, DMS reached forward to arm the Strikemaster's guns and missiles.

Impossible to tell, he thought as listened to the BATT controller's voice, *whether or not the situation on the ground is any better*. But he did know that his earlier attacks had had some effect in checking the Adoo assault. And so more of the same was exactly what he set out to do. He crossed the coast just shy of 400 knots, heading towards the Jebel on a track that would take him just to the left of the DG fort. Keeping the perimeter wire to port, he streaked across the broken plain; the rush of the ground below and the low cloud ceiling providing an intense feeling of speed that was completely absent at altitude. Milne-Smith pulled the gun trigger with his index finger, then, after a beat, unleashed the rockets.

Half a mile behind him, Stoker watched his young Flight Leader break right, standing the little attack jet on its wing as he pulled her into a hard 4G turn to starboard. With a kidskin-gloved hand, Stoker flicked up the Armament Master Switch, then with a practised sweep along the instrument panel armed the guns and the SURA rocket pylons under the wings. The circuit indicator light glowed red.

On his first pass, Bill Stoker followed his Flight Leader round. But as he pulled hard round the racetrack behind Milne-Smith, he decided that, on his second, with DMS again laying down fire along the perimeter wire north of the fort, he would try something different. Back at Salalah the 1 Squadron Boss had been briefed by Alistair Morrison about the Shpagin machine-gun position dominating the battlefield from the Jebel Ali. The BATT FAC too had mentioned it in his opening RT exchange with DMS. Manoeuvring with care between the cloud and the sea, Stoker pulled the nose of the jet round towards the low rock hill that stood guard over the route into Mirbat from the north and placed the summit in the middle of the illuminated circular markings projected on to the glass of the gunsight. He fired the guns to cover himself, then he pressed the pickle button with his right thumb to launch the first eight of the darting little missiles. Then a Shpagin bullet punched through his left wing.

As he completed his second pass, DMS horsed the straight-winged jet round into the corner. As he carved through 180 degrees, coasting out over the bay to set himself up for the third strafing run, the RT gave a tell-tale click as Stoker pressed the transmit button in the cockpit of Strikemaster 407.

'I've been hit really badly,' the Squadron Leader said, 'I've got fuel pissing out of the aeroplane. I'm in some trouble here.'

DMS could hear the alarm in Stoker's voice and he imagined that the Boss must be missing chunks from his aircraft.

Christ, he thought, *we may lose a jet here. And someone with it.* DMS told him to pull up and get above the clouds. But as the CO swept up into the *khareef*, DMS kept his own air-craft reefed tight into the turn with the swell smudging past beneath his starboard wing. Then he levelled off for what was going to have to be his final attack run. It was clear that, unlike Sean Creak, Stoker was going to need a wingman, but, Milne-Smith calculated, if he loosed off the two last rows of SURA rockets one straight after the other on a single pass, then he could shepherd the Boss home, and deliver the ordnance he'd carried with him to Mirbat to help save the BATT; he didn't have to leave them in the lurch. On the ground, using the same frequency as the two Strikemasters, he knew that the BATT had heard what had happened to Stoker's jet. He pressed transmit.

'BATT House, Red Leader,' he said, 'I'm on my last pass. I'll get rid of the weapons, but I have to go back. Over.'

The moment the second salvo of eight rockets sped from the rails under the wings, towards the Fort approaches, Milne-Smith checked his instruments and hauled back on the stick, converting speed to height. As the blunt-nosed little attack jet was swallowed by the cloud he trimmed her into the climb and, his eyes darting from the Artificial Horizon, to the Compass, to the Airspeed Indicator, to the Altimeter, all grouped together on the flight panel, he kept her soaring skyward through the pale clag.

The screaming of the jets, Tak thought for the second time in the space of barely three quarters of an hour, *is the best sound I've ever heard*. The arrival of the cavalry. Looking up at the sky he watched the two Strikemasters thunder past, rockets hissing off the rails and chewing up the Adoo advance. He was struck by how low they were.

Fifty, maybe one hundred feet, he reckoned, *I'm sure the pilots can see everything*. He was also sure, as the gun and rocket attacks finally began to stem the flow of the guerrilla attack, that the SOAF jets were the only thing that had saved them.

As the jet stabbed out from the top of the cloud at around 3,500 feet, the morning sun streamed into the Strikemaster's cockpit. Squinting in the bright light, Milne-Smith reached up and lowered the bonedome's black sun visor down over his face and searched the skies to the west for Stoker's jet. Four miles ahead of him, what might have been a difficult to spot speck in the sky was signposted by the stream of white fuel pouring out of the port wing. Stoker was flying slowly, still climbing.

They were thirty-five miles away from Salalah and Stoker, watching his fuel gauges spin down in the cockpit, didn't think he was going to make it. But any extra height was going to give him a chance of gliding in. But he wasn't sure he was even going to be able to do that. He knew that neither he nor Milne-Smith were going to see the ground, let alone the runway, at Salalah until they were a few hundred feet from it.

Gliding into the runway without power was something all the 1 Squadron pilots practised regularly. They enjoyed it. In visual flight conditions it was rarely more than a satisfying test of one's eye, judgement and coordination. And they practised

SRA – Surveillance Radar Approach – landings under instruction from the radar controllers on the ground. But by their very nature they tended to involve lots of small corrections to speed, heading and altitude; and, as a result, lots of small control inputs and subtle throttle movements. To combine the two – for real – was no picnic at all.

Every student pilot has the mantra 'Aviate. Navigate. Communicate' drummed into him. First and foremost you've got to keep the aircraft flying safely. If you can do that, fly it where you want it to go. And if you've got the first two nailed, then tell people what you're up to. But if just keeping the aircraft flying is soaking up all of a pilot's capacity, then trying to navigate and communicate on top is going to lead to disaster. A significant part of a combat pilot's ability to cope with the complicated, exacting demands of military flying comes from familiarity, routine and repetition. In an emergency, with too much, too unfamiliar, too fast, it was very easy indeed for a pilot – even an experienced one – to reach the limit of his capacity. And, it was clear from the anxiety in his voice that Stoker was in danger of that. With his wingman in trouble, DMS stepped in.

Accelerating to catch up with the damaged jet ahead, Milne-Smith positioned himself off his CO's port flank. The Boss was losing fuel at a huge rate through the jagged fist-sized hole in the wing.

'I'll do the radio, you fly your aeroplane, and I'll formate on you.'

The Strikemaster used the fuel in the wingtip tanks first, then the wings. Stoker's tip tanks were already empty.

While Stoker kept his jet straight and level, the throttle setting fixed in order to avoid burning extra fuel with little changes, DMS kept asking him to check his fuel. If Stoker was going to run out, better to anticipate. Then Milne-Smith stretched forward to his radio Station Box and switched frequencies to Salalah Tower.

'Mayday, Mayday, Mayday,' he began, then passed details of the emergency to the RAF controller on the ground. 'On recovery, six thousand feet,' he continued, 'into the overhead for a precautionary approach.' In reply to each transmission from the Flight Leader, Salalah gave a series of steers to bring the Strikemaster pair into the overhead.

Steer Two Four Zero.

Steer Two Five Zero.

In the cockpit of Strikemaster 403, DMS checked them against the Compass and DME – Direction Measuring Equipment – tuned into the radio beacon at Salalah. Milne-Smith repeated each correction to Stoker, gently insisting on repetition and acknowledgement that the other pilot was responding.

Overhead Salalah, but unable to see the airfield beneath the cotton wool expanse of the cloud, Stoker, with his left hand, pulled back the throttle lever, cutting the power from the Viper engine to idle. Now certain that he could reach the runway whether his engine, starved of fuel, flamed out or not, he had to make sure that its sudden loss or return didn't interfere with the equilibrium of his spiral down through the clag. Now gliding, Stoker tipped his jet on to her wing and pulled her into a tight, fast, descending spiral towards the cloud. DMS watched 407 dissolve into the soft white lake below and disappear.

And then he followed him in.

At Um al Gwarif, BATT HQ welcomed the news from the radio room that G Squadron were safely on the ground and ready to take the fight to the Adoo.

Get in there, lads, they urged them, *and hit the bastards.*

Chapter 40

After watching the second Strikemaster finish its final attack run and pull up into the cloud, Morrison divided his assault force into two groups, each in turn to provide cover while the other advanced to contact. As they skirmished forwards under the overcast towards Mirbat, every third man carried a Gimpy in the light role, held at waist height like a personal weapon. Twice they'd come under fire from Adoo positions and on both occasions they had responded with overwhelming force, pouring GPMG rounds in against the more lightly armed rebel fighters.

Then, as they closed on the south-east of the town a stream of Adoo bullets came in from the flanks. Morrison's platoon dived for cover, except for one Corporal who, under heavy fire, singlehandedly stormed the enemy position and took it out. The Adoo dead were searched and their weapons taken, but the G Squadron men didn't waste time. Ahead they could hear the sounds of the battle for the DG fort and Mirbat's northern perimeter. Morrison's force swept on towards the tumbledown mud-brick buildings of Mirbat's southern boundary, effective, well-practised fire and movement clearing the path ahead from the east to the perimeter to the sea. Whatever restraint might have been exercised before news of Laba's death was gone. This was a demolition.

Bill Stoker finally lost his engine completely as he spiralled down through the cloud like a falling sycamore seed. But with his engine throttled back he was already working on the assumption that it could not be relied on. Its failure made no difference to the tight helix he was flying. As he pulled back on the stick, checking the sideslip with the rudder, he presented the grey, gunsmoke-stained belly of the jet to the outside of his descending curve. He was following a path within the confines of a vertical cylinder in the air as surely as a motorcycle rider revolving round the Wall of Death. And, gliding or not, it had to be fast. When Stoker emerged from the cloud, only airspeed would give him options. Speed could be converted into distance.

When Stoker and Milne-Smith emerged underneath the cloudbase, they could see the airfield below them. But they were high and fast and Stoker didn't have the luxury of going round again. The 1 Squadron Boss had no alternative but to get the Strikemaster down safely on to the ground from where he was.

'You're on your own,' DMS told him, as he chased the Squadron Boss in.

'Fine,' Stoker replied.

With his speed still above the 145 knot limit, he reached forward with his left hand and pushed the 'Undercarriage Down' button. On the instrument panel in front of him, three green lights blinked on to indicate that the gear was locked down. Still high and fast, and in danger of overshooting the runway completely, Stoker pushed the stick forward, trying to push the Strikemaster's nose down towards the threshold of the runway.

DMS pushed his throttle forward and accelerated away to come round again for his own circuit. There was nothing more he could do but leave the Boss to it.

From outside the Squadron building, Nobby Grey watched the two Strikemasters come in, emerging on short finals from the gloom. As DMS broke off from his position on Stoker's wing, Grey kept his eyes on the Squadron Commander's aircraft. The powerful landing light in the nose sparkled brightly in the moist air. Like a passenger in a car willing their driver to brake, Grey tensed, silently urging Stoker to get the jet down on to the ground. But while diving for the threshold certainly got rid of height, it added speed at the same time. It was no way to land an aeroplane. Grey, following his recent tour as a flying instructor on the very similar Jet Provost, knew the flying characteristics of the Strikemaster inside out. If Stoker was going to get the jet down he needed to boot the left rudder and cross the controls to bleed off height and speed; in essence, make the thing fly more like a barn door and less like an aeroplane. But it wasn't happening.

While Stoker swooped low along the centreline of the runway, he must have still been doing 150 knots plus. And the maximum speed over the threshold for a heavy Strikemaster was supposed to be 115 knots. So far in excess of that, the jet just didn't want to stop flying. It was past the halfway point before Stoker finally managed to get the wheels down on the ground. That, though, gave him no chance of bringing the aircraft to a halt before he ran out of runway.

Grey watched the RAF firetrucks rumble north from the airfield buildings in anticipation of trade.

Four Adoo trapped between the advance of G Squadron's left flank and the sea were offered the same choice as the two who'd laid down their weapons. But this group, which included the Adoo assault force's Political Commissar, made a different decision. Cornered, they waded into the surf to try to take refuge in a sea inlet. But, waist-deep in water they had nowhere to go. Instead of accepting the invitation to surrender, one of the younger guerrillas levelled his Kalashnikov at the BATT men and opened up, spraying automatic fire at them. But only briefly. The response from the SAS was immediate and irresistible. The combined firepower from two Gimpies, churning out 7.62mm rounds at over 700 rounds per minute, hit him square in the chest. The force of the fusillade picked him up out of the water and dumped him with a splash yards back from where his hopeless resistance had begun. What was left of his torso slipped beneath the surface and rolled back into the beach with the incoming waves. Alongside him, two of his companions were killed, while an older man had his legs sawn off below the knees as the Gimpies raked across the group.

By the time Morrison arrived, the seawater was red with blood as the rebels lay dead and dying in the wake of the Regiment advance. Pink foam stained the fine white sand as it lapped at the beach; while the troopers responsible for the carnage continued north towards Eight Troop's position on the other side of town.

Later, two RAMC medics attached to B Squadron, Taff Baker and Eric Reach, made their way along the beach, doing their best for the Adoo injured G Squadron had left behind. Leaving a trail of blood, Baker dragged the legless man up the beach, dosed him with morphine and tried to stem the flow of blood from his legs. But as the relief force pushed forward, there was nothing more he could do. When they returned, he lay dead where they'd left him. There were crabs clicking and picking at his bloody stumps, gorging on a prize piece of carrion.

The tide had turned.

The momentum of the Battle for Mirbat now appeared to have swung in favour of the town's defenders. The second Strikemaster attack from David Milne-Smith and Bill Stoker seemed finally to have broken the Adoo's conviction that they would win. But nothing was certain. While the Adoo's surprise attack on Mirbat had failed, there could be no safe assumption that it was over.

The Adoo had learnt the tactics of their guerrilla campaign from their Chinese sponsors well. And that aggression and sophistication had first been evident on the only occasion on which the body of a Chinese advisor fighting as part of an Adoo unit inside Oman had been found among the enemy dead.

In January 1968 a force of fifty guerrillas ambushed a SAF patrol on the eastern Jebel. After a fierce three-quarter-of-an-hour firefight, the Adoo withdrew, allowing the SAF men to evacuate their wounded, but only to lead the Desert Regiment convoy into another ambush. Despite the presence of SOAF air cover, the Adoo were only fought off with bayonets. And yet, as darkness fell, the Adoo attacked the SAF soldiers again. Although half of their total assault force had been killed or injured in the face of superior SAF firepower, they'd kept coming back for more.

That the Adoo assault on Mirbat appeared to have been beaten back did not mean that they were either incapable or unwilling to regroup and come back for more. But even as the rebels began to withdraw towards the north across the Jebel from the DG fort, at RAF Salalah urgent reinforcements were being organized.

Because now was the perfect time for the Adoo to counter-attack.

Eight Troop were shattered. Amongst the detritus of the battle on the roof of the BATT House, there was also vomit, from where sheer exhaustion had taken its toll. But irrespective of the men's doubtful physical ability to continue their resistance, they simply didn't have the ammunition to do so.

After five hours feeding heavy disintegrating-link belts of .50 ammunition into the side of the Browning with the palm of his left hand, Snapper was as tired as the gun itself. At his feet was a single green metal case of bullets. It wasn't yet midday but, in their ferocious defence of Mirbat, Eight Troop had torn their way through three months' supply of ammunition. At the point when the second Strikemaster pair had run in across Mirbat Bay, the BATT were on the verge of becoming defenceless.

After shutting down and unstrapping, DMS climbed out of his jet and went straight to the Ops Room, where Bill Stoker was already talking to the Ops staff.

The Squadron Boss had finally managed to force the wheels down on to the Salalah strip, but not soon enough to prevent his Strikemaster running off the end of the runway into the dirt and bouncing to an undignified halt. But beyond the damage from the Adoo guns, Stoker *had* been able to bring her in in one piece. And, more importantly, was unharmed. He'd been picked up by the Ops Officer and driven back to the Squadron.

When DMS found him he'd thrown himself into the conversation about the air assets needed over Mirbat. He'd already told Nobby Grey to saddle up and get airborne to provide further Top Cover at Mirbat – to Grey's delight, his flight north to Muscat for R&R had been put on hold – and he'd designated another one of his pilots to fly an ammunition resupply in one of the Squadron's piston-engined DeHavilland Beavers. But as much as Stoker was in the thick of the discussion, Milne-Smith could tell that, while he was OK, he was still badly shaken. The big man was having to work at the easy confidence and authority that was usually so natural. It was hardly surprising, given that, just fifteen minutes earlier, he'd been facing the prospect of ejecting through low cloud.

And that, thought Milne-Smith, imagining the scene, *is not great*.

Perhaps the best response to Stoker's apparent shock was simply distraction. If so, the Ops Room was providing it. DMS left him to it and returned to the Squadron while the Ops staff scheduled a Skyvan for another ammunition resupply mission for the afternoon. With the cloudbase still rising, they'd be able to get one of the bigger fixed-wing transports in. And outside on the dispersal Graeme Smyth-Piggott finally began loading his men from the two Northern Frontier Regiment standby platoons on to a pair of waiting Hueys. They too were finally on their way to Mirbat. But while the tone at Salalah was beginning to reflect a belief that they were now dealing with the aftermath of a battle, the situation on the ground along the coast was still uncertain.

From the roof of the BATT House, Snapper glimpsed movement against the skyline beyond the fort. On high ground half a mile east of the fort, a line of figures emerged over the horizon, briefly silhouetted against the light, spread out in an extended infantry line. The soldiers were working their way forward quickly and efficiently: disciplined, well-drilled and purposeful.

The Adoo, he thought, *we're in the shit now. They've regrouped. This is the counter-attack.*

Winner knew from time studying Warsaw Pact military doctrine back at Bradbury Lines that, unlike Western forces – and particularly the Regiment – initiative and individuality were anathema to Communist-trained armies. Their troops were command-controlled from the top; deployed almost like machines. Snapper wanted to pull the plug.

If I can take the leader out, he reasoned, *the rest should fall like a pack of cards.* He lined up the front sight blade of the Browning on the officer leading the advance. Snapper was down to single rounds, but that didn't matter. For this, he only needed one. The Browning had been used as a sniper's rifle in both the Korean War and the Vietnam War, where one US Marine Corps sniper had set a distance record when he chalked up a confirmed kill at a range of well over 1.3 miles.

From behind him, Bob Bennett followed Snapper's movements, raising his binoculars to his eyes to try to make a clearer assessment of the new threat. The two of them looked out across the battlefield. Beneath the *khareef* still draped overhead, there were thin columns of smoke rising from small fires and sporadic gunshots; the odd brief rattle from a machine gun as the Adoo who had been committed to the frontal assault covered their withdrawal north towards the Jebel. The relative quiet seemed to cloak them, but Bennett and Snapper, their eyes fixed on the emerging front to the east, barely noticed it. After the relentless hammering intensity of the battle, the will o' the wisp plumes and stuttering silence felt almost peaceful, but faced with the prospect of a fresh Adoo assault, Bennett seemed reluctant to engage them. But, outwardly composed and calm as ever, the Troop Sergeant's mind was racing with the possibilities.

Then as Bennett and Winner watched, the advancing infantry line, apparently on command, broke to the right as one, descending into the cover of broken ground beyond Mirbat's eastern perimeter. As the troops vanished from view, the sound of gunfire ripped across the plain. Bennett turned to Snapper.

'Go down again,' he said, his usually gentle West Country tones now biting, 'and get a sitrep from base.'

While Bennett continued to scan the eastern approaches, Snapper jumped down from the .50 sangar and disappeared down to the radio room. It was 1030 hours. A couple of minutes later, Snapper ripped off the PRC316 headset, tossed it on to the trestle table carrying the radio equipment, and, adrenalin surging through him, clattered up the ammunition cases and ladders up on to the roof.

As he emerged on to the roof, the Lance Corporal couldn't hide his euphoria. The good news was painted all over his grimy, blackened face before he needed to say a word.

In the brief Morse code exchange with BATT HQ at Um al Gwarif, he'd learnt when G Squadron had been lifted from Salalah on board the helicopters and when the Ops Room had received the report from Morrison's signal sergeant confirming that insertion had gone as planned. As he'd listened, he'd tried to marry this new information to the appearance of the infantry line to the east. And as he assembled the timeline, it dawned on him that the characteristics of the soldiers he'd seen advancing on Mirbat – the control, precision and confidence – fitted the picture. It was G Squadron. He and Bennett had been watching the relief force. And he'd had his finger on the trigger, ready to take down their Boss.

Bennett, taking good news and bad news with equal composure, acknowledged Snapper's confirmation of the soldiers' identity.

'I guessed as much,' he said. He'd already been sufficiently sure of his own conclusion to pull Fuzz Hussey off the mortar in order to help tend the men injured over at the DG fort. Bennett raised his SLR and began sniping at any guerrillas still out in the open on the plain.

Why not? thought Snapper. He yanked back on the

Browning's heavy cocking handle with his right hand, and took aim at the retreating Adoo.

Fuzz grabbed the second patrol medical kit and slung it over his shoulder. He thought of G Squadron's arrival. *There is a God,* he smiled to himself.

In the shadow of the old fort at Taqa, fifteen miles to the east, Neville Baker, Charlie Gilchrist and Stan Standford milled around their battle-damaged Huey waiting for clearance to go in and pick up the wounded. But with news reported over the SAS radio net that the Adoo were now on the run, one of the Taqa BATT troop came jogging out to the helicopter and made his way towards the lean, silver-haired Squadron Leader.

'OK,' the Trooper told him, 'you're clear to go in to pick up the casualties. Still some sniping from long range, but it is only long-range stuff. Should be safe to get in at low level. Communicate using SARBE.'

Baker and his crew climbed back on the aircraft and strapped themselves into their seats. The 1 Squadron Boss reached up to the overhead console with a gloved hand and switched on the electrics, set the throttle to start, then pressed and held the starter. The T-53 turboshaft began to whine and, above the cabin helicopter's fuselage, the main blades slowly started to turn.

Now the shooting had stopped, Baker's casevac helicopter had become the most important piece of kit available to Mirbat's defenders.

Chapter 41

Slumped back against the shredded sandbags of the gunpit, Tak knew they'd won the battle. But there was no joy or elation. No exhilaration. Surrounded by the fallen bodies of comrades and friends and scores of Adoo dead, there was barely relief. Just sadness. The normally impassive Fijian's feelings were running wild. Laba, the friend he'd first met in 1961 in Fiji's capital, Suva, when they'd both responded to the British Army's call for volunteers, was lying in the dirt, his eyes open and his throat shot away. Exhausted, wracked with pain and heartsick, the stoic bulldog of a Fijian Trooper blinked back tears.

The shooting had stopped, but Kealy's men were still fighting for survival. Laba might have gone, but the young Captain knew that Tak and Tommy Tobin needed urgent medical attention. Tobin's wound, in particular, was horrendous, but there was little that could be done for him here. If, Kealy thought, he could get them to the BATT House, they'd stand a better chance. But that was 500 yards away. Then he remembered the Land Rover parked inside the DG fort. If he could just get Tak and Tommy into the back of the vehicle it would be possible to cover the distance with ease.

If hardly unscathed, Mike Kealy was the only man fighting next to the DG fort who'd escaped death or very serious injury. He clambered up over the sandbags and out of the ammunition dump and walked to the fort fifteen yards away. Unable to speak anything but the most basic Arabic greeting, the SAS Captain was reduced to hammering on the door and shouting in English. It seemed, initially, that he'd have no more success than Tak had earlier in enticing the Omani soldiers out of the fort, but, with the battle spent, the thick, carved wooden door eventually began to groan open. Behind it slumped the ruined remains of the Land Rover. Riddled by shrapnel, its tyres cut to ribbons, the 110 sat low on its rims in a slick of oil and water. Damaged beyond repair by the mortar fire that had rained down within the walls of the fort it was going nowhere. It had somehow escaped the spark to the petrol tank that would have completed its destruction.

And inside the fort they had casualties of their own, the most badly wounded being the young Omani Artillery Gunner who'd bravely ventured beyond the walls of the fort only to be thrown back inside by a bullet that punched through his waist.

But without the vehicle there was no way Kealy could get any of the casualties the care they so desperately needed. Exhausted beyond measure, the officer didn't know where else to turn. But he had done enough.

When the G Squadron Boss, Alistair Morrison, crossed the open ground to the DG fort from Mirbat town, he was dumbstruck by what he found.

The whole scene, he thought, *is one of absolute chaos.* His assault force had pushed the Adoo back by splitting into two groups, one of which had fought its way north through the streets of Mirbat, while the other had flanked around east and so nearly found itself on the receiving end of Snapper Winner's Browning. But the violence the Major had witnessed during his men's scorched-earth advance was nothing compared to what confronted him when he arrived at the gunpit.

The pale stone walls of the old fort were pockmarked and blackened with soot. Hanging head down from the crenellation around the ramparts was the lifeless body of one of the DG guards. Driven deep into one of the stone walls was an unexploded 84mm Carl Gustav anti-tank round. Morrison didn't yet realize it was British, left behind in Aden in 1967 only to be turned on its original owners by the Adoo. There were bullet holes clean through the armoured shield of the 25 pounder, the protection it had offered Laba and Tak exposed as inadequate. It was at ground level where the carnage was most evident. The hard ground around the fort was scarred with shallow craters from both Adoo and BATT mortar fire. The gravel outside the bunkers was scattered with bullet cases and the rings from hand grenades. There were unexploded grenades and mortar blinds that gave the hill around the fort the appearance of a badly laid minefield. The sangars themselves were deep in clinking brass. In the gunpit, the bigger cases from the 3.45in 25-pounder rounds floated in a sea of spent cases from the smaller SLR rounds. There were empty, splintered ammunition boxes. In amongst it all were stained field dressings, used to staunch the bleeding from Tak and Laba's gunshot wounds. And there was plenty more blood to be found: splashed on the shredded hessian of the sandbags; in drying, red ochre puddles in the dirt and on the walls of the fort, where, peppered with hair and gore, it painted gruesome pictures of where Adoo fighters had fallen to accurate fire from Tak and Kealy's rifles. From the fall of the Adoo bodies, Morrison could tell that Kealy and his men had been all but hand-to-hand fighting with the enemy. The guerrillas had made it to within five or ten feet of the edge of the two sangars.

Then there were the Regiment casualties. Tak was bandaged and broken, caked in soot, dirt, sweat and congealed blood. Laba was dead. And, between the gunpit and the ammunition bunker, Fuzz Hussey, sent up to the fort by Bob Bennett, tended to the grievously injured Tommy Tobin, reaching through the pulp of his ruined face to clear his airway and keep him from swallowing his own tongue, then wrapping what was left in a field dressing tied round the injured medic's head. Poor Tobin's fight had barely begun.

It's obvious, the G Squadron Boss thought, *that a very heroic action has been fought here.* But if Morrison was left speechless at the devastation around him, it was one of his soldiers who most eloquently captured the sight that had greeted them at the gunpit.

'Jesus wept,' said the Trooper as he surveyed the scene.

Behind them, they could hear the rising noise of an approaching helicopter.

Neville Baker's Huey came in low over the sea from the west. Directed by Bob Bennett on the SARBE beacon the helicopter Squadron Boss skirted inland straight towards the DG fort. With Tommy patched up as well as could be managed, Fuzz skidded down the hill to the flat ground behind and guided the aircraft in to land, the downdraught from the powerful rotor kicking up a vicious storm of dust and stones until Baker took the pitch off the two blades as, when the skids touched down, he relaxed his grip on the collective. Stan Standford was already out of the open cabin door and making his way up the hill to help load the wounded men into the Huey's cabin.

Still sitting in the gunpit, raw with sadness, Tak watched as the two other wounded men, Walid Khamis and Tommy Tobin, were carried on stretchers down the slope and loaded on racks in the cabin of the waiting casevac helicopter. But when Standford jogged back up the hill to the gunpit to stretcher Tak down to the screaming, thumping aircraft, the big Fijian refused his help.

'I'm OK,' he said, biting back a swell of emotion, before, with his deep voice cracking, he told Standford: 'Take Laba first . . .'

Chapter 42

Alistair Morrison was struck by the Eight Troop Boss's composure. After fighting a fierce close-quarter battle, while Mike Kealy's red-rimmed eyes betrayed his deep fatigue, he remained completely in control. And after watching the casevac helicopter accelerate away towards Salalah with his wounded on board, Kealy talked the G Squadron Commander through the day's sequence of events, explaining where the Adoo attack had come in from, and how, in the desperate final hours, they'd tried to flank him and Tak from round the side of the fort. But Kealy's greatest concern was for the returning Firqa patrol. Called back from the Jebel by Tak over the radio as the Adoo attack had begun, Kealy realized that Bahait would be leading his men straight into the retreating rebel troops. And that even after taking heavy casualties in the assault on Mirbat, the Adoo still greatly outnumbered the Firqa force. Kealy also wanted to learn the fate of the night picquet on the Jebel Ali. He asked Morrison if he could lead a small group of men to the 300ft summit of the hill. From there, he argued, not only would he discover what had happened to the Dhofar Gendarmerie guards, but he could either cover the Firqa's return or direct SOAF jets against the Adoo. As they spoke, they heard the crack of small-arms fire to the north.

Reluctantly, Morrison let the exhausted young officer do as he'd requested. Kealy had earned the right, he thought, to make his own decisions. In the end, though, Kealy was headed off at the pass.

*

The helicopters carrying Smash Smyth-Piggott and his Northern Frontier Regiment soldiers landed inside the perimeter wire on the gravel plain between the Jebel Ali and the BATT House. Barely half an hour earlier, it had been the forward edge of the battle area. As the two SAF platoons de-planed, the first person Smash met was Kealy. Despite the BATT officer's ragged appearance, Smyth-Piggott, too, noticed his calm.

Cool as a cucumber, the SAF Captain thought as Kealy greeted his arrival.

'Thank God,' Kealy smiled as he cast an eye over the influx of sixty fresh troops, 'can you go and take Jebel Ali for me?' Then he told Smyth-Piggott that he also wanted men down at the South-Eastern Area too. Smash sent one of his platoons under the command of Staff Sergeant South, while he led the other up towards the Jebel Ali.

To avoid presenting his men as a walking target to any defenders who remained on the Jebel, Smyth-Piggott took them out to sea. Instead of the obvious routes up the rocks, the platoon of Omani soldiers waded knee-high through the surf to where the boulder slopes of the Jebel descended into the water. Smash calculated that an ascent from this direction was the most unlikely and therefore safest. Then from the sea, they pepper-potted their way up; fire and movement to the summit. It was slow going, but necessary. At the top, Smyth-Piggott learnt the sad fate of the night picquet. It was a pitiful sight. All eight of them lay dead in their sleeping bags, bayoneted by the Adoo as they slept. There had been no firefight, no resist-ance of any kind; nor even any warning. It was horribly clear to Smash that, instead of maintaining a sentry, all of the men had been asleep when the rebels had, barefooted, crept up the slopes towards their position. It had been too easy. Now all that was left were dead men in sleeping bag coffins, circled round the ashes of a campfire, and a clinking carpet of spent brass cases spewed out from the Adoo Shpagin heavy machine gun as it fired on Mirbat.

From the Jebel, Smyth-Piggott had a panoramic view of the battlefield, the fort and the open gravel plain across which the Adoo had advanced. It offered almost no cover until a few boulders emerged from the rising ground around the fort well inside the perimeter wire. Whatever else the Adoo attack had lacked, it had not been courage.

As he looked out over the town, he watched the SOAF helicopters shuttle in and out. And, flying towards him from the south, the distinctive shape of a Skyvan transport, flying flat and low past the fort.

When Barrie Williams was visited by the BATT men in Headley Court, they'd delivered exactly what the injured pilot most needed: support, encouragement and a good laugh. They also brought whisky. Now Williams, in the co-pilot's seat of a heavily loaded Skyvan, had the chance to reciprocate. Behind him in the cargo hold were pallets of ammunition to replenish the BATT's depleted armoury; exactly what the SAS most needed.

Like the helicopter squadron, the Skyvans flew into locations where they could expect trouble with two pilots, a precaution in case one was shot. Alongside Williams in the left-hand seat, Squadron Leader Barry West was the Captain of the resupply flight. After cruising to Mirbat beneath the cloud at 120 knots, West pulled the two throttle levers back to prepare for the paradrop. Instead of reducing the rpm of the two constant-speed Garrett AiResearch engines, the pilot's control input reduced the thrust by altering the pitch of each engine's three-bladed propellor. Once the speed had dropped below 100 knots, West trimmed the aircraft into what amounted to a low, slow bomb run. Flying north at 300 feet, he instructed the Air Despatcher in the back to crank down the cargo ramp under-neath the Skyvan's tail.

Through the cockpit glass, Barrie Williams watched the town slip past beneath the nose. Ahead of them, he could see Mirbat's two forts. West's route was taking them straight between the two. As they passed the northern edge of the town and flew out over the plain, Williams twisted back in his seat to give the command to the Loadmaster to drop.

Once it was clear that the action in Mirbat had been exceptional, Airwork engineer Andy Dunsire was told to grab his cameras and get on board the resupply Skyvan. It was important to record the scene. Now, holding his cine camera to his eye, with his 35mm still camera around his neck, he tried to keep out of the way of the two Despatchers as they heaved the ammunition pallets out of the back. He watched the parachutes billow as they were caught in the Skyvan's slipstream, slowing the heavy cargo's fall through the air. The two men stood right at the edge of the open back of the Skyvan's hold, confident that they were tethered to lashing points on the floor. In theory it was impossible for the harnesses to come free from the double-latch clips. But as Dunsire watched, he realized that one of the Loadmaster's straps was loose. Any mistake as he pushed out the cargo, or the aircraft hit a patch of rough air, and there was nothing at all stopping him from following the pallets out of the back of the aeroplane. With a surge of adrenalin, Dunsire lunged for the end of the strap and grabbed it, holding it tight for the rest of the run until, with the paradrop complete, he offered it to the Despatcher as he turned back into the hold of the Skyvan.

'Is this yours?' the Scot asked gently, his dry sense of humour intact. *He'd have been out!* Dunsire thought, surprised by the soldier's apparent lack of concern. He raised the camera to his face and continued snapping. *We could've lost a Loadie.*

It was another piece of luck for the Sultan's forces on a day that had so far hinged on it. But not everyone had been so blessed.

After putting the Huey down on the helipad outside the Salalah FST, Neville Baker left the engine burning and the main rotor turning. As soon as the casualties were safely in the hands of the medical team, he was heading straight back to Mirbat. Baker jumped out of the cockpit door and walked round the nose to the port cabin door to help get the stretchers offloaded. The surgeons, barechested and wearing green scrubs trousers, helped carry the injured from beneath the roar of the helicopter into the relative sanctuary of the field hospital. Wearing his yellow Mae West life-jacket, Baker put a hand round Takavesi's back as the Fijian eased himself out of the cabin of the Huey.

At Mirbat, Tak had refused a stretcher to carry him the thirty yards to the waiting helicopter. He was a little off-balance, he thought, but he could walk. And so he was damned if he wasn't going to.

Just a bit of pride, he told himself, but he wasn't going to let the Adoo take that from him too. They'd taken too much already. It was vitally important that he ended the battle on his own terms. And that meant walking unaided and undefeated from the battlefield, his head held high. Now, twenty minutes later, he once again walked by himself from the casevac helicopter, treating a serious gunshot wound through his chest with the disdain he'd afford an inconvenient scratch.

Tommy Tobin was the last to be stretchered off the aircraft but the first into theatre.

The only time during his career as a doctor that the anaesthetist, Bill de Bass, had so far been appalled by anything he'd seen was when, as a young medical student, he'd witnessed his first post-mortem. Now, while some of the injuries that came into the FST were distressing, his reaction tended to be more practical: *how do we sort this out?* But there were exceptions. And the injury to Tommy Tobin's jaw, he thought, was *pretty horrific*. As a frontline surgical team, the FST's job was to stabilize the patient, stop the bleeding and make the cavities safe. All that was required was to prevent any further deterioration before the patient could be medevaced to a base hospital. But there were such massive injuries to Tobin's face that their ability to do that was by no means certain. It was as close as they had come to admitting: *we really have got a massive problem here.*

'Can you get a tube down?' Surgeon Joe Johnston asked him. The alternative was to perform a tracheotomy, but, despite the bleeding and the extreme swelling to the young Trooper's tongue and pharynx, de Bass still thought he'd be able to get the laryngoscope down into Tobin's airway.

'Yes,' he told Johnston. But after putting Tobin to sleep and letting the paralysing agent take effect, it proved impossible to keep the instrument in place. With half his lower jaw missing it was like one hand clapping. So in the end, the surgical team were forced to perform a tracheotomy and insert a breathing tube into Tobin's neck.

On arrival in theatre, they gave Tobin two pints of blood. But despite walking to the FST, Tak had needed two as well. It was already clear, with four very seriously injured men on board the first casevac flight and with a taxi rank of helicopters now bringing SAF and Adoo wounded in from Mirbat, that they were going to need more blood. And not just from Salalah. As well as putting the call out for volunteer blood donors from the airfield and army camp at Um al Gwarif, they contacted the RAF airbase on Masirah Island, 400 miles away to the north-east. Masirah's 'Walking Blood Bank' was tapped, while one of Bill Stoker's Strikemasters, the fastest aircraft available, was tasked with a mission to Masirah to bring it back. Along with blood and other medical supplies, the jet fighter also returned to Salalah with a theatre nurse from the RAF Masirah hospital in the right-hand ejection seat. Working at the limit of what the small Salalah FST could cope with, any help was likely to be crucial.

Bill de Bass hand-pumped the halothane anaesthetic in and out of Tobin's lungs, while the two RAMC surgeons, Johnston and Nick Cetti, got to work on the soldier's multiple injuries. While the 25-year-old Trooper's most obvious wound was to his jaw, the surgeons also had to clean and pack gunshot wounds to his chest, shoulder and hand, as well as cutting through Tobin's abdominal wall to explore and repair the damage done by the bullet to his stomach. But two hours into the operation, with his blood pressure dropping, the strain proved too much for his heart, and, at 1415 hours, Tommy Tobin suffered a cardiac arrest.

*

On the ground floor of the BATT House, Roger Cole was struggling to bring up a vein on the arm of one of the injured Adoo fighters. Unless he could get an IV line and a drip into him he was going to die. Although the chances were the gruesome, bubbling hole in the man's throat was going to kill him anyway. The suck and whistle that gurgled from the guerrilla's neck as he fought for breath filled the room. After guiding the jets in, Cole had left Jeff Taylor, the Irish Corporal from the G Squadron advance party, to man the GPMG alone, while he'd come downstairs to try to treat the wounded. Now he was surrounded by death and the dying; a scene from Dante's seventh circle. The room was thick with the ammonia stench of piss and sweat; the dirt floor stained with brown pools of dried blood and strewn with used field dressings. Propped up against the pale stone walls were lines of old men with near identical scalp wounds: Askar guards fighting from the roof of the Wali's fort who'd been winged by Adoo bullets as they'd raised their heads above the battlements. Those who had the strength waved away the flies that buzzed around the room, swarming wherever there was the nourishing damp of an open wound.

When Snapper clambered down the stairs from the roof, asked by Bob Bennett to help Cole with the casevac, he thought he'd walked into an abattoir. But it was worse than that. The sound of the strained wet hiss leaking in and out of the Adoo's wrecked windpipe like a pair of broken bellows never left him.

It was a long, long way from the excited, optimistic end-of-term feel that Eight Troop had been enjoying just twelve hours earlier. They'd all been alive then. Snapper couldn't help wonder how this had been able to happen. Bahait, the Firqa Commander, had warned them that something was brewing.

With both hands placed on his sternum the surgeons pumped Tobin's chest; sharp, quick jabs; at a rate a little less than twice a second. While Johnston and Cetti performed cardiopulmonary resuscitation, Bill de Bass gave him hydrocortisone, adrenalin and sodium bicarbonate antacid, in case excess acidity in his blood had triggered his heart's arrhythmia and arrest.

It was rare for the FST to lose a man on the operating table. If the casualty had made it alive this far, then it meant that it was likely, however severe, to be an inherently survivable injury. And so even after the urgent combination of CPR and drugs brought Tommy's pulse falteringly back, de Bass couldn't help but wonder whether their own efforts had overloaded the injured Trooper's circulation. Had they put too much fluid into him?

With Tobin's heartbeat growing stronger, de Bass gave him a small dose of thiopental and atropine to stabilize his heart. Twenty minutes later they were done, sluicing down the operating table with water before bringing Gunner Walid Khamis in for surgery to his stomach.

But Tommy Tobin, for all that he was going to suffer as doctors in the UK did what they could to repair the damage to his jaw, had been stabilized. He was survivable.

Chapter 43

The instructions Neville Baker received over the RT from Salalah were that he was to take the Omani dead straight to Um al Gwarif army camp. There they would be buried quickly before sundown according to the Muslim custom. But when he heard that there were Fijians among the dead, he realized he had to get the bodies of the men in the back checked before he left Mirbat. If there was any possibility that one of the half-dozen bodies he was carrying was a Fijian, he needed him identified.

I don't want him to be mixed up with the Omanis and shoved in a pit, he thought. Instead of Um al Gwarif, he needed to fly them to Salalah, where they could be returned to the UK.

From the cockpit of the thrashing Huey, Baker stuck his arm out of the window and waved to catch the attention of one of the SAS men through the door of the BATT House. When he caught the eye of one of the Regiment soldiers he beckoned him over.

When Snapper saw the grey-haired helicopter pilot with the neatly trimmed moustache calling him over to the aircraft he was grateful for the opportunity to get out of Roger Cole's makeshift dressing station on the ground floor. Outside, the camouflaged helicopter was sitting on its skids, engine whining, barely thirty yards from the front door. Instinctively, Snapper bent down beneath the churning rotor and ran to the cockpit window.

'I need you to go and check the bodies in the rear,' Baker

shouted above the noise of the aircraft. The soldier seemed reluctant. Perhaps, Baker, thought, he hadn't made himself clear enough. 'Tell the crewman which bodies are which. *Which are BATT* . . .' Eventually Baker convinced the BATT man to take on the job.

Battered by the downdraught, Snapper moved back along the helicopter's fuselage to the open sliding door without enthusiasm. Stan Standford was kneeling on the cabin floor waiting for him. The Aircrewman gestured towards the six stretcher racks, slotted in across the cabin in two stacks of three. Draped over each was a blanket covering a recognizably human shape underneath. Snapper started at the bottom back. He took a breath and turned back the blanket. Underneath was the apparently unblemished face of an Arab man; almost peaceful looking. But behind his fine features his ear had been torn off and his skull smashed. It was probably a shrapnel wound, Winner thought. Softly, he pulled the blanket back over the man's face.

The BATT Corporal climbed up on to the edge of the Huey's cabin to get a look at the middle stretcher. The dead man was barely more than a boy. He couldn't have been much more than seventeen. There was no visible injury to the Omani teenager, but his open lifeless eyes were as conclusive an image of death as the older man's panelled-in head.

Give me combat any time, Snapper thought. He stood up, crouching under the helicopter's low roof, and lifted the blanket. Beneath it, the body was face down, his right forearm tucked underneath his head as if he was sleeping. But he was cold and hard to the touch when Snapper tried to gently move him to look at his face. Shifting his weight to give himself a little more leverage, he tried again, hauling the whole body over by its elbow. And then he saw Laba. His jaw badly grazed by a bullet and his eyes open. But it was Laba all right. His friend. Images of the big, laughing Fijian washed through his mind. It seemed unreal to think of such a force of nature laid out like this. It was a hammerblow to his emotions.

I've got to get away quickly, he thought.

Swallowing back the saliva flooding his mouth, with bile rising in his throat, Winner jumped down from the helicopter.

His reaction left Standford in no doubt. The ex-Navy Aircrewman tucked up the blankets around the three stretchered bodies and told Baker over the intercom that they could return to Salalah.

And as the Huey lifted into the air, dipped its nose and swept out over the sea, Winner stared out over the battlefield, engulfed with sorrow.

When Mike Kealy returned to the BATT House, he was greeted by the sight of rows of Adoo bodies laid out on the gravel. There were twenty-nine of them, many carried north to the Mirbat plain from the trail of destruction left by G Squadron's advance. Another twelve injured Adoo prisoners were already on their way back for treatment by the FST surgeons. Nearby, the enemy's weapons, ammunition and kit were piled high, coveted by the handful of Firqa who'd remained in Mirbat. Each, they argued, would earn them a financial reward from the government if they turned them in. Inside the building, Roger Cole was interviewing the only two unwounded prisoners. They were the two men who, on confronting Alistair Morrison on the beach immediately after G Squadron's insertion by helicopter, had had the good sense to surrender. Over tea and cigarettes, they opened up to the BATT Corporal. And the first details of the Adoo's ambition that morning began to emerge.

To the north, beyond the Jebel Ali, Nobby Grey, in a lone Strikemaster, went hunting for their comrades in arms, firing another eight SURA rockets and 690 rounds of machine-gun ammunition at the retreating Adoo guerrillas to deter any possibility of a re-attack. Unusually, he was flying without a wingman. With two jets riddled by bullets and others in routine maintenance, 1 Squadron was simply unable to generate more aircraft. 403 was the same jet that had been flown by David Milne-Smith, 1 Squadron's only airworthy

Strikemaster. It wasn't just Eight Troop who were on their last legs.

Beneath him, pockets of retreating Adoo were ambushed by the fighters from Bahait's returning Firqa al Umri, further swelling the total number of Adoo dead by another nine.

At 1750, surgeon Joe Johnston opened Tak's chest cavity. Until that point, the biggest issue they'd faced was just turning him over. When Bill de Bass put him to sleep he'd been lying on his back. But anaesthetized and paralysed, fourteen stone of Fijian back row forward takes a lot of shifting. With Tak lying on his front though, they shaved the back of his head to clean up and stitch the bullet graze on the back of his head. Then putting in a Heimlich Valve to drain blood and fluid from his chest, Johnston cut a long straight line across his back, from left to right to explore and mend the damage done by the Adoo bullet. Destroying the vacuum within the chest cavity, the procedure changed the physiology of Tak's lungs; a factor that, in keeping him effectively anaesthetized, de Bass had to take into account.

It was only after opening him up that the extent of the damage became clear. And how lucky he had been. He was half an inch from being paralysed from the chest down. No more than two from being shot through the heart. But after two hours in surgery they closed him up and dosed him with Neostigmine to reverse the paralysing agent, and their thoughts turned to the next patient. They'd already been in theatre since midday and Tak was only their third.

Johnston, Cetti and de Bass still had another thirty hours in theatre to endure until they'd operated on the final casualty from Mirbat. They chose who to operate on solely on the basis of clinical need. BATT, SAF and Adoo were all given the same treatment. It meant that, just after midnight, they saved the life of the man whose shredded larynx had so disturbed Pete Winner in the BATT House.

And it also meant that they had to engage in a battle of wills with the Governor of Dhofar. The Wali sent men from Salalah to the FST with instructions to remove the injured Adoo from their beds, take them into town and execute them. Johnston, the CO of the small surgical team, laughed it off from the operating theatre. But the Wali's men were heavily armed and insistent. Once again, a message came through from the door of the FST Twynham hut demanding that they give up the Adoo injured. Barely looking up from his patient, Johnston glanced in the direction of his anaesthetist.

'Bill, will you go outside,' he said, 'and tell them to fuck off.'

'Thanks, Joe,' de Bass smiled, but called his anaesthetic technician over to man the Haloxaire pump and stuck his head outside. Their patients, he told them, were staying where they were.

But, while it may not have been delivered by the men of 55FST, the Wali was to get the Adoo he wanted *pour encourager les autres*.

Barrie Williams returned to Mirbat in the later afternoon. After landing on the strip, he was told to taxi over towards the BATT House. By now the sun had burnt away the *khareef* mist and, low in the sky, cast long shadows across the Mirbat plain. As the empty Skyvan bounced over the ground, neither he nor his co-pilot knew the reason for their mission to Mirbat. It soon became horribly clear.

Approaching the Wali's fort, Williams saw the familiar BATT face stride out in front and cross his arms over his head to instruct him to park up. Williams dabbed at the brakes, with a dip of the nose the Skyvan came to a standstill and he applied the parking brake. Leaving the engines running, he feathered the twin propellors. On either side of the cockpit, their red-painted tips spun noisy circles in the air. Behind the two pilots, as two Land Rovers drove out from the BATT House, the Loadmaster lowered the cargo ramp at the back.

In the back of the Land Rovers, their bodywork sitting low on the springs, were heaps of Adoo bodies. One by one they were pulled off the piles and thrown into the back of the

Skyvan. The 2 Squadron crew couldn't help but react with revulsion at the sight of it. And the smell.

The twenty-nine bodies belonged to soldiers who'd been living in the Jebel for weeks, marching and fighting in the damp and heat wearing clothes that were unlikely to have been washed since they were first handed out. But on top of that was the smell of death. The twenty-nine had been dead since before noon. Piled one on top of the other like bin bags on a rubbish tip, blood, bodily fluids and waste seeped out of them under their combined weight and pooled on the floor of the cargo hold. The flies followed their bounty into the Skyvan.

The stench, within the confines of the aircraft's fuselage, was almost overpowering. In shock, the two pilots had to fight a powerful gagging reflex. They opened their side windows, desperate to get moving. And as they released the brakes and nudged the throttles, they kept the ramp partially open to try to ensure that there was a strong draught through the cabin. It was the Loadmaster in the back Williams really felt sorry for. As the Welshman pushed forward the two pitch levers and accelerated down the Mirbat airstrip, the Loadie stood between the two pilots' seats, facing forward, gripping them tightly with both hands.

And as they climbed away, the nose of the Skyvan pointing skywards, the foul slick on the floor of the transport plane slopped back along the hold and washed out of the open ramp. Whipped up in the powerful vortices trailing in the wake of each propellor, it was silhouetted against the setting sun as a fine mist.

When Williams landed back at Salalah, the RAF controller in the Tower told him to taxi to the far side of the airfield, where the Army would be waiting for them. On the ground, without the airflow through the fuselage they'd enjoyed en route, the smell of death returned with all its earlier repulsive intensity. Parked up out of plain sight of the Squadron buildings, Williams and his crew suffered a little longer, their aircraft's engines turning and burning, while SAF soldiers threw the bodies into the back of a waiting Bedford three-tonner.

Then, as the British pilots taxied back to the SAF dispersal, shut down and left Skyvan 906 to the ground crews to scrub down, the Adoo bodies were driven into the centre of Salalah town. In the main square, outside the Wali's palace, they were dumped in a foetid tangle of arms and legs as a terrifying, rotting symbol of the Adoo defeat. And as a warning.

It was a forceful, unforgettable indication of how, since their humiliation at Mirbat earlier in a battle they *should* have won, the course of the war in Dhofar had now turned permanently and irretrievably away from them and towards the Sultan.

Chapter 44

The telephone rang. John Graham was staying at his mother's flat in Chelsea. After nearly a month in the UK, he'd recovered his strength and looked forward to returning to Oman to complete the last two months of his posting as CSAF. It remained a job half done. Bold efforts like Operations JAGUAR and SIMBA had enjoyed some success but also came at a cost to Oman's small, stretched Armed Forces. And neither, so far, had secured the required breakthrough in attracting significant support from potential Middle Eastern allies. But while Graham recuperated in West London and had been kept abreast of developments in Oman, he was still in the dark about the fighting in Mirbat. Graham lifted the phone from the cradle.

The call was from Hereford 2124, ext. 59. SAS Headquarters. And, over the line, he recognized the clipped Harrovian tones of Lieutenant Colonel Peter Edgar de la Cour de la Billière. The Regiment's Commanding Officer introduced himself, before beginning to detail the morning's events.

'There's been a very significant battle,' he told Graham, before going on to pass on as much as he knew, allowing himself to admit: 'We've done rather well.' The Commander of the Sultan's Armed Forces knew that was true.

'Bloody fools,' Graham replied, unable to understand why the enemy had launched their attack against Mirbat. 'Why weren't they going for Taqa? The broken ground goes right down to Taqa village. They would have taken Taqa.' But the

Brigadier knew at once that the Adoo's unlikely defeat at Mirbat had the potential to be of real importance. He appreciated the difficulty they must have had in raising such a substantial force. And he and de la Billière discussed the crushing effect their failure would have on their morale. He shuddered to think of what reprisals the rebels might inflict against their own survivors of the battle.

And it soon became clear that fewer guerrillas would fight another day than the twenty-nine bodies dumped in Salalah town square suggested. It was always the Adoo custom, where possible, to carry their dead and injured with them and so the bodies flown back to Salalah were not the total. And subsequent SAF intercepts of Adoo radio traffic suggested that, along with those injured and captured, the loss to the Adoo was actually in the high eighties; roughly a third of the entire Mirbat assault force.

John Graham thanked the SAS Lieutenant Colonel for making the call and replaced the receiver. He was already calculating the odds.

Meanwhile, DLB, like Takavesi, knew that, aside from Eight Troop's own resistance, the reason his men survived the Adoo onslaught until G Squadron's arrival was because of Bill Stoker's Strikemasters. Without the intervention of the 1 Squadron jets, it was evident that the outcome would have been very different – and so too the outlook for the whole Sultanate.

A *show*, he believed, *of rare skill and courage* from the airmen who'd flown in under the clouds to beat back the Adoo advance. It warranted, he felt, some thanks and acknowledgement.

The Special Forces Club is located in a town house behind Harrods. There's no brass plaque next to the front door confirming the address. Inside, black-and-white photographs of Special Forces heroes and heroines line the walls of the staircase to the bar and restaurant on the first floor, where members can enjoy a straightforward menu of comfort food staples and steamed puddings. Founded by the last head of the wartime Special Operations Executive in 1945, the Knightsbridge club's motto is 'Spirit of Resistance' and membership is open to 'anyone involved in clandestine or covert roles in and out of uniform'. That certainly covered the job Bill Stoker was doing as Boss of the SOAF Strikemaster Squadron.

And DLB wrote the pilot a personal letter inviting him to join the Special Forces Club. For the SAS officer and the fighter pilot, Mirbat marked a slight return to the terrible events of 1964 in the Radfan, when DLB's friend Robin Edwards and his patrol were caught and besieged by enemy guerrillas, then defended by RAF flyers until nightfall. Eight years on, both men had been fated to reprise the roles they'd played in that earlier campaign. Once more the survival of men under DLB's command had been dependent on support from the air; from Bill Stoker's squadron. And, along with the invitation to become a member of the Club, de la Billière also included an SAS tie, in recognition of the vital part Stoker and his flyers had played in one of the most significant actions ever fought by the Regiment.

Another indication of the growing appreciation that Mirbat had been exceptional was the cable outlining in detail the course of the battle which was sent by the Regiment to British embassies around the globe.

Before leaving the SAS to go up to Oxford, Shaun Brogan had had one final task to complete. While some of his contemporaries were completing gap years, Brogan, following service in Oman, was spending four months travelling around South America training British ambassadors' bodyguards, using the experience he'd gained training Jomo Kenyatta's BG team in Kenya. He visited Nicaragua, El Salvador, Honduras, the Dominican Republic, Mexico, Bolivia and Colombia. And it was in the latter's capital, Bogotá, that Brogan was handed a four-page signal about the attack on Mirbat. The Defence Attaché, a naval officer, did so with extremely bad grace, angry that his staff had been forced to decrypt such a long communication.

'This is brilliant news!' Brogan told him as he skim-read the document. 'The Adoo attacked Mirbat and we've beaten them off. It's a hell of a victory; a hell of a defeat for them . . .'

The naval Commander couldn't have cared less. He didn't know who the Adoo were, where Mirbat was or what the Dhofar war was and wasn't interested. The Attaché's irritation only sweetened the moment for Brogan. But as he re-read the transcript, it was clear that Mike Kealy's Troop had paid a heavy price.

Takavesi and Tommy Tobin were flown out of Salalah aboard an RAF medevac on 21 July. Back in the UK, Tak was sent to Cambridge military hospital in Aldershot where, despite having walked on and off Neville Baker's helicopter without assistance, he remained on the Very Seriously Injured list for another two weeks. Three weeks later, he was up and about though, after suffering what one of the FST surgeons had described as 'one of the worst chest wounds I've seen'. As Tak recovered in Hampshire, Tommy Tobin was sent to Princess Mary's RAF Hospital within the grounds of a Royal Air Force training base at Halton in Buckinghamshire to recover from his wounds. He faced a hard road ahead.

While Tak and Tommy were treated for their injuries in the UK, their Regiment comrades left in Oman marked the victory at Mirbat. And they were in no doubt about the importance of 1 Squadron's intervention during the battle. For all the death and injury suffered by the men of Eight Troop, they had held the line until the arrival of Bill Stoker's Strikemasters had prevented them, and Mirbat, being overrun. And the BATT men still in theatre wanted to make their appreciation felt as much as their Commanding Officer, DLB, had done. First of all, Stoker was gifted a captured Adoo AK47.

'If it hadn't been for your arrival, sir,' the soldier told him as they handed it over, 'they'd have killed me with it.' The gesture meant a great deal to the RAF Squadron Leader, who managed to bring the Kalashnikov back home with him to Sussex. For the next fifteen years or so it enjoyed pride of place in the family home until, one day, Stoker's son James came home to find his grandmother with a spring in her step.

'Don't you worry, dear,' she said, 'I've sorted out that gun thing.' After the announcement of a nationwide gun amnesty, the well-meaning old lady had wrapped the Chinese-made, wooden-stock assault rifle in a bag, taken it into Pulborough Police Station and handed it in. It was gone for good.

But as well as the gift of the AK, Stoker and his pilots were invited by the Regiment to Um al Gwarif camp for drinks. Inevitably enough, it was hardly your average cocktail party.

Seared by the sun and dry as chalk, most of Arabia is as hostile an environment for amphibians as the Sahara desert. But the south-west of Oman, with its *khareef*, wadis and waterfalls, was home to the Dhofar Toad. And, in Salalah, they were thoroughbreds. Racing on trestle tables, under the canvas accommodation of BATT Lines, it was hardly the sport of kings, but it made for a great night out. Bill Stoker and Sean Creak drove down to the army camp with David Milne-Smith. Since escaping from Mirbat unscathed, the blond, good-looking young Flight Lieutenant had been on the receiving end of banter from the rest of the Squadron, jealous, they said 'of his technique – both at flying and on the ground'. The pilots all had to bring their own animals for what, despite the competitors actually being toads, was called a *frog* racing evening. Fuelled by plenty of beer, success or failure was taken seriously. Rumour had it that one of the surgical teams rotated through the FST had tried doping their toads, preparing them with injections of, the troopers guessed, amphetamines and adrenalin. It was all very well until the little amphibians' hearts popped. Death or Glory. One usually followed soon after the other. There were other ways to top a toad, however.

Sean Creak placed his racer on the table next to a BATT competitor. To wild cheers from the men crowded around the table, each choosing which competitor to back. But the amphibians didn't always go straight towards the finish line. And as Creak urged his toad on, it hopped off the table on to the floor. Creak's BATT rival looked him in the eye, raised his boot and slowly brought it down on top of the pilot's animal.

'Oi!' Creak complained as he heard his toad crunch underfoot. The look he received back suggested: 'You lose. Do you *really* want to argue about it?'

Creak paused, then smiled. 'OK,' he said, 'fair enough, I didn't really like it anyway . . .' Toadless and laughing, he took a long slug from his beer and stood aside for the next race. Another victory for the SAS. Who Dares Wins.

When, four days after the defeat of the Adoo at Mirbat, John Graham returned to Oman it was the second anniversary of the coup that brought Qaboos to power. There were already encouraging signs that, while the battle certainly didn't mark the end of the war, it did, perhaps, mark the point at which the outcome became inevitable. Radio intercepts and a rush of SEPs turning themselves in to SAF units provided ample evidence of the magnitude of the Adoo's defeat. They *should* have won. And while FCO officials in London acknowledged that the victory for the Sultan's forces had been 'a close-run thing', only the outcome mattered. The Adoo had given it their best shot and failed – conspicuously. And it was soon clear that they would never again enjoy such an opportunity to reclaim the initiative in the war.

Within ten days of the victory, the first desert-camouflaged Lockheed C-130 Hercules airlifter of the Imperial Iranian Air Force landed, without prior notification, at Salalah. It caused some consternation within the ranks of the RAF Regiment defending the airfield until the Iranian Army Major was able to explain his intentions to Gerry Honey, the Station Commander, over a beer.

The arrival of the IIAF Hercules was the first of sixty Iranian flights into Salalah carrying men and materiel that followed over the next couple of months. John Graham, in his last months as CSAF, christened the airlift Operation CAVIAR and it marked the beginning of a substantial Iranian contribution that, over the next three years, included troops, Special Forces, helicopters and, ultimately, supersonic McDonnell Douglas F-4 Phantom fighter-bombers. The influx of men and machines made possible both the establishment of effective blocking lines across the enemy's supply routes and the retention of Simba position, which one Adoo commander described as 'like having someone's hands round your throat'.

Neither could have been done without the men and machines supplied by Iran. Nor their willingness to take casualties in defence of the Sultan's cause. Alongside the Sultan's bridgebuilding with the Shah, Graham's careful, assiduous cultivation of the Iranian Ambassador, Mr Zand, had been as important a factor in changing the course of the war as the skill and bravery of SAF's soldiers and airmen.

The end of 1972 also marked a change in Chinese policy and a decline in their support for the rebellion. They were replaced by the Soviets, who supplied the Adoo with SAM-7 'Grail' man-portable heat-seeking missiles which cruelly exposed the limitations of the little Strikemasters in the face of modern anti-aircraft weapons and forced changes in tactics to try to protect them. But there was hope on the horizon. The effort started by Graham and Qaboos to internationalize the war that began to bear fruit with the arrival of Jordanian intelligence officers and guns in 1971, and which continued with the massive influx of Iranian men and weaponry, also delivered to the Sultan's Air Force another war-winning weapon. In spring 1975, King Hussein of Jordan gifted his Air Force's powerful Hawker Hunter FGA9 attack jets to Oman. They represented a step-change for SOAF, as, while the fifteen-year-old British aircraft were hardly state of the art, they remained enormously capable machines, able to absorb great punishment and fly tactics that could defeat the Russian SAMs. When the new fleet of swept-wing jet fighters arrived overhead the rebuilt airfield at Midway, flown south in a large loose balbo by Jordanian pilots, SOAF Aircrewman Hamed Nasser felt as if Oman had become a superpower.

And barely six months after the arrival of the Hunters, during Oman's national celebrations on 18 November, the Commander of the SAF Dhofar Brigade, Brigadier John Akehurst, suggested to Sultan Qaboos that he would soon be in a position to announce victory. A month later, the Sultan announced that the war was won. The rebellion had been choked by the growing strength of the military, and starved by the pace of change throughout the country. There was simply nothing left to fight for. As a result, Dhofar was now safe for civil development. And while John Graham's tenure as CSAF had ended three years earlier, it was during his time as head of the Sultan's Armed Forces that all the seeds of victory were sown. First, and most important, was his support for the accession of Qaboos to the throne, then Operation JAGUAR and the effort to establish a permanent presence on the Jebel for the first time; the recognition that Oman needed to win real and substantial support from local allies; the seizing of Simba position in the west and the first attempts to block Adoo supply routes; and, finally, the Battle of Mirbat, the culmination of it all, when the Adoo, realizing that the initiative was slipping away from them, attempted a spectacular offensive that had the potential to destroy the population's faith in the Sultan. And failed.

Hamed Nasser was one of a growing number of Omanis in the Air Force who were taking on more substantial roles as the Omanization of the country's Armed Forces also continued apace. Both he and Malallah, the first Omani to join the embryonic Air Force in 1959, trained as pilots. For Nasser there was never any possibility that he would choose to fly the Hueys in which he'd flown as an Aircrewman at the Battle of Mirbat, while Malallah, after flying Skyvans, eventually decided to forgo the opportunity to join a Strikemaster squadron to lead the process of Omanization. The uneducated boy from Muttrah retired in 1990 as an Air Vice Marshal and

Deputy Commander of the whole Omani Air Force. His boss, Air Vice Marshal Sir Erik Bennett, was the last British Commander of the Air Force.

The last British Commander of Oman's Army was a familiar face in Oman. Sultan Qaboos personally requested Lieutenant General John Watts as the man he wanted to oversee the transition. Disappointed to leave Dhofar before he'd finished the job he started with Operation JAGUAR and the offensive of the eastern Jebel, Watts was back with the Regiment as Director SAS and Commander SAS Group in 1975 when the war was won. What he instigated in 1970 when he flew out under the alias of Mr Smith to assess the contribution the Regiment could make to the deteriorating situation in Oman, he saw to its satisfying conclusion as head of the SAS.

By the autumn of 2010, only a tiny handful of British expatriates still served with SAF, mainly in support roles. Only one British contract pilot remained. A Qualified Flying Instructor with Neville Baker's old squadron at Salalah, he had less than a year to run before he, too, retired. But he was in no doubt, after a top-flight career as a Fleet Air Arm helicopter pilot before travelling to Oman, including operations in the Falklands War, that the Royal Air Force of Oman, as it was renamed in 1990, was 'a pretty slick outfit'.

The health of the Air Force was reflected throughout the country. Rising oil prices in the mid-seventies had allowed the Sultanate to make the most of her relatively meagre oil reserves. But in contrast to some of her neighbours, Oman, under Qaboos, had not squandered the income on skyscrapers and showpieces, but had spent it on her infrastructure, on roads, schools and hospitals. Blacktop roads link Sarfait in the far south to the Musandam peninsula and all points in between. In 1999, 89 per cent of the population had access to health care. In 2000 the figure was 99 per cent. In 2001, in the World Health Organization's first ever analysis of global health care systems, Oman ranked eighth overall, higher than the USA, UK, Germany, Japan, Australia, Canada, New Zealand and all of Scandinavia. And, in November 2010, the

United Nations Development Index, based on life expectancy, literacy, health care, school enrolment and income, listed Oman first out of 135 as the country that had improved the most over the last forty years, noting particular strides made in education.

Faced with declining oil reserves and the issue of succession, Oman certainly faces economic and political challenges ahead, but that does nothing to negate the country's remarkable journey over the last four decades. In early 2011, people in Syria, Tunisia, Egypt, Jordan, Yemen, Libya and Bahrain packed the streets and public squares in protest at the corruption and misrule of their long-serving rulers. Such was the remarkable momentum of the movement that, eventually, protestors made their way on to the streets of Oman in Soha, Muscat and Salalah. It may be that appetite for change in the region is irresistible but there appears to be more ambivalence in Oman. Democracy may well be an ideal, but that doesn't mean, necessarily, that Oman would have been – or would be – better governed as a result. And in 1970 in Oman the prospect of it was a nonsense. There were far more pressing concerns facing the country. What Oman needed, far more than democracy, was good governance. And in Sultan Qaboos that was what it got.

In 1970, the country faced a fork in the road. Down one route was the success and stability of present-day Oman. Down the other was the chaos, misrule, subversion and poverty of her neighbour Yemen, whose last four decades have hardly been as fruitful, or as happy.

Tommy Tobin died in hospital at RAF Halton on 25 October 1972, three agonizing months after the battle. He never recovered, and his last weeks were plagued with fevers, fear and nightmares. It wasn't the grievous injury to his jaw that killed him. Nor the four other gunshot wounds that had peppered his body at Mirbat. It was a fragment of tooth, buried deep in his lung, that became infected and poisoned him. Tommy was Mirbat's last victim. And for his bravery that day the ex-Catering Corps cook was awarded the posthumous Distinguished Conduct Medal.

There were others too. Mike Kealy received the Distinguished Service Order, Tak, along with Tommy, the Distinguished Conduct Medal and Bob Bennett was awarded the Military Medal. Laba, the giant, thirty-year-old Fijian who had, singlehandedly, held the gunpit during the first hours of the battle, and fought on with Tak until an Adoo bullet killed him, received a posthumous Mention in Despatches.

When many people close to the battle felt he deserved a Victoria Cross, Laba's award never seemed to be a remotely adequate recognition of his bravery, spirit and sacrifice. Snapper was adamant that the award of an MiD was an insult. The debate continues to this day. There may never be a satisfactory formal *public* acknowledgement of what Laba did in Mirbat on 19 July 1972, but the Regiment has never forgotten.

Nor, forty years later, does it show any signs of doing so.

Epilogue

The weather in Hereford was chill and damp, a typical late-autumn weekend. Just warm enough for people to breathe without condensation blowing from their mouths. It was Saturday, 10 November, the day before Remembrance Sunday. And, once again, Sekonaia Takavesi was making his way to the Headquarters of 22 SAS. Sitting alongside him as he drove north-west out of town was a man called Labalaba. But it was 2009, thirty-seven years after Laba's death in the Battle of Mirbat. And Tak wasn't returning to the familiarity of Bradbury Lines, the base on the southern outskirts of Hereford that had been home to the SAS during his time in the regiment.

Tak had been out of the Regiment for twenty-three years. Since then he'd trodden a well-worn path, working 'The Circuit' alongside many ex-colleagues as part of a private military company. And since 9/11 business had been brisk. At an age when most people are contemplating retirement, Tak was still fighting. But not today.

Credenhill had been an old RAF station. Now renamed Stirling Lines, after the Regiment's founder, it had been home to 22 SAS since 1999. Compared to the cramped residential location of Bradbury Lines it afforded a good deal more privacy. But the traditions remained the same. The clocktower, recording the names of every SAS man killed on duty, remained. Laba's name was there.

Tak and his passenger were checked through by the guard-house. It wasn't often that the Fijian veteran had gone through that routine while wearing a suit. But today was different, a gathering of the Regiment's great and the good. And while the Colonel, out leading Task Force Black in Iraq, couldn't be there, his Second-in-Command was a willing deputy. Other senior officers not on operations also attended. Alongside them, one of the Regiment's most distinguished veterans had been invited. General the Lord Guthrie of Craigiebank, ex-Troop Commander, Squadron Commander, Colonel Commandant of the Regiment and Chief of the Defence Staff during Britain's campaigns in Kosovo and Sierra Leone, had accepted. The Fijian High Commissioner had been driven up from London for the occasion. And, so too had Prince William. But the heir to the throne was not the day's most important guest. He had travelled much further to attend.

Laba's son, Usaia Dere, had been flown from Fiji by the Regiment for the occasion. He was staying with Tak and his family in Hereford.

Since Laba's death, Tak had taken the boy under his wing; looked out for him and visited him in Fiji every time he returned to the islands. It would still be another year before the house Tak was building for him would be complete, but it was on its way.

For many years there had been a campaign to award Laba the posthumous VC he so richly deserved, but it had come to nothing. But the Regiment knew it was an injustice. When Andy, the Regimental Sergeant Major, received a large donation from outside the Regiment, it was decided that it should be used to finance a statue of Laba. The pose was taken from an old photograph, snapped during Operation STORM in Oman, that had been found discarded by a comrade and kept. Dressed in combat fatigues, one leg up on rocks, draped in bandoliers of 7.62mm ammunition and cradling a GPMG, Laba looks every inch the warrior he was. And, since his death at Mirbat, it had become the iconic image of the Fijian Lance Corporal.

During drinks, Tak and his friend's son were introduced to Prince William and Lord Guthrie. While people talked, sharing memories, discussing SAS operations past and present, the Regiment 2ic asked Tak for a quiet word. He wanted to hear for himself what had happened at Mirbat.

After the reception, everyone was ushered outside for the unveiling. With barely a trace of a southerly wind, the speeches were loud and clear. First, drawing on his conversation with Tak, the Lieutenant Colonel spoke, then Prince William, before the congregation bowed their heads as the padre said a short prayer.

A good ceremony, Tak thought, his reaction a little measured. It was true, he appreciated, that it could be argued that the men at Mirbat had simply performed the task which had been handed to them, but he had, on occasion, felt let down that not *all* those involved had been recognized. *Blokes*, he believed, thinking of other, more public conflicts, *got medals for nothing compared to what my lot went through*. So there was a quiet satisfaction that Laba's statue did something to redress that balance, an acknowledgement of what *all* his Eight Troop comrades had done that day. But, in the end, it was not so much the fact of the statue that warmed him as the manner in which it had come about.

'Tell me something, Andy,' he had asked the RSM when he'd first been told about the Regiment's plans, 'why did they do Laba's statue?'

'Everything,' Andy said, 'that's been done has been done by the officers. I wrote to all the senior ranks in the Regiment asking them what they'd like to do with the money. Would *they* like something to remember the Regiment by?' The letters that came back were near unanimous: it should be a statue of Laba.

That's the best thing, Tak thought as looked at the figure of his friend standing tall once again, for ever in his prime. *It's come from the Regiment.*

Postscript

On 22 January 1974, a day before being scrambled to attack an Adoo camel train with 540lb bombs, SURA rockets and machine-gun fire, Sean Creak introduced another young fighter pilot, just seconded from the Royal Air Force to SOAF, to the joys of the piston-engined DeHavilland Beaver. During his one-and-a-half-hour conversion sortie in the old propellor bush plane, Flight Lieutenant Jock Stirrup flew with Creak down the coast from Salalah to the beach at Mughsayl, where the massive Jebel rocks press close to the sea. Stirrup would spend the next two years in Dhofar, flying Strikemasters and Beavers in the campaign against the Adoo. And while Stirrup returned to the UK in 1975 to fly SEPECAT Jaguar attack jets with 41 Squadron, it was not the end of his association with Oman.

In September 2001, Air Chief Marshal Sir Jock Stirrup was appointed as Commander of Operation VERITAS, the code-name for Britain's initial military operations in Afghanistan after the 9/11 attacks. In that role, as well as enjoying responsibility for the British contribution to the US-led Operation ENDURING FREEDOM, Stirrup was Senior British Military Advisor to US General Tommy Franks, Commander-in-Chief of US Central Command and the man tasked with leading America's military response to Al Qaeda's attacks.

Part of Britain's effort was to deploy a detachment of English Electric Canberra PR9 spyplanes to Oman – always described in vague terms as a Gulf state or a location in the Gulf region.

From here, less than a month after the destruction of the Twin Towers, they flew valuable long-range reconnaissance missions out over Afghanistan in support of Operation ENDURING FREEDOM.

Two of the aircraft involved, XH131 and XH135, were veterans of 13 Squadron's reconnaissance efforts over the Arabian peninsula thirty years earlier. But the war in Afghanistan outlasted them. For both of the old recce jets, their detachment in Oman represented their last operational deployment. When they returned home to RAF Marham in June 2006 they were retired. The long war in Afghanistan out-lasted Jock Stirrup too.

When the ex-SOAF Strikemaster pilot retired from the RAF in October 2010 as Chief of the Defence Staff, the UK's most senior military figure, the war in Afghanistan continued. So too did the RAF's presence in Oman. In the month Stirrup left the Air Force, on the far side of Oman's main Seeb International Airport, away from the civilian passenger terminals, a substantial RAF detachment of VC10 air-refuelling tankers, Sentinel R1 battlefield surveillance jets and Nimrod R1 electronic intelligence spyplanes continued to play its part in one counter-insurgency campaign, from the country in which another had been won.

There were valid comparisons to be made. And, writing about the Dhofar war in 2009, his last year as the professional head of the British military, and as the Afghan war entered its ninth year, Sir Jock acknowledged as much:

> In the end, the campaign is all about politics . . . [Success] requires a sustained and credible effort by those who run the existing system; reconciliation is an internal issue, and cannot be imposed from without. It must address people's concerns for the future and give them a stake in the governance structure, not surrender governance to a competing group . . . As for the military line, the first thing to understand is that it's indispensable. It cannot deliver strategic success, but it is essential to its delivery . . . the

experiences of Dhofar, at least as I perceived – and still perceive – them, resonate strongly with our contemporary security challenges . . . looking at Oman today, there is ample evidence that the principles, when properly applied, do work.

And yet, somehow, understanding the nature of success in Oman only makes the prospect of a similar outcome in Afghanistan seem more remote than ever.

Glossary

25 pounder – British field gun

81mm mortar – standard British Army mortar

A41 – standard British Army VHF radio

ACR7 radar – air traffic control radar

Adoo – Arabic for 'enemy'. The term used by SAF and the SAS to describe DLF fighters

AGRA – Artillery Group Royal Artillery

Agusta-Bell AB20 – Bell Jet Ranger light helicopter built under licence in Italy

Agusta-Bell AB205 – Bell UH-1 Iroquois utility helicopter built under licence in Italy

Airwork – British-based aviation services company

AK47 – Soviet-designed Kalashnikov 7.62mm assault rifle, licence-built in China and elsewhere

Akoot – SAF position in the Eastern sector north of the Jebel

Al Ghaidah – old British-built airfield in South Yemen about sixty miles west of the border with Oman

AOP – Airborne Observation Post

ArmaLite – US-made 5.56mm assault rifle

Askar – local guards

Avtur – jet fuel

BAF – Bait al Falaj. Home to SAF and SOAF HQ and, in 1971–2, Oman's only international airfield

BASO – Brigade Air Support Officer

BATT – British Army Training Team. The term used to describe the SAS in Oman during the Dhofar war

belt kit – SAS webbing. A cut down version of British army webbing used to carry ammunition, food, water and medical supplies

Belvedere – British-built tandem rotor transport helicopter

Bergen – British Army rucksack

BOAC – British Overseas Airways Corporation

Bofors – 40mm anti-aircraft cannon

Bradbury Lines – SAS Headquarters in Hereford

Bren – standard British Army light machine gun

BRIXMIS – British Commander-in-Chief's Mission to the Soviet Forces of Occupation in Germany

Browning .50 – heavy-calibre machine gun used by the SAS and the RAF Regiment in Oman

Browning 9mm – standard British Army automatic pistol

burmail – term universally used in Oman to describe a standard oil drum

C-130 Hercules – American-built four-engined turboprop transport aircraft

Canberra – British twin-engined jet bomber, developed into a high-altitude reconnaissance aircraft

Capstan – codename for a position south of Simba position at Sarfait that dominated the coastal plain

Carl Gustav – recoil-less 84mm anti-tank weapon

CAS – Close Air Support

CAT – Civil Action Team. A term used by small SAS teams concentrating on the 'hearts and minds' effort in Oman

CO – Commanding Officer

Coy – abbreviation of Company, an army unit of around 100 men

CPR – cardio-pulmonary resuscitation

CSAF – Commander, Sultan of Oman's Armed Forces

DC-3 Dakota – American-built Second World War vintage twin piston-engined transport aircraft

DeHavilland Beaver – Canadian-built single piston-engined utility aircraft

DeHavilland Caribou – Canadian-built twin piston-engined short take-off and landing medium transport aircraft

DG – Dhofar Gendarmerie

Dhofar Gendarmerie – a SAF garrison force. Not a trained infantry unit

DLF – Dhofar Liberation Front. The original title of the rebellion in Oman

DR – SAF Desert Regiment

Empty Quarter – One of the world's largest sand deserts. Occupies over a quarter of a million square miles of Oman, Saudi Arabia, Yemen and UAE

F-111 – American twin-engined jet strike aircraft

F-4 Phantom – American-designed twin-engined supersonic fighter bomber

FAC – Forward Air Controller

FAN – Firqa al Nasi

FAU – Firqa al Umri. Firqa based in Mirbat

FCO – Foreign and Commonwealth Office

FGN – Firqa Gamel Abdul Nasser

Firqa – Arabic for 'unit'. Used in Dhofar to describe units of irregular guerrilla fighters fighting on both sides of the conflict, but especially alongside the SAS

FN – Common name for FN FAL, a Belgian 7.62mm assault rifle. Short for Fabrique Nationale

Force de Frappe – Strike Force

FSD – Firqa Salahadin. The first SAS-trained Firqa

FST – Field Surgical Team

futta – sarong-type garment typically worn around the waist by Jebali men

GCA – Ground Controlled Approach

Gimpy – Army slang for the GPMG

GLO – Ground Liaison Officer

GPMG – 7.62 mm General Purpose Machine Gun

GPMG Light Role – General Purpose Machine Gun used without the tripod

GPMG SF – General Purpose Machine Gun, Sustained Fire. Version of the GPMG used with a tripod. Used a chrome-lined barrel to allow longer periods of fire between barrel changes

Green Archer – British mortar-locating equipment used by the RAF Regiment in Oman

Green Slime – slang for army intelligence

Gwadar – from 1783 until 1958, an Omani-owned enclave in Baluchistan, part of mainland Pakistan

Habrut – Location of a SAF fort near the Yemeni border. Also the location of a Yemeni fort on the other side of the border

Hawf – Yemeni border town close to Oman. Used as a safe haven and HQ by the Adoo

Hedgehog – term used to describe RAF Regiment forts built from sand-filled burmails and ammunition boxes surrounding RAF Salalah

HF – high frequency

HMG – Her Majesty's Government

Hunter – British single-engined jet fighter bomber

Il-28 Beagle – Soviet-built twin-engined jet bomber

Insha'Allah – Arabic for 'God willing'

Jebel – from Jabal, the Arabic word for a hill or mountain

Jet Provost – British single-engined two-seat jet training aircraft

Jibjat – SAF position in Dhofar Eastern Jebel

Kalashnikov – Soviet weapons designer. Often used as a generic term for the AK47

khareef – local word for the Dhofar monsoon, a meteorological phenomenon unique on the Arabian peninsula

KIA – Killed in Action

Lightning – British twin-engined supersonic jet interceptor

LP Cock – Low Pressure Cock

Lympne – SAF airstrip in Dhofar Eastern Jebel

LZ – Landing Zone

M79 – American-built grenade launcher

Mae West – slang for an airman's life jacket

Mahra – tribe whose territory straddles Omani and Yemeni territory

Mainbrace – name given to the location of the airstrip at Simba position

MiG-17 Fresco – Soviet-built single-engined jet fighter

MiG-25 Foxbat – Soviet-built twin-engined high-altitude jet reconnaissance aircraft

MoD – Ministry of Defence

mortar – muzzle-loading indirect-fire weapon that launches shells on ballistic trajectories

NAAFI – Navy, Army and Air Force Institutes. British military shop

NATO – North Atlantic Treaty Organization

NDB Beacon – Non-Directional Beacon. Sends out a unique signal used by aircraft to home in on an airfield

NFR – SAF Northern Frontier Regiment

OC – Officer Commanding

Ogs – Olive Greens. Lightweight cotton combat fatigues worn by the SAS in Oman

Operation AQOOBA – codename for SOAF cross-border raids against Hawf in Southern Yemen

Operation INTRADON – codename for SAS operation in 1970/71 on Oman's Musandam Peninsula

Operation LEOPARD – codename for SAS-led operation to try to block Adoo supply routes

Operation SIMBA – codename for SAF Operation to take Simba position at Sarfait on the Western Jebel

Operation STORM – codename for SAS operation in Oman, 1971–1976

PD(O) – Petroleum Development (Oman). Until 1974, Shell was the majority shareholder

PDRY – People's Democratic Republic of Yemen

PFLOAG – People's Front for the Liberation of Oman and the Arabian Gulf. From 1969 the offical name adopted by the rebellion after the DLF combined forces with a rebel movement in the north of Oman

Picquet – sentry

Piston Provost – British single piston-engined two-seat training aircraft

PRC316 – Standard British Army lightweight patrol HF radio. Includes morse key

QGH – Q Code for a ground-controlled letdown

R&R – Rest and Recuperation

RAF Khormaksar – main British airbase in Aden until the withdrawal in 1967

RAF Masirah – airbase leased by the British on the Omani island of Masirah

RAF Muharraq – until the end of 1971, a British airbase in Bahrain

RAF Regiment – infantry unit belonging to the Royal Air Force and specializing in airfield defence

RAF Salalah – British airbase on Salalah plain in Dhofar. Leased from Oman and run by the RAF, it was home to SOAF(Tac)

RAMC – Royal Army Medical Corps

RCL – Recoil-less Rifle

Regiment, The – colloquial term for the SAS

REMF – Rear Echelon Motherfucker. Army slang

RF-4C Phantom – reconnaissance version of the F-4 Phantom

RP – Rocket Projectile

RT – Radio Telephony

Rupert – SAS term for officers

SAF – Sultan of Oman's Armed Forces

SARBE – Search and Rescue Beacon. Used by the SAS in Oman for ground-to-air communications

SAS – Special Air Service

Scout – British single-engined light utility helicopter

SEP – Surrendered Enemy Personnel

SF – Special Forces

Shemagh – Arabian patterned headscarf

Shpagin – Soviet-built 12.7mm heavy machine gun

Shukran – Arabic for 'thank you'

Simba position – SAF position at Sarfait close to the border with Yemen on the Western Jebel

SKS – Chinese-built assault rifle

Skyvan – British-built twin-turboprop light transport aircraft

SLR – Self Loading Rifle. A licence-built version of the Belgian FN assault rifle and the standard British Army infantry weapon throughout the seventies

SNEB rockets – French-designed podded 67mm unguided rockets

SOAF(Tac) – Sultan of Oman's Air Force (Tactical). The umbrella term for all SOAF units based at Salalah and flying operations in the Dhofar war

SON – Sultan of Oman's Navy

SR-71 Blackbird – American twin-engined high-altitude jet reconnaissance aircraft

Strikemaster – single-engined British-built light attack jet

SURA – Swiss-made 80mm unguided air-to-ground rocket

syrette – a device for injecting a single dose of morphine

Tawi Atair – SAF position in the Eastern Jebel and location of a 600-foot-deep limestone sinkhole

Thumeir – British forward operating base during the Radfan campaign in 1964

Tokai – Japanese walkie-talkie used by the SAS in Oman

Trucial Oman Scouts – British-trained and led local army of the Trucial Oman States, now the UAE, before the British withdrawal from the Persian Gulf at the end of 1971

TSR2 – cancelled British twin-engined jet strike aircraft

U-2 – American single-engined high-altitude reconnaissance jet aircraft

UAG – Um al Gwarif. Large SAF camp north of Salalah

UCCA – Universities Central Council on Admissions

VC – Viet Cong

VC10 – British four-engined jet airliner, used by the RAF as a transport aircraft

Vickers Viscount – British four-engined turboprop airliner, used by SOAF as a transport aircraft

wadi – generic term for valley or depression

wazim – term used to describe the Jebali practice of treating pain with pain

Wessex – British-built version of the American Sikorsky S-58 utility helicopter

White City – SAF position in Dhofar Eastern Jebel. Location of the first Sultanate civic centre on the Jebel

Yardarm – codename for a position on high ground dominating Simba position

Z (Zulu) Company – SAF unit used to patrol Salalah plain in defence of the airfield

ZB298 – ground-searching radar used by the RAF Regiment in Oman

ZU-23 – Soviet 23mm anti-aircraft cannon

Bibliography

Books

The Aerospace Encyclopaedia of Air Warfare, Vol. 2: *1945 to the Present* (ed. Chris Bishop), 1997

Akehurst, John, *We Won a War*, Michael Russell, 1982

Allen, Charles, *The Savage Wars of Peace*, Michael Joseph, 1990

Arkless, David C., *The Secret War*, William Kimber, 1988

Ashcroft, Michael, *Special Forces Heroes*, Headline Review, 2008

Asher, Michael, *The Regiment: The Real Story of the SAS*, Viking, 2007

Bain, Chris J., *Cold War, Hot Wings*, Pen and Sword, 2007

Bluffield, Robert, *Imperial Airways*, Classic, 2009

Bowman, Martin W., *Hunters*, Sutton, 2002

Brassey's Annual 1972, William Clowes and Sons, 1972

Carver, Michael, *War Since 1945*, Putnam, 1981

Chartres, John, *Avro Shackleton*, Ian Allan, 1985

Clarke, Bob, *Jet Provost*, Amberley, 2008

Clementson, John, *Eagles: Illustrated History of the Royal Air Force of Oman*, RAFO, 1997

Connor, Ken, *Ghost Force*, Weidenfeld and Nicolson, 1998

Cooper, Johnny, *One of the Originals*, Pan, 1991

Dark, Diana and Sandra Shields, *Oman*, Bradt, 2006

de la Billière, General Sir Peter, *Looking for Trouble*, HarperCollins, 1994

Dewer, Michael, *Brush Fire Wars*, Robert Hale, 1984

Draper, Michael I., *Shadows*, Hikoki, 1999

Fiennes, Ranulph, *The Feathermen*, Bloomsbury, 1991

—, *Atlantis of the Sands*, Bloomsbury, 1992

—, *Where Soldiers Fear to Tread*, Mandarin, 1995

Flintham, Victor, *Air Wars and Aircraft*, Arms and Armour Press, 1989

—, *High Stakes*, Pen and Sword, 2009

Foxley, Harry, *Marking Time: A Soldier's Story*, Trafford Publishing, 2004

Gardiner, Ian, *In the Service of the Sultan*, Pen and Sword, 2006

Geraghty, Tony, *Who Dares Wins*, Arms and Armour Press, 1980

—, *Brixmis*, HarperCollins, 1997

Graham, John, *Ponder Anew*, Spellmount, 2009

Gunston, Bill, *Fighters of the Fifties*, PSL, 1981

—, *Plane Speaking*, PSL, 1991

Hawley, Sir Donald, *Oman and Its Renaissance*, 1977

—, *Desert Wind and Tropic Storm*, Michael Russell, 2000

Holland, James, *Together We Stand*, HarperCollins, 2005

Jackson, Robert, *Hawker Hunter*, Ian Allan, 1982

—, *Canberra: The Operational Record*, 1988

Jeapes, Major General Tony, *SAS Secret War*, Greenhill, 2005

Jones, Tim, *SAS: The First Secret Wars*, I. B. Tauris, 2010

Kennedy, Michael Paul, *Soldier 'I' SAS*, Bloomsbury, 1989

Kimbell, Alex, *Think Like a Bird*, Matador, 2004

Lee, Air Chief Marshal Sir David, *Flight from the Middle East*, Air Historical Branch, 1978

Mason, Robert, *Chickenhawk*, Corgi, 1984

Oliver, David, *British Combat Aircraft in Action since 1945*, Ian Allan, 1987

Oliver, Kingsley M., *Through Adversity: The History of the RAF Regiment*, Forces and Corporate Publishing, 1997

Peterson, J. E., *Oman's Insurgencies*, SAQI, 2007

Ramsay, Jack, *SAS: The Soldiers' Story*, Macmillan, 1996

Ratcliffe, Peter, *Eye of the Storm*, Michael O'Mara, 2000

Ray, Bryan, *Dangerous Frontiers*, Pen and Sword, 2008

Ross, Wing Commander A. E., *Through Eyes of Blue*, Airlife, 2002

Scholey, Pete, *The Joker*, André Deutsch, 1999

Scutts, Jerry, *UH-1 Iroquois/AH-1 HueyCobra*, Ian Allan, 1984

Sibley, Paul, *A Monk in the SAS*, Trafford Publishing, 2006

Skinner, Stephen, *British Airliner Prototypes since 1945*, Midland, 2008

Smith, E. D., *Malaya and Borneo*, Ian Allan, 1985

Smith, Peter C., *Close Air Support*, Orion Books, 1990

Taylor, John W. R., *Warplanes of the World*, Ian Allan, 1968

—, *Jane's All the World's Aircraft 1973–74*, Samson Low, 1973

Thesiger, Wilfred, *Arabian Sands*, Penguin, 2007

Thomson, Major General Julian, *The Imperial War Museum Book of Modern Warfare*, Sidgwick and Jackson, 2002

Walker, Jenny et al., *Oman, UAE & Arabian Peninsula*, Lonely

Planet, 2010

Warner, Philip, *The SAS*, William Kimber, 1971

Magazines, journals and newspapers

'Arabian Fledgeling', *Air Enthusiast*, June 1972

'BAC Strikemaster', *Today's Pilot*, November 2002

'Beaver in the Air', *Flight*, 26 January 1950

Delve, Ken, 'Strikemaster over the Cape', *Flypast*, July 1999

Dickey, Christopher, 'Sultans of Slow', *Newsweek*, 8 May 2007

Dye, Air Vice-Marshal Peter, 'The Jebel Akhdar War: The Royal Air Force in Oman 1952–1959', *RAF Air Power Review*, Vol. 11, No. 3

Foster, Peter, 'Aden Action', *Air World*, May 1995

Hewish, Mark, 'Air Power in Oman', *Flight International*, 20 February 1975

'Il-28 – A Soviet Canberra', *Air Enthusiast*, December 1971

Journal of the Sultan of Oman's Armed Forces, The, Issues 1–11, 58

Lake, Jon, 'English Electric Lightning', *Wings of Fame*, Vol. 7

—, 'Hawker Hunter', *Wings of Fame*, Vol. 20

Lambert, Mark, 'Strikemaster Sortie', *Flight International*, 12 October 1972

Obituaries:

'Brigadier Mike Harvey', *The Times*, 7 August 2007

'Colonel David Smiley', *Daily Telegraph*, 9 January 2009

'Colonel David Smiley', *The Times*, 14 January 2009

'David Smiley', *Independent*, 2 February 2009

'Lieutenant General John Watts', *Daily Telegraph*, 15 December 2003

'Lieutenant General John Watts', *The Times*, 15 December 2003

'Wing Commander Bill Stoker', *Daily Telegraph*, 17 May 2010

'Oman Album', *Flypast*, December 1998

Royal Air Force Historical Society Journal 45

'Short Skyvan: In the Air', *Flight International*, 1 August 1968

'Skyvan Prospects', *Flight International*, 28 August 1969

'Skyvans for Duty', *Flight International*, 19 May 1966

'Strikemaster – A Versatile Tutor', *Air Enthusiast*, March 1973

Sunday Times, 5 June 1972

'Supporting a Sensitive War', *Air Enthusiast*, September 1972

Taylor, Steven, 'Strike Fast, Strike Hard!', *Flypast*, November 2008

'Turbo-Skyvan', *Flight International*, 28 May 1964

Wynn, Humphrey, 'Sultan's Air Force', *Flight International*, 8 July 1971

DVDs and videos
Film of Oman, 1972, David Milne-Smith and Nobby Grey
SAS: The Real Story, Windfall Films, 2003
Special Forces Heroes: Last Stand in Oman, Dangerous Films, 2008

Websites
www.55fst-ramc.org.uk
www.acig.com
   'Oman (and Dhofar) 1952 to 1979', Tom Cooper and Stefan Kuhn
   'South Arabia and Yemen 1945 to 1995'
www.britains-smallwars.com
   'A British Soldier of Fortune's Journey to an African Civil War'
   'Contract Pilot in the Dhofar'
   'Squadron Business'
www.flightglobal.com
www.mod.co.uk
   'Security and Stabilisation: The Military Contribution', 2009
http://naval8-208-association.com
www.pprune.org
   'WingCo Peter Hulme (SOAF) R.I.P.'
www.radfanhunters.co.uk
www.specialforcesroh.com
www.spyflight.co.uk
   'Foxbats Over Sinai'
   'Into Russia – from Iran'
   'Israel vs the RAF – Caught in the Middle'
http://world.guns.ru

Unpublished accounts
Baker, Neville
   'Helicopter Crewmen Selection and Training'
   'Helicopter Operations – Dhofar 1970 to 1974'
   'Helicopters in SOAF 1970–1974'
   'History of the Royal Air Force of Oman'
   'Pilot Training and Selection'
   'The Battle at Marbat'
   'Wg Cdr Neville Baker'
Colley, Colonel Hugh, 'Cracker Battery and the Dhofar War', Royal
   Artillery Historical Society
Downie, Nick, 'Rhodesian Guerrilla Warfare: A Study in Military
   Incompetence'
Hanning, Hugh, 'Defence and Development', Royal United Service
   Institution

Hirst, Wg Cdr P. J., 'The Sultan of Oman's Air Force: A Personal Account'
Knocker, Colonel Nigel, Op Order, Operation SIMBA
Ladwig III, Walter C., 'Supporting Allies in Counterinsurgency: Lessons from Dhofar'

Archives and official documents
55 Field Surgical Team – Anaesthetic Record Cards
Aircrew logbooks:
    Neville Baker
    Sean Creak
    Nobby Grey
    Curly Hirst
    Nick Holbrook
    David Milne-Smith
    Bill Stoker
    Barrie Williams
Operator's Manual, Army Model, UH-1H/V Helicopters, Headquarters, Department of the Army
Pilot's Notes: Strikemaster Mk 88 Aircraft for the Royal New Zealand Air Force, British Aircraft Corporation, Publication B.A.C. 167(88)

Imperial War Museum Sound Archive
Interviews conducted by Charles Allen with three SAS veterans

National Archives of the United Kingdom
AIR 2/16600 – RAF Personnel: Loan to Muscat (SOAF)
AIR 20/10474 – Formation of Sultan of Oman's Air Force
AIR 20/12115 – Radfan Operations: Mission Reports
AIR 20/12294 – RAF Salalah Ground Defence against External Threat
AIR 20/9780 – Operations in Oman
AIR 23/8634 – RAF Masirah and RAF Salalah: Station Histories
AIR 23/8657 – Operations in Radfan, Aden
AIR 27/2991 – No. 208 Squadron: Operations Record Book
AIR 27/3013 – No. 8 Squadron: Operations Record Book
AIR 27/3020 – 13 Squadron: Operations Record Book 1966–71
AIR 27/3095 – No. 43 Squadron: Operations Record Book
AIR 27/3282 – 13 Squadron: Operations Record Book 1972–1975
AIR 28/1509 – Salalah
AIR 28/1851 – Masirah
AIR 28/1852 – Masirah

AIR 28/1876 – Salalah
AIR 28/2081 – Masirah
AIR 28/2106 – Salalah
AIR 28/2106 – Salalah
AIR 29/3668 – Sultan of Muscat and Oman's Air Force
AIR 29/3669 – Sultan of Muscat and Oman's Air Force
AIR 29/3980 – 1417 Flight Fighter Reconnaissance
AIR 29/4009 – No. 2 Squadron
AIR 8/1887 – Muscat and Oman: Potential Operations
AVIA 18/3423 – Skyvan Series 3
AVIA 18/3424 – Skyvan Series 3: Brief Engineering Assessment
AVIA 18/4657 – 653 Squadron Army Air Corps: the Scout Attack
    Helicopter (AH) Mk 1 in the Radfan Operations
CAB 148/121/23 – Defence Assistance to Sultanate of Oman
CAB 185/10 – Joint Intelligence Committee (A) (JIC(A)) meetings
DEFE 11/736 – Oman
DEFE 11/759 – Oman
DEFE 11/760 – Oman
DEFE 13/779 – Historical Details of the Dhofar Campaign
DEFE 15/12575 – Visit of a member of the Mine Warfare Branch to
    Salalah
DEFE 24/1866 – Oman: historical report by 22 SAS Regiment on
    their operations in the Oman, 1958–1959
DEFE 24/575 – Oman: Subversive Activities and Counter-Subversive
    Measures
DEFE 25/187 – Operations in Muscat and Oman
DEFE 25/293 – Muscat and Oman
DEFE 25/294 – Muscat and Oman
DEFE 25/368 – Operational Planning
DEFE 5/192/37 – Future United Kingdom Defence Activity in Oman
DEFE 5/193/15 – Directive to the Commander – Sultan of Oman's
    Armed Forces
DEFE 5/194/13 – Military Assistance in Support of the Sultan of
    Oman: Joint Theatre Plan (East) No. 20 – Op ROBIN
DEFE 5/194/5 – Air Defence of Salalah
DEFE 71/374 – RAF Salalah: Telegrams relating to the deposition of
    Sultan Said bin Taimur by his son
FCO 46/833 – UK Armed Forces in Oman
FCO 46/834 – UK Armed Forces in Oman
FCO 8/1669 – Annual Review for Oman 1970
FCO 8/1688 – Attachment of SAS Personnel of UK to Armed Forces
    of Oman
FCO 8/1689 – Attachment of SAS Personnel of UK to Armed Forces

of Oman

FCO 8/1690 – Attachment of SAS Personnel of UK to Armed Forces of Oman

FCO 8/1702 – South Yemen: Annual Review for 1970

FCO 8/1715 – Soviet Military and Naval Movements in South Yemen

FCO 8/1856 – Military Assistance to Oman from UK

FCO 8/1857 – Military Assistance to Oman from UK

FCO 8/1861 – Military Assault by South Yemen against Armed Forces of Oman

FCO 8/1862 – Military Assault by South Yemen against Armed Forces of Oman

FCO 8/1863 – Military Assault by South Yemen against Armed Forces of Oman

FCO 8/1865 – Military Assistance to Oman from UK: November Review

FCO 8/1872 – South Yemen: Annual Review for 1971

FCO 8/188 – Annual Review for Oman 1971

FCO 8/2006 – Annual Review for Oman 1972

FCO 8/2032 – People's Democratic Republic of Yemen: Annual Review 1972

FCO 8/2237 – SAS in Oman

FCO 8/6860 – Assault by South Yemen on Oman

OD 36/227 – Use of Royal Engineers for Civilian Work Overseas

PREM 15/1761 – Visits of Sultan Qaboos to UK: Records of Meetings with Prime Minister

WO 32/19814 – 22 SAS Regiment

WO 32/19818 – 22 SAS Regiment

WO 337 – War Office HQ British Forces Gulf Area: Files

WO 386/22 – Radfan: Report on operations between 14/4 and 30/6 1964

Appendices

Strikemaster Jet Cutaway
Huey Helicopter Cutaway

BAC 167 Strikemaster

Structure
1 Front pressure bulkhead
2 Windscreen (⅜in Perspex)
3 Power-jettisoned canopy
4 Canopy-actuating motor
5 Canopy sea lever
6 Canopy rack drive
7 Manual operation handle
8 Inflating canopy-seal
9 Rear pressure bulkhead
10 Cabin pressure-relief valve
11 Cockpit pressure-floor
12 Martin–Baker Mk 4 ejection seats
13 Canopy jettison gun
14 Jettison rail
15 Crash pylon
16 Access for engine removal
17 Top panel hinges
18 Front firewall
19 Slinging points
20 Rear fuselage access (port, stbd)
21 Jet pipe-mounting rail
22 Fin front attachment
23 Tailplane front attachment
24 Inverted-section tailplane
25 Jet pipe rail and thermocouple access
26 Jet pipe mounting access
27 Removable tail-cone
28 Steel-bushed wing main-spar attachments
29 Main-spar, web and L-section boom
30 Rear (subsidiary) spar
31 Leading-edge false spar

C – Controls
C1 Aileron control cables
C2 Aileron rod and quadrant
C3 Trim/balance tab
C4 Balance tab
C5 Interchangeable elevators
C6 Elevator control run
C7 Elevator control levers
C8 Rudder control runs
C9 Rudder control lever
C10 Elevator mass balance
C11 Infinitely variable (to 50°) flap
C12 Flap selector
C13 Flap jack
C14 Flap cross-connecting cable
C15 Lift spoiler
C16 Airbrakes
C17 Airbrakes/spoiler jack

A – Air system
A1 Compressor-bleed to air system
A2 Cabin-air gate-valve
A3 Demist/rain-clearance gate-valve
A4 Heat-exchanger (demist/rain air)
A5 Heat-exchanger exhaust
A6 Cooling pack
A7 Turbine exhaust
A8 Water separator (Normalair)
A9 Distribution duct
A10 Demist air
A11 Rain-clearance air

F – Fuel
F1 Filler
F2 No 1 bag-tank cell
F3 No 2 bag-tank cell
F4 No 3 bag-tank cell
F5 Integral tank
F6 Collector-tank and booster pump
F7 Fuel feed line
F8 L-p filter
F9 H-p pump
F10 H-p cock
F11 Main fuel delivery
F12 Tank transfer line
F13 Tank pressurising air (ram or bleed)
F14 Tip-tank pressure line
F15 Tip-tank transfer
F16 Contents unit

H – Hydraulics and Electrics

H1 Reservoir (DTD 525 fluid)
H2 H-p filter
H3 Servicing pressure and suction
H4 Brake accumulator pressure
H5 Main accumulator pressure
H6 Main accumulator air charging
H7 Varley 24V 25Ah batteries
H8 Rotary invertor, 115V
    200Hz(2)

H9 External power-supply socket
H10 Electrical panel
H11 Main junction box
H12 High-energy igniter
H13 Taxi lamps, Type A
H14 Landing lamp

P – Powerplant

P1 R-R Viper 535
P2 Main access to powerplant
P3 Forward access
P4 Bay venting air
P5 Rear firewall
P6 Engine-mounting struts
P7 Adjustable front mounting
P8 Engine-bay steel floor
P9 Throttle control
P10 Fire doors

O – Oxygen

O1 Oxygen bottles (2,130 litres
   total)
O2 Oxygen charging point
O3 Oxygen demand panel

R – Instruments

R1 Compass amplifier
R2 RAE fatigue meter
R3 Accelerometer
R4 Standby compass

U – Undercarriage

U1 Liquid-spring nose unit, fully
   castoring
U2 Main-geartyres, 21×6.75
   (90lb/sq in)
U3 Dowty Rotol main-gear unit
U4 Main-gear pivot
U5 Oleo charging-point access
U6 Retraction sprocket
U7 Folding strut
U8 Down-lock
U9 Mechanical door linkage
U10 Pre-closing door
U11 Dunlop multi-disc brake
U12 Toe brake-cylinders, nosewheel
U13 Down-lock warning light (on
    nosecone)
U14 Selector buttons

W – Weapons

W1 Gunsight
W2 7.62mm FN gun (port and stbd)
W3 ML 100lb, practice bomb
   carrier
W4 Matra 155 rocket pack

© FLIGHT
INTERNATIONAL

F17 Tank access panel
F18 Pipe-run access
F19 Contents-gauge access
F20 48 Imp gal tip tank

Bell UH-1H Iroquois

1 FM homing aerials
2 Nose compartment access door
3 Radio and avionics equipment
4 Battery
5 Downward vision window
6 Yaw control rudder pedals
7 Footboards
8 Fire extinguisher
9 Windscreen de-misting air duct
10 Instrument console
11 Instrument panel shroud
12 Windscreen panels
13 Windscreen wipers
14 Starboard jettisonable cockpit door
15 Cockpit eyebrow window
16 Handgrip
17 UHF aerial
18 Cockpit fresh air intakes
19 Overhead systems switch panel
20 Pitot head
21 Pilot's seat (armoured type)
22 Cyclic pitch control column handgrip
23 Safety harness
24 Centre instrument console
25 Control column
26 Cockpit door jettison mechanism
27 Seat mounting rail
28 Collective pitch control lever
29 Cockpit step
30 Port lower navigation light
31 Door latch
32 Co-pilot's seat (conventional type)
33 Sliding side window panel
34 First aid kits
35 Cabin roof frame construction
36 Cabin skin panelling
37 OF loop aerial
38 Litter installation (maximum six stretchers)
39 Stretcher mounting post
40 Forward, hinged, cabin door, port and starboard
41 Cabin side pillar construction
42 Winch mounting pad (four alternative positions)
43 Heater distribution ducting
44 Forward external stores pylon mounting lugs
45 Landing skid front strut
46 Winch motor
47 Rescue hoist/winch
48 Heating air distribution ducting
49 Cabin floor panelling
50 Floor beam construction
51 Underfloor fuel tank; total fuel capacity 220 US gal (833 l)
52 Underfloor control linkages
53 External load-slinging cargo hook
54 Cargo hook stabilizing spring
55 Medical attendant's folding seat
56 Port upper navigation lights
57 Ventilating air intake
58 Detachable rotor-head front fairing
59 Generator

60 Ventilating air intake
61 Starboard upper navigation lights
62 Two-bladed main rotor
63 Laminated blade-root stiffeners
64 Blade-root attachment joints
65 Semi-rigid rotor head mechanism
66 Rotor stabilizing beam
67 Blade counterbalance weights
68 Pitch angle control rods
69 Main rotor mast
70 Rotor head control rods
71 Swash plate mechanism
72 Swash plate control rods
73 Main rotor gearbox
74 Gearbox mounting sub-frame
75 Gearbox support structure
76 Control rod hydraulic actuator
77 Rearward sliding main cabin door panel, port and starboard
78 Centre section fuel tank
79 Ammunition feed chute

80 Hand-held gun swivelling mounting
81 Ammunition box
82 Gun pintle mounting
83 Pylon mounting struts
84 Port landing skid
85 External fuel tank, capacity 60 US gal (227 l)
86 Fuel filler cap
87 Tank mounting adaptor
88 Landing skid rear strut
89 M-23 0.30-in (7.62-mm) machine gun (carried with cabin door removed)
90 Heater distribution ducts
91 Fuselage flank fuel tanks, port and starboard
92 Cabin rear bulkhead

93 Maintenance access step
94 Handgrip
95 Fuel system filter
96 Bleed air control valve
97 Engine bay forward fireproof bulkhead
98 Engine intake guard
99 Engine/gearbox shaft coupling
100 Filtered air intake
101 Detachable engine cowling panels
102 Cooling air scoops
103 Engine accessory equipment
104 Aveo-Lycoming T63-L-13 turboshaft
105 Engine bearer struts
106 Fireproof engine mounting deck
107 Sliding cabin door rail

108 Voltage regulators
109 Maintenance access steps
110 Electrical equipment bays
111 0.50-in (12.7-mm) machine gun
112 Cartridge case collector bag
113 Ammunition box
114 Ground power socket
115 Static inverters
116 Centrally mounted oil cooler
117 Engine bay rear fireproof bulkhead
118 Tail rotor shaft coupling
119 UHF aerial
120 Anti-collision light
121 Exhaust pipe
122 Smoke generator
123 Engine exhaust nozzle
124 Tail rotor control cable linkage

125 Tailcone attachment joint frame
126 Tailcone extension section
127 Longeron bolted joints
128 Tailcone lower longeron
129 Frame and stringer construction
130 All-moving tailplane control linkage
131 Upper longeron
132 Tail rotor transmission shaft
133 Shaft bearings
134 Dorsal spine shaft housing
135 Main rotor blade honeycomb core construction
136 Extruded aluminium D-section blade spar
137 Leading edge anti-erosion sheathing (stainless steel)
138 Laminated glass-fibre blade skins
139 Fixed tab
140 Starboard all-moving tailplane
141 Tailplane torque shaft

142 Port all-moving tailplane construction
143 Radio compass transmitter
144 VHF navigation aerial
145 Control access panel
146 Sloping tail pylon spar joint frame
147 Bevel drive gearbox
148 Tail rotor control cables
149 Tail rotor drive shaft
150 Tail pylon construction
151 Final drive right-angle gearbox
152 FM communications aerial
153 Two-bladed tail rotor
154 Blade root attachments
155 Tail rotor blade pitch control mechanism
156 Honeycomb core blade construction
157 Laminated glass-fibre blade skins
158 Tail navigation light
159 Tail rotor protecting tailskid

Mike Badrocke

Picture Acknowledgements

Although every effort has been made to trace copyright holders and clear permission for the photographs in the book, the provenance of a number of them is uncertain. The author and publisher would welcome the opportunity to correct any mistakes.

First section

Brigadier John Graham: © John Graham; DeHavilland Beaver and BAC Strikemaster: © Neville Baker; Blackpool Beach: © Sean Creak; Colonel Hugh Oldman: © Barrie Williams

John Graham greets Sultan Qaboos: © John Graham; G Squadron, 22 SAS, in Musandam: Captain Shaun Brogan inoculating a Jebali: members of BATT in Dhofar: all © Shaun Brogan; RAF Salalah from the air: © Sean Creak; Adoo leaders in Peking, 1971: © Nobby Grey; RAF Salalah putting green: © Charlie Gilchrist

1 Squadron, SOAF(Tac) with Strikemaster: © Nobby Grey; Squadron Leader Neville Baker: © Neville Baker; wreckage of Barrie Williams's Strikemaster: © Barrie Williams; SOAF(Tac) headquarters: © Nobby Grey; Flight Lieutenant Sean Creak with Spoon: © Sean Creak; Flight Lieutenant David Milne-Smith: © Andy Dunsire; Nick Holbrook: © Nick Holbrook; Flight Lieutenant Denis 'Nobby' Grey: © Nobby Grey

SOAF AB206 helicopter landing at Mirbat: © Shaun Brogan; the Jebel: © Rowland White; Lieutenant Colonel Johnny Watts: © Lady Watts; SAS on patrol on the Jebel: SAS patrol: SAS trooper with GPMG: Shaun Brogan taking a break: briefing the Firqa: all © Shaun Brogan

3 Squadron AB205 Huey helicopter: © Shaun Brogan; resupply by SOAF Hueys: © Charlie Gilchrist; goats boarding SOAF Skyvan: © Andy Dunsire; 'The Fresh' delivery: © Shaun Brogan

Second section

Firqa guerrillas on the Jebel: Trooper Sekonaia Takavesi: Shaun Brogan being treated in Salalah field hospital: Shaun Brogan's map: all © Shaun Brogan

Lieutenant Colonel Nigel Knocker with Neville Baker at Akoot: © Nigel Knocker; Neville Baker pins up a map: Neville Baker during flood: both © Neville Baker; Skyvan seen from Strikemaster: © Shaun Brogan; DeHavilland Caribou taking off from Salalah: © Stephen Scott-Davies; SOAF helicopter flying in supplies: © Charlie Gilchrist; Capstan: © Rowland White; helicopter over Capstan: © Andy Dunsire

1 Squadron Strikemasters over Capstan: © Sean Creak; building runway at Tawi Atair: © Shaun Brogan; take-off from Tawi Atair: © Andy Dunsire; Browning .50 machine gun: © Shaun Brogan; Squadron Leader Bill Stoker: © Nobby Grey; Shaun Brogan prior to dusk rocket strike: © Shaun Brogan; 1 Squadron pilots: walking to jets before raid against Habrut: both © Nobby Grey

Pre-flight inspection: © Nobby Grey; Nobby Grey in cockpit: heavily armed Strikemasters: Strikemasters flying towards Habrut: the fort: all © Andy Dunsire; Strikemaster being loaded with 540lb bomb: © Barrie Williams; Sultan Qaboos: © John Graham

Cross-border attack against Hawf: © Shaun Brogan; Nick Holbrook with AB206 helicopter: © Andy Dunsire; smoke from targets hit by SOAF jets: stickers produced by 1 Squadron: both © Sean Creak

Third section

Canberra PR9 spyplane: © RAF Masirah website; 'Hedgehogs': © Bill de Bass; shrapnel damage to accommodation block: © Charlie Gilchrist

FST operating theatre: FST inspect damage from Adoo RCLs: both © Bill de Bass; B Squadron, 22 SAS, returning to Oman, 1972: © Gerry Honey; BATT House: Dhofar Gendarmerie fort: inside the BATT House: Skyvan with Mirbat fort in the background: all © Brian Harrington Spier

Index

ABOUT THE AUTHOR

Rowland White is the author of the No. 1 bestselling *Vulcan 607*, the extraordinary true story of the RAF's raid on Port Stanley airfield, and the *Sunday Times* bestseller *Phoenix Squadron*, his acclaimed account of HMS *Ark Royal*'s little-known intervention in Central America in the early 1970s.

His writing has appeared in *Esquire* magazine as well as a number of specialist aviation magazines. He lives near Cambridge with his wife, Lucy, and their three children and works in publishing. *Storm Front* is his third book.